AF477549

SCHOLAR, PATRIOT, MENTOR

HISTORICAL ESSAYS IN HONOR OF DIMITRIJE DJORDJEVIĆ

Edited by

RICHARD B. SPENCE

LINDA L. NELSON

EAST EUROPEAN MONOGRAPHS, BOULDER
DISTRIBUTED BY COLUMBIA UNIVERSITY PRESS, NEW YORK

1992

EAST EUROPEAN MONOGRAPHS, NO. CCCXX

Contents

Part III: The Balkans and Eastern Europe in the Eighteenth to Nineteenth Century

Part IV: The Balkans and Eastern Europe in the Twentieth Century

Part V: Other Fields

ACKNOWLEDGEMENTS

In addition to those who have contributed works to this volume, there are several persons deserving special thanks for their help in its preparation. Foremost are Nan Djordjević and Alain Dubie, and additionally Seka Allen, Nancy Dafoe, Helen Nordhoff, and Marj Pon.

PREFACE

I first met Dimitrije Djordjević in the fall of 1973, not long after he had begun his career at the University of California, Santa Barbara. At the time I was just beginning a Masters program in History and was, quite frankly, not all that certain of just what direction I wanted to take. In the years that followed, through my Masters and on through the Ph.D., I credit "Mita" Djordjević with being the most important influence on my development as an historian, scholar, and teacher, and I know that I am not alone in that estimation. He was an outstanding mentor, learned and rigorous, but also patient and understanding. He was always willing to offer advice and, equally important, he was always willing to listen. He was a friend and, without putting too fine a point on it, something of a father as well. Mita often referred to his graduate students as his "Balkan family," and there was, indeed, a strong bond of comradeship and affection. In the years since he has continued to take an active interest in the careers of his students and to take satisfaction and, justifiably, pride in their accomplishments.

Its only fitting, therefore, that many of us, along with other friends and colleagues, have chosen to mark his retirement with this volume of essays. At first it was thought to limit contributions to essays dealing with Balkan and Eastern European histories, but it was quickly decided that this would not only exclude too many people but also would not suggest the full range of Mita's influence and associations. Thus the present collection is a rather broad one, although the emphasis remains on the Balkan/East European field. I hope the reader will find something of interest and value in its pages, and I hope you Mita, will accept this humble effort as a token of our affection and esteem.

Richard B. Spence

This Volume is Dedicated to the Memory of

Mihailo "Misha" Dordević

PART I

THE LIFE AND WORK OF DIMITRIJE V. DJORDJEVIĆ

THE SHAPING OF A BALKAN SCHOLAR
THE BACKGROUND, YOUTH, AND EDUCATION OF
D. V. DJORDJEVIĆ

Milorad M. Drachkovitch

Those who know or know of Dimitrije Djordjević may be interested in learning more about his background and early life in his Balkan homeland. As a friend of several decades, and with help of many mutual friends, I think I can write about these matters with some expertise. "Mita" (as he is known to family and friends) and I have much in common in our early lives. We are rougly the same age, both born in EJlgrade to families of comparable social position, and our early intellectual and political develpoment wa virtually identical.

Family Background

Mita's father Vladimir Djordjević (1884–1967), was a scion of an old Belgrade Family and as head of the highly successful "Brothers Djordjević" commercial firm reputably one of the richest men in the city. Vladimir studied law in Germany and obtained a doctorate from the University of Berlin in 1907. The following year he became a reserve officer of the Serbian Army, and as such saw action in World War I. Badly wounded in the celebrated Battle of the Cer in 1914, Vladimir was decorated for bravery and took part in the Serbian Army's perilous retreat through the Albanian mountains.

During the interwar years Vladimir Djordjević had a diverse and promiment career. He was a wealthy and influential industrialist and in 1937 became a member of the Serbian Cultural Club headed by the eminent Serbian political historian Professor Slobodan Jovanovic, later premier of the Yugoslav Government-in-exile. Vladimir chaired the Club's financial section.

Mita's mother, Jelena, was from the noted Rasic family whose members held many important military and diplomatic posts. His maternal grandfather, General Mihailo Rasic, belonged to the elite of the Serbian officer corps and distinguished himself on the Salonika Front and in his liaison work with the French High Command.

Dimitrije Vladimirović Djordjević was born February 27, 1922, and soon afterwards was joined by his brother Mihailo ("Misha"). Mita graduated from high school in 1940and enrolled in the University of Belgrade with the intention of studying law. But the German invasion of 1941 cut short his scholarly career.

War, Occupation, and Resistance

Along with his brother, Mita was a member of the youth section of the Serbian Cultural Club. Although not a formal political party, the Club attracted many Serbian intellectuals and professionals, as well as university and high school students. Through its organ, *Srpski glas [Serbian Voice]*, the Club did seek to influence public opinion and government policy. In the years preceding the outbreak of war, it took a staunchly pro-Allied position, was adamantly opposed to the Rome-Berlin Axis, and mistrustful of Soviet Russia. As a member of the Club, Mita absorbed a democratic patriotism that served as a guide both during and after the war—even to the present day.

In the wake of the German occupation of Belgrade (April i941), Mita and Misha sought the relative freedom of the Serbian mountains. Along with many contemporaries, they joined units of the Chetnik resistance movement led by Colonel Draža Mihailović. The brothers served in a special Youth Command 501, the largest unit of its kind in the organization. Mihailovic's guerilla's soon found themselves at war not only with the Axis occupiers but also looked in a bitter civil war with domestic foes. The most powerful of these was the Communist Partisan Army led by Josip BrozTito. In the years to come, the Communists would neither forget nor forgive Mita's participation in the Chetnik movement.

World War II had a profound effect on the Djordjević family. Returning to Belgrade for a clandestine visit, Mita and Misha, along with their father, were arrested by the Gestapo in the night of October 12, 1942. Along with other Chetniks and Mihailovic sympathizers, they were sent to the sinister Banjica camp outside Belgrade. Here some were executed and others dispatched to concentration camps in Germany. A few lucky ones were released, but thereafter regarded as hostages liable to rearrest at any time. Vladimir and Misha were among the latter, while Mita was sent to the notorious Mauthausen camp in Austria in late December 1942. Mita's German "visit" was

one of privation and constant movement. In January, he was moved
from Mauthausen to the Gestapo prison in Vienna, and from there to
jails in Maribor, Zagreb, and finally back to Belgrade. By this time
(February 1943) he had fallen seriously ill with a kidney infection,
but this led to his being released to his family for medical treatment.
In September, although still not fully recovered, Mita and his brother
returned to the mountains and rejoined their unit. There they would
remain until August 1944.

Trials of an "Outcast"

Vladimir Djordjević died a heartbroken man in 1967. All that
he had believed in and worked for he saw destroyed during and after
the war. Perhaps worst of all, his son's lives and careers seemed shat-
tered. Still, Vladimir retained one satisfaction: having participated
in Serbia's triumph in 1918 and the creation of a Yugoslav state, he
belonged to a generation of "historical victors." But for Mita and
Misha, an much of their generation, a different fate was in store. As
supporters of a defeated and villified cause, they had no victory to
look back upon, and faced a future of persecution. Nazi barbarities
were replaced with Communist vengeance. While this did not alter
their basic convictions, it did play havoc with their lives. The lament
of their generation today fills the works of Serbian poets, writers, and
historians.

When Partisan and Red Army forces entered Belgrade in late
1944, Mita was again in the city working with the 501 staff. While
most of the unit fled Belgrade to avoid arrest, Mita and Misha, for
family reasons, whose to remain. But Mita, in particular, was determined to continue fighting against Communist rule. He now played
a leading role, and gathered a large body of courageous followers.
He drafted the statutes of a new organization based on democratic
principles that he hoped would provide the basis for continued political action. But the new regime was not to tolerate such defiance.
From the outset, Mita's organization was infiltrated by Communist
informers and *provocateurs*. On the night of November 29, 1945, Mita
and forty-four other members of his group were arrested. They were
imprisoned and interrogated for months, before facing trial in May
1946. On the 20th of that month, Mita and seventeen of his comrades were sentenced to prison for their "illegal" activities. The trial
itself created a sensation in Belgrade and was moved to a large hall at

the city's university to accommodate the crowd of onlookers. Mita received four years imprisonment. Once again, he was transferred from one place to another, serving time in two of Yugoslavia's toughest prisons, Zabela and Sremska Mitrovica.

Fortunately, he was released in general amnesty in May 1947. But this did not end his troubles with Communist authority. The police had compiled a secret dossier, a cornerstone of their security apparatus. This *Karakteristika* detailed every facet of Mita's life, marked him as a enemy of the new order, and would dog his every step in the years to follow.

A New Direction

With his deliverance from prison, Mita's career of political militancy came to an end. He exchanged the life a a defeated warrior for that of an unwanted scholar. Freed from the depression of incarceration, Mita's mind sought renewal and fulfillment in the pursuit of knowledge. He returned to his studies interupted by the war, but encountered obstacles in every direction. His father, impoverished and powerless, could offer little help. As a "reactionary," Mita was barred from Belgrade University which was under the firm control of the Party faithful. He tried to enroll at the University of Zagreb, but was quickly ferreted-out and subsequently banned from all Yugoslav universities. During 1948–49, he was compelled to discharge his military duty to the new state. He bided his time and hoped that the regime would relax its hostility towards him. returning to civilian life, he held a brief job on the staff of an economic magazine. In 1950, he finally enrolled as a part-time student in Belgrade University's Department of Philosophy, and received his diploma in 1954. Two years later he was offered a job in the Serbian State Archives. He only worked there three months, however, when a review of his *Karakteristika* caused his dismissal. He ultimately found a secure haven in the Serbian Academy of Arts and Sciences, where he worked from 1958 through 1969. Here he finally was able to devote himself to historical research and received a Ph.D. in 1962, with an emphasis in diplomatic history. His dissertation examined the tariff war between Serbia and Austria Hungary in the decade prior to World War I. It was a seminal work, later published as a book and widely translated. Mita became a recognized and respected scholar, but still lacked security from the lingering hostility and caprice of the Tito regime. He realized that his dream of holding Belgrade University's chair in Balkan history would be forever frustrated be the regime's watchdogs.

His persecutors, however, did make one important concession. They granted him a passport that allowed him to pursue research and teaching interests in Europe and the United States. He established close ties with the Thessoloniki Historical Institute in Greece, and in 1966 Cambridge University invited him to teach a course on Balkan history. That same year, he secured a coveted Fulbright Scholarship that allowed him the visit American universities, including the University of California, Santa Barbara. In February 1967, a tour of West German universities was interrupted by the death of his father in Belgrade.

In 1968, Mita was invited to teach a one-quarter course at UCSB. The University hoped to enrich its curriculum by establishing a permanent position in Balkan history, and saw in Mita just the erudite, prolific, and cultivated European scholar they were seeking. They could hardly imagine, nor did they care, that this well-groomed, soft-spoken gentleman had been treated as a despicable bandit by the Nazis and a despised class enemy by Tito's Communists. UCSB was only interested in his solid scholarship. In 1970, Mita accepted a permanent position at Santa Barbara. It was not an easy decision; he left behind family and friends and a country he loved. But the powers in Belgrade were glad to see him go. Their loss was Santa Barbara's gain.

THE SCHOLARSHIP OF DIMITRIJE DJORDJEVIĆ

Wayne Vucinich

When Dimitrije Djordjević, or "Mita," as he is known among colleagues and friends, accepted the appointment as Professor of History at the University of California at Santa Barbara in 1970, he was already an established historian. As a graduate student at Belgrade University he had shown signs of becoming a promising historian, and graduated with distinction in 1954. After receiving his Ph.D. in in 1962, it would have been usual for him to be appointed a teaching assistant at that institution. Mita welcomed such an opportunity because he liked teaching and working with students. But a teaching assistantship was not available to a young man of his class and political background. Fortunately, a group of senior historians recommended that Mita be appointed first as an archivist and then to a research position in the Institute of History of the Serbian Academy of Arts and Sciences.

Mita's presence in the Institute was felt at once. Among other things, he published two first rate short studies, one on Serbia's Adriatic policy[1] and the other on Milovan Milovanovic, prominent foreign minister,[2] both of them considered classics in Serbian historiography. He also published his doctoral dissertation on the "Customs War between Serbia and Austria-Hungary," popularly referred to as the "Pig War."[3] This is Mita's best, largest, and probably most enduring published work. The study is heavily documented and shows how Serbia succeeded during 1906–1911 in emancipating itself from Austro-Hungarian economic and political domination. Within a relatively short time, Mita became one of the Institute's most highly regarded members. With the support of senior scholars, he was named Secretary of the Yugoslav National Committee for Historical Sciences and the Secretary of the National Committee for Balkan Studies (1962–1970). In these capacities, Mita played a leading role in the renewal and establishment of professional contacts between the Serbian and Yugoslav historical circles and their counterparts in Europe and America. He figured prominently in organizing the participation of Yugoslav scholars in the world congresses of historians and Balkanologists in Vienna (1965), Sofia (1965), Moscow (1970). and Athens (1970).[4] Mita himself attended these gatherings, organized panels, read papers and commented on those read by others.

It should be pointed out that there are very few complete Balkan historians, and Mita is one of them. While his principal research and writing is on Serbia and Yugoslavia in the nineteenth century, he has a solid knowledge of the history of all Balkan peoples and countries during this period, and has written on most of them. He is a versatile historian in that he has investigated and written on nearly every aspect of modern Balkan history. Mita believes that to be a good historian of Serbia and Yugoslavia, one must have a solid grasp not only of the history of the South Slavs but also of Europe, especially of those European states and the Ottoman Empire which at various times ruled parts of the South Slav world. He has spent a great deal of his professional time in archives, especially those in Belgrade and Vienna, possesses a solid knowledge of the bibliography and historiography of modern Europe, and has an impressive command of languages. Mita closely follows the trends and currents in West and East European historiography. One of his enviable traits is that he writes objectively yet sympathetically about people in South Eastern Europe. He writes about events and individuals as if they were a part of his personal experience.[5] Another of his attributes is the ability to present local history in the content of broader European history.

Although an urbanite by birth and upbringing, Mita feels deeply for the plight of the peasantry and appreciates the role it played in general Balkan and Serbian history. He recognizes the fact that the peasantry was the heart and soul of the Serbian nation and the preserver of national traditions and customs. The peasant of patriarchal Serbia has long personified the Serbian nation and given it its special characteristics. In his isolated village, Mita writes, the peasant perpetuated the legacy of the medieval Serbian state, and preserved the traditional social organization, the patriarchal code of morality, and the awareness of belonging to the Serbian people. He goes on to eplain how during Turkish rule the Serbs were dispersed far and wide, taking with them their tradition, customs, folklore, and awareness of ethnic and religious unity.[6]

According to Mita, the Radical Party in Serbia, organized in the second half of the nineteenth century, was the first political organization that fully recognized the importance of the peasantry in Serbian society and made it a significant plank in its platform. In his studies Mita links the peasantry to the development of Serbia, discusses the peasants' aspirations and attitude toward the bureaucracy, and tells about their suspicion of the government officials (*činovnici*) whom they considered intruders in their own inherited culture and traditions. These characteristics are valid for the entire Balkan region.

Mita's *Weltanschauung* is cosmic and his culture cosmopolitan. He is equally at home in Paris and Santa Barbara as he is in Belgrade, and yet, not completely. Once while strolling on the Santa Barbara campus grounds, Mita exclaimed in his ekavian Serbo-Croatian:

> Voja, it is wonderful here but how nice it would be if there were somewhere our kind of coffee shop to drop in, have a drink and exchange a few words.

This sort of attachment to his homeland and people is revealed by Mita in many other ways. He commands an inexhaustable repertoire of stories about life in the Serbian village and in the old Belgrade. He lives to tell stories about the peasant's philosophy of life and those describing the experiences of the political leaders, men of learning, and other prominent individuals. The stories are generally true, sometimes apocryphal, but nearly always humorous or satirical. A born raconteur, Mita knows how to tell and embellish a story. His stories and anecdotes are of little importance as sources of historical data, but they are invaluable as portraits of the society and life in preWorld War II Belgrade when seemingly everyone know everyone. Mita is a prodigious writer. Along with the three books already mentioned, he has published, co-authored, or edited a total of twelve books, a large number of book reviews and many solid articles in leading historical journals (American, Yugoslav, British, Greek, French, and German) as well as in *Enciklopedija Jugoslavije* and *Encyclopedia Britannica*.[7] eleven of his articles on a number of different subjects appeared recently in a book entitled *Essays in Recent Balkan History*.[8] Most of Mita's work is on Serbia, and the rest is on other Balkan and East European peoples and the Habsburg Empire. His interests are many and varied.[9] He has published on demography,[10] social, agrarian and peasant problems, the similarities and differences between the Enlightenment in Western Europe and in the Balkans,[11] the First Serbian Uprising (1804–1813),[12] the revolutionary movements and the struggle of the Serbs and other Balkan peoples for national liberation,[13] the Western philosophical and cultural influences in the Balkans, and the diplomatic involvements there of the Great Powers. He has also written on the genesis and development of Serbian nationalism and the role of historicism in the formation of the Balkan states.[14] Mita has written on Serbian culture, education and learning.[15] The progress of Serbia's development was slow. After all, Mita rightly observes, when Serbia emerged at the beginning of the nineteenth century as an autonomous political community, it embraced only a part of the Serbian nation. Its destiny was to serve as a rallying point around which those not yet liberated would unite.

In his writings, Mita has shown great interest in the emergence of the Serbian intelligentsia, the development of Serbian social and political thought, and the French influence in Serbia in the time of Napoleon III. He has studied and written on the movements for the national and economic independence of the Balkans in the nineteenth and twentieth centuries,[16] the constitutional struggle and Western constitutional influence in the Balkans, Serbia's "defenders of the constitution [*ustavobranitelji*), inter-Balkan relations, proposals for Balkan federation,[17] and the agrarian reforms in the Balkans after World War I.[18]

Another topic of Mita's strong research interest is Austro-Hungarian relations with Serbia before and during World War I. He has written several articles on this subject,[19] including one impressive and well-documented article on the Monarchy's occupation of Serbia in the time of World War I.[20] Mita is a strong believer in South Slav unity and the Yugoslav state, and he has written a number of short studies on the South Slav movement, the Yugoslav idea and the formation of Yugoslavia.[21] He justifies his Yugoslavism on ethnic, linguistic, historical and political grounds. Mita argues that there are more forces that unite the South Slavs than divide them. In his opinion, a democratic association of the South Slavs is the best political solution for the Yuguslav nations. Any other solu tion would create "mini-Yugoslavias." Yugoslavia, he thinks, serves best not only the interests of the South Slavs, but also those of Europe.

Although Mita writes about Serbian history critically, he at the same time exudes sympathy and admiration for his Serbian nation and Serbian Church, both of which have long been under oppressive foreign rule but have never ceased to struggle for freedom. He credits the legacy of St. Sava (Rastko Nemanijić), the founder of the Serbian autocephalous church in 1919, and the Kosovo tradition, for shaping the Serbian national destiny and character, and for having enabled the Serbs to survive and to regain their independence.

Many years of study of Serbian history have convinced Mita that the work of Saint Sava, who reformed the Serbian Church and gave it the Serbian ethnic stamp, has been of great significance for the Serbs. The Serbian Church instilled in its people a spirit of freedom and independence, and imbued them with pride and confidence. In Mita's opinion, no other institution did more than the Church to prevent in the peasant community the denationalization of the Serbs. In monasteries and churches, nothing was a precious or guarded more closely than the relics of the Serbian saints.

Mita says that the Serbian Church, which outlasted the Serbian medieval state, and in some ways was its heir, played a major role in the survival of the Serbian nation. The Church, he adds, was "the custodian of the medieval (Serbian) statehood."[22] The Church, he reasons, outlived all other Serbian institutions and movements. It suffered with its nation and identified with it. The influence of the Church on the Serbian culture, literature, art and music has been enormous. The Church buttressed and sometime spearheaded the struggle for freedom and independence, and nurtured in its faithful Serbian national awareness. The Patriarchate of the Serbian Orthodox Church linked the scattered Serbian communities throughout the Ottoman Empire; it perpetuated the tradition of St. Sava and the memories of the Serbian independent state. Mita shares the conclusion of Dimitrije Bogdanović that "without the Patriarchate of Peć, restored in 1557, Kosovo would have been lost forever."[23]

Like most prominent Serbian historians, Mita has also recently written on the cult of Kosovo and the various stages through which it evolved.[24] In a paper he gave in 1989, at the conference at Stanford University commemorating the six hundredth anniversary of the Battle of Kosovo, Mita observed that the Kosovo testament was deeply planted in the soul of the Serbian man, and proceeded to explain the place of the Kosovo tradition in the birth and development of the modern Serbian state.

Mita is fully aware that in studying the Battle of Kosovo, one must endeavor to separate myth from fact. But at the same time he recognizes the important role which "myth has played in shaping (Serbian) people's psychology and determining its destiny." He goes onto say that "Fictitious or true, the Kosovo legend offered the fatherland to people who had lost it."[25] He says that the Kosovo myth, built on martyrdom, injustice, and hope, called for national liberation and the restoration of the national state. These lofty principles incited the first Serbian uprising against the Turks in 1804. Karageorge drew his inspiration from Kosovo; followers of the Obrenović family included Kosovo on their coat of arms. Kosovo, Mita says, became synonymous with word "battlefield." In medieval sources the region of Kosovo and Metohija were called Serbia. The new Serbia of the Nineteenth century consisted of Sumadija and the valley of Morava. To distinguish these the former is called "Old Serbia." But he says that in Serbian minds, the two Serbias are one.[26]

The success in fighting the Turks in the First Serbian Uprising, Mita writes, had profound impact on the Serbs as well as other Balkan peoples; it instilled in the people national pride and a powerful desire to achieve liberation from the Turks. The Kosovo legend became merged with Serbian nationalism and "avenging Kosovo" became the battle cry. Karageorge appeared as the avenger of the Kosovo defeat. He appealed to the Serbs to rid themselves of the yoke they had been carrying since the Battle of Kosovo, and started restoring monasteries and urging commanders to take Milos Obilić as their model.

The persons of pen, such as Vuk Karadžić, the distinguished language reformer, ethnographer, and collector and publisher of popular songs, linked the Kosovo epic to national awakening and the idea that there is no freedom without sacrifice. "Kosovo," writes Mita, "was the leittmotif in the poems of the Montenegrin Prince, later King Nikola,"[27] and before him Peter II Petrović Njegoš, the famous Bishop of Montenegro with his "Mountain Wreath" (1847), exerted enormous influence on the development of the Serbian national movement, and was the first to codify the link between Serbian national identity and the Kosovo myth.

Mita discerns the powerful impact that the Kosovo tradition had in Djordje Petrović and Miloš Obrenović, the founders of the Modern Serbian state, the statesmanship of Ilija Garašanin, the author of "Načertanije"—the plan for the liberation of the Serbs, Prince Mihailo's Serbian and Balkan visions, and on the wars between the Serbs and the Turks in 1876–1878, the Balkan Wars of 1912–1913, and the World War I.[28]

Yet Mita correctly points out that the tradition of the pre-Kosovo state of the Nemanjići was more attractive than the Kosovo tradition to the Serbian insurgents in 1804–1813. After all, he says, the

Nemanjići symbolized the ascendancy and glory of the state while Kosovo marked its collapse.[29] In other words, the Cult of Stevan, the First-Crowned King, overshadowed the cult of Prince Lazar, the fallen ruler. As Serbia grew stronger, and its national program became broadened in the Nineteenth century, the cult of Stevan was replaced by the worship of Emperor Dusan under whose rule Serbia attained its greatest power and territorial size.

According to Mita, the Kosovo tradition was utilized in support of the monarchical system in nineteenth-century Serbia and Montenegro. King Milan referred to himself as "the First King after Kosovo" and spoke about the restored throne of the great Nemanjići. Both the conservative and liberal circles in Serbia, in the second half of the nineteenth century, nurtured the Kosovo tradition, and called for the fulfillment of the Kosovo legacy.[30] Mita sees the Kosovo tradition as a thread that goes through the entire existence of the Serbian nation. The Kosovo idea in the past served as a force unifying the Serbs, and it continues to play the same role today. The celebration of the Battle of Kosovo, he says, is an expression of a deeply rooted mission which the Serbian people have inherited. In that mission, Mita explains, the Serbian nation finds its being and its future.

In the words of Mita, the First Serbian uprising (1804–1813), and the developments that followed, set Serbia on a course of Western cultural orientation and development into a modern European state. Serbia entered the European cultural orbit. He explains that the geopolitical position of Serbia subjected her to Western, Central and Eastern European influences. The Serbian state developed more rapidly than did Serbian society. Mita points out that the Serbs learned technical and financial sciences from the Germans and Austrians, and law and philosophy from the French. Russian influence reached Serbia through Russian realists, such as Turgenev, Tolstoi, and Dostoyevski. The first Serbian military men were sent to Russia for training as these were linked closely to the Russian people ethnically, confessionally, and through common struggle against the Ottoman Turks. Later, in the time of Napoleon III, the Serbs began to send military experts to Paris. The result, Mita concludes, was that Serbian civilization in the course of the nineteenth century became an amalgam of different cultural influences.[31] Extending his studies to the Balkans, Mita searched for European influences in Balkan constitutions which tried to accommodate the organization of Balkan states to the European model.[32] In this respect he investigated the role which the military played in modern Balkan history.[33]

The prominent persons who contributed substantially to the liberation of the Serbs, the building of the modern Serbian state and the formation of Yugoslavia have also fascinated Mita. He has published articles and essays on Naradjordje (Djordje Petrović/Karageorge), Miloš Obrenović, Ilija Garašanin, Jovan Ristić, Milovan Milovanović, Radomir Putnik, Nikola Pasic, Stojan Novaković and Slobodan Jovanović.[34] He has studied the character, activities and leadership qualities of these men, and makes insightful observations about them. Mita sees Karadjordje as a great soldier, remarkable strategist, and a skilled revolutionary, and Miloš Obrenović as an astute reformer who established the foundations of the modern Serbian state. Like historian Slobodan Jovanović, he sees Miloš as a figure less epic than Karadjordje but as the greatest political mind in nineteenth century Serbia.[35] Though illiterate and lacking formal education, Miloš was, according to Mita, a skilled diplomat, who, during the acute rivalry among the European powers over the Eastern Question, knew how to take advantage of the opportunities available to him.[36]

As for Ilija Garašanin, Mita sees him as a man of vision and admires him for his proposals for the liberation of the Serbs, Balkan revolution, and the confederation of countries in the area extending from the Baltic Sea to the Aegean Sea, ideas that are still being discussed. Garašanin, Mita reasons, came at the right time and his ideas corresponded to the needs of the growing Serbian national society. Mita says that the visionary ideas of Garašanin and Prince Mihailo can be best appreciated when one considers the time to which the two men lived. While they were planning to clear the Turks from Serbia, the Ottoman Pasha still sat in the Kalemegdan fortress, over which the Turkish flag waved, and the Turkish nizam patrolled the streets of Belgrade.[37]

Mita sees the quality of superior statesmanship in Jovan Ristić, whose labors led to the liberation of the Serbian towns from Turkish occupation in 1867, an important achievement accomplished through compromise at a time when Serbia was not yet ready to engage the Turks militarily. Another Serbian statesman whom Mita studies is Milovan Milovanović, whose policy is reflected in his statement that little Serbia could not achieve its objectives alone and must "tie its small boat to the ship of the great European powers." Finally, Mita singles out one other Serb political leader, Nikola Pašić,[38] whom he admires greatly and who in his opinion was endowed with extraordinary qualities of statesmanship. Regardless of the extent to which Pašić has been criticized and maligned, Mita finds him an exceptionally astute politician, who knew what had to be accomplished and how to do it, and a realist, who know where Serbia's interests lay. Though attacked from all sides, in the words of Mita, Pašić held to his program, never losing sight of his principal objective. Mita writes that during the Austro-Serbian Customs War, Pašić shaped Serbia's foreign policy with great skill and finesse. In 1906–1911 Pašić knew that Serbia's chances of winning the Customs War with Austria-Hungary were slight, and that the only choice for Serbia was to secure the support of friendly Western democratic powers and Russia. Pašić sought friends and got them, assuring Serbia's victory.

Much has been written about the relations between Pašić and the Serbian government which he headed during World War I, and the iugoslav Committee, representing the South Slavs in Austria-Hungary, especially in regard to the Yugoslav question. Some writers praise Pašić, more or less, for the position he took while others praise and apologize for the activities and policies of the Yugoslav Committee. Mita contends that most of the criticism of Pasic was not warranted. It must be understood, he says, that while the Yugoslav Committee worked for the union of the South Slavs during the war, the Serbian government faced a plethora of challenges of which the Yugoslav Question was only a part.

In founding Yugoslavia, he writes, only two forces were of consequence—the Serbian army and the Serbian government allied with the Entente, and adds that the borders of Yugoslavia were established at the points the Serbian soldier reached in 1918.

Alone or in collective endeavors, Mita has written short syntheses and surveys of the history of the Serbs and other Yugoslavs, including the Bulgars. He published in Greek a history of modern Serbia[39] and contributed to the multi-volume *History of the Serbian People,* a 180-page section on Serbia's relations with Austria-Hungary, covering the period preceding World War I.[40] Finally, it should be added that Mita wrote a number of Articles on the status of modern Yugoslav historiography and on Balkan and Yugoslav research and publication in the United States.[41]

Mita is an imaginative, inquisitive, and productive historian, unafraid to ask and answer questions and to articulate his views. But doing historical research and writing about it is not his only attribute. He is also a superb teacher. At the University of California at Santa

Barbara (UCSB), he obtained his first real opportunity to teach history. He offered a variety of courses on the history of the Balkans and Eastern Europe and introduced them into the UCSB curriculum for the first time.

As a result of his teaching excellence, Mita was asked to take charge of the introductory courses on the History of Modern Europe. With his knowledge of university history, his breadth of historical interest, and his pedagogical skill, he was uniquely qualified to offer such a course—tracing the origin and development of modern society in a coherent and meaningful way. Mita quickly became one of the most beloved teachers on campus.

Mita is an inspiring lecturer who prepares his lectures meticulously and presents them interestingly and effectively. He is generous with the time he allows his students as an advisor on both the undergraduate and graduate level. This, combined with his loyalty and assistance to the graduate students, directing their research, finding financial assistance for them, and making arrangements for study abroad, had made Mita one of the most respected and appreciated members of faculty. He founded and directed a Graduate Program in Balkan Studies at UCSB. Under his guidance, some twenty young historians obtained a Ph.D. with dissertations dealing with Balkan and East European history.

Mita's professional work is boundless. At Santa Barbara, he served as Chairman of the Russian Area Studies Program. Mita was instrumental in bringing to UCSB the precious "Nikić Collection," purchased in Belgrade. It comprises of some 15,000 volumes concerning the history of Serbia and the Balkans. For several years he was the University's delegate to the International Research and Exchange Board (IREX), which selected junior and senior scholars in the field of Russian and East European Studies for study abroad. He also served on the Advisory Committee for Slavic and East European Studies of the CIES in Washington, DC (1987–1990). He never abandoned connections with the historical circles in Yugoslavia, especially in Serbia, where he is treated as a native historian. He has worked closely with the centers for historical research in Belgrade, and even after accepting the teaching position at Santa Barbara, he has had articles and books published in Yugoslavia. In 1985 Mita was elected to the membership of the Serbian Academy of Science and Arts, Serbia's foremost learned society, and in 1987 concluded an agreement of collaboration between UCSB and the Balkan Institute of the Serbian Academy of Science and Arts. He is looked upon as both an American and Yugoslav historian.

For many years Mita was a member of the American Historical Association, the American Association for the Advancement of Slavic Studies, the Bulgarian Studies Group, the Modern Greek Studies Association, the Association for South East European Studies, the North American Society for Serbian Studies (President in 1986), the Society of Nikola Tesla, and the United Nations Society (Santa Barbara). He served as President of the Conference on Slavic and East European History (1984–1985) affiliated with the American Historical Association, and has been of the editorial boards of the periodicals *The Austrian History Yearbook (1974–1978)*, *East European Quarterly* (Boulder, since 1970), *Historical Abstracts* (Santa Barbara, since 1970), *Serbian Studies* (since 1981), and *Balcanica* (Serbian Academy of Sciences, Institute for Balkan Studies, in 1970). Because of his prominence in the historical profession, Mita has been included in *Who's Who in America* and in the *International Who's Who in Education* (Cambridge, England, 2nd ed., 1981).[42]

Although Mita has retired from teaching, there is no indication that he will cease being a productive historian. In fact, he is currently working on his memoirs, which will focus on his experiences in World War II and the years immediately following. Those of us who admire Mita as a scholar and man hope that after formal retirement as a teacher of history he will continue his productive work and professional activities.

NOTES

1. Dimitrije Djordjević, *Izlazak Srbije na Jadransko More i Konferencija ambasadora u Londonu 1912* (Stamparija "Slobodan Jović," Belgrade, 1956), 160 pp.

2. *Milovan Milovanović* (Prosveta, Belgrade, 1962), 179 pp.

3. *Carinski rat Austro-Ugarske i Srbije 1906–1911*, (Istorijski Institut, Belgrade, 1962), 733 pp.

4. For a brief description of Mita's professional activities, see Dimitrije Djordjević, "Biografije i bibliografije," *Godisnjak Srpske Akademije nauka i umetnosti za 1986 godinu*, XCIII (Belgrade, 1987), pp. 491–499, published on the occasion of his election as a full member of the Academy in 1985.

5. Radovan Samardzić, "Pogovor," in *Dimitrije Djordjević, Ogledi*

iz novije Balkanske istorije (Srpska književna zadruga, Belgrade, 1989), pp. 223–229.

6. Dimitrije Djordjević, "The 1883 Peasant Uprising in Serbia," *Balkan Studies*, XX (1979) pp. 235–255. By the same author, "Agrarian Factors in Nineteenth Century Balkan Revolutions," in Bela K. Kiraly and Gunther E. Rothenburg, eds., *War and Society East Central Europe*, I (Brooklyn College Press, 1979), pp. 163–182. By the same author, "The Balkan Peasantry 1740–1814—A Synthesis," in Stephen Fischer-Galati and Bela Kiraly, eds., *War and Society in East Central Europe 1740–1920*. (Atlantic Studies on Society Change, New York, 1987), pp. 193–222.

7. See, Dimitrije Djordjević, "Marke Djuričić," *Enciklopedija Jugoslavije*, III (Zagreb, 1958) , p. 211, "Ilkin atentat," p. 344, "Dimitrije Isailović," p. 369, IV (1960); "Mladoturska revolucije," and "Milovan Milovanović," V (1962) , pp. 145, 119–120; "Stojan Ribarac," "Sanstefanski mir" and "Srbi," VII (1968), pp. 69, 135, 526–532.

8. Dimitrije Djordjević, *Ogledi iz novije Balkanske istorije* (Srpska knjizevna zadruga, Belgrade, 1939), 229 pp.

9. For a list of his complete works, see the bibliographic essay by Jelisaveta Allen in this volume.

10. Dimitrije Djordjević, "Migrations during the 1912–1913 Balkan Wars and World War One" in *Migrations in Balkan History* (Belgrade, 1989), pp. 115 & 129. By the same, "Prilog prčavanju migracija iz Habsburske Monarhije u Srbiju 60-tih i 70-tih godina XIX veka" in *Oslobodjenje gradova u Srbiji od Turaka 1862–1867* (Belgrade, 1970), pp. 313–336.

11. Dimitrije Djordjević, "Balkan Versus European Enlightenment—Parallelism and Dissonances," *East European Quarterly*, IX, 4 (Boulder, 1975), pp. 487–497.

12. Dimitrije Djordjević, "The Impact of the First Serbian Uprising on Balkan Peoples" in Wayne S. Vucinich, ed., *The First Serbian Uprising 1804–1813* (Columbia University Press, 1982), pp. 361–3B9.

13. Dimitrije Djordjević, "National Factors in Nineteenth Century Balkan Revolutions," *War and Society in East Central Europe*, I (Brooklyn College Press, 1979), pp. 163–182. By the same author, *Revolutions nationales des peuples balkaniques 1804–1914* (Istorijski Institut, Belgrade, 1965) 2O pp. (Presented at the World Congress of Historians in Vienna in 1965).

14. Dimitrije Djordjević, "Uloga istoricizma u formiranju balka-

nskih drzava XIX veka," in *Zbornik Filosofskog Fakulteta*, X:1 (Belgrade, 1968).

15. Dimitrije Djordjević, "Srbija i Beograd u vreme osnivanja Narodnog pozorista" in *Jedan vek narodnog pozorista u Beogradu 1868-1968* (Belgrade, 1968), pp. 29-39.

16. "Les mouvements pour l'independence nationale et economique des Balkans aux XIX et XX siècles (jusqu'á 1914)," *XII Congres international des historiques. Rapports*, IV (Vienna, 1965), pp. 284-290.

17. Dimitrije Djordjević, "Projects for the Federation of South-East Europe in the 1860s and 1870s," *Balcanica*, I (1970), pp. 117-143.

18. Dimitrije Djordjević, "Agrarian Reforms in Post-World War One Balkans: A Comparative Study," *Balcanica*, XIII-XIV (1983), pp. 255-269.

19. Dimitrije Djordjević, "Srbija i Habsburška monarhija—uzroci sukoba," *Istorijski glasnik*, No. 1, (1969), pp. 31-39. "Vojvoda Putnik, the Serbian High Command and Strategy in 1914" in *East Central European Society in the First World War*, B. Kiraly and N. Dreiszinger, eds. (East European Monographs, Boulder 1985), pp. 569-89.

20. Dimitrije Djordjević, "Austro-ugarski okupacio ni režim u Srbiji i njegov slom 1918," in *Naučni skup upovedu 50-godisnjice raspada Austro-Ugarski Monarhije i stvaranje jugoslovenske drzave* (JAZU, Zagreb, 1969) pp. 205-226.

21. Dimitrije Djordjević, ed., *The Creation of Yugoslavia 1914-1918* (Clio Books, Santa Barbara, 1980), see especially, pp. 1-14. By the same author, "Yugoslavism: Some Aspects and Comments," *Southeastern Europe*, I: 2 (Pittsburgh, 1974), pp. 192-201.

22. Dimitrije Djordjević, "Tradition of Kosovo in Formation of Modern Serbian Statehood in the Nineteenth Century." Scheduled to appear in a book to be published in late 1990. Paper was read at the Conference in Commemoration of the 600th Anniversary of the Battle of Kosovo, 1389-1989, held at Stanford University June 2-3, 1989.

23. Ibid., p 4.

24. Ibid., pp. 4-5.

25. Ibid., p. 2.

26. Ibid., p. 2.

27. Ibid., p. 12.

28. Ibid., p. 27.

29. Ibid.

30. Ibid., pp. 30–31.

31. Dimitrije Djordjević, "Ottoman Heritage versus Modernization: Symbiosis in Serbia During the Nineteenth Century" (To be published by Sud-Ost Europa Institut, Munich, presented at the conference in Bad Homburg, July 1989.

32. Dimitrije Djordjević, "Foreign Influences on Nineteenth Century Balkan Constitutions," *Papers for the V Congress of Southeast European Studies* (Slavica Publishers, Ohio, 1984), pp. 72–102.

33. Dmitrije Djordjević, "The Role of the Military in the Balkans in the Nineteenth Century," *Der Berliner Congress von 1878*, (Wiesbaden, 1982), pp. 317–347.

34. Dimitrije Djordjević, *Ogledi iz novije balkanske istorije* (Srpska književna zadruga, Belgrade, 1989), 229 pp.

35. *Politika*, April 8, 1990, p. 9.

36. *Politika*, April 8, 1990, p. 9.

37. Djordjević, "Evropski ok viri," pp. 1, 12.

38. Djordjević, " Pašić i Milovanovic u pregovorima za Balkanski savez 1912 godine," *Istorijski casopis*, IX–X (1959), pp. 467–486.

39. Dimitrije Djordjević, *Istoria tis Servias (1804–1918)* (Institute for Balkan Studies, Thessaloniki, 1970).

40. *Istorija srpskog naroda*, Vol. VI, Pt. 1 (Belgrade, 1983), pp. 95–174. See also Dimitrije Djordjević, *Pregled istorije jugoslovenskih naroda* (Belgrade 1965).

41. Dimitrije Djordjević, "Contemporary Yugoslav Historiography," *East European Quarterly*, I (Boulder, 1967), pp. 75–86.

42. Dimitrije Djordjević, "Biografije i Bibliografije," *Godišnjak Srpske Akademije Nauka i Umetnosti za 1986 godinu*, XCIII (Belgrade, 1987), p. 492.

THE BIBLIOGRAPHY OF DIMITRIJE DJORDJEVIĆ

Jelisaveta Stanojevich Allen

The lifetime achievement of Professor Dimitrije V. Djordjević rests on his continuous and indefatigable scholarly research and publication in the fields of Balkan, Yugoslav, and Serbian history of the nineteenth and twentieth centuries, as well as their relations to the neighboring states. His methodology, his erudition and his clear judgment have made each study a model of its genre. Since 1956 he had authored, co-authored, edited, and coedited eleven books listed here under Monographs.

Over the years, Professor Djordjević took part in many international congresses, symposia and conferences. At the University of California, Santa Barbara, he organized four international conferences on Balkan studies. He contributed papers to the *Festschrifts* honoring his colleagues and friends, and he has lectured throughout the United States, Europe and Australia. The results of his scholarly investigations (eighty-two articles in addition to the monographs), can be grouped into three major divisions: Essays in Balkan History; Essays in Yugoslav History; and Essays in Serbian History. His articles will be listed here chronologically under whose those heading, following the **Monographs**.

Since 1954 Djordjević has written over sixty book reviews. However, they, as well as shorter notes, newspaper articles, and interviews are not included in this bibliography.

MONOGRAPHS

1. *Izlazak Srbije na Jadransko More i konferencija ambasadora u Lomdonu 1912. [Serbia's Outlet to the Adriatic Sea and the 1912 Ambassadors' Conference in London]* (Belgrade, 1956), 160 pp.

2. *Carinski rat Austro-Ugarske i Srbije 1906–1911. (Jugoslovenske zemlje u XX veku)*, v. 1) ["La guerre douaniere entre l'Autriche-Hongrie et la Serbie 1906–1911"], (Belgrade, 1962). 733 pp.

3. *Milovan Milovanović* (Belgrade, 1962), 183 pp. (a biography).

4. *Revolutions Nationales des Peuples Balkaniques 1804–1914* (Belgrade, 1965), 250 pp.

5. *Istoría tís Servias, 1804–1918* [History of Serbia, 1804–1919], (Idryma meleton Chersonisou tou Aimou, 116) (Thessaloniki, 1970) xiii, 477 pp.

6. *The Creation of Yugoslavia 1914–1918*, (editor) (Santa Barbara, 1980), viii, 228 pp.

7. *The Balkan Revolutionary Tradition* (co-authored with Stephen Fischer-Galati), (New York, 1981), xv, 271 pp.

8. *Istorija srpskog naroda* [History of the Serbian People], Vol. 6, p. 1, *Od Berlinskog Kongresa do ujedinjenja 1878–1918*, (co-editor and author of three chapters, pp. 95–207) (Belgrade, 1983).

9. *East Central European Society and the Balkan Wars* (co-edited with Bela K. Kiraly), *War and Society in East Central Europe*, Vol. 18; (Atlantic Studies on Society Changes, no. 37) (Boulder/New York, 1987) xii, 431 pp.

10. *Ogledi iz novije balkanske istorije* [Essays in Modern Balkan History] (Belgrade, 1989), 229 pp.

11. *Migrations in Balkan History* (co-edited with Radovan Samardžić) (Belgrade, 1989), 170 pp. Proceedings from the conference, Population Migrations in the Balkans from the Pre-History to Recent Time, held in April 1988 at the University of California, Santa Barbara jointly with the Institute for Balkan History of the Serbian Academy of Sciences.

ARTICLES

1. ESSAYS IN BALKAN HISTORY

1. "Italijansko-turski rat 1911–12 godine i njegov uticaj na Balkan," ["The Italo-Turkish War of 1911–12 and Its Influence in the Balkans], *Istorijski pregled*, Vol. 1, pt. 4 (Belgrade 1954), 46–54.

2. "Kako su velike sile saznale za sklapanje Balkanskog Saveza 1912 godine." ["Comment les grandes Puissances on apris la formation de la Ligue Balkanique"], *Istorijski glasnik*, 4 (Belgrade 1954), pp. 127–143.

3. " 'La société', L'Alliance des peuples des Balkans en Serbie en 1890–1891. Contribution a l'histoire des alliances balkaniques." *Balkan Studies*, 4 (Thessaloniki, 1963), 137–154.

4. "Les mouvements pour l'independence nationale et economique des Balkans aux XIX et XX siècle (jusqu'á 1914)." *Rapports IV:*

Methodologie et histoire contemporaine. *XII Congres International des Sciences Historiques* (Vienna, Comite International des sciences historiques, 1965), 237–254.

5. "Pregled studija moderne balkanske istorije u Grčkoj," ["Studies on Modern Balkan History in Greece"], *Istorijski časopis*, 14–15 (Belgrade 1966), 49-5-503.

6. "Srbija i Balkan na početku XX veka, 1903–1906," ["La Serbie et les Balkans au debut du XXe siècle"], in *Jugoslovenski narodi pred Prvi svetski rat*, (Posebna izdanja SANU, vol. CDXVI, *Od⌐ljenje drustvenih nauka*, 61) (Belgrade, 1967), pp. 207–230.

7. "Raspad Habsburske monarhije 1918; slucajnost ili neiz bežnost?" ["The Collapse of the Habsburg Monarchy: Accidental or Inevitable"], *Jugoslovenski istorijski časopis*, 1–2 (Belgrade, 1968), 25–42.

8. "Uloga istoricizma u formiranju balkanskih država XIX veka" ["Le role de l'historicisme dans la formation des états balkaniques du IX siècle"], *Zbornik filozofskog fakulteta*, 10/I (Belgrade, 1968), 309–326.

9. "Les Balkans dans la politique internationale du XVIIe au XIXe siècle. Les pays Yugoslaves aus XIXe siècle." Co-rapport, II Congres International des études sud-est européennes. (Athens, 1970), 1–10.

10. "Projects for the Federation of South-East Europe in the 1860s and 1870s," *Balcanica*, 1 (Belgrade, 1970), 119–145.

11. "Osvrt na savremenu američku balkanologiju" ["Balkan Studies in the United States"], *Balcanica*, 2 (Belgrade, 1971), 425–427.

12. "History of the Balkans, 1815–1914," *Encyclopaedia Britanica*, Vol. 2 (1973-74), 624–631; *Bibliography*, p. 640.

13. "The Impact of the State on Nineteenth Century Balkan Social, Economic and Political Development," Corapport, III Congrès International des études sud-est européennes. *Mouvements sociaux et nationaux dans les pays du sud-est européen* (Bucharest, 1974), 70–83.

14. "Balkan versus European Enlightenment: Parallelism and Dissonances," *East European Quarterly*, 9/4 (Boulder, 1975), 487–497.

15. "My Dear Friend Basil." *Essays in Memory of Basil Laourdas* (Thessalokiki, 1975), 91–94.

16. "The Balkans and the Mediterranean in the Nineteenth Century," Association Internationale d'études du sud-est européen, *Bulletin*, 13–14 (Bucharest, 1975-76), 11–24.

17. "An Attempt at the Impossible: Stages of Modernization of the Balkan Peasantry in the 19th Century." *Balcanica*, 8 (Belgrade, 1977), 321–335.

18. "Agrarian Factors in Nineteenth-Century Balkan Revolutions." *War and Society in East Central Europe*, Vol. 1, Bela K. Kiraly and Gunther E. Rothenberg, eds. (Brooklyn, 1979), 163–182.

19. "National Factors in Nineteenth Century Balkan Revolutions," *War and Society in East Central Europe*, Vol. 1, B. K. Kiraly and G. E. Rothenberg, eds. (Brooklyn, 1979), 197–213.

20. "The Impact of the First Serbian Uprising on the Balkan Peoples," *The First Serbian Uprising 1804–1813*, Wayne Vucinich, ed. (Boulder/New York, 1982), 361–389.

21. "The Role of the Military in the Balkans in the Nineteenth Century." *Der Berliner Kongress von 1878. Die Politik der Grossmächte und die Probleme der Modernisierung in Südosteuropa in der zweiten Halfte des 19, Jahrhunderts.* R. Melville and H. J. Schröder, eds. Veröffentlichungen des Instituts für Europäisch Geschichte, Mainz. Beiheft 7 (Wiesbaden, 1982), 317–347.

22. "Agrarian Reforms in Post World War One Balkans. A Comparative Study," *Balcanica*, 13–14 (Belgrade, 1983), 25–269.

23. "Balkan Revolutionary Organizations in the 1860s and the Peasantry," *The Crucial Decade: East Central European Society and National Defense, 1859–1870*, Bela K. Kiraly, ed. (Boulder/New York, 1984), 270–283.

24. "Foreign Influences on Nineteenth Century Balkan Constitutions," *Papers for the V Congress of Southeast European Studies, Belgrade, September 1984* (Columbus, Ohio, 1984), 72–102.

25. "The Present State of Studies of Nineteenth Century History of Balkan Peoples in the United States," *Conference Internationale des Balkanologues, Belgrade, 7–8 septembre 1982*, Institut des études balkaniques, Editions speciales, 23 (Belgrade, 1984), 127–136.

26. "The Serbian Peasant in the 1876 War," *Insurrections. Wars and the Eastern Crisis in the 1870s*, Bela K. Kiraly and Gale Stokes, eds. (Boulder/New York, 1985), 306–316.

27. "The Balkan Peasantry, 1740–1914: A Synthesis," *Essays on War and Society in East Central Europe, 1740–1920*, Stephen Fischer-Galati and Bela K. Kiraly, eds. (Boulder, 1987), 193–222.

28. "Centralization versus Decentralization in the Formation of Nineteenth Century Balkan States," *Ekmečićev Zbornik*, Yearbook of the Association of Historian of Bosnia and Herzegovina, 39 (Sarajevo,

1988), 84–90.

29. "Migrations during the 1912–1913 Balkan Wars and World War One," *Migrations in Balkan History.* (See also under Monographs, no. 11), 115–129. Also: "Preface," 7–8.

30. "Balkanski ustavi u devetnaestom veku" ["Balkan Constitutions in the Nineteenth Century"], *Zbornik: Dva veka savremene ustavnosti*, Srpska Akademija nauka, naučni skupovi, 47, Odeljenje društvenih nauka, 9. (Belgrade, 1990), 543–551.

ESSAYS IN YUGOSLAV HISTORY

1. "Bosna i Hercegovina od 1878 do 1903 godine"; "Bosna i Hercegovina od 1903 do 1914 godine"; "Srbija od 1903 do 1912 godine"; "Jugosloveni u Prvom Svetskom Ratu (1914–1918)," chapters: *Pregled istorije jugoslovenskih naroda*, Vol. 2. (Belgrade, 1965), 71–75; 99–103; 114–118; 146–158. (*History of the Yugoslav Nations*, chapters: "Bosnia and Herzegovina"; "Serbia 1903–1912"; "The Yugoslavs in World War I, 1914–1918").

2. "Contemporary Yugoslav Historiography," *East European Quarterly*, 1 (Boulder, 1967), 75–86.

3. "Yugoslav Migrations from Austria-Hungary to Serbia in the Second Half of the XIX Century," *Oslobodjenje Kradova u Srbiji od Turaka 1862-1867* (Belgrade, 1968), 313–336. Conference held at the Serbian Academy of Sciences and Arts.

4. "Yugoslavia—Work in Progress," *Contemporary History in Europe: Problems and Perspectives*, D. C. Watt, ed. (London, 1969), 250–262.

5. "Les Yougoslaves au XIXe et au XXe siècle. Rapport pour la seance pleniere: Les peuples de l'Europe du Sud-Est et leur role dand l'histoire," I Congres International des études balkaniques et sud-est européen, Sofia 1966, *Actes. III. Histoire* (Sofia, 1969), 117–130.

6. "Fascism in Yugoslavia: 1918–1941," *Native Fascism in Successor States, 1918-1945*, Peter Sugar, ed. (Seattle, 1970) 125–134.

7. "West European and American Post-War Historiography on Macedonia and Macedonian People" (Skopje, 1970), 147–162.

8. "La Communede Paris et les Yougoslaves," *Dimensions et resonances de l'année 1871. (Revue d'histoire moderne et contemporaine*, 19 (Paris, 1972), 345–353.

9. "Yugoslavism: Some Aspects and Comments," *Southeastern Europe*, 1/2 (1974), 192–201.

10. "Schooling and Public Education," *Sudost europa Handbuch*, 1. Jugoslawien. Klaus-Detley Grothusen, ed. (Göttingen, 1975), 383–395.

11. "The Idea of Yugoslav Unity in the Nineteenth Century," *The Creation of Yugoslavia 1914–1918*. (See also *Monographs* no. 6), 1–17.

12. "Serbia and the Adriatic Sea: One Aspect of the Yugoslav Question in the Nineteenth Century," *Serbian Studies*, 1 (Chicago, 1980), 5–16.

13. "Three Yugoslavias–A Case of Survival," *East European Quarterly*, 19/4 (Boulder, 1986), 385–393.

14. "Mavro Orbini," "Lucius Ivan," "Vitezovic Ritter Pavao," "Brankovic Count Djordje," "Rajic Jovan," *Great Historians from Antiquity to 1980—An International Dictionary*, Lucian Boia, ed. (Greenwood Press, 1989), 85–88; 341–344.

15. "Great Historians–Yugoslavian:" "Gavrilović, Mihailo," "Jovanović, Slobodan," "Kukuljević, Sakcinski Ivan," "Novakovic, Stojan," "Ostrogorski, Georgije," "Racki, Franjo," "Ruvarac, Ilarion," "Sišić, Ferdo," "Smiciklas, Tadija," "Stanojević, Stanoje," *Great Historians of the Modern Age—An International Dictionary* Lucian Boia, ed. (Greenwood Press, 1991), 783–798.

3. ESSAYS IN SERBIAN HISTORY

1. "Projekt Jadranski železnice u Srbiji (1896–1912)," ["The Adriatic Railway Project in Serbia, 1896–1912"], *Istorijski Glasnik*, 3–4 (Belgrade, 1956).

2. "0 dramatizaciji Ivkove slave" ["On the Dramatization of Ivkova slava"], *Prilozi za književnost, jezik. istoriju i folklor*, 22/1-2 (Belgrade, 1956), 115–119.

3. "Austro-srpski sukob oko projekta Novopazarske želiznice" [" Austro-Serbian Conflict over the Novi-Pazar Railway Project"], *Istorijski časopis*, 7 (Belgrade, 1957), 213–248.

4. "Velikoškolska omladina u borbi protiv ličnog režima kralja Aleksandra Obrenovica" [" University Youth against the Personal Regime of King Aleksandar Obrenović"], *Istorijski pregled*, 4/2 (Belgrade, 1957), 115–120.

5. "Genčić, Djordje," "Grunberg, Karl," "Djuričić, Marko," "Ilkinatentat," "Isailović, Dimitrije," "Iswolsky, Aleksandar Petrovic," "Momzen, Theodor," "Mladoturska revolucija," "Milovanović,

Milovan," "Protić, Stojan," "Petrović, Nastas," "Popović, Stojan," "Rafailović, Zivojin," "Ribarac, Stojan," "San Stefanski mir," "Sazonov, Sergije Dimitrijević," "Srbi: Istorija: od 1858 do 1918," *Enciklopedija Jugoslavije*, Vols. 3–7 (Zagreb, 1958–68).

6. "Trgovinski pregovori Srbije i Austro-Ugarske 1869–1875" ["Commercial Negotiations between Serbia and Austria-Hungary, 1869–1875"], *Istorijaki Glasnik*, 3–4 (Belgrade, 1958), 51–73.

7. "Pašić Milovanović u pregovorima za Balkanski savez 1912. godine" ["Pašić and Milovanović in Balkan Alliance's Negotiations 1912"], *Istorijski časopis*, 9–10 (Belgrade, 1959), 467–486.

8. "Milovanović i Izvoljski u Karlsbadu 1908. godine" ["Milovanović and Iswolsky in Karlsbad 1908"], *Jugoslovenska revija za medjunarodno pravo*, 7/3 (Belgrade, 1960), 40–547.

9. "Obrazovanje i raspad vlade cetvorne koalicije u Srbiji 1909. godine" ["The Formation and Collapse of the Four-Party Government in Serbia in 1909"], *Istorijski časopis*, 11 (Belgrade, 1960), 213–230.

10. "Pokušaji srpsko-ugarski saradnje i zajedničke akcije 1906. godine" ["Tentatives de collaborations serbo-hongroise 1906"], *Istorija XX veka*, Vol. 2 (Belgrade, 1961), 354–384.

11. "Filozofski fakultet Univerziteta u Beograd u 1905–1918" ["The Philosophical Faculty at Belgrade University, 1905–1919"], *Spomenica stojodina beogradskog Filozofskog fakulteta* (Belgrade, 1963) , 53–89.

12. *Historiographie yougoslave 1955–1965* (Belgrade, 1965); chapters: "L'essor de la Serbie (partie de 1878–1903): La Serbie et la première alliance balkanique de 1878 à 1930," 256–261; "Histoire Culturelle," 284–290.

13. "Parlamentarna kriza u Srbiji 1905. godine" ["La crise parlementaire de 1905 en serbie"], *Istorijski časopis*, 14–15 (1963–1963, published 1966), 157–172.

14. "The Serbs as an Integrating and Disintegrating Factor in the Habsburg Monarchy," *Austrian History Yearbook*, 3 (1967), 48–82.

15. "Srbija i Beograd u vreme osnivanja Narodnog pozorišta" ["Serbia and Belgrade at the Time of the Foundation of the National Theater"], *Jedan vek Narodnog pozorišta u Beogradu, 1868–1968* (Belgrade, 1968), 29–39.

16. "Austro-ugarski okupacioni režim u Srbiji i njegov slom 1918" ["The Regime of the Austro-Hungarian Occupation of Serbia 1914–1918 and Its Collapse"], *Naučni skup u povodu 50-godisnjice raspada Austro-Ugarske monarhije i stvaranja jugoslovenske države* (Za-

greb, Jugoslavenkska Akademija znanosti i umjetnosti, 1969), 205–226.

17. "Srbija i Habsburška monarhija; uzroci sukoba" ["Serbia and Habsburg Monarchy: Origins of Conflict"], *Istorijski glasnik*, 1 (Belgrade, 1969), 31–39

18. "The Influence of the Italian Risorgimento on Serbian Policy during the 1908–1909 Annexation Crisis." *Balcanica*, 3 (Belgrade, 1972), 333–347.

19. "Historians in Politics: Slobodan Jovanović," *Journal of Contemporary History*, 8/1 (1973), 21–40. Reprinted in Historians in Politics. Walter Laqueur, ed. (London, 1974), 253–272.

20. "The Echo of the 1866 Cretan Uprising in Serbia." *Third International Congress of Cretan Studies, Rethymnon, Crete, September 1971* (Athens, 1975), 94–109.

21. "Economic Emancipation of Serbia and the Great European Powers on the Eve of World War I." *Velike sile i Srbija pred Prvi svetski rat. Zbornik radova prikazanih na Medjunarodnom naučnom skupu Srpske Akademije nauka, septembar 1974* (Belgrade, 1976), 95–108.

22. "The 1883 Peasant Uprising in Serbia," *Balkan Studies*, 20 (Thessaloniki, 1979), 235–255.

23. "Die Serben," *Die Habsburgermonarchie 1848–1918*, Vol. 3, pt. 2, *Die Volker des Reiches* (Vienna, 1980), 734-774.

24. "Nikola Jovanović–Amerikanac: The First Serbian Representative in the United States," *Serb World*, Vol. 3, no. 2 (1982), 16.

25. "The Serbs: A Historical Survey," *Landmarks in Serbian Culture and History* (Pittsburgh, 1983), 1–16.

26. "Srbija i srpski društvo 1880-tih godina" ["Serbia and Serbian Society in the Year 1880"], *Istorijski časopis*, 29–30 (Belgrade, 1983), 413–426.

27. "Vojvoda Putnik, the Serbian High Command, and Strategyin 1914," *War and Society in East Central Europe*, Vol. 19, *East Central European Society in World War I*, Bela Kiraly and Nandor Dreisziger, eds. (Boulder, 1985), 568–569.

28. "Stojan Novaković: Historian, Politician, Diplomat," *Serbian Studies*, 3/3 (1985–86), 39–57. Reprinted in *Historians as Nation Builders—Central and Southeast Europe*, Dennis Deletant and Harry Hanak, eds. (London, 1988), 51–69.

29. "Vojvoda Radimir Putnik," *War and Society in East Central*

Europe, Vol. 25, *East Central European War Leaders: Civilian and Military*, Bela K. Kiraly and Albert Nofi, eds. (Boulder, 1988), 223–248.

30. "Serbian Society 1903–1914," *East Central European Society and the Balkan Wars* (see *Monographs*, no. 9), 227–239.

31. "Seljastvo u Srbiji u devetnaestom veku," ["The Peasantry in Serbia in the Nineteenth Century"], *Glas CCCLIV SANU. Odeljenje istorijskih nauka*, 6. (Belgrade, 1988), 17–31. This article was Djordjević's inaugural address read at the Serbian Academy of Sciences and Arts November 11, 1986.

32. "The Role of St.Vitus Day in Modern Serbian History," *Serbian Studies*, 5/3 (1990), 33–40.

33. "Tradition in Kosovo in Formation of Serbian Statehood in the Nineteenth Century," *Kosovo—The Legacy of a Medieval Battle*, Thomas Emmert and Wayne Vucinich, eds. (University of Minnesota, Minneapolis, 1991), 309–330.

WORKS FORTHCOMING IN 1992

"La Peninsola balkanica. 1900–1950," *Instituto della Enciclopaedia Italiana, Storia del XX Secolo*, Vol. I, Part II.

"The Yugoslav Phenomenon," *The Columbia History of Eastern Europe in the Twentieth Century*, Joseph Held, ed. (New York, 1992.)

DOCTORAL DISSERTATIONS IN
MODERN BALKAN HISTORY AND
RELATED TOPICS
Completed under the Guidance of D. V. Djordjević
at the University of California, Santa Barbara

Frances Radovich, "Aftermath the Regicide—British Policy and Serbian Conspiracy Question 1903–1906," (1975).

James Barringer, "Alexander Petrovich Izvolsky 1906–1908, A Reevaluation," (1975).

Nikolai Altankov, "The Bulgarian Americans," (1977).

Richard Woytak, "On the Border of War and Peace—the Role of Intelligence and the Frontier in Polish Foreign Policy 1938–1939," (1977).

Lynn Curtright, "Muddle, Indecision and Setback: British Policy and the Balkan States, August 1914 to the Inception of the Dardanelles Campaign," (1980).

Horst Lorscheider, "The German Economic Penetration in the Balkans 1871–1914," (1980).

Richard Spence, "Yugoslavs, the Austro-Hungarian Army and World War I," (1981).

Bernd Fischer, "King Zog and the Struggle for Stability in Albania," (1982).

Kathy Bangerter, "Three Prominent Philhellenes in the Greek Struggle for Independence," (1982).

Leonard Friedman, "The Anglo-Axis Rivalry in Greece in the Eve of World War II," (1914).

Alain Dubie (Wachhold), "Frank Golder," (1984).

Frank Verna, "Yugoslavia under Italian Rule 1941–1943: Civil and Military Aspects of the Italian Occupation," (1985).

Eric Knudsen, "Great Britain, Constantinople and the Turkish Peace Treaty 1919–1922," (1985).

Thaeib Elbhloul, "Italian Colonialism, the Young Turks and the Libyan Resistance 1908–1918," (1986).

Remi Nadeau, "The Big Three and the Partition of Europe 1941–

1945," (1987).

Wilan Protić, "The Ideology of the Serbian Radical Movement 1881–1903–Sources, Characteristics, Developments," (1987).

Kim Frančev, "France and the Montenegrin Government in Exile 1916–1921," (1988).

Linda Nelson, "Nationalism and Gender Identity: The Bulgarian National Revival, Women's Consciousness, Women's Activism," (Ph.D candidate, anticipated completion, 1992).

Nina Bakisian, "The Danubian Federation Projects: Motion for Unity in an Age of Nationalism and Dissent," (Ph.D candidate, anticipated completion, 1992).

Doctoral Dissertations in Ancient History

Elpida Hadjidaki, "The Classical and Hellenistic Harbor at Phalasarna: a Pirate's Porti?" (1989).

Robert Frakes, "Audience and Meaning in the *Res Gestae* of Ammianus Warcellinus." (1991).

Masters Theses in Modern Balkan History
and Related Topics

Steve Harding, "The OSS and American Covert Operations in Yugoslavia." (1977).

Chester Biedul, "The April War in Yugoslavia," (1941).

Eric Knudsen, "The Failure of European Diplomacy and the Greek-Turkish War 1919–1923," (1979).

Kim daCunha (Frančev), "Comparative Study of Serbian, Bulgarian, Greek and Montenegrin Constitutions in the 19th Century," (1980).

Thaeib Elbhloul, "The Italian Colonial Expansion: A Study of the Italian-Turkish War over Libya 1911–1912," (1980).

Nicholas Vucinich, "From the Adriatic to the Pacific Coast—the Yugoslavs California," (1983).

Milan Protić, "The Characteristics and Ideology of the People's Radical Party in Serbia 1881–1903," (1983).

Linda Nelson, "The Yugoslav Government in Exile and the United States 1941–1944," (1983).

Patricia Brown, "European Immigrations in Rural Illinois 1860–1910," (1990).

During his years at UCSB Professor Djordjević was the comprehensive examiner for forty-three candidates in fields of Modern European history. In addition, he chaired nineteen Ph.D. committees in the area of Balkan history and was a member of eleven Ph.D. committees in other areas.

PART II

THE ANCIENT AND MEDIEVAL BALKANS

THE BALKANS IN THE SEVENTH CENTURY
AN ETHNIC APPROACH

Nikolay G. Altankov

Bulgarian historiography has traditionally maintained that the secret of the national ethnogenesis of the Bulgarians is to be found in the plains of ancient lower Moesia. There in 681 A.D. a wild and illiterate band of Proto-Bulgarians met Slav—and Thracian—settlers and eventually disappeared in their midst, leaving no trace except for the name of the newly founded state of the Slavo-Bulgarians.

Such a view, true or not, necessarily requires an ethnic model. Its proponents generally have assumed that in the Balkans, especially in the territory between the Balkan mountains and the Danube River and between the Black Sea and the Iskur River (roughly the western and southern frontiers of Bulgarian penetration until at least mid-ninth century) there were only two main ethnic groups: the Slavs and the Thracians. A Bulgarian textbook published in 1963, while acknowledging that "a considerable ethnic medley was created" with populations of Germanic, Sarmatian and Turkic origin, asserted that "romanized and Hellenized Thracians were still the majority "by the end of the fourth century.[1]

Since very little substantive evidence has been offered in support of this model, it would seem unfair not to go to the historical records and ascertain if this view is accurate. There is good reason to believe that this limited and parochial view of the ethnogenesis of the Bulgarians stands a good chance of acquiring universal acknowledgment. This is also supported by the inadequate work recently done on the subject by Bulgarian and international scholars.

The purpose of this review, therefore, is to trade and describe, and attempt an analysis of, the various ethnic groups that formed the population of the Balkan Peninsula before and after the foundation of the Bulgarian state in 681. Leaving aside the numbers question, i.e. how many Slavs and the Thracians were there in comparison with other groups, we consider it appropriate to ask if there were

in fact such powerful contingents of Slavs and Thracians to justify
disregard for other populations. The historical records are full of
evidence concerning Dacians, Moesians, Avars, Goths, Huns, Bulgars,
Armenians, and Greeks, while quite reluctant to place Slavs en masse
in Moesia and hardly ever mentioning the Thracians.

Thus, the first question to assess is the character and the diversity
of the various ethnic groups in the Balkans as they are described in the
records. Second, we will attempt to show their distribution as well as
their relative weight, if not absolutely, at least in comparison to one
another. Special consideration will be given to the resettlements and
deportations of population groups—not sporadic but wholesale—as
shown in the sources. Lastly, we will suggest a fuller, and we think, a
more appropriate model of the ethnic diversification in the Balkans,
specifically as it relates to the ethnogenesis of the Bulgarians.

For the sake of clarity we will distinguish three main periods
in the dynamics of ethnic development in the Balkans. The period until the fourth century A.D.—before the barbarian invasions—is
characterized by the gradual emergence of two main language areas:
Greek to the south and Latin to the north of the Balkan mountains.
The "traditional" populations in the south, Thracians, Macedonians,
Greeks, Illyrians, and others, were already drawn into the Hellenistic
orbit, while the ethnic composition in the north was more varied, as
beyond the Danube there often extended barbaricum. The arrival of
the Goths, which marked the beginning of the barbarian migrations
in the fourth century, changed this situation, especially in regards to
the fate of the traditional population groups. The third period, in
the aftermath of these invasions, coincides with the settlement of the
Bulgars on the right bank of the Danube.

Before the arrival of Khan Isperikh and his Bulgars, the Balkans
were a veritable ethnic mosaic. Eastern Thrace and the Black Sea
coast, Thessalonika and the ports of peninsular Greece were more
or less solidly Greek, the populations swelled by refugees from other
areas. Elsewhere, there were pockets of Greeks and Romans, and un-
Romanized Thracians. To the west were Illyrians, Daco-Moesians,
Dalmatians, Slavs, Avars, Bulgars, and Armenians, to mention only
the most prominent ethnic groups.[2] Even some of those designations
no longer denoted ethnicity but rather residency, as we shall see.

We should remember that when talking about the disappearance of historic populations, we rarely mean their physical extinction.
Rather, we are describing the loss of important characteristics per-

taining to their distinct identity and singular development, usually, but not always, as a result of their loss of political dominance. Neither the Thracians, the majority of whom were Hellenized, nor the Slavs, who became Hellenized in Greece and Bulgarianized in the north, nor the Macedonians, whose kingdom was destroyed by the Romans, were physically annihilated. We do not claim that the Avars, about whom we hear very little after the destruction of their empire by the Franks and the Bulgars, simply vanished. On the other hand, we have to make the clear distinction between "traditional," that is, historic ethnic groups, such as Greeks, Thracians, Macedonians, and groups such as the Huns, Avars, and Bulgars, whose origins, distinctive features and, specific identity are less clear. The latter groups usually carried geographical names, or names given to them by others. Such was the case with inhabitants of Moesia, simply called Moesians, designating thereby not the peculiar characteristic of a tribe, nation, state, but rather the inhabitants of a geographic area. Later on, the terms Thracian, Macedonian, Greek, and also, Dacian took on similar connotations, offering few clues as to the ethnic identity of the regions' inhabitants. Such might have been the case with many of the Balkan Slavs, who became known by the names of their areas of settlement. Early Greek sources speak of Timochani, Strimonzi, and Dragoviti, names derived from rivers and districts, areas settled by the Sclavi, or Slavs. This development was by no means unique and had many equivalents in the life of Byzantium; Emperor Basil I, the founder of the "Macedonian" dynasty was really of Armenian extraction, although he was born in Macedonia.

Archaeology tells us that the Balkans have been inhabited since Paleolithic times, and diggings have yielded rich remains from the Abbevillian Culture onwards, probably due to the unique climate and geography of the area.[3] Evidence also suggests that the ethnic composition has always been varied.[4] The Thracian plain, in particular, was famed for its dense population in the Bronze Age and also in Hellenistic times. The original populations, Greeks, Macedonians, Illyrians, Thracians, and others, later became diluted with Roman colonists and immigrants from Asia Minor, Syria, and Greece.[5] The Thracian lands lay to the east of the Balkan peninsula and the Illyrians to the west; Greeks lived in the Peloponnesus, while the Daco-Moesians were settled between the Balkan mountains and the Danube River and beyond.[6]

The Thracians, first mentioned in the eighth century B.C., were conquered by the Macedonians in the fourth century. They were traditionally divided into tribes and had no native alphabet or literature. The kingdoms they formed were usually short-lived.[7] The Romans destroyed the Macedonian kingdom in 168 B.C. and by 46 A.D. all Thracian territory formed two Roman provinces, Thrace and Moesia.[8] Thracians were gradually drawn into the orbit of Hellenistic culture (although the Moesian Thracians became Romanized), and the process seems to have been fairly complete by the time of the barbarian invasions of the sixth century.[9] It is doubtful if Thracian speech, culture, or ethnic consciousness had survived as far as the fourth century.[10] The modern Vlachs are, according to some authors, descendants of the ancient Thracians, or, in other views, the remnants of the Roman settlers or "provincials" from Dacia. Vlachs, as a group, were first mentioned in 976 when a brother of the Bulgarian King Samuil was reported slain by a Vlach.[11]

Modern Bulgaria was part of the Roman Empire from the time of Augustus (63 B.C.–A.D. 14). Moesia was divided by Domitian (81–96) into Upper (western) and Lower (eastern) Moesia separated by the river Cebrus. In 274 Emperor Aurelian abandoned Dacia (present-day Transylvania and western Wallachia) to the barbarians and at that time many Romanized Dacians resettled in Moesia, the central part of which became known as Dacia Aureliani.[12] The Dacians and the Getae were natives of the lands between the Dniester and Danube Rivers, while the Venedi, also called Slavs or proto-Slavs, lived north of the Dacians in approximately the same area.[13]

The Sarmatians disappeared by the fourth century, while the Celts probably vanished before the arrival of the post-Hunnic invasions of the Balkans (ca. 600), and very few of the older Germanic pockets remained after the fifth century.

By the fourth century the southern Balkans, roughly the territory of present-day Greece, was still mostly Greek speaking, and the few non-Greek communities there—Roman, Italian, and remnants of the original Macedonians—were probably largely Hellenized. The Greeks outside Greece proper were mostly colonists from Miletus to the Black Sea, who had emigrated from the seventh century B.C. to the Black Sea littoral. Greek is still spoken today in the streets of Nessebur, Bulgaria, as well as in other places along the coast. North of the Balkans, however, Latin was the dominant tongue. We should keep in mind, of course, that language, however important, is only one of the distinguishing characteristics of an ethnic entity, therefore not all

Greek-speaking groups in the south were necessarily ethnic Greeks, nor were all Latin-speaking inhabitants of Dacia and Moesia Romans.

We generally consider the Goths to have started the so-called barbarian invasions of the Balkans. They appear in the records after 166 A.D. In 214 they took Dacia away from the Romans and held it until 375 when they, in turn, were conquered by the Huns. The Goths invaded Moesia and Thrace as early as 250 and again in 376 during the reign of Emperor Valens, who permitted them to settle in Moesia. Those who remained there were henceforth known as Moeso-Goths and it was for them that Bishop Ulfilas (311–383) translated the Bible into Gothic around 350. Ulfilas himself lived for a few years in a Goth settlement not far from present-day Turnovo in Bulgaria.[14]

The Goths, who were of Germanic descent, gave birth to a new, so-called Gotho-Gepid culture. In 376 the Iranian-speaking Alans overran the Ostrogoth empire in the Ukraine and pushed the Visigoths from the Dniester region. The refugee Goths were later settled south of the Danube as *foederati* of the East Roman Empire (Byzantium), but eventually revolted and defeated a large Roman army under Emperor Valens (378).[15]

In 375 the Huns conquered the Goths between the Don and the Danube rivers. It is this period, from the end of the fourth century through the fifth, that the ethnic picture north of the Black Sea changed considerably.[16] After 470 the Ostrogoths settled in lower Moesia and Dobroudzha. Later, in 488, they were induced by Byzantium to leave and battle the usurper Odoacer in Italy. It is conceivable, of course, that many of them stayed behind and joined the earlier Gothic settlers.[17]

The Huns appeared south the Danube in the second half of the fourth century but did not remain long.[18] But after 378, chiefly because of Hun pressure, other peoples crossed the Danube and invaded Valeria. The records mention Sarmatians, Sciri and Carpodacians.[19] Some Huns settled in Thrace in 390. Either alone, or allied with other groups, the Huns raided and devastated whole districts of the Balkans for the next fifty years. In 441–447, for instance, they destroyed Serdica.[20]

The Bulgars were mentioned in Byzantine annals before 430. Later thev were often linked with such groups as the Utigurs, Kutrigurs, and Onogurs. They are clearly identified after the collapse of the Huns (ca. 460–500). A Turkish people, the Bulgars had come to Europe from central Asia in the Second century A.D., settling in the region between the Caspian and the Black Sea.[21] By the fifth century they appeared along the Danube. In 482 the Byzantine Emperor Zeno employed Bulgar troops against Theodoric the Ostrogoths.[22] By 487 some Bulgars had already settled in the lands of present-day Romania, north of the Danube, while others penetrated as far south as Thrace.[23] They raided into Byzantine territory in 493, 499 and 502, and in 528 they invaded Thrace and in 539 the overran Dobroudzha, Moesia and the rest of the Balkan Peninsula as far as Thrace.[24]

In 545 Emperor Justinian was offered land and *foederati* status to the Antae to guard the Empire against the Bulgars, but new invasions were reported in 558–559 and in 562. Romans and Utigurs fought against the Kutrigurs in 551. Greek sources reported that the Avars subjugated the Kutrigurs in 562 and six years later the Utigurs were reported defeated by the Turks.[25] Apparently under the pressure of the Avars, the Bulgar groups migrated to the steppes of the Kuban River, into the Kama-Volga basin, to Lombardy and to the region of the lower Danube, where Khan Isperikh established his people around 650.[26]

Recent research has given rise to the designation of the Saltovo, or Saltovo-Mayatska (or Balkan-Danubian) Culture, which is ascribed to Bulgars, Avars and Khazars. It was distinguished, according to some authors, by growing cities, flourishing trade and a developed feudal system.[27]

In 562 Baian organized a vast Avar empire that stretched from the river Don to the middle Danube. The Avars, like the Huns and Bulgars, were well-known in Asia before their appearance about 550 in the Caucasus. They conquered the Antae and after 561 approached the Danube. About 580 some 600,000 of them crossed the Danube from Illyria to Scythia (Dobroudzha), demolishing entire settlements of local Sclavini (Slavs).[28] The Byzantines reportedly offered them the lands of the Herules who were settled north of the Sava River. Justinian I was also alleged to have turned the Avars against the Slavs.[29] The Avars reached the peak of their might in 626 with an unsuccessful siege of Constantinople.[30] Eventually their power declined until in Khan Krum's time (803–814), there came a total collapse of their empire. The Bulgars took over their land and led many Avars into captivity.[31]

The Antae, also known to the ancients as Wends, and identified by some scholars as Slavs, lived between the rivers Oder and Dnieper, or between the Volga and Don. Mention has been made of their "mysterious state."[32] The Slavs reportedly had long periods of "contacts" (probably an euphemism for being subjugated) with peoples like the Sarmatians, Scythians, and Cimmerians—all of them Iranian speakers—and later with the Germanic-speaking Goths, and still later with Huns, Avars and Bulgars. Moses of Chorene mentions twenty-five Slavic tribes living in Dacia. Later on they apparently crossed the Danube, invaded Thrace and Macedonia, and spread south to Achaia and Dalmatia.

The Bulgarian scholar Vladimir Georgiev in his distribution map of the earliest Slavic toponyms, finds them between the rivers Timok and Morava and around Nish-Sofia, and less frequently in northeastern Bulgaria, including Dobroudzha.[33] Another Bulgarian scholar, Iordan Zaimov, who has researched Bulgarian toponymy, after studying the distribution of site names in the Balkans, came to the conclusion that the main route of the "penetration" of the Slavs in the Balkans was the area between the Morava and Timok Rivers, with a secondary route through Dobroudzha and lower Moesia. The author, however, was unable to discover toponymic data in the latter area. It follows, and Zaimov makes this clear, that the Slavs had not passed through the Danube-Moesia-Balkan Mountains-Thrace and the Rhodope Mountains, nor through Dobroudzha-eastern Moesia-Thrace-Macedonia and the Peloponnesus. The spread of patronymics as well as toponymic data demonstrates that the most compact Slav settlements were not in Moesia but in Macedonia, i.e. areas which do not join the Bulgarian state until the middle of the Ninth century.[34] It has been asserted–again with little evidence–that the Slavs assimilated the Illyrians, Daco-Moesians, Thracians and the local Roman population between the Sava River and the Black Sea.[35]

In Justinian's time there were invasions of Slavs in conjunction with Bulgars, Avars and Huns. Slavs were reported along the Danube by the end of the fifth century. In 530 the Antae invaded from the north and were followed by Huns and Kutrigurs in 550. It is reported that in 551 12,000 Kutrigurs raided the Balkans, but were later attacked by the Utigurs. Later about 2,000 of them settled in Thrace.[36] In 582 a Slav-Avar invasion reached Anchialos, and in 586 and 97–Thessaloniki. The direction of the invasions was generally through the Struma Valley, and the Slavs were usually mentioned as satellites of the Huns, Avars or Bulgars. In 626 Slavs and Bulgars joined the Avar siege of Constantinople.[37]

The East Roman Empire, despite temporary setbacks and loss of control over some of its territory, did not cease to regard such areas as belonging to it *de jure*, and used every opportunity to revive the political and economic life in the devastated, abandoned, and sometimes even partially depopulated areas, resettling there population groups from other parts of the Empire. Resettlement was widely practiced and was actually used as a method of subjugating conquered peoples as well as to facilitate Byzantine rule over the diverse ethnic groups through their dispersal and atomization. Resettlement played an important role in the further mis of the ethnic picture in the Balkans. Most of them were, in fact, mass deportations, practiced, although for different reasons, by Byzantines, Avars, Bulgars and Huns. The Avars, for instance, deported large groups from Illyria and Thrace north to Sirmium. Later those groups reportedly revolted, fled and re-emigrated to Constantinople.

The government of the Byzantine Empire would remove as a matter of policy, or necessity, whole groups of peoples from other regions, mostly from Asia Minor, but frequently also from the northern provinces, especially in the early days. Records from that time mention the Germanic Goths, Bastarnae and Heruli, the Sarmatians, Scythians and the Iranian-speaking Alans, as well as the Karpi, a Dacian tribe, which was also Iranian-speaking.[38] After 450 A.D. Isaurians from Asia Minor were settled in Moesia to serve in the garrisons along the Danube.[39]

The largest contingent of newcomers, deported by the Byzantines, or arriving voluntarily, appears to have been the Armenians. There is evidence linking Bulgarians and Armenians from the second century A.D. on the steppes near the Sea of Azov, and later with those Bulgarians who full under Khazar domination, and formed the nucleus of the latter-day Balkars.[40] In 460 Armenians led by the Arshakid princes Artavan and Ghazrik settled in Nicea.[41] A second large wave came in the 570s after the unsuccessful Armenian uprising against the Persians (Armenia had lost its independence and by 450 was divided up between Byzantium and Persia).[42] In 582 large numbers of Armenian soldiers were sent hy the Byzantines against the Azars. After the military action many of them did not return to Armenia but settled in the Balkans, some along the Danube, but mostly in Thrace. The Armenians were already the majority of the population of Philipopolis in the sixth century.[43]

Armenian resettlements in Thrace began in earnest with Justinian I (527–565). Emperor Maurice (582–601) also transplanted them on a large scale. Thousands of Armenians and Monophysite Syrians were deported to the Balkans by Constantine V Copronymus (740–775) and Leo IV the Khazar (775–780).[44] Constantine V removed large numbers of Armenians from Theodosiopolis and Syrians from Meltene to the Thracian frontier. This action was probably the reason for the outbreak of a war between Byzantium and Bulgaria, as the latter challenged the newly built fortresses in Thrace, which were settled by Armenians and Syrians.[45] The deportations in the eighth century were also religiously motivated as the majority of the deportees were Paulinian heretics.

The Empress-Regent Irene resettled Armenians in Thrace and Emperor Nicephorus settled many peasants from Anatolia to Macedonia as well as Paulician Armenians to Thrace.[46] Armenians continued to arrive until late in the tenth century. Emperor John Tsimiskes, himself an Armenian, resettled Armenians from Anatolia to Philippopolis, and also Anatolians and Capadoccians to areas in the Balkans. Basil II settled Armenians in Macedonia, and it was reported that Bulgar King Samuil's mother, Hripsime, was also Armenian.[47] The influx of foreign elements continued even later. The Cumans or Polovtsians appeared in the Balkans between the eleventh and the thirteenth centuries. A Cuman lady married the Bulgar Tsar Kaloyan in the beginning of the Thirteenth century, and both the Terter and Shishman dynasties had Cuman blood. After 1020 we encounter Pechenegs, whose descendents are believed to be the Shops of today, who inhabit an area near Sofia, the Bulgarian capital.[48]

No less interesting are the well-known removals and the resettlements of ethnic groups away from the Balkans to other areas. These cases concern mostly Slavs. Constance II (641–668) in 658 attacked and defeated the Slavs in Thrace, and took many of them *away* from the Balkans. According to Theophanes some 5,000 Slavs were resettled to Asia Minor by the Byzantines in 664. Justinian II (686–695) fought Slavs and led "a large number" into captivity from Thrace and Macedonia to Asia Minor in 687.[49] Two years later he deported Slavs from Thessaloniki. Later, in 693, 30,000 Slavs assisted the Byzantines in their war against the Saracens, but their assistance was ineffective as they reportedly betrayed their masters and dispersed in Asia,[50] In 758 Constantine V Copronymus was reported fighting and subduing the Slavs in Thrace and Macedonia. He eventually resettled many of them in Bithynia, by the River Artanas.[51] Over 200,000 Slavs were removed from the Balkans and settled in Asia Minor in the 760s. Patriarch Nicephorus mentions a number of 208,000 Slavs deported in 762.[52] In 783 Empress Regent Irene's general Stauracius was hailed as the conqueror of the Slavs in Greece.[53] In 809 Emperor Nicephorus was reported colonizing formerly Slav-inhabited areas in Macedonia with Christians from Asia.[54]

Many Slavs left the Bulgarian state voluntarily and for other reasons. The same 208,000 Slavs reported above were said to have run away from the Bulgars and to have given up to the Byzantines who resettled them in Asia Minor.[55] During Khan Omortag's time (814–831) many Slavs deserted the Bulgarian state. In 818 the Timochani tribe went over to the Franks and the Abodriti and the Branichevtsi, living respectively north and south of the Danube, sent messengers to Louis the Pious (814–840) asking him to take them under his protection. In 819 the Timochani, together with the Croats, fought the Franks and lost. By 822–823 all three tribes were forced to bow to the Franks.[56]

The Bulgarians were also known to practice resettlements and mass deportations. One of the first tasks of Khan Isperikh after defeating the Byzantines was to remove the Slav tribes and the Severi from Moesia to critical points on his new frontiers. In 811 Khan Krum was reported to have transported some 10,000 inhabitants of Adrianople north of the Danube. Two years later he took into captivity and resettled more Byzantines (and Armenians?) north of the Danube.[57] During the winter of 813–814, Krum attempted new deportations from conquered areas in Thrace; 50,000 prisoners were removed from Aracadiopol, including women and children.[58]

It might be easier to conclude if we begin by comparing the prevailing view in the formation of the Bulgarian ethnogenesis with the historical evidence. The two—or three—component thesis assuming the existence of only, or mainly, Slavs and Bulgars—or Slavs, Bulgars and Thracians—in the Balkans prior to, and after, the establishment of the mythical Slavo-Bulgarian state in 681, lacks foundation. It is also illogical and difficult to accept. It presupposes either the "vacuum" model: desolate areas in the Balkans filled easily and uninterruptedly by Slavs, or, the "assimilation" variant, juxtaposing Slavs (and Thracians) with the local populations, only to have the latter quickly melt away. In the first place, there is no evidence regarding the physical disappearance of the older, traditional population groups, although the sources sometimes mention deportations, resettlements and emigration effected by Byzantium or by the invaders.

We may never find out the ultimate fate of the Thracians, or of the Macedonians, the Goths in Moesia, etc., but we have no clear proof of annihilation. On the other hand, it seems clear that the Peninsula has never been an uninhabited land in historical times, least of all in the seventh century. Despite the barbarian invasions, the local inhabitants still remained there. Some of them might have withdrawn to more quiet and better protected areas, such as the larger cities along the Adriatic or the Aegean, as well as the fortified cities in Thrace, while others might have fled to the mountains where they waited-out the recurrent raids. And Roman-Byzantine power was usually fairly easily restored. It is important to note that, losses and devastations inflicted by the barbarians notwithstanding, the only piece of real estate ever permanently lost to the Empire in this period was lower Moesia, annexed by Bulgaria after the war of 679–680, and recognized by Byzantium with the peace treaty of 681.

The "assimilation" model is also unacceptable. Nowhere in the Balkans do we hear of Slavs assimilating other ethnic groups. Cases to the contrary, however, abound: the fate of the Slavs in Asia Minor, in Thessaly and the Epirus, in the Peloponnesus and elsewhere in the Empire is known; they lost their identity and disappeared in the midst of more advanced civilizations. There is even less evidence of the assimilating capabilities of the Thracians. Finally, we are faced with the relatively sparse Slav contingents in the Bulgarian Khaganate. Archaeological, toponymic and historical data agree that the Slavs were most numerous outside the state borders of Bulgaria, namely in Macedonia and northern Greece, parts of which did not join the Bulgarian state before the middle of the ninth century.

If anything, the ethnic situation in the Balkans in the Seventh century was as diverse as it has ever been. Far from distinguishing only—or mainly—between Slavs, Thracians and Bulgars, particularly in lower Moesia, the medieval authors inform us in detail about the uninterrupted existence of several other ethnic groups.

Is there, then, an ethnic model, which might be closer to the historical reality? Chronologically we distinguish between the older, "traditional" population groups and the newcomers, the barbarians. The emergence of the two main language areas, Greek in the south and Latin in the north, however simplistic, probably holds true until the mass arrival of the barbarians. Subsequently, and especially after the invasions subside, we note the substitution of geographical designations for the older, generic appellations, and the division of existing ethnic groups into "generics" and "geographics" becomes important. We speak of Macedonians not as descendents of the ancient Macedonians of Philip and Alexander, but rather as the inhabitants of the geographical area known as Macedonia.

Speaking of the relative weight of the various ethnic groups we have to exercise some caution and to try to distinguish between the advantage in numbers (i.e. who were most numerous) and the extent of influence which a group could exert on others in spite of relatively small size. The exact dimensions of each ethnic group is difficult to fathom. It seems clear, for example, that there must have been more Greeks than Daco-Moesians, or Goths, and more Bulgarians than Armenians. But how many of each we do not know. The best we can do is to try to make a reasonable estimate. The situation is also complicated by the fact that the Empire was not a nation-state in the present sense of the term, and the common language–Greek during the period under consideration–was more of a convenience, a *lingua franca*, than an ethnic distinction. Still, it seems safe to assume that the most numerous single ethnic groups must have been Greeks, Avars, Bulgars, Slavs and Armenians, not necessarily in this order. The Greeks were established on the peninsula for the longest period of time and there were many Greek colonies outside of Greece proper. The Avars ruled over a huge empire and it stands to reason that they also enjoyed prominence in numbers, also considering their Asian credentials. The Bulgarians were very numerous, too. They were able to defeat both the army and the navy of the only superpower of that time, and managed to conquer, impose and maintain their rule over large territories (we often forget that the larger part of Bulgaria lay outside the Balkans–to the east and to the north). The Slavs were large in numbers, but they were concentrated mostly outside the Khaganate, and their size was reduced by wars, deportations and resettlements, not to mention their apparent assimilation by the Greeks below the north Aegean coast and in Asia Minor. The Armenians emigrated to the Balkans in the course of several centuries, and it is quite possible that their role was substantially more important than assumed hitherto.

More significant than the numbers game, however, is the influence each of those groups could yield, that is to say, its political influence and the cultural impact it could deliver. From the point of view of the Bulgarians, the influence wielded by the Avars was probably not of an adverse nature, as they were not far removed from the Bulgarians in culture and language, if not in origin. Retrospectively, it is apparent that the greatest foreign influence exerted on the Bulgarians had come from the Greeks, who in the ninth century supplied the alphabet, the literary medium of the Bulgarian state, and also the Christian religion, probably the single monumental development in the medieval history of the Bulgarians, although for reasons other than celebrated. If the Greeks obliged the Bulgars by baptizing them and by providing a new state model, the Armenians were probably most influential in the inception, if not the spread, of a unique Bulgarian heresy, which came to be known as *bogomilstvo*, and which has been hailed by some as the first substantial manifestation of social protest in the Middle Ages, and by others as the forerunner of Protestantism. The influence exerted by the Slavs appears to be minimal in comparison, and the one of the Thracians very questionable.

If neither the Slavs nor the Thracians participated actively in the formation of the Bulgarian ethnogenesis, and if the role of the Avars had been supportive, while those of the Greeks and the Armenians influenced the Bulgarians at a much later date, when they apparently already existed as a distinct ethnic group. It is then logical to ask what remains of the so-called formative years of the ethnogenesis of the Bulgarians in the Balkans. If no ethnic group was either strong enough, or influential enough, to leave its imprint, how then did the process of the ethnic formation of the Bulgars proceed?

We think the answer is simple and suggests itself: the Bulgarians did not develop their ethos in the Balkans. This process was already complete before their arrival, probably long before they appeared at the Danube. In order to discover its secrets and development one has to step back a few hundred years and to remove oneself from the narrow confines of Balkan history. The ethnogenesis of the Bulgarians, as Professor Vasil Zlatarski pointed out sixty years ago, is not to be found in Europe, it is hidden in Asia. Perhaps someone will decide to take the trip someday.

NOTES

1. D. Kossev *et al.*, *A Short History of Bulgaria* (Sofia: Foreign Languages Press, 1963), p. 20.

2. Robert Browning, *Byzantium and Bulgaria: A Comparative Study Across the Early Medieval Frontier* (Berkeley and Los Angeles: University of California Press, 1975), p. 43.

3. David Marshall Lang, *The Bulgarian* (Boulder, Colorado: Westview Press, 1976), p. 21. Kossev, p. 9, mentions the Middle Paleolithic and the Monsterian Era.

4. Browning, p. 21.

5. Lang, p. 21.

6. V. Georgiev, "The Genesis of the Balkan People," *Slavonic and East European Review*, 44 (1965–6), pp. 28–97.

7. Kossev, p. 12.

8. Ibid., p. 17

9. Lang, pp. 21–22.

10. V. Besevliev, *Personennamen bei den Thrakern* (1970), pp. 69-136; despite some assertions made by Besevliev, the presentation is far from convincing. See also Alexander Fol and Ivan Marazov, Thrace and the Thracians (New York: St. Martin's Press, 1977).

11. Lang, pp. 27-28.

12. Ibid., pp. 22–23.

13. Gimbutas, *The Slavs* (1973), pp. 68–70. The description is according to an old (fourth century) Roman road map known as Tabula Peutingeriana.

14. Lang, p. 23.

15. Browning, p. 25.

16. Gimbutas, pp. 76–8; Kossev, p. 20.

17. Browning, p. 29.

18. Otto J. Maenchen-Helfen, *The World of the Huns* (Berkeley: University of California Press, 1973), pp. 29–30.

19. Zosimus, *Historia nova*, IV, 34, 6, p. 190.

20. Lang, p. 24.

21. Kossev, p. 25.

22. John of Antioch, *Fragments*, p. 619.

23. Lang, pp. 33–34.

24. Marcellinus Comes, *Chronica minora*, 94–96.

25. Menander Protector, *Hist. Byz.*, pp. 5, 55, 87.

26. Lang, p. 34.

27. Gimbutas, p. 93. See also N. Ia. Merpert, *Za Genezisa na Saltovsko-Maiatskata kultura* (1951), I. I. Liapushin, *Pametnitsi na Saltovsko-Maiatskata kultura v donskiia basein* (Moscow, 1958).

28. Menander Protector, *Hist. Byzt.*, p. 102; Theophylactus Simocatta, *Hist.* 6.3.

29. Browning, p. 35.

30. *Sancti Demetrii Martyris Acta*, p. 1284; Theophylactus Simocatta, pp. 250–60, Theophanes Byzantius, *Chronographia*, p. 532—he calls the Avars Bulgars.

31. Suidas, *Greek lexicon*, 2 vol.: "The Bulgarians liked themselves so much in the attire of the Avars that they adopted it and until now they are still clad in it." See also Vasil Zlatarski, *Istoriia na bulgarskata durzhava prez srednite vekove* (Sofia: Isdatelstvo Nauka i Izkustvo, 1970, Vol. I), p. 373.

32. See Browning, p. 31.

33. VI. Georgiev, p. 295.

34. Iordan Zaimov, *Zaselvane na bulgarskite slaviani na balkanskiia poluostrov. Prouchvane na zhitelskite imena v bulgarskata toponimiia* (Sofia: BAN, 1967), pp. 99–103.

35. See Gimbutas, p. 109.

36. Procopius of Caesarea, *De bello vandalico*, 18–19, 550; Menander Protector, *Hist. Byz.*, p. 3. See also Steven Runciman, *A History of the First Bulgarian Empire* (London: G. Bell & Sons, Ltd., 1930), pp. 8–9.

37. See Lang, pp. 24–25.

38. Ibid., p. 25; Browning, p. 24.

39. Ibid., p. 28.

40. See for fuller documentation in S. V. Ovnanian, *Armianobolgarskie istoicheskie sviazi i armianskie kolonii v Bolgarii vo vtoroi polovine 19 veka* (Erevan: INASSR, 1968), pp. 17–19.

41. Georgi Cedreni, *Historiarum compendium*, pp. 437, 557.

42. Ovnanian, p. 26.

43. Ibid., p. 27; *The History of Bishop Sebeos*, translated in Russian (Erevan, 1939), p. 49.

44. Nicephori patriarchae, *Opuscula Historica*, pp. 66, 36; *Istoriia halifov armianskogo virdapeta Gevonda*, translated by K. Patkanian, (1863), p. 91; Chronography of the Syrian patriarch Michael; Theophanes, *Chronoxraphia*, p. 364. See also E. E. Lipshits, "Pavlikianskoe dvizhenie v Vizantii v VIII i pervoi polovine IX v.," in *Vizantiiskii vremennik*, t. V, 1952; K. Iuzbashian, "L istorii pavlikianskogo dvizhenia v Vizantii," in *Voprosi istorii religii i ateizma*, 1956, No. 4; D. Angelov, *Bogomilstvoto v Bulgaria* (Sofia, 1968).

45. Nicephori patriarchae, pp. 66–8; Theophanes, p. 662. See also Runciman, pp. 35–36.

46. Theophanes, p, 755.

47. See Lang, pp. 38–39.

48. Ibid., pp. 39–41.

49. Theophanes, *Chronographia*, p. 364; Constantin Porphyrogeneti, *De thematibus et de administrando imperio*, p. 50; Nicephori patriarchae, *Opuscula historica*, p. 36.

50. Ibid.; Theophanes, p. 557, pp. 365–366, p. 486; see in Zlatarski, pp. 223, 329.

51. Theophanes, pp. 662–665; Runciman, pp. 36–38.

52. Nicephori patriarchae, p. 67.

53. Theophanes, pp. 699–707.

54. Ibid., p. 486; Zlatarski, p. 329.

55. Theophanes, p. 432; Nicephori patriarchae, pp. 18–69.

56. Einhard, *Annales*, s.an. 818, 822, p. 205, 209. See Zlatarski, p. 401.

57. Theophanes, pp. 785–786; Scriptoris incerti, *De Leone Bardae Armenii filio*, pp. 342–344; Leonis Grammatici, *Chronographia*, p. 231; Theophanis Continuati, *Chronographia*, p. 216; cf. in Zlatarski, p. 357.

58. Scriptor incerti, pp. 352–362, 346–347.

HELLENISTIC CRETAN PIRACY

Elpida Hadjidaki

Introduction

Anyone who visits Crete today will recognize that it is a wild place, and it has always been so. The people have always been seafarers, and amongst them a share of pirates. We know this as far back as Homer, although the practice of piracy on Crete reached its peak during the Hellenistic period,[1] but many questions remain unanswered. The topic is quite important for the historian of Hellenistic Crete, for piracy seems to have been one of the main sources of the island's wealth and reflects the social and economic conditions of the times.[2]

Cretan piracy goes back to the Middle and Late Bronze Age, a period during which Creto-Mycenaean maritime expansion resulted in at least fifty-four settlements in the Middle East, reaching as far as Babylon, to Egypt in the south, and Sicily and Italy in the west.[3]

In ca. 1240 B.C., Crete had such a large navy that she could afford to participate with eighty ships in the Trojan war.[4] However, despite Creto-Mycenaean policing of the seas, it was during this period that the first indications of seaborn raiding appear, and it is very likely that they came from the Greeks themselves. Jason's expedition to the Black Sea in quest of the Golden Fleece,[5] and the Trojan War itself could be considered acts of raiding and piracy. Odysseus's boast that he is a Cretan pirate[6] reflects the honor given to piracy. The pride that is described in his love for oared ships and war indicates that raiding and great spoils were highly reputable in aristocratic Creto-Mycenaean circles in the Late Bronze Age. Furthermore, the raid of Odysseus's men on the Egyptian shores[7] fits well with a description of the Ekwesh people "from the countries of the sea" who joined Libyan invaders off the Egyptian coast during the reign of Merneptath (circa 1225–1215 B.C.).[8]

Seventeen years later, during the reign of Ramses III (circa 1198–1167 B.C.) new sea raiders attacked Egypt. Among them were the

Peleset who came from the "northern isles" and ". . . were warriors upon land and sea,"[9] the Peleset being identified as the Philistines, who had migrated from Crete.[10]

The Cretan sea-raiding at sea lasted until the times of the Dorian invasion, circa 1150 B. C., or the "return of the Herakleidai," that brought the island into the Dark Ages for 400 years.

Piracy in the Hellenistic Period

Prehistoric notions and traditions did not die out during the centuries, and up to the Hellenistic period or later, there remained Minoan people on Crete still speaking a non-Greek language[11] Crete is an island that sticks to old customs and legends, while its people have always been different from the rest of the Greeks. They are primitive and proud people, mountain warriors who love their freedom, and daring sailors with a special feeling for the sea, often not out of love for it, but of necessity, as a source of livelihood. During the days of Polybios they were considered good in raids, ambushes, and night attacks,[12] and the island had a reputation for greed and money. Thus Bevan writes,

> the Cretans were born to arms, to ambushes in steep places, and stealthy clambering. When they were not fighting at home, they went to fight abroad in the service of foreign kings.[13]

Piratical acts in the eastern Mediterranean Sea had resumed during the late fourth century B.C., after the weakening of the Athenian navy, which had policed the seas for almost 150 years. The rivalry between the Greek states, the rise of Macedon, and Macedon's use of mercenaries who were often pirates left the Aegean free for raiders. Those in the east included the Aetolians,[14] inhabitants of the islands of Mylonesos,[15] Skiathos,[16] the Tyrrhenians,[17] and the Cilicians[18] the Tyrrhenians seem to have plundered during the late fourth century B.C. and early third century B.C.,[19] and were succeeded by the Cretans.

Although only a few names of specific piratical towns are mentioned in ancient literature—those of Allaria in west Crete[20] and Hierapytna[21]—there is no lack of evidence for Cretan piracy. Ancient authors such as Polybios,[22] Strabo,[23] and Plutarch[24] all report on Cretan raiding, which seems to have been very successful during the third and second centuries B.C. Strabo, who had a good knowledge of Cretan affairs, writes that[25]:

$$Μετα \; γαρ \; τους \; Τυρρηνους, \; οι \; μαλιστα \; εδηωσαν \; την$$
$$καθ \; ημας \; θαλατταν, \; ουτοι \; εισιν \; οι \; Κιλικες \; κατελυσαν$$
$$δε \; παντας \; Ρωμαιοι, \; την \; τε \; Κρητην \; εκπολεμησαντες$$
$$και \; τα \; πειρατικα \; των \; Κιλικων \; φρουρια$$

He also emphasizes the close relations between pirates and mercenaries, commenting on a certain military expert named Dorylaos. Dorylaos was a friend of king Mithridates V, and often sailed to Crete on his behalf looking for private military personnel:

$$συχνου \; δ'οντος \; εν \; αυθ \; του \; μισθοφορικου \; και$$
$$στρατιωτικου \; πληθους \; εξ \; ου \; και \; τα \; ληστηρια$$
$$πληρουσθαι \; συνεβαινεν.[26]$$

An inscription from the island of Thera dating probably to 260 B.C. records that pirates from Allaria in west Crete raided the island of Thera, but the Egyptians who had the island under their influence drove them out with the help of the natives.[27]

A decree from the island of Amorgos dating to the third century B.C. honors two men for their help during an incursion of pirates from either Aetolia or Crete.[28] Aetolians and Cretans seem to have collaborated in raids and piracy, and probably used each others harbor facilities.[29] An inscription dating to 217/216 records a certain pirate Bucris carrying off to Crete Athenian citizens for ransom. Later on, the Cydonian officer Eumaridas saved other Athenians from Aetolian pirates by exchanging the captives for twenty talents,[30] quite a handsome profit for the slave traders. Eumaridas was now honored by the Athenians for his services, and for intervening to preserve good relations with all the inhabitants of Crete, thus preventing further Creto-Aetolian raiding.

The words "good relations with all the inhabitants of Crete" appear in the caption text twice. This leads to the suggestion that all Cretans agreed on this form of activity. "The practice was not merely condoned, but actively pursued with the protection and authority of the Greek States in antiquity."[31] That is probably why few specific pirate towns are mentioned in ancient sources. Piracy must have been

a common practice in Hellenistic Crete, and the individual alliances
that the Greek world tried to form with the Cretan city-states are
further indications that the Cretans engaged in piracy. Evidence for
this comes from the treaty, dated to between 293 and 260 B.C. between Miletus on the coast of Asia Minor and various Cretan cities
forbidding the purchase of citizens and slaves. The names of twenty-
eight Cretan states appear on the decree: each dominant power on the
island such as Knossos, Phaestos, and Gortyn with their respective
allies.[32] As the city-states of Crete were independent and constantly
at war with one another, only an alliance with all of them simultaneously could protect one against piracy. There is little doubt that the
towns of Phalasarna, Knossos, Kydonia, Hierapytna, Olous, Gortyn,
Phaestos, and Itanos, to mention only a few, were among those states
which blessed this barbaric act.

Apart from Miletus and Athens, Rhodes also made alliances with
individual Cretan states in order to protect free trade. Rhodes had
tried to control the Mediterranian throughout the second and first
centuries B.C., by being the watchdog of the Romans, proclaiming
the freedom of the seas, and trying to destroy piracy.[33] She allied
with Knossos in 220 B.C.,[34] and with Hierapytna around 200 B.C.[35]

The inscription involving Rhodes and Hierapytna is important
for four reasons:

(1) it implies that Hierapytnians were involved in raiding;

(2) it reports the existence of Cretan pirate bases on the island;

(3) it describes the conditions by which the town was required to
abide; and

(4) it refers to the recruitment of Cretan mercenaries,[36] a second
source of large profit for Crete.

The mercenary service of the Cretans and their distinction in
military matters has been well documented by Willetts in his excellent
chapter on piracy and mercenary service.[37] He points out that:

> The warfare between the Cretan cities from the end of the
> fourth century until the Roman conquest must have caused
> a continuous drain on the manpower resources of the citizen
> military classes. Yet these cities were able not only to supply
> forces for these in internal wars, but to engage in two other
> forms of agressive activity.[38]

Thus, in 171 B.C. Phalasarna and Knossos sent 3000 mercenaries
to assist Perseus under the command of Susus of Phalasarna and Syl-

lus of Knossos[39] Furthermore, a recruitment officer named Cnopias of Allaria is described by Polybios as being second to none,[40] further evidence of the prestige the Cretan mercenaries enjoyed in the Hellenistic world.

Willetts argues that mercenaries were almost exclusively citizens who provided their own arms.[41] Thus, they must have been people of some wealth. Where did such wealth come from so that thousands of mercenaries could travel abroad, leaving their own cities undefended? The island was mountainous and forested, and the few fertile valleys in between would provide enough food only for the local population. The Cretan economy was based on aristocratic land ownership, and remained predominantly agricultural

> with no advanced forms of industry or commerce . . . where the land continued to be owned by a relatively few families . . . and where small ownership never had a chance to develop.[42]

There was ample food and wood for shipbuilding, but many raw materials such as copper would have to be imported.

Apparently, for the first 150 years of the Hellenistic period, Crete enjoyed a large portion of the Mediterranean's spoils, brought through piracy, the slave market, ransom money, and mercenary service. By the third century B.C., the island was so rich that it was able not only to send mercenaries abroad, but also to engage in strenuous wars at home that little affected its economy. Large hoards of coins found all around the island date to that period.[43] For example, in October 1987, Ms. V. Niniou of the Archaeological Museum of Chania, while excavating a small Hellenistic country temple near Sougia, at the southwest coast found thirty silver coins in excellent condition, all dating to around the third century B.C.

After around 150 B.C. Crete's large profits must have been shared with Cilicia, on the southeast coast of Asia Minor, which became a second plague in the Aegean, and as a matter of fact surpassed Crete in raiding and piracy. The Cilician rocky coast, like the Cretan one, is ideal for ambushes.[44] The country was under Hellenistic rule until the mid-second century B.C. when the kings of Syria left it partly independent.[45] Thereafter, the Cilicians, starting out as mercenaries for Mithri dates,[46] became so rich and powerful that they impressed Plutarch, who writes about them that:

> there embarked with these pirates men of wealth and noble

birth and superior abilities. . . . They had divers arsenals, or piratic harbors, as likewise watchtowers and beacons, all along the sea coast; and fleets were here received that were well manned with the first mariners, and well served with the most expert pilots, and composed of swift-sailing and light-built vessels adapted for their special purpose. . . . Their ships had gilded masts at their stems; the sails woven of purple, and the oars plated with silver, as their delight were to glory in their iniquity.[47]

Ancient texts indicate that there was contact and collaboration between Cilicia and Crete.[48] Ormerod states that the Cilicians "possessed everywhere fortified bases and watchtowers and carried out their raids on all sides."[49] but it seems to me more likely that these corsairs probably used some Cretan harbors for their operations, and that they probably split the spoils. Plutarch says that Crete was the second source of pirates after Cilicia,[51] , and the Romans accused the Cretans of assisting the pirates[52] as well as King Mithridates. There followed a war between Crete and Rome in 71 B.C., in which Rome was humiliated by the Kydonian leader Lasthenes and the victorious Cretan pirates off the coast near Kydonia.[52] As a result, the Romans demanded the surrender of Lasthenes with all ships over four oars, 4,000 talents, and the return of the Roman captives.[53] No confident Cretan warrior or pirate would ever have yielded to these demands!

Thus in 67 B.C., the Roman general Q. Caecilius Metellus was dispatched to Crete, crossing probably from Gythion on the south coast of the Peloponnese to the harbor at Kisamos, since this was the best and fastest route to attack Kydonia.[54]

Metellus destroyed Kydonia, as well as other Cretan pirate strongholds, with the utmost brutality,[55] and proceeded to subdue the whole island. During the same year Pompey the Great destroyed all Cilician harbors; and thus came the end of the savage years of piracy in the Mediterranean.

Archaeological Evidence of Piracy

It is likely that the geographical position of Crete, its rocky coast ideal for pirate hideouts, and its harbors hidden behind promontories, all contributed to the success of Cretan raiding. Unfortunately, the ports and coastal cities of these great mariners were largely destroyed by the later Romans, Venetians, and Turks, so that only small sections and foundations survive today as evidence of their great past.

The Hellenistic ports of Hierapytna, Knossos, and Kydonia have been overbuilt by the modern ones. At the harbors of Phaestos and Gortyn on the south coast of central Crete, which are Matala and Kommos, little has been found. At Matala there remains only a single shipshed and a line of bollards[56] while at Kommos only Minoan harbor installations have been found so far.[57] Naturally there were other ports of lesser importance such as Olous, Itanos, and Allaria, but their harbor installations are either underwater or have not yet been discovered.

The island of Crete has been subjected to many geological changes over the past 2,000 years as it lies near the African-Aegean tectonic fault, Which deforms Crete, uplifting the west end and submerging the east.[58] Thus, the ruins of Itanos are lying -2.0 m underwater, whereas the port of Kisamos has its Roman mole 5.0 m above water. This geological misfortune has become the cause for the preservation of the ancient harbor at Phalasarna, on the extreme west coast of Crete, a town that had supplied mercenaries and pirates to King Perseus in 171 B.C.[59] Today, what was once the harbor lies 100 m from the sea, and 6.6 m above it. This town may turn out to be the major archaeological source for the island's maritime activities in the Hellenistic period. Since excavations began in 1986,[60] several well-preserved monuments have been revealed, all covered by sediment from tsunamis and centuries of erosion from hillsides above. The town had never been reinhabited since it was destroyed in the middle of the first century B.C., thus leaving behind intact walls and defenses standing up to 5 or 6 m in height. Although excavations at Phalasarna are still in preliminary stages, they already shed light on ancient harbor engineering, support of piracy by the state, Roman military practice, and the size of the Cretan pirate ships.

Phalasarna had an elaborate and skillfully constructed artificial harbor well hidden behind its steep cliffs, which caught the attention of geographers such as Skylax, Dionysius Kalliphontis, and the author of the Stadiasmus.[61] They described the harbor as '$\lambda\iota\mu\eta\nu$ $\kappa\lambda\epsilon\iota\sigma\tau o\varsigma$,' which meant that its installations were enclosed for protection within the city's fortifications.

Excavation and surveys have found that the military port measures only 100 x 100 m, but is surrounded by at least four towers and other connecting defensive walls. A narrow, artificially cut channel 120 m long connected the port to the sea (Fig. 1). The large towers and the walls that have been excavated so far, together with remains of temples, public buildings and other massive fortifications that are visible today protruding from behind bushes, bear clear evidence of elaborate work (Figs. 2–4), which only a wealthy nation with large resources in manpower could afford. Phalasarna had few natural resources and her revenues must have come mainly from piracy, from the hiring out of mercenaries, and from slave trade. A second source of income might have been the export of stone, as suggested by Lawrence.[62] Reports of a shipwreck in the bay with a cargo of worked stone support this view.

As all signs of habitation on the site disappear after the first century B.C., we presume that the harbor at Phalasarna was among the first sites attacked by the Romans on their sweep through Crete in 67 B.C.[63] Archaeological evidence of Roman destruction comes from the main entrance channel at the harbor at Phalasarna. A trench excavated in 1987 revealed the harbor mouth to have been forcefully blocked by large rectangular stones coming apparently from nearby sea-walls.[64] The same method was used by Scipio in his attack on the harbor channel at Carthage,[65] where archaeolgical remains of the destruction have also been found.[66]

The harbor of Phalasarna is lying today 100 m away from the sea, and 6.6 m above water, due to the local uplift of west Crete. However, during the late fourth century B.C., the time during which it was constructed, the water level in the basin was around 1–1.20 m deep. This suggests that pirate ships in the Hellenistic period were relatively small in size with a small drift, not requiring much displacement. According to L. Casson, the favorite ships of the pirates were the haemiolia and the myoparo.[67] They were light and and fast two-banked galleys, traveling under sail as well as oars at a speed up to 5 knots, but no one knows about the size and appearance of these boats. We know also that Mithridates' main body of pirate ships seems to have consisted of dicrota (biremes) , another type of two-banked gallery.[68]

No source is more likely to inform us about the nature of these ships than future excavations at the harbor of Phalasarna. Even if we are not fortunate enough to discover actual remains of a warship, which may have sunk inside the harbor and been preserved by silt, the sizes of shipsheds suspected to lie nearby and other installations will give us a notion of their dimensions. The picture which arises to date from the present excavations is that piracy was a practice supported and condoned by the state, which provided the military installations to make it possible. During the three centuries in which

Cretan pirates terrorized the Mediterranean sea, they built great harbors, ships, and towns, which even the large Rhodian navy could not defeat. They continued a tradition of maritime activity which began with the Minoan navy, and has continued to the present day.

NOTES

1. The major works on Hellenistic Cretan piracy are, H. A. Ormerod, *Piracy in the Ancient World*, (Liverpool 1924), R. F. Willetts, *Aristocratic Life in Ancient Crete*, (London 1955) , S. Spyridakis, *Itanos and Hellen Crete* (Berkeley 1970), and P. Brule, *La piraterie Crétoise Hellénistique*, (Paris 1978).

2. M. Rostovtzeff, *The Social and Economic History of the Hellenistic World*, (Oxford 1941) pp. 199, 201–204, 607–610, 782–785.

3. For references to Minoan marine trade and communication, see the following: R. W. Hutchinson, *Prehistoric Crete*, (London 1962) pp. 102–115;   1983) pp. 64–69; A. Malamat, "Syro-Palestinian Destination in Mari Tin Inventory," *Israel Exploration Journal*, 21 (1971), pp. 30–38; E. Vermeule, *Greece in the Bronze Age*, (Chicago 1964) pp. 254–258; A. H. Sayce, "Krete in Babylonian and Old Testament Texts," in *Essays in Aegean Archaeology*, S. Casson, ed., Oxford (1927) pp. 107–110; G. Childe, "The Minoan Influence on the Danubian Bronze Age," in *Essays in Aegean Archaeology*, S. Casson, ed., Oxford (1927) pp. 1–4; D. J. S. Pendlebury, *The Archaeology of Crete* (London 1939), pp. 72–175, 258–259, 286–257; and N. Platon, *Zakros: The Discovery of a Lost Palace in Ancient Crete*, (New York, 1971) pp. 240–246.

4. *Iliad.* 640–646.

5. Appolonius Rhodius, *Argonautika.*

6. *Od.*, 14.224–231.

7. *Od.*, 14.257–265 1906) pp. 249.

8. J. H. Breasted, *Ancient Records of Egypt*, Vol. 3, (Chicago, 1906), p. 249.

9. Breasted, (supra no. 8) Vol. 4, pp. 24 and 37.

10. Hutchinson, (supra no. 3) p. 108; A. Jones, *Bronze Age Civilization: The Philistines and the Danites*, (Washington DC, 1975) pp. 15–16, 101–102; R. A. S. Macalister, *The Philistines, Their History and Civilization*, (Chicago 1965) pp. 7–28.

11. Hutchinson, (supra no. 3) p. 23.

12. Polybios, 4.8.

13. E. R. Bevan, *The House of Seieucus*, (London 1902) p. 286.

14. Polybios 4.3; Dittenberger, Syll[3], pp. 520 and 521; Gk. Hist. Insc., p. 178.

15. Aeschines, 2.72

16. Appian, *Mithndates*, 94.

17. Strabo, 10.4.9; 6.2.67.

18. Plutarch, *Pompey*, 24.1.

19. Ormerod (supra n. 1), p. 127.

20. *IC*, II.I pp. 1–5.

21. Dittenberger, Syll[3], p. 581.

22. Polybios, 4.8, 6.46, 8.21.

23. Strabo, 10.4, 10.9–10.

24. Plutarch, *Pompey*, 29.1.

25. Strabo, 10.4.9.

26. Strabo, 10.4.10.

27. *IG*, 12.3.291; 12.3.328.

28. Dittenberger, Syll[3], p. 521; Gk. Hist. Inscr., 186.

29. Rostovtzeff, (supra no. 2),p. 199.

30. *IG*, ii.2.844.

31 R. F. Willetts, *Everyday Life in Ancient Crete*, (London 1969) p. 112.

32. *IC*, I.viii. p. 60, no. 6.

33. Strabo 14.2.5; C 3, pp. 31-36, no. 3A

34. Polybios, 4.53; Diodoros, 20.88

35. *IC*, (supra no. 32). Rhodes, being unable to subdue the rebellious Cretans, made another appeal in 168 BC. However, war broke out in 155 B.C.; the Cretans raiders fought so successfully that Rhodes had to ask for Roman intervention in order to terminate the matter.

36. *IC*, (supra no. 32).

37. Willetts, (supra no. 1) pp. 241–248; see also Strabo, 10.4.10; Ormerod, (supra no. 1), pp. 145–147; G. I. Griffith, *The Mercenaries of the Hellenistic World*, (Cambridge, 1935) pp. 234–235, 245; and E. R. Bevan, *The House of Seleucus*, (London 1902) Vol. 2, pp. 218 and 286.

38. Willetts, (supra no. 1) p. 241.

39. Livy, 42.51.7.

40. Polybios, 5.63–65.

41 Willetts, (supra no. 1), p. 248

42 Willetts, (supra no. 1) p. 177.

43. Svoronos, J. N., *Numismatique de la Crète Ancienne*, (Macon 1890).

44. Strabo, 14.671.

45. Ormerod, (supra no. 1), pp. 203, 204.

46. Ormerod, (supra no. 1), p. 210; Appian, *Mithridates*, 63 and 78.

47. Plutarch, *Pompey*, 24.1.

48. Appian, *Mithridates*; Dio Cassius 36.23, and 36.18.

49. Ormerod, (supra no. 1), p. 223

50. Plutarch, *Pompey*, 29.1.

51. Appian, *Sicelica*, 6; Livy, Ep. 97.

52. Florus, 3.7; Diodorus, 40.1.

53. F. Frost, "The Last days of Phalasarna," *Ancient History Bulletin*, 3.1 (1989) p. 2.

54. I. Sanders, *Roman Crete*, (Wilts 1982) p. 3.

55. Diodorus 40.1; Appian, *Sicelica*, 6.2; Plutarch, *Pompey*, 29.1.; F. Frost, (supra. no. 53)

56. D. J. Blackman, "The *neosoikos* at Matala," *Proc. 3d Cretoiogical Congress, 1971* (1973) pp. 14–21.

57. J. Shaw, "Excavations at Kommos (Crete) during 1984–1985," *Hesperia*, 55 (1986) pp.219–269.

58. P. Pirazzoli, J. Thommeret, Y. Thommeret, J. Laborel, and L. Montagnoni, *Crystal Block Movements from the Holocene Shorelines: Crete and Antikythera* (Greece), *Tectonophys.*, 86 (1982) 27–43.

59. Livy, 42.51.7.

60. E. Hadjidaki, "Preliminary Report of Excavations at the Harbor of PhaLlsarna in West Crete," *American Journal of Archaeogogy*, 92 (1988) 463–479.

61. Skylax, 47; Dionysius Kalliphontis 118; Stadiasmus 336.

62. A. Lawrence, *Greek Aims in Fortification*, (Oxford 1979) pp. 395, 438.

63. F. Frost, (supra no. 53).

64. Hadjidaki (supra no. 60) p. 475–476, fig. 20.

65. Appian, *Sicelica*, 8.121

66. Professor D. Esse of the Oriental Institute of the University of Chicago, participated in the excavation of the commercial port of Carthage, tells me that the Romans systematically dismantled the Punic quay walls down to the foundations, and used the stone to block the harbor mouth.

67. L, Casson, *Ships and Seamanship in the Ancient World* (Princeton 1971).

68. Appian, *Mithrzdates*, 17.

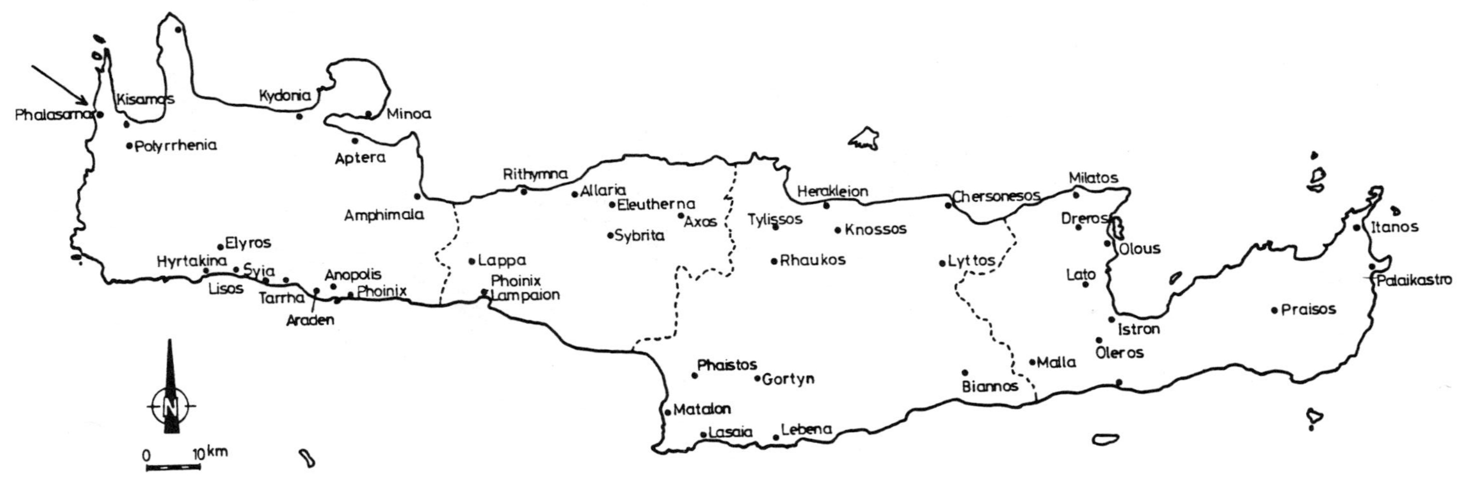

1. MAP OF CRETE WITH HELLENISTIC TOWNS

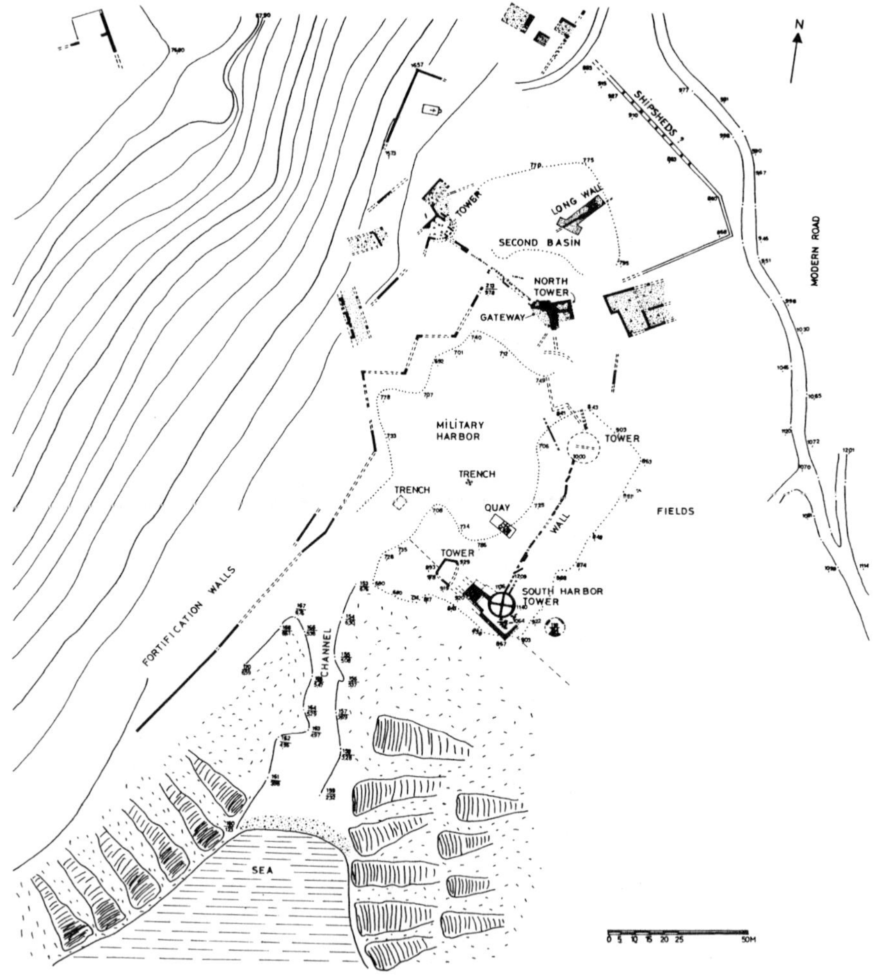
N
MODERN ROAD
SHIPSHEDS ?
LONG WALL
SECOND BASIN
TOWER
NORTH TOWER
GATEWAY
MILITARY HARBOR
TOWER
TRENCH
TRENCH
QUAY
WALL
FIELDS
TOWER
SOUTH HARBOR TOWER
FORTIFICATION WALLS
CHANNEL
SEA
0 5 10 15 20 25   50M

3. Bay of Phalasarna

4. Line of fortifications

5. South harbor defense tower

ON RAGUSAN PATRICIANS'
MISBEHAVIOR IN DUBROVNIK AND SERBIA
IN THE EARLY FIFTEENTH CENTURY

Bariša Krekić

The early fifteenth century marked the period when the patrician class of Dubrovnik (Ragusa) recovered fully from the consequences of the Black Death, which had struck the city very hard in mid-fourteenth century. Records of patrician attendance at the meetings of the Major Council of Dubrovnik show this very clearly. The recovery and growth of patrician numbers continued vigorously throughout the fifteenth century and lost very little steam in the sixteenth. However, as usual in periods of rapid expansion, everything was not functioning ideally. There were, in fact, many severe problems accompanying the dynamic development of Dubrovnik, including serious difficulties with the behavior of the patricians, especially younger ones. Various kinds of reprehensible patrician behavior were not limited to Dubrovnik alone, but appeared in other places, such as Serbia, where Ragusan patricians visited, lived, and worked for protracted periods of time.

Of course, the most common trouble in which people, including patricians, became involved were altercations in the streets and squares of Dubrovnik. For example, in January 1403, the Rector of the city and his court investigated two fights among patricians. One was a minor incident, but the other involved three men and occurred in the city *loggia*, one of the most prestigious places in Dubrovnik, where patricians would congregate, to talk and to spend time together. The incident started as a verbal altercation between two patricians and ended with bloody punches, in which a third patrician participated, until they finally were separated by other patricians standing nearby. The instigators of both fights were punished by fines of six hyperpers (ca. two ducats) each.[1]

Besides troubles among patricians, there was violence also in relations between patricians and commoners. In June 1404, a man complained against two brothers, patricians who had beaten him with a wooden stick over his head and had hit him with fists in his chest, all of this on the main street, Placa, near the *loggia*.[2] More importantly, there were serious cases of sexual assault by patricians against commoner women. Several incidents of this sort took place in the year 1406. On January 17th of that year, the patrician *ser Michael de Restić* (Restić) was accused of having grabbed on the previous evening a female servant. who was carrying on her head a bucket with water near the cathedral, and of "wanting to shame her." In the ensuing struggle the bucket fell and broke into several pieces. A witness declared that he had heard the woman screaming and had seen the bucket fall. When the witness approached the woman and asked what was the matter with her, she replied that Michael Restić "wanted to abuse me."[3] Restić seems to have been a rather restless young man. A few days later, on January 25, 1406, together with three other patricians and a doctor, he was accused of a very grave assault by a woman named "Stana, daughter of Tvrtko." According to the accusation, in the middle of the previous night, the five men had knocked on her door, demanding that she let them in. When she told them: "Why should I open? There are no bad women here," they broke down the door, entered the house, stayed there over two hours "and violated me and did many bad things to me." A female neighbor stated that she had not seen who the men were, but she had heard the knocking at the door, the noise that the men made inside the house, and Stana screaming, "For God's sake, for God's sake, you are choking me." This story was confirmed by two other women witnesses.[4]

Sexual assaults involving patricians occurred outside the city as well as inside it. In April 1406, two patricians attacked a young servant, named Vellica in a vineyard in the Ragusan suburb of Gruz. One of them

> came over Vellica and violently threw her on the ground and, having lifted her clothes, climbed on her with the intention of knowing her carnally, squeezing her mouth with his hand, so she could not scream, and holding a nude dagger in the other hand.

During that time the other patrician stood guard. Nevertheless, the intervention of a boy and of another girl-servant named Vellica, who was also beaten. A major investigation of the case by the Rector and his court followed.[5] The next month, May 1406, a young patrician attempted to "violate" a girl-servant in a house located inside a garden, while two other patricians stood guard outside. Here, too, the girl screamed so hard that neighbors intervened, and the return of the landlady frustrated the attempt of the young patrician.[6] The misbehavior of some patricians went so far that they even abused their official duties to satisfy their illicit lust. Thus, in July 1408, *ser Georgius de Gozze* (Gučetić), while selling communal salt, grabbed a young servant-girl, locked her in the hut where salt was stored, and witnesses testified that she was screaming inside.[7]

Patricians committed still other offenses. In 1408, the abbey of one of the biggest nunneries in Dubrovnik, *Sancta Maria de Castello*, accused a patrician of having deliberately gone to the property of the monastery and there ordering the cutting down of a vineyard and fruit trees belonging to the nunnery.[8] As before, patricians continued to insult commoners[9] and to offend and menace each other.[10]

It is easily understandable that such behavior did not endear the patricians in the eyes of the commoners, nor did it contribute to commoners' respect for their rulers. More than one instance from this period, the early fifteenth century, illustrates such negative feelings and bad dispositions among the common people of Dubrovnik. In February 1408, *ser Gauze de Pozza* (Pučić) was attacked by three commoners on the main street, Placa, "and they told him many insulting words."[11]

More vivid and significant was a case that occurred in March 1407. As three patricians were leaving the cathedral, one of them, *ser Georgius de Gozze* (Gučetić) was accosted by the tailor Ivan Goić, who said to him:

> Thank you, sir, for the punch that you gave me in my face
> last night and for drawing your dagger three times to hit
> me, but tell me why?

In the ensuing altercation, Gučetić raised his dagger to strike Goić, but another patrician stopped him. For his part, the tailor declared: "O noblemen, do not offend and beat the people this way, because God will make stated you lose your reign."

A witness testified that Goić had said: "My lords, if you persist in humiliating the commoners this way, you will not govern any more."[12]

These were "revolutionary" words indeed. When one recalls that only a few years earlier, in 1400, there had been an attempt to overthrow the government of Dubrovnik, in which both patricians and commoners had been implicated, and which was put down with bloodshed, the 1407 document clearly demonstrates continued unrest and dissatisfaction among the common people in the city—a fact which could only make the authorities more suspicious and vigilant.

The presence of such a mood is confirmed by other cases from this period. During a brawl, in November 1409, a commoner insulted a patrician by telling him: "Son of a jackass, why are you beating merchants?" According to another witness, the commoner's insults were even worse: "Son of a jackass, tadpoles, everybody is fed up with you."[13] In November 1412, when a town crier demanded a payment from a man and said that criers enjoyed public trust, the man answered: "May the devil take those who ordered that town criers enjoy public trust,"to which the crier replied: "May the devil take you, because you are blaspheming against all noblemen of this land, for they made those ordinances."[14]

Lingering discontent among commoners was probably additionally stimulated by the purported behavior of patricians in governmental councils. Although the meetings of those councils (Major, Senate, and Minor) were closed to the public, there can be no doubt that much information and many rumors filtered out and became common gossip. This is confirmed by later decrees enforcing secrecy, order, and discipline and prohibiting the presence of non-authorized persons during councils' sessions.[15] Among the numerous rumors that circulated, those concerning patrician misbehavior were frequently well-founded.

On July 21, 1418, for instance, "in the hall of the Major Council, in the presence of the Lord Rector and of the Minor Council," a patrician insulted another one by "saying offensive words to him," and their verbal altercation persisted even after the Rector admonished them.[16] Worse still, that same day a patrician "said insulting words to the . . . Lord Rector, who was sitting in the [Minor] Council."[17] In April 1427, *ser Marinus de Bona* (Bunić) was condemned to five days in jail "because of words pronounced against the Lord Rector and the Council."[18] Another patrician, *ser Petrus de Lucari* (Lukarević), that same year was allowed to receive in jail "noble men and women and others who would like to visit ser Petrus . . . on condition that they always stay inside [the cell] with closed doors."[19]

Personal clashes among patricians also continued. In August 1427, the Rector had to impose an enormous fine of 100 ducats each on three patricians "lest they use dishonest words against each other."[20]

Three years later a fine of 50 ducats was imposed on a patrician "lest he dare utter in this (sc. Major) Council provocative or insulting words against anyone."[21]

Patrician dissent and interpersonal conflict no doubt forced the government, in August 1427, to change the rules for the election of counts from the rich and newly acquired region of Konavle. Indeed, it was stated explicitly in a decree that these modifications were made "for the peace and unity of all noblemen of Dubrovnik, lest delays should take place in the election of the count of Konavle."[22] This is, certainly, an indication of political disunity and of the existence of antagonistic groups in the most important governmental bodies of the Republic.

Finally, let us consider one more example of patrician misconduct, and against young ones. On October 4, 1429, a group of young patricians "entered the hall of the Major Council and there they playfully made noises and squabbles." The Rector, an elderly man and one of the ablest and most distinguished Ragusan patricians at the time, *ser Pasqualis de Restis* (Restić), sent his servants to tell the youngsters to leave the hall, but the young men refused to obey the order. At that point,

> the Lord Rector personally went to the door of the said Major Council, which was locked, and knocking on the door, ordered those inside to get out. When one asked, 'Who are you?,' he said, 'I am Pasqualis de Restis, Rector of Dubrovnik.'

Several youngsters retorted, "What major part do you have in government and in this place than we have?" This was an outrageous insult to the government and to the Rector personally. Not surprisingly, the young patricians, "in view of the disgrace [inflicted] on the government," were sentenced to spend twenty days in jail under strict regime.[23] The incident is another confirmation of patrician misbehavior, particularly the lack of respect for age and authority on the part of younger noblemen.[24]

* * * * * *

Such misbehavior was not limited to the city or the territory of the Republic of Dubrovnik. Sometimes it manifested itself among Ragusan patricians abroad. It is well known that since the thirteenth and fourteenth centuries Ragusan merchants, among them numerous patricians, had played an active role in mining enterprises in Serbia and Bosnia. This led to the rapid growth of Ragusan colonies in the main mining and commercial centers of those regions.[25] Some of these Ragusans became important figures in the royal and princely courts of Serbia and Bosnia.

Nevertheless, the behavior of these people was far from impeccable. In January 1413, two Ragusan commoners complained to the Dubrovnik authorities about an incident in Novo Brdo. They had gone "outside the city [of Novo Brdo, Nouaberda] to play with bows and balists," when three patricians "attacked the plaintiffs with denuded knives" and wounded one of them three times "and in addition told them many insults."[26] This was, obviously, very reprehensible behavior on the part of Ragusan patricians, especially since it occurred in a foreign country and in an extremely sensitive spot—the biggest and richest silver mine in Serbia (and in Europe), in whose operation Ragusans played a major role and from which they extracted huge profits.[27]

Much worse, however, was what happened in 1418. In May of that year, Dubrovnik authorities received reports "not from malevolent or suspicious persons, but rather from true, trustworthy and honest ones that the Serbian ruler, Despot Stefan Lazarević, was able to learn of the plans of the Ragusan government

> on the matter of the conflict over Srebrenica and Novo Brdo
> before the said government sent its intentions in writing to
> its ambassadors in the court of the said Lord Despot.

The conflict over Srebrenica and Novo Brdo mostly concerned the matter of customs fees that Ragusan merchants were supposed to pay in those centers. This controversy had developed into a major snag in the relations between Dubrovnik and Serbia and it had led to the expulsion of Ragusans from Novo Brdo in 1417.[28] The reports that the Despot was able to obtain information on Dubrovnik's diplomatic moves constituted a matter of great concern for Dubrovnik. Quite naturally, its leaders could not accept the idea that the Serbian ruler might be spying on the innermost functioning of the Ragusan government.

On May 25, 1418, an interrogation of *ser Georgius de Gozze* (Gučetić), who had spent January of that year as Dubrovnik's envoy in Despot Stefan's court (and later played an important role in Dubrovnik's relations with Serbia and with the Ottomans), re-

vealed that Serbian noblemen had told Gučetić that Ragusan patricians were instigating the Despot to introduce new, unfavorable measures.[29] Asked by Gučetić who these Ragusan patricians were, the Serbians replied: "*ser Marinus de Gradi* (Gradić) perpetrates all of that and informs the Lord Despot on everything you do, and induces the Lord to do bad things against your Ragusans."
Gučetić further reported that he had heard rumors that every time the Ragusan government sent couriers to its ambassadors in the Serbian court, a courier also went to Marin Gradić. Moreover when the official Ragusan couriers returned to Dubrovnik, Gradić sent along a courier of his own. Gučetić added that he had personally seen one of Gradić's couriers travelling with government couriers during his recent return to Dubrovnik.

The government was eager to learn more about this disturbing situation and, on May 31, 1418, examined George Gučetić again, this time concerning his stay in Srebrenica in November 1417. Gučetić recounted that one day he sat with Marin Gradić in the customs house of Srebrenica and they talked about the recently arrived Ragusan ambassadors, who were on their way to the Despot. Gradić reportedly said, "The Lord Despot knows all the reasons for the visit of those ambassadors," and Gučetić replied, "It is a bad sign if the Lord Despot knows what the ambassadors want to say and do even before they have arrived in his presence." Three days earlier the Ragusan government had examined another patrician, *ser Marinus de Gondula* (Gundulić), who had been in Srebrenica in October 1417, and who also had conversed with Marin Gradić. On that occasion Gradić supposedly told him that the ambassadors had been elected in Dubrovnik to visit the Despot "because of differences over Srebrenica" and that the Despot already knew of their coming and of their business, "and that the Lord [Despot] also knew everything that was contained in the commission of the said ambassadors." According to Gradić, Stefan Lazarević even knew ahead of time that the envoys were not bringing him any gifts and was surprised and angry because of that. Gundulić added that he had told Gradić: "It seems to me it is very bad that the Lord (Despot) knows that, and from where does he know it?"

Yet another patrician examined on that same day, *ser Matheus de Crosi* (Krusić), who had been in Pristina three months earlier, testified that:

> he had heard several merchants, Ragusan and Serbian, publicly stating that Marin Gradić was and is the cause of all

the troubles existing between the Lord Despot and the commune of Dubrovnik. He also claimed that even before the Ragusan ambassadors went into the presence of the Lord Despot, the latter knew everything that was in the commission of the ambassadors and what they wanted to negotiate with him.

Finally, two other depositions were taken on May 30, 1418. *Ser Marinus de Bona* (Bunić) testified that he had heard from several people in Dubrovnik that the Serbian Despot knew the contents of ambassadorial instructions ahead of their arrival in his court.[30] Another patrician, *ser Benedictus de Gondula* (Gundulić) described how he had learned "while he was in Krusevac, in the court of the Lord Despot," that Marin Gradić had bought from the Serbian ruler the customs rights at Srebrenica under circumstances unfavorable to Dubrovnik.[31]

Clearly, Marin Gradić was the source of Despot Stefan's information and the cause of deep concern for the government of Dubrovnik. Gradić had spent a long time in Serbia, since the beginning of the fifteenth century, and he would eventually die there in 1422. His relationship with Despot Stefan Lazarevic was a very close one (he even left 105 lbs. of silver to the Despot when he died) and Gradić, doubtless, exercised considerable influence in the Serbian court, especially in dealings with Dubrovnik. Gradić's son, Junius, later also lived in Serbia and was a knight in the service of Despot Djuradj Branković, Stefan's successor.[32] Why Marin Gradić acted against the interests of his country is not clear, although he is not the only case of this sort.[33] However, in all fairness, it should be emphasized that the majority of Ragusan patricians who lived and worked abroad, and sometimes reached very high positions in the service of foreign masters (in Bosnia, Serbia, Hungary, the Papacy, Spain, etc.), remained loyal to Dubrovnik and performed numerous and very valuable services for their native city.

Probably the most disturbing aspect for the Ragusan government of the case just described was the realization that Gradić must have had collaborators in the innermost circle of Dubrovnik's government. These were men who knew exactly what was going on in the decision-making bodies: what discussions took place, what decisions were made, and when and what instructions were being sent to Ragusan envoys in Serbia. Being well-informed, these people were evidently willing and able to quickly and efficiently send the information to Gradić in Serbia, thus acting directly against the laws and interests of their country. This breach of trust and discipline constituted an act of treason, in which, beyond doubt, more than one person was involved.[34]

Unfortunately, we do not have further information on this case. Did the government of Dubrovnik try to do something against Gradić? The fact that he died in Serbia and that his son stayed there might indicate that his return to Dubrovnik would have been dangerous for him. It is also possible that decisions concerning this case were made secretly and noted in separate, closed books, which were later destroyed, as happened with many delicate and unpleasant decisions. In any case, Marin Gradić's behavior was a drastic example—to put it mildly—of political misbehavior by a Ragusan patrician at a time and in a place of greatest interest and importance for Dubrovnik.[35]

* * * * *

When looking at the incidents of Ragusan patrician misbehavior in the early fifteenth century, one cannot escape noticing the high degree of similarity with the behavior of Venetian patricians, in its colonies and elsewhere.[36] To a lesser degree, one also finds similarities with patricians in cities on the eastern coast of the Adriatic Sea.[37]

None of the above behavior by Ragusan patricians should be really surprising. Nevertheless, one should not imagine that the majority of those patricians were men lacking dedication to duty and bent only on fulfilling their selfish, and frequently illicit, urges. Had that been so—either in Dubrovnik or Venice—neither of those cities would have survived and prospered for centuries, leaving behind a wealth of information which allows us to study, among many other things, even the negative characteristics of their rulers and the unpleasant aspects of their rule.

Of course, the phenomena described here were not limited to the period of Dubrovnik's growth and prosperity in the fifteenth and sixteenth centuries. They persisted, grew and took additional forms in times of economic, political, and social difficulties in the seventeenth and eighteenth centuries, but that is a topic which deserees another, separate study.

NOTES

1. Historical Archives, Dubrovnik (hereafter HAD), *Lamenta de criminale*, Vol. 1, p. 125v.

2. HAD, *Lamenta de intus*, Vol. 1, p. 4.

3. Ibid., f. 164. On the less than exemplary behavior of another Ragusan patrician at this time see B. Krekić, "Ser Basilius de Basilio," in *Zbornik radova Vizantoloskog instituta*, Vol. XXIII (Belgrade 1984), 171–182.

4. It is interesting to note, that the scribe, an Italian, wrote those words in the Slavic language (*Saboga, saboga, vdauisme*) in an otherwise Latin text. *Lam. de intus*, Vol. 1, f. 166. On sexual violence in Venice, especially on rape, see S. Chojnacki, "Crime, Punishment and the Trecento Venetian State," in *Violence and Civil Disorder in Italian Cities*, L. Martines, ed. (University of California Press, 1972), 184–228; G. Ruggiero, *Violence in Early Renaissance Venice* (Rutgers University Press, 1980), 16–170; the same author, *The Boundaries of Eros: Sex, Crime and Sexuality in Renaissance* (Venice, Oxford University Press, 1985), 89–1O8.

5. *Lam. de intus*, Vol. 1, f. 182; cf. D. E. Queller, *The Venetian Patritiate. Reality versus Myth* (University of Illinois Press, 1986), 208–210.

6. *Lam. de intus*, Vol. 1, p. 186v.

7. *Lam. de crim.*, Vol. 2, p. 138.

8. Ibid., p. 280.

9. In October 1408, a patrician called a commoner "a thief" and his wife "a whore;" ibid., Vol. 2, f.153v. In April 1411, a woman complained that a patrician, with the aid of his two servants, had stolen money from her house in Gruz. HAD, *Lamenta de foris*, Vol. 2, p. 89v.

10. *Lam. de crim.*, Vol. 2, p. 258v.

11. Ibid., p. 93v.

12. Ibid., separate sheet. See also B. Krekić, "Developed Autonomy: The Patricians in Dubrovnik and Dalmatian Cities," in *Urban Society of Eastern Europe in Premodern Times*, B. Krekić, ed. (University of California Press, 1987), 200.

13. The last statement is quoted in Slavic in a document written in Italian: "Pulogl auzi, doi edoste su emu suietu." *Lam. de crim.*, Vol. 2, sep. sheet. Krekic, ibid.

14. *Lam. de crim.*, Vol. 3, p. 6v.

15. For disorderly conduct of Venetian patriciates in governmental councils see Queller, o.c., 240–245.

16. HAD, *Lamenti politici*, Vol. 2, p. 182v.

17. Ibid., p. 183. Krekić, "Developed Autonomy," 201.

18. HAD, *Consilium Minus*, Vol. 4, p. 81v.

19. Ibid., pp. 67, 68.

20. Ibid., p. 103v.

21. HAD, *Consilium Maius*, Vol. 4, f. 88. On verbal insults and physical violence among patricians in Venice see Queller, o.c., 234–239.

22. *Cons. Minus*, Vol. 4, p. 105.

23. It seems that the warden and three family of the government refused the orders concerning the strict regime of the condemned and ended up in jail themselves; ibid., pp. 267v–268.

24. On Ragusan attitudes towards old age see B. Krekic, "Slike iz gradske svakodnevnice: prilozi proucavanju zivota u Dubrovniku u doba Humanizma i Renesanse," in *Anali Zavoda za povijesne znanosti JAZU u Dubrovniku*, Vol. XXVI, Dubrovnik 1988, 18–22.

25. For Ragusan presence and their colonies in Serbia and Bosnia see, among others: B. Hrabak, "Proslost Pljevalja po dubrovackim dokumentima do pocetka XVII stoljeca," in *Istorijski zapisi*, Vols. 1–2 (Titograd 1955), 1–38; M. Dinić, "Dubrovcani kao feudalci u Srbiji i Bosni," in *Istorijski zasopis*, Vol. IX–X (Belgrade, 1959), 139–149; D. Kovacević, *Trgovina u srednjovjekovnoj Bosni* (Sarajevo, Naucno drustvo Bosne i Hercegovine, 1961), 65–88; D. Kovacević-Kojić, "Zvornik (zvonik) u srednjem vijveku," in *Godišnjak Društva istoricara Bosne i Herrecovine*, Vol. XVI, (Sarajevo, 1965), 19–25; the same author, "Dubrovcani zanatlije u srednjovjekovnoj Srebrenici," in *Godisnjak Drustva ist. B. i H.*, Vol. XVII (Sarajevo, 1966), 35–45. The same author, "Dubrovacka naseobina u Smederevu u doba despotovine," in *Oslobodjenje Eradova u Srbiji od Turaka* (Belgrade, Serbian Academy of Sciences and Arts, 1970), 103–120; the same author, "Pristina u srednjem vijeku," in *Istorijski casopis*, Vol. XXII (Belgrade, 1975), 45–74; the same author, *Gradska naselja srednjovjekovne bosanske države* (Sarajevo, Veselin Maslesa, 1978), 159–167. S. Cirković, "Prijepolje u srednjem veku," in *Simpozijum Seoski dani S. Vukosavljevica*, Vol. III (Prijepolje 1976), 211–223.

26. *Lam. de crim.*, Vol. 3, pp. 30, 33v.

27. On Novo Brdo at this time see, among others: K. Jirecek, "Trgovacki putevi i rudnici Srbije i Bosneu srednjem vijeku," in *Zbornik Konstantina Jirečeka*, Vol. I (Belgrade, Serbian Academy of Sciences, 1959), 268–270. M. Dinić, *Za istoriju rudarstva u srednjevekovnoj Srbiji i Bosni*, Vol. II (Belgrade, Serbian Academy of Sciences and Arts, 1962), 27–99. The same, "Novobrdska okolina"

and "Novo Brdo" in M. Dinić, *Srpske zemlje u srednjem veku* (Belgrade, Srpska književna zadruga, 1978), 113–120, 331–334; *Zakon o rudnicima despota Stefana Lazarevica,* N. Radojčić, ed. (Belgrade, Serbian Academy of Sciences and Arts, 1962); D. Kovacević Kojić, "Prilog proucavanju zanatstva u Novom Brdu i okolini," in *Zbornik Filozofskog fakulteta,* Vol. VIII, *Spomenica Mihailu Diniću,* II, (Belgrade, 1964), 525–532; S. Cirković, "The Production of Gold, Silver and Copper in the Central Parts of the Balkans from the 13th to the 16th Century," in *Beiträge zur Wirtschaftsgeschichte,* Vol. 2, *Precious Metals in the Age of Expansion,* H. Kellenbenz, ed. (Stuttgart, Klett-Cotta, 1981), 41–69.

28. I. Bozic, *Dubrovnik i Turska u XIV i XV veku* (Belgrade, Serbian Academy of Sciences, 1952), 30–32. M. Dinic, *Za istoriju rudarstva,* Vol. I (Belgrade, 1955), 64–70; Vol. II, 2–54. M. Al. Purković, *Knez i despot Stefan Lazarević* (Belgrade, Sveti arhijerejski sinod Srpske pravoslavne crkve, 1978), 110–111. *Istorija srpskog naroda,* Vol. II, J. Kalic, ed. (Belgrade, Srpska knjizevna zadruga, 1982), 108.

29. K. Kirecek, *Istorija Srba,* Vol. I (Belgrade, Naucna knjiga, 1952), 358; Bozić, o.c., 86, 149. I. Mahnken, *Dubrovacki patricijat u XIV veku,* Vol. I (Belgrade, Serbian Academy of Sciences and Arts, 1960), 253; Purković, o.c., 111.

30. *Lam. polit.,* Vol. 2, ff. 153–155. N. Iorga, *Notes et extraits pour servir à l'histoire des croisades,* Vol. II (Paris 1899), 166–168.

31. Dinic, *Za ist. rud.,* Vol. I, 103–104.

32. Bozic, o.c., 28. Mahnken, o.c., 284. Purkovic, o.c., 11.

33. One year later, in 1418, there was a big investigation in Dubrovnik of hostile activities of the Ragusan patrician ser Michael de Caboga (Kabuzic) in the Bosnian royal court. S. Cirkovic, *Istorija srednjovekovne bosanske države* (Belgrade, Srp. knjiz. zadruga, 1964), 242, 246–247; P. Zivkovic, *Tvrtko II Tvrtkovic. Bosna u prjov polovini XV stoljeca* (Sarajevo, Institut za istoriju, 1981), 67.

34. On the problem of guarding secrecy in Venice see Queller, o.c., 212–224.

35. The Gradić family ranked eleventh in importance on a list of 34 patrician families in the fifteenth century, see B. Krekić, " O problemu koncentracije vlasti u Dubrovniku u XIV i XV vijeku," in *Zbor. rad. Vizant. inst.,* Vol. XXIVXXV (Belgrade, 1986), 399.

36. See D. E. Queller and F. R. Swietek, "The Myth of the Venetian Patricianate: Electoral Corruption in Medieval Venice," in D. E.

Queller, *Two Studies on Venetian Government* (Geneva, Libraraie Droz, 1977), 101–170.

37. See Krekić, "Developed Autonomy," 201–205.

THE OLD TESTAMENT HIGH PRIESTS IN ARILJE
Their Representation, Related Images, and Theological Significance

Ljubica D. Popovich

The church dedicated to St. Achileos of Larisa, commonly called Arilje, serves as the focal point for a Serbian provincial town bearing the same name. This church and its monastic structures, the royal foundation of Kings Stefan Urog Dragutin and Stefan Urog Milutin, served as the cathedral of the bishops of Moravica and the mausoleum of King Dragutin. Built in the style of the Raška School in the last decade of the thirteenth century, it combines features both distinctly Byzantine and Apulian Romanesque.[1] The church and its fresco decoration represent one of the most completely preserved thirteenth-century ensembles, not only in the territories of medieval Serbia, but in the Byzantine world as well. The frescoes, Byzantine in style, were painted in the year 1296 by unknown masters who most likely came to Serbia from Thessalonika. Studied by N. L. Okunev in 1936, and mentioned subsequently by a number of scholars, these recently cleaned frescoes still await modern evaluation.[2] Although the stiff drawing and harsh color pigments make them inferior in quality when compared to other Serbian royal foundations of the thirteenth century, such as Žiča, Mileševa or Sopoćani, the fresco program of Arilje emerges as one iconographically rich and, therefore, historically significant. The Arilje frescoes inherited some aspects from the immediate artistic past, while at the same time, they signalled the iconographic innovations so characteristic of the preserved fully developed Palaeologan paintings.

As indicated by the title, this study will concentrate on one group from Arilje comprised of six standing figures, representing the Old Testament high priests, and its parallels. The unusual features of this group are not found in the subject matter, an iconographic theme well known in Byzantine art, but in the placement and organizational arrangements of the images. It would also be of interest to try to reestablish their lost identities and to decipher the theological message they once conveyed.

Undeniably, the dome, or domes, structurally dominates a Byzantine church while the dome decoration concludes the iconographic program of the same.[3] Ideologically, Arilje conforms with its tradition but in its own particular manner (Fig. I). Damage to the calotte of the drum destroyed the image of Christ the Pantocrator, but the paintings in the drum of the dome directly below that representation remain almost completely preserved. In this two-tiered pictorial organization, standing figures, the focus of our attention, occupy roughly the upper two-thirds of the drum. Windows pierce this area and the figures adorn the interfenestral spaces. Directly below the standing figures , bust representations with extended arms and scrolls form a visually uninterrupted frieze. The latter group will be discussed only briefly in so much as is needed to further comprehension of the message of the figures above. The structural nature of the six-sided drum limits the figures in both tiers to the less frequently used number of six. In this respect, Arilje's drum differs from the more usual eight- or twelve-sided drums of domed Byzantine churches.

So far identified only in general terms as "prophets," all six heads of the standing figures, as well as their identifying inscriptions, are almost completely lost. Obviously, the damages sustained by the roof of the cupola, which caused of the loss of the Pantocrator representation and parts of the painting directly below it, also affected the standing figures. The loss of the heads with their icon-portraits makes positive identification of these figures somewhat more difficult, although not impossible. Due to the characteristic sacerdotal garments and some of the attributes carried by the figures, we can dispense with the rather generalized appellation of "prophets," this label being a specific iconographic category to which they do not belong. As their garments and attributes indicate, they are not prophets, e.g. authors of the Old Testament books, in the specific sense of the word. Furthermore, by means of the garments and attributes, it is possible to establish a positive identity for some of the figures and to tentatively suggest the same for the others. To begin with, the priestly robes, described in Exodus 29:6, establish that the Arilje frieze contains representations from the category of high priests, the forefathers of the Old Testament outside the Genealogy of Christ.[5] All of the Arilje figures are richly clad, their sticharia and phelonia embellished with varied patterns, such as lozenges or running scrolls, and sometimes encrusted with simulated gems. Each high priest is rendered frontally in a formal pose warranted by placement and very slightly indicates a contrapposto stance. In general, the figures are very broad, their phailonia spread open in such a manner as to fill the available architectural space.

Examining these figures, moving clockwise in relation to the main east-west axis of the church, one finds the first figure to be that of Moses, easily identified through his attribute, the Tablets of the Law (Fig. I:1).[6] Next to him stands another high priest who should undoubtedly be identified as Melchizedek. He holds a paten with three loaves, Melchizedek's characteristic attribute as mentioned in the "Painter's Manual" by Dionysius of Fourna[7] and confirmed by many similar representations in Byzantine art (Fig. I:2).[8] Another sacerdotal figure, the only one within this cycle carrying an calligraphically outstanding, is well preserved: *Tako glagolaet Gospod, izmiite se i čisti budite.* These words, "Thus spoke the Lord: wash up and be clean," most likely Paraphrase I Moses 35:2 in which the Lord instructs Jacob about the purification and the building of a sacrificial altar. Should one, then, on the basis of this text, identify this figure as Jacob? This is difficult to answer and certain elements must be taken into consideration in any discussion of the identity of this figure. First, it is not an absolute rule that the texts carried by Old Testament characters must be Biblical quotations written by them or directly related to them. Rather, quotations are selected on the basis of their appropriateness to the underlying theme of the entire iconographic program. For example, in the main dome of the Resava Monastery, dated ca. 1415–18, it is Aaron among the priests represented who carries a scroll with a text.[9] In this case, the selection comes from V Moses 10:14. Moses spoke these words after Aaron's death (V Moses 10:6) at a time when Eleazar was the high priest.[10] Second, many difficulties arise with the seemingly obvious identification of this Arilje figure as Jacob. When represented in Byzantine art, Jacob the Just, the Old Testament patriarch and one of the forefathers according to the genealogy of Christ, wears a classical garment not sacerdotal robes. Most likely, the Arilje masters would not have substituted Jacob's dress thereby causing a substantive iconographic change.

Who then is the figure with the scroll in the Arilje drum? Although his identity cannot be positively established, this author tentatively suggests that it may be Zachariah the Elder, father of St.

John Prodromos. In addition to the garment, other elements seem to fit well with this hypothesis. Zachariah the Elder is one of the most frequently selected figures to be included in drum cycles in which the number of prophets was augmented by the addition of Old Testament high priests. He frequently carries a scroll inscribed with text, the source for which often varies. For example, in the Church of the Virgin Peribleptos in Mistra, dating from the second half of the fourteenth century, the text carried by Zachariah the Elder comes from the prophecy of Zechariah the Younger.[12] Similarly, in the Resava Monastery, Zachariah the Elder holds a scroll with the text from Luke 1:68[13] the same quotation suggested for this Biblical character by the *Painter's Manual* of Dionysius of Fourna.[14] Therefore, Zachariah the Elder could conceivably be the third figure of the Arilje group. The quotation he carries in this church is by no means incongruous with his role as high priest, and it complements the overall program of this zone of the drum.

The fourth figure in Arilje can most readily be identified as Samuel (Fig. I: 4). Traces can still be seen of a long beard reaching to the middle of the chest, a characteristic of Samuel explicitly mentioned in the *Painter's Manual.*[15] Two other attributes seem to confirm this identification , the swinging incense burner and a pyxis. The latter substitutes here for the horn of anointment, another symbol of priestly function. Both attributes frequently accompany representations of Samuel.[16]

Because of its location in the northernmost section of the drum, the figure next to Samuel sustained more damage at shoulder level than the others (Fig. I : 5). The body proportions, more slender than the others in this group, differentiate this figure from the rest. The general outline is also less broad, especially in the hip area. The figure holds his only visible attribute, the rolled scroll, closely against his chest. According to the *Painter's Manual,* Hur alone, in the category of Old Testament high priests, is given the rolled scroll as an attribute.[17] Although infrequently represented, Hur can be found in the repertory of Byzantine monumental painting as witnessed by his image in the Kariye Djami.[18] Therefore, this identification is a very likely possibility for the Arilje image.[19]

Completing this group is the high priest standing directly north of the east-west axis and complementing the image of Moses. His standard attributes, the golden vessel,[20] inspired by the text of Exodus 16:33, and the flowering rod, also from Exodus, 17:5, readily identify him as Aaron. Both objects are well recognized symbols , the interpretations of which frequently vary in accordance with the iconographic context within which they are depicted.

Before examining formal and iconographic parallels from the Palaeologan period (1261–1453), one should look briefly at the usage and meanings of the representations of the Old Testament high priests in Christian art. Many of the Old Testament priests were represented in compositions and as individual figures in Early Christian and Byzantine art both prior to the Iconoclastic period (711–843) and afterwards. A scene of the meeting of Melchizedek with Abraham in the fifth century mosaic from the nave of the Church of Santa Maria Maggiore in Rome provides an early example.[21] The preserved sixth century monuments show two formal traditions: the individual standing figure of the high priest, as exemplified by the illustrations in the Rabbula Gospels,[22] and the Old Testament scenes with high priests explicitly charged with liturgical conotations. One of the best examples of this latter type, the Sacrifice of Melchizedek, combines with the *Sacrifice of Abel,* to occupy a lunette of the presbytery in the mosaic ensemble of San Vitale in Ravenna[23] This close association between the placement of the Old Testament high priest and the actual altar of the church continued in the iconographic tradition after the Iconoclasm. A characteristic example is the eleventh century mosaic representation of Aaron in the apse of St. Sophia in Kiev. In this church, Aaron is located on the north side of the belly of the apsidal arch. Clad in sacerdotal robes, he carries a pyxis and swings an incense burner. Lazarev believes that its priestly figure represents the sole survivor of an entire group of the Old Testament high priests and kings which once decorated the vault of the bema.[24] Possibly, this type of apsidal iconographic program follows the Constantinopolitan tradition which remains undocumented owing to the loss of monumental paintings in that city.[25]

The tradition of representing Old Testament high priests in the apsidal region, especially in the bellies of the arches which frame the apse, continued in subsequent centuries as witnessed by the early twelfth century mosaic in Daplni,[26] the thirteenth century frescoes in Sopočani, and the fourteenth century examples found in the churches of Gračanica and Dečani, among others.[28] However, Arilje, the central monument considered in this work, differs from these in some basic ways. In Arilje, the Old Testament high priests, placed in the upper zone of the drum, create a formally and iconographically cohesive group. Does this church, then, represent a late thirteenth century infusion of new ideas and theological interpretations into the Palaeologan iconographic program? Or does this type of sacerdotal group predate the thirteenth century, thus making the Arilje case only a confirmation of its existence? It is unlikely that a provincial monument such as Arilje would have served as the place in which some newly formulated theological shtements would have been originally visualized in ideas rather than fostered their origin. If this is the case, does the drum decoration of Arilje reflect an older, now lost, iconographic tradition?

When and where do we find the representation of the Old Testament high priests first depicted in the drum of a dome? From the time it was first introduced into the vaulting systems of Christian buildings, the dome assumed a very special role.[29] As its form evolved, its decoration changed but always rehined an iconographically preeminent function. This decoration could be allegorical, symbolic, narrative, or iconic.[30] In the latter case, the image of the Pantocrator dominated not only the calotte and the dome, but the entire church and, figuratively, the Christian universe. Standing figures, placed in the drum of the dome between the windows, accompanied Christ. As far as the rare preserved evidence permits us to judge, the standing figures of the apostles were depicted in the drum as survivors of the Ascension composition, one of the scenes chosen for the decoration of the dome.[31] The scant remains of the eleventh century mosaic figures in St. Sophia in Kiev documents this tradition and provides an example of the figures of the apostles in a drum.[32] Also exceptional is the combination of apostles and prophets around the Pantocrator in the dome of a Byzantine church dating from the third quarter of the thirteenth century, the Church of St. Sophia in Trebizond.[33] In the majority of the preserved Byzantine churches with single domes, the images of the prophets occupy the drum area. Occasionally, when either the size of the dome or a tall drum required a large group of the Old Testament figures, representative of the Old Testament high priests were intermingled with the prophets.[34] Is this then what happened with the images of the high priests, who had occupied an important place in the concept of apsidal iconography during the late Macedonian period (the second quarter of the eleventh century) as witnessed by the already mentioned example from St. Sophia in Kiev?[35] As the entire apsidal decoration underwent iconographic replanning, the group of the high priests was either placed elsewhere in the church[36] or survived in the bema area, but was numerically reduced.[37] As the preserved evidence attests, this important category of figures was not eliminated from the iconographic program, but flourished in its own unique way.

Are there any preserved representaions of the Old Testament high priests, formally separated from the group of prophets as in the case of King Dragutin's church, in the drum of a dome which predate their depiction in Arilje? Bearing in mind that much evidence has been lost, this author can cite only one example, that of *Cappella Palatina* in Palermo. Previously studied by Otto Demus and others,[38] thus, mid-twelfth century mosaic ensemble is currently under investigation by Ernst Kitzinger. As of this writing, Kitzinger's conclusions from his imminent publication about *Cappella Palatina* are unknown to this author. Yet, certain suggestions about the iconography of this dome's decoration and its formal solution can be made. Undoubtedly inspired by Byzantine sources, it is nevertheless a clear example of a compilation of elements not always understood in the West. Images of the four archangels and the four angels surround a Pantocrator encircled by text.[39] In the area of the squinches below are represenhtions of eight prophets in bust and, in four niches placed at the cardinal points, the figures pertinent to this discussion. Two of them, Old Testament king-prophets David and Solomon, are modern restorations, but the other two date from the period. In the north niche, St. John Prodromos prominently holds a scroll with the text from John 1:29: "Behold the Lamb of God, which taketh away the sin of the world," a standard reference to the sacrifice of Christ. On the opposite side is the image of Zachariah the Elder, father of St. John Prodromos. Appropriately, he wears sacerdotal garments and swings an incense burner with his right hand, a distinct priestly action. The inscription identifies him as the prophet Zachariah. His actions as narrated in the Gospel of Luke, Luke 1: 1–38) justify the epithet; Dionysus of Fourna also mentions it as proper for this figure in the *Painter's Manual* [40] and indeed , he is thus entitled in other monuments as well.[41] However, here at *Cappella Palatina*, a substitution was made in the text that Zachariah the high priest exhibits so prominently on the scroll held in his left hand. He borrows the text from his namesake, the minor prophet Zechariah the Younger, the Prophet who proclaims the exalted Christ.[42] One of his most famous and most frequently quoted passages, Zechariah 9:9, "Rejoice greatly, 0 daughter of Zion; for behold, thy king cometh unto thee, riding upon an ass, and upon a colt, a foal of an ass," the texts forms part of the liturgical reading for Saturday of the Palm Week.[43] Thus, in this pair, the ideas of sacrifice and triumph are clearly stated and well-balanced visually. Considering the decoration of the dome as a whole, however, it appears that the artist incorporated various ideas and interpolated different images into a single dome system, mixing the prophets, the kings, and a high priest into a composite ensemble. While the iconography of the dome decoration of Cappella Palatina and Arilje differ greatly, as does the selection of figures included , certain superficial similarities of a formal nature ought to be mentioned. In both churches, the decoration of the drum contains whole figures and busts, the latter being reserved for the prophets. In the Sicilian church, the busts occupy the higher zone and the standing figures the lower, while in the Serbian church, the opposite holds true. In the drum of the latter, the presence of the Old Testament high priests is formally underlined and visually emphasized as a separate garb of a high priest, remains a sole representative of this category. His inclusion in this group of figures is undoubtedly due to the presence of St. John the Baptist rather than due to the need to express through iconography and text a certain sacerdotal meaning.

Are there any preserved painting ensembles chronologically closer to the date of the Arilje figures which contain a group of Old Testament high priests? To the best of this author's knowledge, the closet comparison is found in the painting of a small chapel dedicated to Saint Nicholas , in the village of Markova Varos, near the city of Prilep in Macedonia. This one-nave structure most likely dates from the eleventh or twelfth century. Its fresco decoration conhins several chronological layers, the one pertinent to this study belonging to the year 1298, thus postdating Arilje by only two years.[44] St. Nicholas features a domeless chapel. The iconographic program normally found in the dome here occupies the barrel vault of the main nave. In the vault, sixteen spaces, eight on each side of the east-west axis, were reserved for the standing representations of the Old Testament figures. Eight of these are prophets, distributed in the western half of the barrel vault, four on each the south and north sides. The other eight standing figures occupy the eastern half of the same vault and, thus, are physically closer to the apse.

Two among these are Solomon and David, the king-prophets, easily identified by their royal garments. They are depicted on the north side of the vault and, counting from the east, occupy the third and fourth places respectively. The remaining six figures in this part of the vault are Old Testament high priests. Four of them are located on the south; the other two join David and Solomon on the north side of the vault. It is this gathering together of high priests that thematically relates these two basically very different monuments, Arilje and St. Nicholas near Prilep. All of the priests are dressed in very elaborate sacerdotal robes , setting them clearly apart from the eight prophets who wear classical garments and the two king-prophets dressed in royal robes. The first figure on the north side of the vault is Aaron who carries his characteristic attributes, the vessel and the rod. The somewhat younger personage standing next to Aaron can be easily identified as Moses through the Tablets of the Law which he holds in addition to the menorah.[45] On the south side, balancing Aaron, is Samuel, identified by the preserved inscription, his characteristically long beard , and the bejewelled horn of anointment carried as his attribute.[46] He differs in that respect from the figure in Arilje identified as Samuel who carries an incense burner and a pyxis. In spite of attribute variations and stylistic differences, the priestly robes of these two figures share many common decorative details: the running scroll on the border of the long tunic and the identical diamond-shaped pattern of their respective phelonia.[47]

Since he holds a gold paten like the corresponding figure in Arilje, the figure next to Samuel is most likely Melchizedek. The frescoes of the two Old Testament priests following Melchizedek in St. Nicholas' church need further cleaning before their identities can be established. Both hold scrolls with very faded texts, impossible to transcribe and, therefore, to identify in their present state. All of the high priests are represented frontally, assuming a formal, hieratic position, very much like the figures in Arilje and in sharp contrast to the highy animated figures of some of the prophets who follow their suite on the vault of St. Nicholas.[48] Despite many differences between the churches of Arilje and St. Nicholas, their respective groups of the Old Testament high priests show remarkable similarities in garments, attributes and, above all, in the figure selection. At least four of the latter, Aaron, Moses, Samuel and Melchizedek, are identical. This suggests that both churches follow a well-established tradition.

The Old Testament high priests continued to be included in the iconographic program of Byzantine churches of the fourteenth and subsequent centuries. Found in various locations within the church, they often join other Old Testament characters, frequently the prophets.[49] Nowhere, among the preserved monuments, are they represented so clearly isolated as an iconographic and theological unit as in the drum of Arilje's dome and, to a lesser degree, in the tunnel vault of the church of St. Nicholas near Prilep. To the best of this author's knowledge, only one gathering of the Old Testament high priests in the upper zone of a drum matches in clarity of idea and somewhat in figure selection those represented in Arilje and St. Nicholas. These high priests, unfortunately heavily damaged, are depicted in the drum of the dome of the catholicon of the Kalenić monastery, dated about 1415. In Kalenić, very much as in Arilje, the standing figures occupy the interfenestral spaces of the drum (Fig. II). Kalenić's drum, tall and eight-sided , required the iconographic program to expand to include eight frontally depicted figures. The pair which occupy the two lateral spaces of the drum's west window wear royal dalmatica with gem-encrusted loros and can be identified as the king-prophets David and Solomon. Both heads and name inscriptions are lost, thus, more specific distinction is not possible at this time. Certainly, both kings held scrolls, one of these was definitely open, yet only several letters remain from its text (Fig. II: 4 and 5). The same two king-prophets can be found grouped with the high priests in St. Nicholas, but are absent from the drum in Arilje. In the eastern side of the drum in Arilje, stands the pair which this author proposes to identify as follows. To the north of the eastern window is the figure of St. John Prodromos, clad, in contrast to the others, in a classical garment (Fig. II: 8). A himation drapes his shoulders, cascading down his right side. He wears a short chiton which leaves the lower part of his legs exposed, an iconographic feature typical of St. John. His gesticulation also characterizes him; his right hand, raised to the height of his shoulders, points upward, his fingers arranged in the gesture of blessing. His left hand holds a once-inscribed, unrolled, hanging scroll.[51] To the south of the east window is a figure easily identified on the basis of his garment and the text of his scroll as the prophet Elijah (Fig. II: 7). He wears a typical fur-lined cloak over a long, belted chiton. His right blessing hand is placed in front of his chest, the left holds the hanging scroll. The remaining letters permit the five lines of text to be identified as III Kings (I) 19:10.[52] Elijah has a full head of hair and a medium length beard. His head, slightly uplifted, gives the impression that he glances upward. In this aspect, he differs from all of the other figures in this drum, the heads of whom are represented strictly frontal.

Such rendering of the prophet Elijah's head may have served multiple purposes. To begin with, it visually indicates the formal beginning of the group and connects the standing figures with the representations above them. In addition, the head movement is inspired by the text which deals with the conversation between Elijah and the Word of the Lord, thus indicating the prophet's personal theophany. Furthermore, this text was read on July 20th, the Feast of the Ascension of the prophet Elijah. This event in his life, in turn, was interpreted as the Old Testament prefiguration of the Ascension of Christ.[53] In this case, the prophet Elijah and St. John Prodromos bracket the whole group of figures, indicating its beginning and end.

The remaining four figures in the Kalenić drum are clad in priestly robes and, therefore, belong to the category of Old Testament high priests. Due to the damage to the frescoes in ffis area, all of the identifying inscriptions have been lost along with two of the four heads, thus making positive identification difficult. The first figure south of Elijah represents a very old high priest, his age indicated by his very long beard (Fig. II: 2). In his right hand, he holds a paten, upon which rests a vessel. Nothing indicates that this vessel contained an image depicted in a medallion on its belly. The type of beard and the presence of the vessel favor the identification of its figure as Aaron.[55] The upper half of the next figure can barely be discerned. The figure possibly wore an elaborate hat and sported a rather short, rounded beard (Fig. II: 3). The right hand, lifted to shoulder height, exhibits the blessing gesture while the left hand rests against the chest. No preserved details indicate the presence of an object, the symbol of the given figure. With so little information, the identity of this Old Testament high priest cannot be positively established. Only a hypothetical proposition can be made. If the first priest in this group is Aaron, the following figure could be Moses. To begin with, the groups of figures , such as the ones discussed here, are logically constructed. Second, Moses and Aaron are frequently depicted as a complimentary pair. When Moses appears alone, it is within a very different iconographic context.[56]

The two remaining high priests occupy the northern segment of the drum, between a king-prophet and St. John Prodromos. The high priest adjacent to the king-prophet suffered damage to the head and shoulders (Fig. II: 6). He seems to wear the elaborate head gear typical for his iconographic category and may also have had a pointed beard of medium length. He holds his arms in front of him and in his hands carries a rolled scroll, an attribute also seen with one of the high priests from Arilje (Fig. I : 5). His tunic appears to be somewhat shorter than those worn by the other figures in this Kalenić group and his phelonion is less elaborately decorated. Unfortunately, the above provides evidence too meagre to propose even a tentative identification.[57] The most completely preserved high priest in this group stands next to St. John Prodromos (Fig. II: 8). The attribute held in his right hand, the horn of anointment, clearly identifies him as Samuel. The same Old Testament high priest holds this attribute in the group of high priests painted on the tunnel vault in the church of St. Nicholas.[58]

In order to interpret the meaning of these figures in the window zone of the Kalenić drum, it is necessary to mention that above them traces of feet, fragments of garments and details of altar tables remain (Fig. III). These represent the remnants of a continuous frieze of angels who formed a procession celebrating the Divine Liturgy. The frieze occupied the area just below the now completely lost image of the Pantocrator in the calotte of the dome. Below the window zone, a second continuous frieze of figures decorates the drum. In this case, the frieze takes the form of twelve standing representations of the prophets, easily recognizable by the inscribed scrolls, garment types and, in some instances, partially preserved name inscriptions. Undoubtedly, all of these figures comprise an iconographic and theological unit that should be interpreted not as individual representations but as a total message.

Although separated by many decades, formally not identical, and stylistically very different, the dome decorations of Arilje and Kalenić, in addition to the vault images from St. Nicholas, seem to testify to the existence of a particular iconographic tradition of the Old Testament high priests with a specific theological exegesis. The meaning of this tradition certainly warrants closer examination.

What happened, one might ask, to the group of the high priests, which formed a part of Byzantine apsidal iconography as documented by the already mentioned mosaics of St. Sofia in Kiev? What was their context in that church? Did only selected members of that iconographic category survive and migrate to another part of church decoration , such, for example, as the dome as shown by the representations from Cappella Palatina in Palermo? How can one account then for the re-emergence of a numerically large and formally separated group of high priests in the drum of the dome of a late thirteenth century monument such as Arilje? Is it an iconographic innovation found in the peripheral region of the Byzantine empire, far from the leading center, the capital itself, Constantinople? Or was there another way or place within which the group of Old Testament high priests could have been used during the Comnenian period (1081–1204)? It might be worthwhile to explore an idea whose iconographic application seems plausible, although it cannot be substantiated due to the lack of preserved evidence. Middle Byzantine architecture, not limited to single-dome churches, witnessed the erection of ecclesiastical buildings with multiple domes, among those the petatrurion or five-domed type.[59] In the latter type, the five domes had five calottes and five drums to be decorated. The sources and preserved monuments demonstrate that it had become customary to represent the prophets in the main drum. Combined, the five drums of a pentatrurion totalled a minimum of twenty four sides (eight sides for the main dome and four for each of the subsidiary domes), thus, exceeding by eight the combined number of the four major and twelve minor prophets. Obviously, in order to reach the needed number, other figures of an iconographically similar nature had to augment the number of prophets to be painted in the spaces between the windows of the drums. To understand the iconographic category selected for that purpose, it is important to enumerate the iconographic depictions of Christ in the calottes of a pentatrurion. The Pantocrator occupied the main dome. Images in the subsidiary ones included: Christas the Emmanuel, Christ as himself, Christ as the Priest, and finally, Christ as the Elder of the Days.[60] Logically, representations of the Old Testament high priests in the drum below it would have iconographically complimented the image of Christ as the Priest. Little preserved visual documentation remains in the domes of the pentarurions dating from the Comnenian period. In one example, St. Panteleimon in Nerezi (1164), only the images of angels surrounding the four represetations of Christ in the damaged and repaired subsidiary domes have been preserved.[61] Other churches of this type with fourteenth century and show, in an old theme, the infusion of new liturgical and theological ideas. Some characteristic representatives are the churches of the Virgin Ljeviška in Prizren, St. George in Staro Nagoričino near Skopje, and, finally, Gračanica in Kosovo.[62] Perhaps confirmation of this hypothetical arrangement of Christ as the Priest with the Old Testament high priests is to be found in a rather confused eighteenth century account of the decoration of the upper parts of a church, ex-

clusive of the bema. In the *Painter's Manual,* Dionysius of Fourna
makes reference to the decoration of architectural substitution could
be explained by the chronologically late compilation of this instruction book. In this account, Dionysius clearly mentions several figures
in priestly robes which should occupy the groin vaults or the lunettes
directly below them. Dionysius's list includes a number of sacerdotal
characters discussed in this paper. He writes the following instructions to painters:

> Lower down, in the spaces formed by the groin-vault, paint
> Moses holding the tablets of the law, Aaron holding the
> golden vase and the flowering rod, both of them dressed
> in bishops' robes and mitres . . . lower down . . .
> paint the prophet Samuel holding a horn of oil and a censer,
> Melchizedek holding a plate with three loaves the prophet
> Zachariah, the father of the Forerunner, with a censer.

This list coincides with the identifications of some of the high priests
represented in Arilje. It is also noteworthy, and perhaps has bearing
on this discussion , that in the subsidiary domes of Aphentiko in Mistra (dated ca. 1310), four of the Old Testament high priests occupy
the shallow calottes.[64] There, the represented high priests are Aaron,
Moses, Melchizedek, and Zachariah the Elder, thus, mirroring some of
the characters who play an important role in the groups found in Arilje, St. Nicholas, and most likely in Kalenić as well. It seems that the
Aphentiko case represents a mature Palaeologan iconographic elabo-
ration of the priestly theme which also found its application in other
churches.[65] Such iconographic usage of the representations of the Old
Testament high priests certainly must have served as a basis for the
instructions given in the *Painter's Manual* for the depiction of the
priests in post-Byzantine churches.[66]

If the idea cannot be proven here that the group of the Old
Testament high priests, as depicted in the dome's drum in Arilje or
that on the vault of St. Nicholas, is a revival of an iconographic
program of a Comnenian pentatrurion type church, it can at least
be safely assumed that it was not a totally new creation. Rather,
it seems that the group of the high priests was borrowed from the
Middle Byzantine period and rearranged ahere in combination with
the prophets. One can further ask why such a group of figures was
selected for the drum of Arilje's dome, when it was not the only option
for the iconographic program of such a special place.

Finally, one must ask how to interpret the meaning of the high priests in Arilje, which in turn might provide a clue to understanding the other two groups of high priests discussed here. Very often, some of the representations of the Old Testament high priests bear the symbols of Mary and are given Marianic context.[67] Should one interpret the Arilje, St. Nicholas and Kalenić groups of high priests in the same vein? Such an explanation would make the above-mentioned groups similar in emphasis to the theme expressed in the painting of the main dome of the church of the Virgin Peribleptos in Mistra dating from the second half of the fourteenth century.[68] The themes expressed in the iconographic program of the latter church, dealing with Mary's virginity and her role in the Incarnation, were central to Byzantine theology and art. However, this author does not believe that each and every Byzantine dome decoration incorporated references related to these concepts. Furthermore, this author's studies of dome decoration seem to indicate that there were many variations on the generally accepted themes. The figures selected and the messages, textual or otherwise, were subtly adapted to suit the particular iconographic emphasis of the given monument.[69] The images in the dome provide indication that the Arilje high priests could not and should not be interpreted in the same manner as the high priests from the Peribleptos in Mistra. The arrangement of figures in the Arilje drum is formally different from that of the Peribleptos where that Old Testament high priests are intermingled with the representations of the prophets and where the image of the Virgin is included among them as well. The Arilje high priests are conceived as a formal entity by being placed in their own zone just below the image of the Pantocrator. Although not as clearly as in Arilje, grouping isolations exist in two other churches examined in this study. Such a formal treatment suggests a specifically closer theological emphasis. The attributes that the high priests in this church carry make reference to the Law and the Eucharist, the Altar and the Ritual, sacerdotal authority and , through the written word, express the prefiguration of Redemption.[70] Therefore, it seems clear that the sacerdotal idea is underscored. In Arilje specifically, it concurs with the entire iconographic emphasis as the cathedral of the bishops of Moravica.[71]

Sacerdotal figures of the Old Testament do occur interwoven with the prophets and more rarely with other Old Testament figures in the main or subsidiary domes of Byzantine churches. Besides the already mentioned examples in Cappella Palatina in Palermo, and the Virgin Peribleptos in Mistra (Moses, Aaron, Zachariah the Elder), one should indicate that such figures are found in other churches of Serbia and Macedonia such as in the Church of the Virgin Hodegetria in the patriarchate of Peć and in the monasteries of Lesnovo, besides the already mentioned Ravanica and Resava.[72] It is important to stress that in all of these churches the number of Old Testament high priests does not exceed four and that when they are painted in the main dome, they share the same zone with the images of the prophets. Their meaning can be fully understood in the total iconographic concept of each individual dome. It goes beyond saying that none of these can compare formally and theologically with the groups of the high priests represented in the churches of Arilje and St. Nicholas and, to a lesser degree, in Kalenić.

The above presented material led this author to conclude that these groups of sacerdotal figures, and above all, the one from Arilje, should not be interpreted as Marianic Old Testament prefigurations. Rather their meaning ought to be found in the context of the Christological priesthood. Paraphrasing Psalm 110:4, "The Lord hath sworn, and will not repent, Thou art a priest for ever in the order of Melchizedek," St. Paul introduces the idea of Christ as the high priest into the New Testament in his epistle to the Hebrews (Hebr. 5:6, 6:20 and 7:21).[73] Its relevant parts were incorporated into the liturgical readings as documented by the typicon of the Great Church.[74] The same idea, the priesthood of Christ, continued to live in the writings of both Greek and Latin authors. It suffices to mention only two examples here. A passage in Eusebius' *Church History*, in the panegyric of the church of Tyre (ca. 317), expresses this priestly idea:

> As for the holy, great and single altar, what else can it be than the Holy of Holies, the pure soul of the universal Priest?[75]

St. Augustine, in his commentary on the text of the prophet Malachi 1:10–11 dealing with the priesthood and the sacrifice, said the following:

> Since we can already see this sacrifice offered to God in every place, from the rising sun to his going down, through Christ's priesthood after the order of Melchizedek . . .[76]

Although his further comments are aimed against the Jews, he brought the idea of priesthood from the Old and New Testaments together

once again. Such an idea seems to fit well with the principle theological exegesis and the iconographic thrust of the drum's upper
zone in Arilje. Furthermore, could it be just placed in the lower part
of the Arilje drum (Fig. I) directly underneath the figure with the
scroll (whom this author has tentatively identified as Zachariah the
Elder)?[77] The text on the scroll held by the prophet Malachi, now only
partially preserved, clearly contains the word *vsedrzitelj* [Pantocrator],
the Lord God of the Old Testament, confined in Malachi's prophecy
and selected for commentary by St. Augustine. The presence of this
prophet and the quote from his prophecy may serve ever so slightly
toward strengthening the hypothesis about the priestly and sacrificial
meaning of the dome decoration of Arilje and of those other vaults
and domes preserved in Byzantine art in which the images of the Old
Testament high priests are represented without Marianic symbols.

NOTES

1. Aleksandar Deroko, *Monumentalna i dekorativna arhitektura
u srednievekovnoi Srbiji*, S.A.N. (Beograd, 1953), 58–63 and 84–85.

2. Nikolai L. Okunev, "Arilie, pamiatnik serbskavo iskusstva
Xlll vieka," *Seminarium Kondakovianum* VIII, (1 936), 221–254. In
this study, however, the decoration of the dome is mentioned in most
general terms; also, Vojislav J. Diurie, *Vizantiske Freske u Juaoslaviii*
(Beograd, 1974), 44–46 and note 46 with bibliography.

3. Otto Demus, *Byzantine Mosaic Decoration* (Boston, MA,
1964), 3rd edition), 10–22.

4. Branislav Živković, *Arilje, rasoored fresaka* (Beograd, 1970),
6, fig. III.

5. Dionysius of Fourna, *The "Painter's Manual,"* translated by
Paul Hetherington (London, 1974), 27–28 lists them as following:
Melchizedek, Job, Moses, Aaron, Hur, Joshua, Samuel, Tobit, To-
bias, Ananias, Azarias, Misael, Joachim, and Simeon.

6. D. of Fourna, *The "Painter's Manual,"* 1974, 27.

7. Ibid.

8. Paul A. Underwood, *The Karive Djami*, Bollingen Series LXX
(New York: Pantheon Books, 1966), Vol. 2, 84, fig. 78b.

9. Stevan Tomić and Radomir Nikolić, *Manasiia* (Beograd, 1964),
pl. XCVII, fig. 110.

10. As of this writing, this author was unable to locate a single
representation of Eleazer in Byzantine monumental painting.

11. P. Underwood, *The Karive Djami*, 1966, Vol. 2, 54, fig. 25.

12. Doula Mouriki, "The Old Testament Prefigurations of the Virgin in the Dome of the Peribleptos of Mistra," *Archeoloaikon Deltion*, 25 (1970), (Athens, 1971), 232.

13. S. Tomić and R. Nikolić, *Manasija*, 1964, 74. In this study the text is quoted, but it was not identifed.

14. D. of Fourna, *The "Painter's Manual,"* 1974, 29.

15. Ibid., 28.

16. Branislav Živković, *Sopoćani, crteži fresako* (Beograd, 1984), 8, drawing no. 7.

17. D. of Fourna, *The "Painter's Manual"*, 1974, 28.

18. P. Underwood, *The Karive Djami*, 1966, Vol. 2, 83, fig. 75a, where Hur does not carry any attributes.

19. As drawn by B. Živković, *Arilje . . .*, 1970, 6, fig. 10, it seems that the rolled scroll is the attribute. The only other possibility would be that due to the surface losses of the fresco, this detail was not sufficiently clear, and that, instead of a rolled scroll, the figure originally held a horn. Such a mistake could have been possible, but it was not likely the case in this monument.

20. D. of Fourna, *The "Painter's Manual,"*. 1974, 28.

21. Henrich, Karpp, ed., *Die frühchristlichen und mittlealterlichen Mosaiken in Santa Maria Magiore zü Rom* (Baden-Baden, 1966), figs. 29 and 30.

22. Carlo Cecchelli, Guiseppe Furlani, and Mario Salmi, *The Rabbula Gospels* (Olten and Lausanne, 1959), fol. 3b (Moses and Aaron), and fol. 4a (Samuel).

23. Pietro Toesca, *San Vitale di Ravenna: i mosaici* (Milano, 1952), 14, and pls. II–III.

24. Viktor N. Lazarev, *Mozaiki Sofii Kievskoi* (Moscow, 1960), 98, drawing no. 5, and pl. 26.

25. For examples, among the preserved mosaics from Hagia Sophia in Constantinople, and the drawings which document now lost mosaics, there are no traces of representations of the Old Testament high priests. See: Cyril Mango, *The Mosaics of St. Sophia at Istanbul, Dumbarton Oaks Studies* VIII, (Washington, DC, 1962), *passim*, and figs. 1–118. From the literary descriptions of Constantinopolitan church decoration from the Macedonian period (867–1056), it is impossible to identify specifically the representations of high priests. See A. Frolow, "Deux églises byzantines d'après des sermons peu connus de Léon Vl le Sâge," *Etudes Byzantines*, III, 1945, 43–91.

26. Ernst Diez and Otto Demus, *Byzantine Mosaics in Greece: Hosios Lucas and Daohni* (Cambridge, MA, 1931), 46, figs. 72 (Zachariah) and 74 (Aaron).

27. Vojislav J. Djurie, *Sopogani* (Beograd, 1963), 54 and drawing on page 122.

28. For the location of the Old Testament high priests in Gračanica, see: Branislav Živković, *Gračanica, crteži fresaka* (Beograd, 1989), VI: Moses (S.-E. pier); Zachariah the Elder (S.-W. pier); of the same figures in Dečani, see: Vladimir R. Petković, *Manastir Dečani* II (Beograd, 1941), 28, 51–53, 57 and 68; and pl. CLXVI.

29. E. Baldwin Smith, *The Dome: A Study in the History of Ideas*, Princeton Monographs in Art and Archaeology XXV (Princeton, NJ, 1950), *passim*; Karl Lehmann, "The Dome of Heaven," *Art Bulletin* XXVII, 1945, 1–27; Richard Krautheimer, "Introduction to an Iconography of Medieval Architecture," *Journal of the Warburg and Courtauld Institutes*, V (London, 1942), 7–33.

30. Suzy Dufrenne, "Les programmes iconographiques des coupoles dans les églises du mond byzantin et post byzantin," *L'information d'histoire de l'art*, 5, 1965, 185–199.

31. André Grabar, *The Art of the Byzantine Empire* (New York, 1966), 122, and pl. 83.

32. V. N. Lazarev, *Mozaiki . . .*, 1960, 83–85.

33. David Talbot Rice, *Church of Hagia Sophia at Trezibond* (Edinburg, 1968), 115–116.

34. Branislav Živković, *Ravanica. crteži fresaka* (Beograd, 1990), drawings on pages 10–11, and Branislav Živković *Manasija, crteži fresaka* (Beograd, 1983), drawing 1: the great dome and the pendentives.

35. See above, note 24.

36. B. Živković, *Gračanica . . .*, 1989, drawing VI.

37. V. R. Petković, *Dečani* II, 1941, pl. CIXVI.

38. Otto Demus, *The Mosaics of Norman Sicily* (London, 1949), 38–39.

39. 0. Demus. *The Mosaics . . .*, 1949, 39 and note 105.

40. D. of Fourna, *The "Painter's Manual,"* 1974, 29.

41. B. Živkovie, *Manasiia . . .*, 1983, drawing 1.

42. Gertrude Schiller, *Iconography of Christian Art* 1, (Greenwich, CN, 1971), 20–21.

43. Alfred Rahlfs, "Die alttestamentlichen Lektionen der griechischen Kirche," *Nachrichten von der Königlichen Gesellschaft der Wissenschaften zii Göttingen*, 1915 (Berlin, 1916), 38.

44. V. J. Bjurić, *Vizantiske freske . . .*, 1974, 19 and note 17, with older bibliography. While this small church still awaits its monographic study, the previous works dealing with it did not examine the figures painted on the barrel vault in detail. The observations concerning prophets, prophet-kings and the Old Testament high priests painted in St. Nicholas were made during this author's field trip in 1978.

45. There are other examples where Moses holds more than one attribute. In Gračanica, he holds the Tablets of the Law and a vessel which is cleverly combined with a seven-branched candelabra; see B. Živković, *Gračanica . . .*, 1989, drawing VI. ln Dečani, Moses holds the vessel, from whose neck protrudes the menorah; see: V. R. Petkovig, *Dečani* II, 1941, pl. CLXVI.

46. D. of Fourna, *The "Painter's Manual,"* 1974, 28.

47. This is not to suggest that the textile patterns of a garment are sufficient evidence to provide iconographic identification of the given figure. It is interesting to note that one of the Old Testament high priests in Sopoćani, also wears a phelonion covered with diaper pattern; see: B. Zivković. Sopoeani . . ., 1984, drawing on p. 8. In Arilje (Fig. I), the same design dominates the priestly cloaks, with variations in shape of the rombi. The Arilje high priest, identified as Samuel (Fig. 1:4) wears a phelonion whose diaper-shaped pattern is extremely close to that worn by the figure of Samuel who is positively identified.

48. Especially animated is the unidentified prophet on the north side of the vault, closest to the west end; see: Gabriel Millet, *La peinture du moven âge en Yougoslavie (Serbie, Macédoine et Monténégro)*, 111 (Paris, 1962), pl. 21–22.

49. See above, note 28; for the inclusion of the Old Testament high priests among the prophets in monuments in Russia during the fourteenth century, see: G. I. Vzdornov, *Volotovo. Freski cerkvi Usoenia na Volotovolm polie bliz Novaoroda* (Moscow, 1989), 62–63, and documentation nos: 10 and 11 (Moses and Aaron), no. 17 (St. John Prodromos), no. 35 (Samuel), no. 76 (Zachariah), and no. 77 (Melchizedek).

50. Branislav Živković, *Kalenić, crteži fresaka* (Beograd, 1982), drawing 1, 1–3. Its should be mentioned that four Old Testament high priests are grouped together in the lower zone of the main dome's drum in the catholicon of Manasija Monastery. They are: Samuel with the horn of annointment and a scroll with text; Zachariah, hold-

ing an incense burner and an inscribed scroll; Aaron carrying the blooming rod and a biblical quotation on a scroll; and Moses holding a vessel with medallion image of the Virgin. See: B. Živković, *Manasiia . . .,* 1983, drawing 1.

51. D. of Fourna, *The "Painter's Manual,"* 1974, 32. Among the early representations of St. John the Baptist with this text, one can cite a sixth century encaustic icon now in Kiev. See: Kurt Weitzmann, ed., *Age of Spirituality, Late Antique and Early Christian Art, Third to Seventh Century* (New York, 1979), 534–535, no. 479.

52. For a further discussion on Elijah and the text that he carried, see: Ljubica D. Popovich, "Hitherto Unidentified Prophets from Nova Pavlica," *Zograf* 19 (Beograd, 1988), 27, 38 and 41.

53. A. Rahlfe, "Die alttestamentlichen Leldionen . . .," *NKGWG* (1916), 51.

54. Vessels with painted representations of the Virgin Mary in medallion certainly contain Marianić symbolism. See Volislav J. Djuri, Sima Ćirković, and Vojislav Korać, *Pećka Patriiaršija* (Beograd, 1990), 150, and note 28.

55. See above, note 20.

56. For example, Moses without Aaron is included among the prophets in the drums. In that case he does not wear the garments signifying his sacerdotal function, but, like all other prophets, he is clad in a chiton and himation, and he carries an inscribed scroll. See: Moses in the church of Panagia tou Arakou, Lagoudera, Cyprus, The Photograph Collection, Dumbarton Oaks Center for Byzantine Studies, Washington, DC, Neg. No. D 71.206; or, for the same figure in Fethiye Camii, see: Hans Belting, Cyril Mango, and Doula Mouriki, *The Mosaics and Frescoes of St. Mary Pammakaristos (Fethiye Camii) at Istanbul,* Dumbarton Oaks Studies XV (Washington, DC, 1978), 49, and fig. 29.

57. For a list of possible candidates, see above, note 5.

58. For the horn as an attribute of the Old Testament high priest Samuel, see above, note 16.

59. Richard Krautheimer, *Early Christian and Byzantine Architecture* (Baltimore, MD, 1965), figs. 97, 101, 108, 109(A-B), pls. 148(B), 168, 177, 182(A), 183(A-B), 184, and 185(B).

60. Gordana Babie and Draga Panić, *Boaorodica Lieviška,* (Beograd, 1975), 49–50, figs. 2–6.

61. France Mesesnel, "Najstariji sloj fresaka u Nerezima," *Glasnik skopskoa naučnoa društva,* VII–VIII, Skoplje, 1929–1930, 121.

62. D. Panić and G. Babić, *Bogorodica Lieviška*, 1975, 47–93; Pera J. Popović and Vladimir R. Petković *Staro Nagoričino, Psača, Kalenić* (Beograd, 1933), 3–23; B. Živković, *Gračanica . . .*, 1989, drawings I–XII.

63. D. of Fourna, *The "Painter's Manual,"* 1974, 84, while mentioning at the same time different iconographic aspects of Christ.

64. David Talbot Rice, *Byzantine Painting: the Last Phase* (New York, 1968), 178, and fig. 147.

65. As for example, in late Palaeologan churches in Greece, D. Mouriki, "The Old Testament Prefigurations . . .," it Archeologikon Deltion, 25, 1970, 217–251; in Yugoslavia, B. Zivković, *Ravanica . . .*, 1990, drawing on page 10, and B. Živković, *Manasija. . .*, 1983, schema 1; in the USSR, G. I. Vzdornov, *Volotovo. . .*, 1989, 62–63.

66. D. of Fourna, *The "Painter's Manual,"* 1974, 84, The Old Testament high priests are depicted on the nave vaults of domeless churches during the Turkish period. One good example is found in partially preserved frescoes in the Church of St. Elijah, in the monastery of Ilienzi, near Sofia, Bulgaria, dating from the middle of the sixteenth century. In the eastern part of the vault, above the altar, Moses, Aaron, and Samuel were painted as whole figures standing under an arcade. There was a corresponding group at the western end of the vault, now heavily damaged. See: Asen Kirin, "The Murals in the Katholikon of the Monastery of Ilientzi," *Acts of the Symposium: Serbian Culture in the Sixteenth Century* (Belgrade, 1989) (in print), and Asen Kirin, "The Literary Sources and the Images of Prophets in a Sixteenth Century Iconographic Program in the Spiritual Life of the Epoch," *Arts of the Symposium: Prophets and Prophecies in Art*, UNESCO (Bucharest, 1990) (in print).

67. See above, notes 50 and 54.

68. See above, note 12.

69. Ljubica D. Popovich, "Figure proroka u kupoli Bogorodice Odigitrije u Peći. Identifikacija i tumačenie tekstova," *Arhiepiskop Danilo II i nigovo doba* (Beograd, 1991) (in press).

70. The Redemption is implied through the sacrifice of Christ as expressed in the text from the Gospel of St. John, and frequently inscribed on a scroll by St. John Prodromos. See above, note 51.

71. It is sufficient to mention a rather large number of church fathers which are found in the apse, diaconicon and on the piers and walls of the nave. A total of twenty-nine is preserved. This sacerdotal theme is continued in the esonarthex, where seven bishops of Moravica

are represented, while on some of the walls of the exonarthex are compositions depicting oecumenical and Serbian church councils. See: B. Živković, *Arilje* . . ., 1970, drawings on pages 4–5, 13, 14–15.

72. Milan Ivanović, "Crkva Bogorodice Odigitrije u Pećkoj patriiaršiji," *Starine Kosova i Metohije,* II–III (Pristina, 1963), 133–154 (Peć); V. J. Djurić, *Vizantiske freske* . . ., 1974, 65, and note 76 (Lesnovo; the representations of the Old Testament high priests are in the narthex dome); for Ravanica and Resava (Manasija) see above, note 34.

73. This quotation is taken from *The Holy Bible*, C. L. Scofeld, ed. (New York, 1917).

74. Juan Mateos, *Le typicon de la Grande Église, II: Le cycle des fêtes mobiles*, Orientalia Christiana Analecta, 166 (Rome, 1963), 39 and 47.

75. Cyril Mango, *The Art of the Byzantine Empire 312–1453*, in Sources and Documents in the History of Art Series, ed. by H. W. Janson (Englewood Cliffs, NJ, 1972), 7.

76. St. Augustine, *The City of God*, intr. Thomas Merton (New York, 1950), 643.

77. The following six minor prophets are represented as figures in bust below the standing high priests in the Arilje drum, from the east window clockwise: Jonah, Joel, Malachi, Zechariah the Younger, Habakkuk, and Zephaniah. They are positively identified due to the well-preserved name inscriptions, and they all hold scrolls inscribed with full or partially preserved texts from their prophecies. A full examination of these texts would have required a lengthy addition to this study. However, the author's preliminary reading and identification of texts does not in any way contradict Christological rather than Mariological interpretation of the meaning of the Old Testament high priests above them.

PART III

THE BALKANS AND EASTERN EUROPE IN THE
EIGHTEENTH TO NINETEENTH CENTURIES

DANUBIAN FEDERATION PROJECTS
ORIGINS AND DEVELOPMENT, 1848–1918

Nina Bakisian

The Habsburg monarchy of the early nineteenth century rested on several supports—the high aristocracy, the German upper middle class as well as the bureaucracy, army, and Catholic Church. This balance was challenged by two other forces which demanded a change of character and sometimes the end of the monarchy. First, there was the traditional nationalism of the smaller nobility in Hungary and Croatia. Then there was the innovative nationalism of the national middle classes and the peasant people. Throughout the empire the revolutionary happening of the nineteenth century was the process of democratization.

Early national movements were created and led by writers— principally poets, linguists, and historians. Their politics were of literature rather than life. Every nation claimed to be the heir to one of the ancient kingdoms on the ruins of which the Habsburg monarchy had been built. The German nationalists looked back upon the Holy Roman Empire, the Hungarians claimed the lands of St. Stephen while the Czechs claimed the lands of St. Wenceslaus. The Croats, in turn, looked back at the Triune Kingdom of Dalmatia, Slavonia, and Croatia, while the Serbs looked to Emperor Dushan and the Bulgarians to Michael the Brave. Each of these national groups sought to recapture its historic past.

Throughout the nineteenth century, the Habsburg monarchy was involved in the Eastern question and the problems that arose in connection with the weakening of the Ottoman Empire and the revolt of some sections of its population. In a European framework, it was expressed in the Anglo-Russian and Austro-Russian rivalry. In the local-regional aspect the biggest problem in both parts of the empire was the position of the non-German and non-Hungarian nationalities who represented well over half of each of their populations. The Hungarian nationality policy was to cause difficulties for both parts of the monarchy. Domestically, Hungarian leaders embarked upon a policy of intense magyarization. This was to cause bitter animosity and raise the national consciousness of the other peoples. Towards Austria they asked national independence and self-recognition.

The evolution of the federal idea in Austria, which includes the consideration if not the full acceptance of the ethnic factor as the foundation of the Empire's reorganization, cannot really be associated with the ideas of a single individual. There were many nationalists and other reformers who sought to change the political organization of the Habsburg monarchy. The elaborate and ingenious reform plans of Croatian Ognjeslav Utjejinović Ostrozinski were in the interest of Austria's preservation and transformation into a federal state power. Austria, in his opinion, had to recognize the limited autonomy of the following nationalities: (1) Germans, (2) Czechs, Moravians, Silesians, Slovaks, (3) Magyars, (4) South Slavs-Serbs, Croats, Slovenes, (5) Poles, Ruthenians, (6) Romanians, and (7) Italians. Ostrozinski insisted that the autonomy of these nationalities had to be established within ethnic frontiers not within existing historic-political crownland frontiers. He considered it impossible to recognize the national rights of small dispersed minority groups but was prepared to offer representation to them in local administration.[2]

In the decade before 1848, there was interest in the Balkans for a possible Balkan federation. This interest penetrated the Austrian empire as well and the various national groups (South Slavs, Romanians) sought to coordinate their plans with their brethren in the decaying Ottoman Empire. During the 1840s, a number of books and articles were published that dealt with the Slavs and the Romanians urging federation as the solution for their problems.

Karl Marx, one of the most famous thinkers of that time, recognized in principle the right of all oppressed nations to independent existence, although he considered the realization of this right difficult in regards to a people whose social structure was entirely based on feudalism. According to him, Croats as well as Czechs, though not Poles, worked during the revolution either intentionally or unintentionally in the interests of Russian Pan-Slav imperialism. He felt that this was clearly exemplified by their natural bent to join together against the empire's nationalities of authority, the Germans and the Magyars. What he did not recognize was that the Slavs had really no other alternative. Marx displayed a flagrant ignorance of the character of Slav cultural renaissance and also a short-range view of the political potentialities of the Slav national revolution. In many ways he symbolized the German approach of his day.

The 1840s were not conducive to cooperation. There was no united action among either the Slavs in the monarchy or the Balkan peoples. In 1848, simultaneous revolutions broke out all over the empire. On March 13, 1848 a revolution occurred in Vienna that resulted in the formation of a new government and the dismissal of Prince Metternich. A Slavic Congress was organized in Prague and opened at the beginning of June. Under Czech influence, the representatives supported a program of Austro-Slavism. They called for a reorganization of the monarchy into separate national autonomous units. This action would strenghten the influence of the Slavic peoples because they made up more than half of the empire. The empire was not to be dissolved but rather transformed into a federation of nations. However, this plan did not satisfy the Poles, Croats, or least of all the Slovenes who had not been invited. The meetings were disbanded only a few weeks later by the Habsburg army. Although the Prague congress met but a short time the Austro-Slav idea was to remain an alternative solution for the reorganization of the monarchy and was to enjoy support among some Slavic groups, especially the Czechs. Through Austro-Slavism they could have protection from both the Russians and the Pan-Germans.

In the meantime a liberal, anti-feudal nationalist, Lajos Kossuth, was working on changing the political organization of the empire in his own way. He was a fiery provincial lawyer from the Slovakian region who wanted full emancipation of the Hungarian peasants, the recognition of Magyar as the national language throughout greater Hungary, including Croatia and Transylvania, the transformation of the relationship with Austria to a confederal association, and the establishment of a separate Hungarian customs territory.

By the end of October 1849, the imperial forces were in full control of Vienna. Habsburg authority had been reestablished over most of the imperial lands. Back in control in Vienna, the government had to face the immediate question of the future organization of the empire. The issue to be decided was the choosing between a centralist or a federal form of government. The most successful of the revolutionary movements in the empire was Hungarian, but it, too, was finally defeated. A strong factor in the Habsburg favor was the extreme dissatisfaction that was aroused among the non-Hungarian nationalities. Vienna was able to rally support from the Croatian,

Serbian, and Romanian populations. The South Slavs themselves attempted to take advantage of the upheavals to forge a united nation. The Belgrade Committee was formed to facilitate a union of Turkish and Austrian Slavs. During the revolution, however, the national movements of the Romanians and the South Slavs was diverted and utilized for the defense of the Habsburg Empire. Nevertheless, a desire for unity remained. An important lesson had been learned. If the subject peoples of the Austrian and Turkish empires wanted to overthrow their oppressors then they should cooperate and not exterminate each other.

In the aftermath of the Hungarian revolution Kossuth recognized the necessity of cooperation with the Serbs, Croats, and Romanians and he did attempt to come to an agreement with them. After the collapse of his government in Hungary, Kossuth fled to Turkey and took up the Danubian federation project seriously in an effort to obtain allies. In the decade after 1849 there were repeated attempts made by the peoples of Southeastern Europe against their oppressors with the goal of setting up a Danubian federation of free nation states.

With the end of the Hungarian revolution, the Habsburg government proceeded with the reoganization of the empire. The new system was associated with Alexander Bach, the minister of the interior. Even though he wanted to establish an enlightened regime, the state went back to the absolutist pattern by which the emperor held complete power unchecked by a representative assembly. This was a reaction to the revolution.

Efforts were made during the course of the war with Italy in 1859 concerning a Danubian federation. The Italian nationalist, Camille Cavour, and the French emperor, Napoleon III, had agreed on a war against Austria and began negotiations with Hungarian émigrés to encourage revolutions within the empire. Kossuth suspected that the allies were interested in using the Hungarians only as tools against Austria and therefore demanded that an Allied force be sent to Hungary, and Napoleon III issue a proclamation in favor of Hungarian independence. Cavour repeatedly suggested that the Hungarians come to an agreement with the Romanians and the South Slavs for common action against Austria. However, just as Austrian neutrality had prevented action during the Crimean War now the unexpected conclusion of peace between Austria and Italy disrupted the anti-Austrian bloc while it was still in the process of formation. These were the boiling 1860s.

Ever since 1848 failed the defeated nations had realized that it was essential to join forces and settle national disputes in order to defeat Austria. Plans for a Danubian federation became closely associated with plans for a Balkan federation. After 1849 the resistance was continued in émigré circles, which included Hungarian, Polish, Italian, and Romanian émigrés. This association for a common cause made them work closely together. Adam Tchartoriski, the Polish nationalist, believed that a federation of Central and Southeast European peoples wedged between East and West would keep both Russia and Austria from imperialistic maneuverings. Giuseppi Mazzini, the Italian nationalist and radical republican, pictured an alliance of Slav and Latin peoples against Austria and Turkey. Active and interested in Balkan affairs, Mazzini advocated that Hungary should form a free confederation with Bulgaria, Serbia, and Bosnia. The basis of his philosophy was the sacred right of nationality.[3]

On a meeting held in London on January 4, 1850, the Romanian representative Balcescu presented a plan for a Danubian confederation. It was conceived on the Swiss example with a common parliament and executive. The purpose was a defense against Austria and Russia and the emancipation of the peoples of the Danubian region. It was called the *Donau Bundesstaaten* and would have included Hungary, Bukovina, Moldavia, Wallachia, Bessarabia, and Serbia.[4]

Of all the federalist plans the best known are those devised by the Hungarian émigrés, most notably Kossuth. The symbol of East European liberal nationalism, he is chiefly associated with the approach to the subject of a Danubian confederation that reached a supranational rather than a national character. He believed that the victory of national freedom in the whole Danube area was to be secured and extended to other national groups by means of a confederation. He promoted the project during his stay in Piedmontat, at the height of the Austro-Sardinian crisis in 1859.

In 1862, Kossuth drew up confederation plans which would fulfill the demands of the Romanians and the South Slavs. He wrote, along with his close associate General Klapka, a plan for federation that would include Hungary, Transylvania, the Triune Kingdom (Croatia, Slavonia, Dalmatia), Montenegro, Bosnia, Hercegovina, Serbia, Moldavia, Wallachia, Bessarabia, and Bukovina. After the failure of 1849, Kossuth realized that the emancipation of Hungary relied on the ability to work with the Balkan people. In a sense, the incorporation of Hungary in a group of Central European and East European nations would reconcile the integrity of a historical Hungary with the principle of nationality. It would be this integrity of a historical Hungary that would eventually lead to the breakdown of the plans of a Danubian federation.[5]

Kossuth wrote that only a federation of small people could safeguard their advancement especially in terms of Russian pressure. He wrote in 1862:

> If the Danube confederation fails, then every Slav element will have to support Russia, which with its giant arms, the Pan-Slav tendencies, will ensnare us down to the Adriatic . . . through this confederation Hungary frees itself from the necessity of being obedient to the policy of a Great European Power.[6]

In a sense he was fighting for the role of influencing the Slavs.

Instead of letting Russia take control of the European Slavs, Hungary could do the same. This was part of the problem—the idea of control rather than equality. Still Kossuth was trying hard to make this confederation work.

On May 1, 1862, Kossuth accepted a modified version of the draft written by Ferenc Pulszky. It was based on the previous summary presented by General Klapka. This draft differed from the one drawn up by Kossuth in 1850 in two major respects. He no longer insisted that the confederation have a permanent capital on Hungarian territory. There were three options for Transylvania. It could reunite with Hungary, have autonomy within Hungary, or have a chance to choose a constitutionally independent state. Special privileges for any of the three member states of the confederation were to be strictly barred. There was also a plan to make neither Magyar, Romanian nor Croatian but French the official language of the Confederation. Kossuth proposed that the seat of the confederate government alternate among the member states. He favored a constitution similar to that of the United States if the bicameral system could be adopted. Foreign policy, defense, commerce, customs, and finance were to be under federal control but in all other respects the individual states were to be independent. Each state was free to write its own constitution. Executive power was to be exercised by a federal council responsible to a common parliament.[7]

Kossuth sent the draft to Ignac Helfy, editor of the Milanese *L'Alleanza,* a paper dedicated to Italian-Hungarian cooperation. The

May 18, 1862, issue carried the draft. The Hungarian exiles felt that the Habsburgs' renewed position of power would be but temporary. They felt that Vienna's insistence on keeping Venice would lead to a renewal of hostilities with Italy, and that it was only a diversion. Therefore, the exiles started to reaffirm their contacts with the Italian government for potential allies. Italian nationalist revolutionary, Guiseppe Garibaldi, was one of these allies. It was part of a secret Italian diplomatic move that brought together Hungarian, South Slav, and Romanian cooperation. The exiles' plans for confederation won its final formulation.[8]

A precondition of the Danubian Confederation was the cessation of national animosities. First, they had to shake off the Great Power's yoke. Then they had to build a free alliance. They realized only too well that under the Great Powers each nation could become at best a second rate nation. It could hardly be able to safeguard its independence. They could develop freely and enjoy the benefits of a larger community by being a part of a confederation. Another function that the confederation would serve would be to fill the power vacuum that threatened to develop when the two eastern empires disintegrated. This would also satisfy Britain's foreign affairs preferences. Britain felt threatened by the emerging strength and power of Russia in this area. A strong confederation of eastern states would make a bulwark against Russian expansionism. Britain was very concerned about its empire in the East, especially India, and did not want any other Great Power rivaling her in her endeavors to remain "the empire on which the sun never set."

Kossuth's plan concerned the future of the Danube basin after it had managed to throw off the yoke of Habsburg and Turkish rule. Representatives of Hungary, Romania, Croatia, Serbia, and any other South Slav provinces that might decide to join would meet together in a legislative assembly. The articles of the confederation would include the joint affairs of defense and foreign policy. The entire confederated area would be an economic community. One house of the federal parliament was to be chosen on the basis of representation by population while the other was to have an equal number of representatives by population. The other house was to have an equal number of representatives from each state of confederation and act as guarantor of their coequality. The supreme executive power was to be in the hands of the Federal Council which was to sit in turn in each of the capital cities of the federated states. In all other matters the state was free to choose its own constitutional form of government. They were to be guaranteed to all irrespective of creed or nationality. These were the civil liberties outlined in Kossuth's Constitutional Draft.[9]

One of the problems with the plan was that it failed to take into account that the Danubian Confederation was not a pact with an oppressor but an alliance made on the basis of the democratically expressed free choice of equal partners. This was unlike any compromise that was considered up to this point and unlike that which would be realized later. Each nation that would have joined it for the mutual aid of safeguarding their hard won liberty would remain autonomous and would be free to withdraw at any point.

The failure of Kossuth's program did not result from his underestimation of the nationalities' psychological "state complex" but from the fact that he was not interested in the organization of the Danube area as a given historical entity or according to ethnic frontiers but as it should be to make possible the restoration of Magyar independence. Nevertheless, Kossuth was able to distinguish between Pan-Slavism (Russian dominated) and the independence and freedom of Slav nations. The ruling classes in Hungary did not accept Kossuth's solution of the Hungarian dilemma: choosing between Central Europe and the Balkans, they gave preference to the former because it guaranteed their undisputed hegemony within historic Hungary. The Resolution Party refrained from overt attacks but were busy behind the scenes. They were actually more detrimental to the cause because they failed to use their extensive illegal information network to compensate for the shortcomings of the censored press. They failed to convey Kossuth's clarifications regarding the long range plan for a Danubian Confederation. They also failed to contradict and in fact promoted Aurel Kecskemethy's argument that the planned confederation was comparable to compromise with the Habsburgs.

Kossuth was upset by this indiscretion. He added a lengthy explanation to the text and mentioned that the draft was not of his wording. However, the basic principles he accepted as his own. For this reason, the plan is generally attributed to Kossuth. His views were not only the backbone of the draft but also the most consistent in accepting political responsiblity for the idea after publication.

In the 1860s, the collapse of Bach's absolutism ushered in a new constitutional age. The October diploma of 1860 represented an attempt at federalization of the Monarchy. This was a period of inner tension that preceded the introduction of dualism in 1867. There were three intermingling concepts according to D. Djordjević: federalism, dualism, and centralism. Federalism would include a program of provincial autonomy that would include historical-political individuality. Centralism was rejected by the majority of the people under the Habsburg crown. In a memorandum to Emperor Franz Josef in 1860, Rieger proposed a federation based on ethnic units in historical regions each with district autonomy.[10] This was representative of the time because there was a general reshaping of Europe in the 1860s and a new map called nationalism.

In 1866, a flurry of excitement occurred as a result of the Austro-Prussian War. Italy and Prussia joined forces to stimulate revolts in Austria which included negotiations with Magyars and Serbs. However, Bismarck was not interested in the subject nationalities. As the Prussian chancellor, his goal was the unification of Germany. He wanted to expel Austria from the German confederation so that he could have control and Prussia would be the leader within the new German state.

The liberalism of the 1860s had its impact on the formulation of ideas concerning relations within the Balkans. These ideas shared the tendency to relate liberation movements to external political factors. The federalist projects that were put forward in Southeast Europe in the 1860s and 1870s were an expression for the desire of liberation of the nationalities within the two empires. The liberal ideas of the European West began to penetrate the Balkans. According to D. Djordjević, there were two European movements that had a great impact on the evolution of federalist concepts in the Southeast. These were the League for Peace and Freedom in the West and the Russian revolutionary democrats and reformers in the East.[11]

The goal of the Ligue de la Paix et de la Liberté was the creation of the United States of Europe. It was to be founded on the brotherhood of European nations and on the principle of broad national autonomy. At the Congress held in Lausanne in 1869, a special committee studied the Eastern question reaching the conclusion that it should be resolved on a democratic and federalist basis. This, in effect, presupposed the autonomy and independence of the Eastern peoples.

At the other spectrum, the writings of the Russian democrats and republicans had an impact on the protagonists of the new socialist ideas in that part of Europe. The revolutionary democrats believed that the future of the Slav nations in the Southeast of Europe lay in their struggle for national and social liberation. Herzen envisioned the future of the Slavs as a union of free and independent peoples. Tchernishevski gave concrete shape to Herzen's Danubian federation. This would integrate both the internal and external aspects of the struggle for liberation, and would help against both foreign and domestic oppressors.

The legal, social, and political conditions that prevailed in the region in the 1860s and 1870s strongly affected the federalist concepts, especially the ones that came from the soil of the Habsburg monarchy in the Balkans. In the Balkans, the idea of federalism was considered a way of solving the Eastern question both foreign and domestic. As a strong, cohesive force, they could stand unified against European intervention. It would also help to settle relations between the new Balkan national states.

One of the biggest problems that the federalist projects encountered was all the internal contradictions that occurred among the various nationalities. Each was trying to implement federal plans that would safeguard against the hegemony of one nation over another. At the same time, they wanted to avoid the hegemony of the external powers, most notably Austria and Russia, and wanted to obtain self-determination.

A politican from the Voivodina, Mihailo Polith Desančić,[12] outlined a project from a Balkan confederation that would replace the failing Ottoman Empire. The combination of Turkish Christian subjects in a Danubian confederation would guarantee the integrity of freedom according to Polith. The Crimean War and the Paris Conference pushed forward the Eastern question. State emancipation of the Christian subjects was an important criteria. Another one was that the European East must remain European. None of the older European countries should be able to take land from the newly emancipated nations/peoples. One of the greatest fears at this point was the great Powers would try and seize certain portions of the decaying Ottoman empire for themselves. There were two trends at this time. One was to break away from multinational states and form smaller more homogeneous states, the other trend was to unify nationally divided states.

Polith also points out that the Christians in Turkey should belong to themselves—no one has a right to them. Turkey, in his opinion must be made neutral for Europe's interest and need. Some believed that Turkey cannot be modernized and therefore could not be Europeanized. On the other hand, Turkey is seen as a marketplace. The idea of a customs union in that area would be in the economic interest of Europe. It would open trade with the East even more and make the Balkan peninsula European through a confederation. This would achieve an equilibrium for the balance of power in Europe. All the different people that live in European Turkey would be closer to Europe.

Polith's solution is that the nationalities would be formed into a confederation. He stated that there is no mathematical solution to historical problems. It is hard to foresee the fate of the Turkish subject nationalities. As with every organism, each nationality has its own characteristic. They each wanted to obtain a goal. This goal being the combining of culture, language, and history into one nation state. Polith thinks that there are three nationalities that could be considered states. These include the following: (1) Slavs (Serb, Bulgarians) (2) Romanians (3) Greeks. Their cultural possiblity is unquestioned while the others require more time to make clear the distinctions. Other nationalities living in the Ottoman Empire that Polith discusses are (1) Tsintzars, (2) Albanians, (3) Osmans (Turks), (4) Armenians, (5) Jews, (6) Tatars, and (7) Gypsies. Polith feels that these nationalities, unlike the former ones discussed, are not historically prepared to form a nation state.[13]

The migration of people before the arrival of the Turks made it difficult to establish specific national boundaries. One or another of the national groups was stronger or weaker prior to the establishment of an empire. First came Byzantium, then Bulgaria, and finally Great Serbia. Each wanted to unify the Balkans into one state. However, no one country became precedent over the others and each of the nations had their own autonomy.

Polith then goes on to discuss the changes that could lead to confederation. He believes that the moment when the solution will come is when the flame will be set off for revolution and the Turks will no longer be able to put down their Christian subjects. It could become an all-European war which can be prevented through alliances, according to Polith. There has to be a division of Christian and Muslim but the freedom of religion must be guaranteed.

The union would be achieved through a confederation of states-Staatenbund.[14] A greater Bulgarian-Serbian state should exist as one of the members of this confederation. The Slavs, the Romanians, and the Greeks would each be one branch of this federation. Every state would have its own local government but they would all adhere to the power of the federation at large. There would be ministries that they would each have in common. Each state would have the independence to govern themselves according to their own wishes. There would be representatives to help smooth out any problems that would occur. A confederation could not become a nation state. This is based on the nationality principle because the nationality of each nation would demand its own independence. There is also the factor of finding a compromise between European and Balkan interests.

According to Polith, these nations are too small and weak to make up their own state. They should form together into a large confederacy. Geographic location and material interest are diverse and therefore no one nation can absorb any other nation into itself. In the case of the Christian subjects of the Turkish kingdom, this would be a good solution because they were not strong enough to survive on their own but within the confederation they can get the recognition and the autonomy they desire. Polith stresses that the Eastern question is not just a Balkan one but rather a European one. It must be remembered that the little countries would be on the side of the Europeans. In Polith's opinion the confederation could perhaps be an Eastern Switzerland and achieve for the East what Switzerland does for the West.

Another Serbian writer in 1866 was Ilja Garašanin.[15] In a letter to Napoleon III, he expressed his views on the Austro-Hungarian monarchy. He views the Austrian empire as a strange agglomeration not of peoples but rather fragments of nations. It is not a system capable of satisfying the various nationalities because any separation will cause an envy in all of them. Each of these nations wish to restore their historic past, according to Garašanin, which consists of the perfect independence. Garašanin presented the Balkan interests in these matters.

Garašanin believed that the Slavs would consent on the principle to sacrifice with some rights but he did not allude to the nature of these concessions. The Slavs did wish to completely paralyze German and Magyar hegemony. There were about 17 million of them at this time and they would have preferred to constitute an ethnographic group such as a federation which would have been presided by a leader of their race. Europe has to be convinced, in Gara'v sanin's opinion, that any combination with Austria is not a solution to the Eastern question.[16]

The best thing to do with Austria, in Garašanin's opinion, is to allow the isolation that she has created to continue. Perhaps it would help to resolve the Eastern question if both of these outdated monarchies (Austrian, Ottoman) would just follow the course of total decomposition. The movement of the Christians of Turkey is on its way. They should obtain the power to involve the Croats and the other South Slavs, the Hungarians, and the Romanians of Transylvania. If at this point, Prussia would make a move to the German provinces then Austria would diminish to little less than the Western Slavs of Bohemia, Moravia, and Galicia.

Garašanin opposed the influence of Russia and believed that the only way to reduce her power was to form a strong confederation of peoples which were situated between the Baltic and the Adriatic Seas. This confederation would have approximately 44 million people and be one day able to take away Silesia, Posnania, and Pomerania from Prussia that are Slavic in origin. That way they will strive to reconstiitute a whole Poland. This kind of barrier would help to counterbalance the two Great Powers on either side.[17]

Garašanin believed that France was the only one that could help to revise the map of Europe and for this reason appealed to Napoleon III, ruler of the Second Empire. Garašanin called it, "an enterprise equal to tantalize the soul of a great sovereign." He goes on to say:

> Everbody's eyes are fixed on Napoleon III. He has already given strong prompting to the national spirit and begun in this sense a great metamorphosis in world politics. We will wait for that which will direct us towards the solution of this gigantic work. And if for some misfortune Turkey will be allowed to drag out its miserable existence or Austria be chosen to succeed the Ottoman Empire then the prophecy of the emperor's famous uncle will not be delayed in its realization: Europe will not become republican but Cossack.

In this way, Garašanin attempted to sway Napoleon III to his cause but eventually it was not successful and soon the French emperor was embroiled in his own battles.[18]

The concepts of Desančić were liberal while those of Miletić[19] were more radical. He discussed how the Eastern question can be looked from several points of view. It can be looked at from the interests of a national movement among the various nationalities within the Ottoman Empire determining their own destiny. The other alternative is to look at it as a question to be left for *Kabinetpolitik*.

Miletić states that there are three phases to the Eastern question.[20] The first stage began when Russia started to slowly chip away at the Ottoman empire. This plan basically began with Peter the Great and lasted until 1829. Therefore, the first epoch is completely Russian. Russia alone was interested in the Eastern question. However, Russia's interest in the Balkans was for imperialistic purposes. She wanted to carve up an empire that would include access to various warm sea ports. This would also give her control over the Christian subjects of the Turkish empire. In this way, they would not really be free.

The second stage began according to Miletić when other European countries started to be interested in Eastern affairs. This epoch is Russian-European. It culminates in the Crimean War when the Great Powers of Europe wanted to keep Russia from spreading her influence too widely. Russia's main competitors in the Balkans were Austria and England. Both of these countries wanted to retain a certain amount of hegemony over the Balkan area. England was interested in Greece partly because of a historic tie, partly because it was a gateway to the empire that lay beyond it. England was very adamant about retaining control over its overseas possessions for they are what made her a great power. Austria's interest in the Balkans was part of empire building, also. Her whole *raison d'être* was the empire that she had acquired in the East. During this period there was a constant rivalry. It was Anglo-Russian and Austro-Russian since Russia had been there first and wanted to retain her position of power. Each of these countries wanted to take the heritage of the Ottoman Empire for themselves.

At this point, Miletić introduced the third stage. This stage is where the Great Powers recognize non-intervention and the liberation of the Christian peoples in Turkey will occur. Miletić saw this as a revolutionary movement. After 400 years of Turkish yoke over the four people (Serbs, Romanians, Greeks, Bulgarians), he feels if they do not unite they will once again be conquered. This time it will occur on the part of the Great Powers. What Miletić stresses is the breakup of the two multinational empires. Once they are no longer, smaller states should be formed. At this stage, they should join into a confederation because without one there would be no chance of survival. The basic premise of Miletić's plans is the prevention of the aggression by the Great Powers. For this reason he was willing to make a compromise. The notion of federal dualism was proposed by the leaders of the Serbian movement in the Voivodina (part of the Austrian empire). Miletić advocated federalist ideas and supported the Hungarian liberals. He was prepared to accept dualism in the sense of a union between two federal states whose peoples would enjoy full autonomy. He related the Austrian and Eastern questions to one another because the majority of the Serbian nationals lived south of the Danube. The question could only be settled by the principle of "The Balkans to the Balkan people."[21]

By 1867, the Hungarians had reached a compromise with the Austrian empire. This compromise known as *Ausgleich* gave the Magyars equal rights in relation to the Austrians. A dual monarchy was set up and the Emperor of Austria (Franz Josef) was also the King of Hungary. Ferenc Deak, a Hungarian nationalist, had been one of the main proponents of this settlement. Kossuth had opposed him in his endeavors because Hungary would still not be independent. The Compromise also completely left out the Slavs. Without the Hungarians to back them, the Slavs also lost any influence they could have had within the framework of the Empire.

A strong movement continued to exist, nevertheless, in radical circles in favor of Balkan federation. In Bulgaria, the revolutionary leaders were beginning to think in terms of social revolution and Balkan federation. One if the leaders of the Bulgarian liberation movement, Ljuben Karavelov, favored a federation of "free Balkan countries" patterned on the United States of America.[22] The young Serbs and Bulgarians at this time (1870s) were inlfuenced by political, social, and philosophical ideas of the Russian radicals. However, there was little opportunity at this time for socialist groups of various Balkan countries to put their theories into practice or to seriously influence inter-Balkan relations. A champion of Balkan federation was the ardent republican, Vasil Levski. The industrial backwardness of the Balkan peninsula made it impossible to build up powerful socialist parties as was done during this period in France, Germany, and other Western European countries. It was not until the time of the Balkan Wars and World War I that the socialists were able to win much support for their antiwar and profederation policies.

By the 1870s, the various Balkan alliances had become quite weak. Working with his foreign minister, Ilia Garašanin, Prince Michael Obrenović of Serbia had tried to maintain contact with other Balkan rulers throughout his reign. Alliances had been signed in 1866,

1867, and 1868 with Greece, Montenegro, and the Bulgarian Committee as well as an agreement on friendship with Romania. However, the movement that had seemed so promising was disintegrating. Prince Michael was assassinated in Serbia and the conservative regency in Serbia was not inclined to adopt an aggressive foreign policy while the Greek government declared its neutrality and joined the Entente of neutral powers. Greece was pursuing an anti-Slav policy while Serbia was going back and forth between Austria and Russia.

The looseness of inter-Balkan ties during this period was further demonstrated by the course of the 1875–1878 Balkan Crisis. War erupted between Russia and Turkey over the Balkans in 1877. The Russo-Turkish War ended in 1878 with a victory for Russia that was not easy to achieve. Ottoman and Russian representatives negotiated a treaty signed at San Stefano on March 3, 1878. This settlement threatened to upset the balance of power. The negotiations were chiefly conducted by Russian Foreign Minister Ignatiev and the terms reflected his concern for Russian interests. The agreements was detrimental to British and Habsburg interests and both powers protested. Russia agreed to attend a European conference that would take place in Berlin under the chairmanship of German Chancellor Otto von Bismarck. The Treaty of Berlin in July 1878 created a new Balkan map: Romania, Serbia, and Montenegro became independent. An autonomous Bulgarian state was established north of the Balkan mountains. Austria-Hungary was given the right to occupy and administer Bosnia-Hercegovina, the strategic piece of land separating Serbia and Montenegro.

For the next two decades there was hardly any activity in the realm of federation projects. Then the projects were revived again by the German socialist in the Austro-Hungarian Empire. The Social democrats had a largely centralist approach of German-Austrian socialism to the nationality problem. It became a fight under German leadership against czarist Pan-Slavism. This justified the existence of Austria as a bulwark against Russian Pan-Slaviam. The Austro-German socialists met at a party convention in Brunn (Brno) in 1899. They adopted a program there that had five steps that included the following:

(1) Austria should be transformed into a democratic federation of nationalities.

(2) Their legislative and administrative agencies were to be elected by national chambers on the basis of general and equal franchise.

(3) All autonomous territories of one nationality should have complete self-administration in national affairs.

(4) Rights of national minorities should be protected by separate law to be passed by central parliament.

(5) National privileges of any kind were not to be recognized. Consequently, the demand for a state language was rejected (a mediation language would be acceptable).[23]

The opinions of the Austro-Germans and the Slavs particularly clashed. The program's basic concept of ethnic federalism had been known since 1848. Karl Renner and Otto Bauer received little attention at Brunn. Socialism was naturally hesitant to recognize situations where institutions could create spheres free of state control. The social democrats were at the forefront of the fight for the introduction of otherwise unequal franchise. The program did influence the work of Karl Renner and Otto Bauer in a broad ideological sense.

Karl Renner joined the Social Democratic party in the new century. He was an academic scholar who became active in socialist party politics. In his work *Selbstbestimmungsrecht der Nationen* he explored and presented an internal state order to replace the political struggle of nationalities. For two decades he proclaimed in speech and writing the idea of the democratic multinational Empire federation. Renner's basic idea rests in the objective of adapting the structure of a federal state to requirements of a multinational state. New autonomous institutions were not to be exempt from state control. Rather they would form a separate branch of state power.[24]

He believed that the trend shifted from the national state to the multinational state. There were to be four main socioeconomic territories of Austria. These were the following: Alpine lands (Vienna), Sudetenland (Prague), Carpathian lands (Lemberg), and the Littoral lands (Trieste).[25] National problems would be of no concern to these units. The legislative branch of government was to consist of a lower house elected by all citizens of eight national member states. A feasible but not essential part was the institution of an upper house one-third to be composed of members representing the national council. The whole plan did not deal with the consitutional organization of Hungary. Renner thought it vitally necessary to solve the Hungarian nationality problem jointly with the Austrian problem on a comprehensive basis.

Renner's analysis of federalism is turning away from doctrinaire concepts. He believed that true federalism commences at the bottom in the municipality. Internal self-determination should be extensive. The influence of the national question on federal administration itself is too limited. German was to be the language of mediation and communication at the highest level of governmental activity. He believed that a solution of the national conflict is vitally important for the preservation of the state and within the state itself it is of supreme importance for the working class. National conciliation will break aggressive nationalism of the petty bourgeoisie in small towns. National strife is the basis and pretext for national competition.

The most obvious criticism raised against Renner's program is the complicated machinery of the set-up—a dual national and state administration each subdivided into several smaller units. The main issue of the Renner proposals was not the complexity but rather the feasibility—was their realization politically possible? Renner was a firm believer in the triumph of reason. It was doubtful that the ruling system in Austria would have submitted to a system which meant sacrifices to all. The crown, the still influential aristocracy, and the liberal German bourgeoisie all stood to lose too much. Even in Austria among the non-German national groups it was rather unlikely that a popular majority would support it. Pan-Germanism was also a movement of consequence at the turn of the century and that stood in the way of reconciliation with the Slavs on the basis of equanimity.

Renner recommended a *Staatenstaat*—a state of states—a supranational synthesis which tried to satisfy the nations by means of cultural autonomy. Oscar Jaszi reflected in 1918 that Renner's plan might have had a chance to succeed if he would have reversed the chronological order of his reforms. The outcome of World War I established national successor states to the empire. This development did not lead to an expected second step—the creation of an East-Central European confederation. The truth may be, according to R. Kann in *The Multinational* Empire, that Renner's proposals were made too late—a half a century too late.

Within the Austrian Social Democratic party there were two oppositions. The Slavs (Czechs) to the right and the predominantly German radical Marxist opposition to the left. During the International Socialist Conference in Stockholm in 1917 the majority of the Austrian Czech delegates advocated a loose confederation of Austrian nationalities. After World War I, Otto Bauer became the actual political leader of the German Austrian Socialist Party. He was perhaps the most influential representative of the Second International. In his work, *Die Nationalitatenfrage und die Sozialdemokratie* (1907), he fully supported Renner's program and in many ways elaborated on it.[26] As far as Brunn was concerned he felt its greatest deficiency was the failure to understand the nationality problem comprehensively.

Bauer was not less "pro-Austrian" than Renner. In some ways he was a good deal more centralistic. He had a strongly positive attitude toward preservation of a great multinational state but implied no sympathy with traditions and actual organization of Habsburg monarchy. He considered the multinational empire a good basis of operation for the realization of a socialist program. After the war, another great state complex was considered—a greater Germany instead of a greater Austria. The rise to power of the working class using a multinational state as a means to its end—this was the primary objective of Bauer. As he put it, "The whole modern history of Austria is permeated with conflict between our Austrian and German character." He goes on to say:

> The strategy could be made possible by the very rule of centralism or crownland federalism. Working classes of all national groups ask for a constitution which will stop the national power conflict by securing for each nationality a legally guaranteed sphere of jurisdiction . . . a constitution that will give each national group the possibility for further development of its culture.

The Social Democratic Worker's Party demands the transformation of Austria into a democratic federation of nationalities. Roughly following Renner's scheme of national organization of the national minorities into corporate bodies with similar autonomous rights in handling their national affairs is specifically demanded.

Bauer was one of the first historians who conceived the full theoretical difference between national groups with and without history with all it's potential for future development of national culture. The nations of a Central European union under more or less outright German leadership such as F. Naumann's *Mitteleuropa* plan were widely acclaimed and supported even by socialists. The idea of *Grossdeutsch* liberal republicans of 1848 was to be revived. Now these demands were linked to the full recognition of emancipation of the central European national groups. This included the far-reaching protection of the national rights of all peoples proclaimed in the earlier writing of Renner and Bauer. The social democratic parties were specifically pledged to fight the incorporation of alien minorities.

After World War I, Bauer said that the disintegration had been national not social. It was the nationalities that had revolted not the classes. Renner's theories—the idea of the democratic multinational state prevailed over the achievement of the socialist revolution. The radicalization of the socialists after 1917 changed that. The most significant fact for Austria is that social democracy and the increasing political strength of the working class had been reconciled to the idea of a multinational empire when there was still time to take advantage of reconciliation.

The plans for Danubian federation took many forms between 1848 and 1918. The proponents changed and the focus shifted but the idea remained. The reorganization of the Habsburg monarchy was the goal of the discontented nationalities and later the socialists. Each of the leaders went about proposing his plans in a different way but their goals were ultimately similar. The idea of a Danubian confederation did not end because it was not attained. On the contrary, the projects have remained an option to this day.

NOTES

1. Ognjeslav Utjesinović Ostrozinski: 1817 – Ostrozin Croatia, 1890, Zagreb. His father was an officer in the Military Frontier, Ogneslav served first in the Frontier (primary school) then moved to Rijeka (Fiume) where he learned Italian and French. He graduated from high school in Zagreb and was promoted to lieutenant in Karlovac (1842). Continuing his law studies in Zagreb, in due time he was gradually promoted to the highest posts in the bureaucracy. In 1851 *sub-soapanus (prod-zupan)* in Varazdin, in 1856 secretary of the minister in Vienna, in 1862 Court Councellor if the Croatian Chancellary and finally grand *zupan* (courtly administrator) in Varaždin in 1875.

Under the pseudonym Ognjeslav Ostrozinski he published a poem: "The Echo from the Balkans" in the *Augsburger Zeitung* and in *Danica*. The poet calls the Enlightened Europe to free, in the sake of humanism, the subjected people in the Balkans. He published later a series of poems (1845, 1860, 1868). He wrote a historical study, *The Biography of Cardinal George Utiesinović*. His political brochures included *About the Organization of Austria on Principle of National Equality* (1848); *Die Haus-Communisnen der Südslaven* (1859); *Die Militärgrenze und die Verfassung* (1861) and *Die Militärgrenze* (1869).

2. Robert A. Kann, *The Multinational Empire, Nationalism and National Reform in the Habsburg Monarchy, 1848-1918* (New York: Columbia University Press, 1950), p. 15.

3. Dimitrije Djordjević, *Projects for the Federation of South-East Europe in the 1860s and 1870s,* (Belgrade: Institute for Balkan Studies, 1970) p. 125.

4. Ibid.

5. G. Y. Szabad, *Hungarian Political Trends between the Revolution and Compromise* (Budapest: Academiae Scientiarum Hungaricae, 1977), p. 128.

6. Ibid.

7. Ibid., p. 130.

8. Ibid.

9. Ibid.

10. Dimitrije Djordjević, *Projects for the Federation of South-East Europe in the 1860s and 1870s,* p. 123.

11. Ibid., p. 121.

12. Mihailo Polit-Desančić, 1833–1920, studied law in Novi Sad and Vienna, as well as Paris. He entered politics and was elected deputy in the Croatian diet in 1861. He supported the Yugoslav policy of Bishop Strossmayer and the Serbo-Croatian collaboration while he opposed the dualistic reorganization of the Habsburg monarchy and wrote about the solution to the Eastern Question. Due to his political activity, Desančić was forced to leave Zagreb for Novi Sad where he lived until 1903 working as a journalist and attorney at law. Replacing Svetozar Miletić he was a deputy in the Hungarian Diet 1873–1913. A distinguished Serbian politician in the Voivodina, Desančić was an author of political treatises, books, pamphlet, and editor of journals.

13. Mihailo Polith, *Die Orientalische Frage und ihre organische Losung,* (Vienna: Franz Leo's Verlagserbedition, 1862), p. 33.

14. Ibid.

15. Ilija Garašanin (1812–1874). A colonel under Prince Miloš, he affected the Prince's abdication. He then became the minister of the interior and one of the leaders of the liberated country of Serbia. Garašanin contributed to the country's organization and was the initiator of the revolutionary liberation movement. Influenced by Adam Czartoriski, he was the architect of the "Načertanije" (1844) which became the national program of Serbian and Yugoslav liberation and unification and applied throughout the century until 1914. Garašanin was minister of foreign affairs in Serbia during Prince Michael's reign.

He obtained the Ottoman withdrawal from the Serbian citied in 1867. As prime minister, Garašanin was one of the most distinguished Serbian statesmen in the nineteenth century.

16. Vojislav Vučković, *Politicka Akcija Srbije u Juznoslovenskim Pokrajinama Habsburske Monarhije* (Belgrade: Serbian Academy of Science, 1965), p. 232.

17. Ibid.

18. Ibid., p. 233.

19. Ibid.

20. Svetozar Miletic, *Die Orientfrage,* (Neusatz: Verlag der Serbisch Nationalen Vereins Buchdruckerei, 1877), p. 2.

21. Ibid.

22. L. S. Stavrianos, *Balkan Federation* (Menasha, WI: George Banta Publishing Company, 1944), p. 117.

23. Robert A. Kann, *The Multinational Empire*, p. 155.

24. Ibid., p. 157.

25. Rudolph Wierer, *Der Foderalismus im Donauraum,* (Graz: Verlag Hermann Bohlaus, 1960), p. 107.

26. Robert A. Kann *The Multinational Empire*, p. 167

BIBLIOGRAPHY

Djordjević, Dimitrije, *Projects for the Federation of South-East Europe in the 1860s and 1870s*, Institute for Balkan Studies, Serbian Academy of Sciences and Arts (Belgrade, 1970).

———and Stephen Fischer-Galati, *Balkan Revolutionary Tradition* (New York: Columbia University Press, 1981).

Jaszi, Oscar, *The Dissolution of the Habsburg Monarchy* (Chicago: University of Chicago Press, 1929).

Jelavich, Barbara, *History of the Balkans, Eighteenth and Nineteenth Century*, Vol. I (Cambridge: Cambridge University Press, 1983).

———, *Modern Austria, Empire and Republic 1800–1980* (Cambridge: Cambridge University, 1987).

Kann, Robert A., *The Multinational Empire, Nationalism and National Reform in Habsburg Monarchy, 1848–1918* (New York: Columbia University Press, 1950).

———, *A History of Habsburg Empire 1526–1916* (Berkeley: University of California Press, 1974).

Macartney, C. A., *The Habsburg Empire, 1790–1918* (London: Weidenfeld and Nicolson, 1968).

Miletić, Svetozar, *Die Orientfrage, Verlag der Serbisch Nationalen Vereins-Buchdruckerei* (Neusatz, 1877).

Polith, Mihailo, *Die Orientalische Frage und ihre organische Losuna* (Vienna: Franz Leo's Verlagserbedition, 1862).

Stavrianos, L. S., *Balkan Federation, A History of the Movement toward Balkan Unity in Modern Times* (Menasha, WI: George Banta Publishing Company, 1944).

Szabad, G. Y., *Hungarian Political Trends between the Revolution and the Compromise (1849–1867)* (Budapest: Academiae Scientiarum Hungaricae, 1977).

A. J. P. Taylor, *The Habsburg Monarchy, 1809–1918* (London: Hamish Hamilton, 1948).

Vucković, Vojislav, *Politička Akcija Srbije u Juznoslovenskim Pokraiinama Habsburske Monarhiie, 1859–1874* (Belgrade: Serbian Academy of Science, 1965).

Wierer, Rudolph, *Der Foderalismus in Donauraum* (Graz: Verlag Hermann Bohlaus, 1960).

SIR ARTHUR NICOLSON, GENERAL CONSUL
AT BUDAPEST, 1888–1892

Cornelia Bodea

Harold Nicolson, son and biographer of Sir Arthur Nicolson Bart, First Lord Carnock, divided his father's diplomatic career into two distinct parts, in accordance with the main traditions of British foreign policy. The first covered the period 1870 to 1900. This corresponded to a time when friendly relations were maintained with Germany and Austria-Hungary, and when the only concern of Great Britain in matters of European balance of power was to stop France and Russia from consolidating their positions and influence within and outside the Continent. The second part of Nicolson's career belonged to the period 1900 to 1914. This is identified with the time when his country believed in the German menace and consequently considered the necessity of abandoning its splendid isolation and making friends and allies throughout Europe.[1]

Nicolson's term as General Consul at Budapest took place between 1888 and 1892, after a rather busy and successful diplomatic experience in the Foreign Office, at Berlin, Constantinople, Athens, and in Persia at Teheran. In 1888, he was thirty-nine years old, with eighteen years of diplomatic background and his abilities in full bloom. The four years in Hungary, however, were devoid of exceptional international events which could have called upon his skills. In addition, Nicolson was displeased with Magyar high-life society and very much so with the haughtiness of its aristocracy. Consequently, at this point his stay there was annoying and dull. In contrast, he became interested in the minority problem in the whole Dual Monarchy, by and large, and in that of its Hungarian portion in particular.[2] It was this latter direction that Nicolson's appointment to Budapest proved its entire value.

There was growing tension among two of the non-Magyar nationalities—the Croats and the Romanians—which captured his attention.

With regard to the former, as it is well known, the Austro-Hungarian Compromise of 1867, by including Croatia under direct Hungarian control, aggravated the already existing animosity against Hungary. The subsequent special Croatian-Magyar arrangement—the *Nagodba*—negotiated in 1868 continued to deepen internal antagonism and strife: The National Liberal Party (Bishop Strossmeyer's followers) showed themselves favorable towards the Habsburgs and Vienna, but not towards Budapest. The resolute extremist Party of the Right, led by Ante Starčević, rejected any collaboration, either with Vienna or with Budapest. In contrast, the Unionists lived up to their nickname—*Magyarones*—championing collaboration with the Hungarian Government. The bloody suppression of the Kvartenick uprising in 1871, added fuel to the whole struggle for an independent Croatia. The state of mind prevailing in the seventies in Croatia is epitomized as follows by A. J. Patterson, a contemporary British expert in Hungarian history and literature, while visiting Croatia and the military frontier, in 1872:

> Conscious as I was that my residence in Hungary and knowledge of the Magyar language rendered me more or less an object of suspicion in the eyes of Croatian patriots, I did not care to imperil my position in national society by intercourse with their political enemies. I continually met in that society young men who had lately been in prison for taking part in demonstrations against the Government, either by cheering the national Bishop Strossmayer, or insulting the newly appointed archbishop . . .[3]

Sixteen years later, in 1888, tensions between the patriots and Magyarones were further exploited by the Government. In addition, the opposition was weakened by its own disunity: the fanaticism of the extremist Stačević Party lately expressed in charges and injuries against Bishop Strossmayer met with strong disapproval even among his own Stačevist adherents; as a consequence some of them resorted to secession. Thus, the principle *divide et impera*, which had been closely observed since 1883 by the newly appointed Ban, Khuen Héderváry, proved all its efficiency: Secession and new parties created among Croatian-Serbian people were evidence all by themselves.[4]

Transylvania experienced a contrasting development. There, Romanians' political rights and existence, which won recognition during the bright interlude in the sixties, were voided by the Austro-

Hungarian Compromise of 1867. And, unlike Croatia, the incorporation of Transylvania into the newly established Hungarian portion brought the complete abolition of the centuries old Transylvanian autonomy. No extra negotiation ensued. An open Romania protest, published in 1868, known as the *Pronunciamentum of Blaj*, changed nothing. Yet at least it marked the existence of a general discontent with the new state of things. Subsequently, by adopting either a "passivist" or an "activist" opposition vis-à-vis the Budapest Parliament, Romanians did not lack unity nor solidarity in their final aims. In addition, they enjoyed a continual encouragement from Romanians across the borders, notwithstanding the fact that after 1883, officially and overtly, the Government in the Regat had to comply with the terms of Romania's secret alignment alongside the Triple Alliance.

Yet, most importantly, in the Romanian case, was the special strategic position that Transylvania had held at the time within the European balance of power, which made it more often discussed in mass media than was Croatia. It was common knowledge, not only among diplomatic and journalistic circles, that Transylvania represented a weak vulnerable point, a real Achilles' heel of the Austro-Hungarian integrity, justly because of the Romanians' disaffection.

In other words, it was anticipated that the Romanians, as the preponderant nationality in the country, in certain possible contingency, could easily be tempted to disconnect themselves from the Hungarian oppressive rule, and gravitate towards the native national state of Romania. As Emily Gerard noted in 1888:

> There is no doubt, that the bulk of Romanians living today in Hungary and Transylvania consider themselves in bondage, and covertly gaze over the frontier for their real monarch. And who can blame them for so doing?[5]

In fact, it was soon after the Congress of Berlin, 1878, that Transylvania became a matter of concern in the European balance of alliances and alignments. As early as the autumn of the same year 1878, Sir Drummond Wolff, the British diplomat, recorded such critical circumstances. While in Vienna, on his way to Constantinople, reports had reached the Austrian capital city that an ultimatum had been sent by Russia to Romania insisting on an offensive and defensive alliance, or threatening the deposition of the Prince and the disarmament of the Army. Wolff noted with apprehension in his recollections, that the *Neue Freie Presse* from Vienna announced that the Romanian Army,

Archives, and Treasury would be on their way to the Transylvanian border. "If crossed into Hungary," he noted, "it was thought there would at once be an explosion."[6]

During the few months of Nicolson's appointment to Budapest, 1888–1889, the political and strategic importance of Transylvania, as well as the role of the Romanian *Regat* in European balance of power, appeared quite obsessive to several Western politicians and columnists of that year. Not to mention that even a "Great War" was anticipated aiming at the final expulsion of the Turks from the Continent.[7]

To make up his own mind about the people and the exact political situation within the Hungarian area, Nicolson directed his first inquiry into the Croat problem. He visited Croatia in the fall of 1889.[8] The information that he was able to collect on the spot from a large number of interviews and informants, in addition to his own findings, was rather elusive, conflicting, and in most cases diametrically contradictory. This altogether led him to a rather pessimistic forecast. By considering the long past development of Croation political life, Nicolson came to an initial conclusion, that matters had really changed in Croatia and had grown worse with the appointment of Count Héderváry as Ban (December 1883). As a most striking instance of change, he pointed to the practical collapse of Croatian parliamentary opposition. Moreover, he certified that the opposition was composed of "several irreconcilable elements," so much so that its powers of attack were greatly reduced. The Ban Héderváry impressed Nicolson as a "man of great energy and decision," but in practice he seemed to him "little more than the agent of the Central Government." However, unlike the high officials at Pest, the Croatian Ban showed not to be much concerned about "elements dangerous to Hungary in Croatia."[9]

Héderváry's optimism was not shared by the British reporter. Nicolson also differed with Héderváry's negative impression on Bishop Strossmayer's great impact as a national leader. In contrast, he proved to be fully aware of the Pan-Slav desires of the Croatians and of their wishes to see a Great Croatia established. Yet in this respect he shared the general opinion of the patriots that questions of such vast importance were dependent largely on the international developments. Subsequently, he could not refrain from calling the Foreign Office attention in anticipation of the current Croat opinion that Croatia's tie with Hungary in its existing form was not only an

anomaly but an injustice. In his report, Nicolson pointed out the fact
that:

> there was no ground, either ethnological, geographical, or
> political, which could be a valid reason for maintaining the
> connection with Hungary. Race, language, customs, all were
> different, and there was not the remotest tendency among
> any class of Croats to gravitate towards Hungary. . . . They
> cannot recognize and accept the pact with the Hungarians,
> who never lost an opportunity of infringing, by direct or
> indirect means, on the rights they had promised to guarantee
> to the Croats.[10]

Nicolson informed the Foreign Office about the desire expressed
to him by the followers of Strossmayer, that Croatia, Slavonia, and
Dalmatia should be formed into an autonomous kingdom under the
dynasty of the Habsburgs, and be placed in the same relations with
Vienna as was the case with Hungary since 1867.

The Nationalities' struggle in forcing Hungary to give up its autocracy seemed to the British observer to have very much in common
with the complaints uttered by the Hungarians before 1867. And his
conclusion followed:

> As the latter did not achieve their desires until Austria had
> been forced by foreign disasters to make terms with her dis-
> contented subjects, so Croatians could not expect to attain
> their wishes till Hungary was compelled by similar misfor-
> tunes to give an ear to their demands.

Nicolson concluded with a warning:

> It remains to be seen whether the policy of the Hungarian
> Government will be successful in breaking the spirit of dis-
> content and in conciliating the majority of the Croatians, or
> whether they can only succeed in silencing the open expres-
> sion of dissatisfaction, while rendering still more dangerous
> at a critical moment, a latent and deep-seated animosity.[11]

A few days after the Croatian journey, Nicolson expressed his
intention to undertake a similar inquiry into the Romanians in Transylvania. In the latter case, his interest was stirred up on two levels:
on the one side, because of their political situation under the same
Hungarian administration; on the other, and more relevantly because
of their geographical position which *"renders them an important factor in certain possible eventualities."* This statement of Nicolson is

to be found already in the cover letter to his report on Croatia. It is dated October 11, 1889.[12] It took him, however, more than sixteen months to fulfill his project: from October 1889 to May 1891. As a matter of fact, his postponed visit took place at a peak time when the governments in Vienna and Berlin were indeed worried that such "certain possible circumstances" might be imminent.[13]

A wave of manifest hostility to Austria-Hungary had arisen at that time in the Romanian Kingdom associated with the oppressive policies pursued by the Magyar administration against Romanians in Transylvania and Hungary. A rift threatened to compromise the Secret Agreement of 1883, when it was justly supposed to be reinforced. The British Cabinet was acquainted with the representations being made by Germany with the Government at Budapest, in order to calm down the tensions in and over the Transylvania area. In April 14, 1891, Nicolson had sent to the Foreign Office a detailed dispatch on a discussion in which the General Consul of Germany at Budapest, Anton Graf von Monts, tried to convince Szilágyi Dezso, the Hungarian Justice Minister about the necessity "to remove as far as possible all causes of discontent which was not likely to prove successful."[14]

Nicolson described his impressions and conclusions on the political situation in Transylvania, in an itemized account dated May 25, 1891.[15] Like his report on Croatia, the British diplomat covered the first part of his exposure with the description of the land, the numbers of the people and a historical sketch on the early relations between Transylvania and Hungary up to 1867. A special mention is made here of that "bright interlude" prior to 1868 when for the first time the Romanians enjoyed an officially recognized political existence. Then, attention was concentrated upon the widespread discontent of the Romanians with the new Dualistic era. In comparison with the Croatian situation, Nicolson assessed that Romanians' discontent was "grounded on more serious and specific grievances than those which existed among the Serb and Croat nationalities." He also set forth that among Romanians "expression and form had been given by a well-organized system of opposition." Furthermore, he considered as being peculiar to the situation in Transylvania, that there had been not only open sympathy in Romania with the grievances of their brethren, but means have of late been adopted in that country towards assisting in their alleviation.

His account goes further into Romanians' political situation and unsatisfactory condition. Nicolson discussed by turns: the religious question, school system, the growth of the intelligent proletariat among them, the press—prosecutions, electoral system, provincial administration, and judicial procedure. Then testifying that the provisions of the Law of Nationalities of 1868 practically were a dead letter, he described the measures the Romanians have taken to meet the difficulties.

Some of the conclusions and statements in the final part of the report resemble those set forth for the Croatians.

> I much fear, Nicolson stated, that, unless there is some relaxation, of which there seems to be little prospect, that the Romanians may adopt the attitude assumed by the Hungarians before 1867 towards the Austrian Government, and consider Hungary's difficulties as their opportunities.

However, in the Transylvanian case, he admitted that there were reasons for stronger worries and fears because of the radical reactions of the Romanian part. Conditions had been much more complex than among Croatians. Nicolson was directly told by Magyar leaders that the Romanians aspired to aims much more ambitious than the requests formulated in their public program. Consequently, abstaining from anticipating the future, he nevertheless insisted on the fact that that large Romanian community, which occupies in compact masses a portion of the Hungarian State, "in possible eventualities, might prove a vulnerable point for hostile attacks."[16]

After the Transylvanian tour Nicolson had a long interview with the Hungarian Justice Minister—the same Szilágyi Dezso from the previous talks with the German Consul General. When challenged by the British Consul, Szilágyi contended that one could not compare the Croatian case with the circumstances in Transylvania. According to the latter, Croatia could never have been the cause of serious uneasiness to Hungary, while an autonomy granted to Transylvania would have meant the very disruption of the Hungarian Monarchy. Therefore, the official Magyar solution was an iron-fisted policy.

Both Nicolson's *Reports* circulated as Confidential print within the British Foreign Office. The latter especially was considered for a long time as the main source of reference in Transylvanian matters.

With these considerations in mind, let us return—in conclusion— to that same short passage devoted by Harold Nicolson to his father's term in Budapest.[17] According to the appraisal of Arthur's son concerning those four years as General Consul, Sir Arthur Nicolson

carried away from Hungary a deep distrust of Hungarian
and indeed Austro-Hungarian policy, an instinctive fear that
the Habsburg Empire was an element not of stability but of
disintegration and decay.

This feeling "became intensified with the passage of time" not only
for him but for British foreign policy in general. However, for the
sake of the European balance of power, neither Great Britain nor any
other of the great powers were in favor of proving the sensitivity of
the Austro-Hungarian Achilles' heel. It took several decades until
the former British Consul General's warning did come true in cases
of Croatia and Transylvania. This trend began to unfold before the
astute diplomat had left the Foreign Office. (N.B.: Since 1910 until
his last day at Foreign Office, June 20, 1916, he had been conducting
it as its Permanent Under Secretary.) Hence, he was no longer there
to record the news of Romania's entry into Transylvania, in August
1916, and even less so, able to participate in the Versailles Peace
negotiations. But he was able to see his predictions and apprehensions
come true.

NOTES

1. Cf. Harold Nicolson, *Sir Arthur Nicolson Bart. First Lord
Carnock. A Study in the Old Diplomacy* (London, Constable & Co.
Ltd., 1930).

2. Ibid., pp. 78–80.

3. J. A. Patterson, "From Agram to Zara," *Fortnightly Review,*
Vol. XI, N.S. April 1, 1972, pp. 359–360.

4. R. W. Seton-Watson, *The Southern Slav Question and the
Habsburg Monarchy* (New York: Howard Fertig, 1969), pp. 65–128.

5. Emily Gerard, *The Land Beyond the Forest. Facts, Figures.
and Fancies* (Edinburgh and London: Blackwood and Sons, 1888),
Vol. I, p. 306–307.

6. Sir Henry Drummond Wolff, *Rambling Recollections* (London:
Macmillan and Co., 1908), II, pp. 176–177.

7. J. D. Bourchier, "Fate of Roumania," *Fortnightly Review,* Vol.
XLIV, N.S. 1888, pp. 785–804.

8. Great Britain, Public Record Office (PRO), Foreign Office
(FO), 800/336, A. Nicolson Papers, 1889–1905, #5846, "Report by
Sir A. Nicolson on the Present Situation in Croatia," October 1889.

9. Ibid.

10. Ibid.

11. Ibid.

12. Ibid.

13. Cornelia Bodea, "A Lady-novelist, and a Diplomat on Transylvania and its People, 1888–1892," *Anuarul Institutului de Istorie se Arheologie A.D. Xenopol*, Supl. IV, (Iasi, 1983).

14. Ibid.

15. The full text of Nicolson's "Report on the Political Situation of Transylvania," in Cornelia Bodea and Virgil Candea, *Transylvania in the History of the Romanians* (East European Monographs, CXVII, Boulder, 1982), pp. 140–160.

16. Ibid.

17. Harold Nicolson, *Sir Arthur Nicolson*, p. 80.

THE FRENCH RADICAL PARTY MOVEMENT
THE RADICAL PARTY IN SERBIA
A Parallel Analysis of Ideologies

Milan St. Protić

Tracing the ideological origins of the Radical Party in Serbia in the late nineteenth century, one is almost bound to search for the roots of Radicalism as a European political doctrine. And here, one comes to the French Radical movement for one major reason. During the second half of the nineteenth century the French Radicals emerged as the most powerful, and at the same time, ideologically, best defined political group belonging to political doctrine known as Radicalism.

Thus, the comparative study of two political conceptions had two major results. First, it established the mutual relations between two political movements in terms of ideological convictions. In other words, the influence of the French Radical ideology on the Serbian Radical Party. And second, it contributed to the formation of a complete picture of Radical theoretical concept, which, in various forms, appeared in most European countries of the time.

* * * * *

It is virtually impossible to establish the exact paths by which French ideas came to Serbia. The only fact which seems unquestionable is that the majority of the Radical leaders read and spoke French, and that most of them visited France in the 1870s.[1] Some, but only a few, made their studies in Paris and were later named the "Parisian doctors."[2] According to Radical newspapers of that time, it appears that by the 1880s they received French political press regularly, including Clemenceau's *La Justice*.[3]

It seems quite logical, therefore, to search for the influences of French Radicals on their colleagues in Serbia in comparison of the two movements' political programs.

The first written program of the Radical Party in Serbia was dated January 1881. This program was originally published in the first issue of *Samouprava*, immediately following the formal organization of the Radical Party. In the introduction, the Radicals stressed two crucial political objectives:

> . . . in domestic policy—national prosperity and freedom and in foreign affairs—State independence, liberation and unification of all parts of Serbdom.[4]

The program was divided into eight sections, each of them defining the Party position on major issues. The Serbian Radicals suggested vast constitutional reform in the following directions: the National Assembly was to be the supreme legislative body and completely elective; elections were to be direct and secret; the Constitution guaranteed universal male suffrage. The Grand National Assembly was designed to summon only in the case of a constitutional change. The Radical constitutional draft abolished the State Council. It introduced the principle of local self-government in the administrative organization of the country. In the judicial system the Radical proposal designed elected judges for all civil cases and juries for criminal acts. In State finances, the program insisted on the "introduction of [a] direct, progressive tax system on property and income." The Radicals suggested the reorganization of the National Bank and its transformation into the central loan institution for agriculture, trade, and industry. The program especially emphasized the introduction of free, compulsory primary education. It also argued for the substitution of the standing army by the national militia. The proposal explicitly demanded the absolute freedom of the press, association and public meeting, and the complete guarantee of personal and property security.[5]

*   *   *   *   *

That same year (1881) the French Radicals came out with their political programs for the upcoming elections. Still not organized as a monolithic political organization, the Radicals in France did not make an official Party program. Rather, their two leading candidates, Georges Clemenceau and Camille Pelletan, made public lists of their political demands. Those two programs, nevertheless, fully expressed the political spirit of French Radicalism. Both programs were almost identical to the proposal made by the Radicals in Serbia.

In his political manifest, Georges Clemenceau, the Radical who, by his attitude and actions in the French National Assembly, deserved the nickname "The Tiger," insisted on following political reforms: (1) constitutional reform which included the abolition of the Senate and the introduction of the single chamber Parliament—fully elective National Assembly; (2) absolute freedom of the press, association and public speech guaranteed by the Constitution; (3) separation of the Church and State; (4) free, compulsory, secular primary education; (5) substitution of the standing army by the national militia; (6) free and equal justice for all citizens; (7) elective officials on all levels of the State administration; (8) personal and criminal responsibility for all public functionaries; (9) universal male suffrage; (10) administrative decentralization on the basis of communal autonomy; and (11) progressive taxation on property and revenue.[6] In the second part of his electoral program which dealt with questions of social legislature, Clemenceau demanded: (1) limitation of the working day; (2) responsibility of the owner in cases of workers' accidents; (3) right of the workers' unions to participate in public affairs; and (4) abolition of the exploitation of the prisoners' work.[7]

The political program of Camille Pelletan was made public also in 1881 and for the same occasion—elections for the French National Assembly. This manifest was written in more detail than Clemenceau's and stands as one of the outstanding examples of Radical political doctrine in France. In its philosophical essence, the program of Camille Palletan is not any different than the manifest of Clemenceau. As his political friend Pelletan put the constitutional change in first place, the change was directed towards the abolition of the Senate, establishment of the Republic headed by the elective President. Pelletan's reform designed the single chamber Parliament, completely elective, responsible for all decisions of national interest. General Councils were to act as supreme representative bodies on the level of departments and to decide about the issues of departmental interest. Pelletan applied the same pattern on the level of municipalities. He advocated an administrative system very similar to the system of convent, based on the principle of representation and local self-government—a kind of governmental pyramid of elective representative bodies on each level of the administrative echelon. This system, Pelletan thought, should secure full and complete democracy in decision making. He set the entire State organization on the principle of communal autonomy where "the commune is to be the master of its administration, finances, and police."[8]

Like all previous Radical political programs, Pelletan's electoral platform also stressed the demand for absolute freedom of the press, association and public reunion, separation of the Church and State, compulsory, secular and free primary education, as well as the revision of the tax system and the application of the principle of the universal male suffrage as the supreme guarantee of the national sovereignty.[9] Like Clemenceau, Pelletan suggested the substitution of the standing armies by the national guard. In the chapter of his program which dealt with judicial reforms, Pelletan insisted on the revision of all legal codes according to the principle of justice and equality. In the last point of his manifest, Camille Pelletan demanded that the exclusive right of declaring war should be given to the entire nation, insisting at the same time on the policy of peacemaking.

The program of social reforms which constituted the second part of Pelletan's political manifest asked for the limitation of the working day to ten hours and prohibited work for children under the age of fourteen. Pelletan insisted on the establishment of retirement funds for the elder workers and labor invalids. And again like Clemenceau, he demanded the responsibility of patrons in cases of accident and the abolition of labor exploitation in prisons. Pelletan openly called for the nationalization of mines and railroads and for the reorganization of the French National Bank along the lines of central loan institution for the economic development of the country.[10]

* * * * *

The similarities between the Serbian radical program of 1881 and the electoral programs of Georges Clemenceau and Camille Pelletan dated that same year were more than obvious. The fundamental issues pointed out in all three documents appear identical, not only in ideas which they expressed but in terminology as well.

Serbian Radicalism, like French, insisted on constitutional reform, which in both cases included the single chamber National Assembly elected by universal male suffrage. Following their French comrades, the Serbian Radicals singled out the principle of self-government as the central mode of territorial organization and the instrument of democratic process. They both insisted on tax reform and on the introduction of a direct tax system on capital and income. The idea of the formation of a popular army instead of professional military corps characterized both ideologies. Finally, Serbian Radicals, again like the French, stubbornly repeated demands for civil liberties.

Their ideas were identical regarding the educational system reform: both argued in favor of free, compulsory primary education.

The differences between the ideologies of the two Radical movements originated mainly from different political, social, and cultural circumstances existing in French and Serbian societies in the last quarter of the nineteenth century. The French Radicals were strongly anti-clerical due to the leading role of the Roman Catholic Church in French politics, social life, culture, and education. In Serbia, on the contrary, the clergy of the Serbian Orthodox Church was neither that powerful nor in an especially advantageous position within the social hierarchy. This was particularly true of the lower clergy, which largely shared the social status of the peasantry, but acted as parochial intelligentsia and became largely affiliated with the Radical movement.[11] The higher members of the clergy in Serbia, however, located in Belgrade and several larger towns, never really accepted Radicalism. Belonging to the State establishment and having close ties with the All-Russian Orthodox Church, the leadership of the Serbian Orthodox Church entered the Liberal Party.[12]

The French Radical movement grew out of the great Republican bloc whose origins lay deep in the French Revolution, and always remained the champion of the Republican cause. This came as a result of specific historical circumstances in France, where the conflict between the Monarchy and the Republic affected the entire nineteenth century. In Serbia, the republican issue was never seriously considered. Although the group of Svetozar Marković developed the theoretical concept of Republicanism in the early 1870s, this idea was soon abandoned by the Radicals despite the fact that several staunch republicans belonged to the Radical Party.[13] The realities of the Serbian political and social development, in which the ruler acquired the pivotal role in politics and, more importantly, in minds of the vast population, the Republic did not have much chance. Instead, the Serbian Radicals became strongly anti-dynastic, endlessly fighting for the limitations of the ruler's prerogatives of power. Thus, the Radical antidynastism became the substitution for republicanism. The French minister in Belgrade could not but notice the anti-dynastic attitude of the Serbian Radicals and underlined it in several reports to the French Ministry for Foreign Affairs: *L'opposition radicale en Serbie est loin d'être une opposition dynastique.*[14]

And again in 1888:

Sans doute, parmi les cinq cents radicaux, que les electeurs

*ont envoyé sièges à la Grande Skoupchtina, plus d'un est
parti de son village avec des dispositions franchement anti-
dynastiques.*[15]

The French Radical movement favored the anti-colonial foreign
policy and the policy of peacemaking. After a devastating defeat in
the Franco-Prussian War (1870–1871), and the unstable political situation in the country, the French Radicals argued for internal political
reforms and opposed Jules Ferry's overseas adventures. The Serbian
Radical Party was purely of national motivation advocating the liberation and unification of all parts of Serbdom. It came as a result of
a historical process of national emancipation and State building. As
a centripetal force, the Serbian State attracted all unliberated parts
of its nation. The Radicals were compelled to join in the great national cause. What both political movements had in common was the
idea that the internal reforms were favored over external expansions.
French Radicals as well as the Serbian viewed the national stability
of their States in Europe only as a consequence of internal stability
and progress, not the other way around.

At this point, it became quite clear that the Serbian Radicals
were influenced only by the political aspects of French Radical programs. There they found a fertile ground for the implementation
of French Radical ideas in Serbia. The social side of French Radicalism, however, could not correspond to Serbian social and economic specifics and was, therefore, unacceptable to the Serbian Radical Party. In industrially-developed France, with a numerous working
class, the demands for the limitations of working hours, workers' in-
surance, and the prohibition of child labor were logical steps in the
process of improvement of working conditions. In this respect, France
was no exception in Europe. Almost all industrially advanced European countries started to introduce social legislature in the closing
decades of the nineteenth century. In peasant dominated Serbian
society, with little industry and virtually no working class, the socio-
economic segment of the French Radical programs was inapplicable.

* * * * *

In conclusion let us note several relevant facts regarding the problem of parallel ideologies of Radicalism in France and Serbia. First,
both movements came out with finely defined political programs almost simultaneously—in 1881. Second, the resemblance between the

two political ideologies is more than obvious, once they were compared. Third, one could safely argue that it was French Radicalism
which influenced the Serbian and not the opposite: the French movement had its long history of development whose origins lay back in
political concepts of Condorcet, one of the great spirits of the French
Revolution. The Serbian Radicals were organized as a political party
in 1881 and their roots do not go back farther than the political
grouping of Svetozar Marković in the early 1870s.[16] Needless to say,
during the last quarter of the nineteenth century, France was in the
center of European political events while Serbia, winning independent
State status only in 1878 at the Berlin Congress, still remained at the
outskirts of European politics.

The external ideological impacts on the formation of the Radical
Party in Serbia were manifold. What was shown here represents the
major foreign source of the ideology of Serbian Radicalism.

NOTES

1. Velizar Ninčić, *Pera Todorović* (Beograd 1956), 58–62.

2. Pera Todorović, Jovan Zujović, Mihailo Vujić and later Milovan Dj. Milovanović to quote only the most important ones. See
Slobodan Jovanović, *Vlada Milana Obrenovica* 3, (Beograd, 1934),
282–283.

3. *Samouprava*, June-July 1883.

4. *Samouprava*, No. 1, January 8, 1881.

5. Ibid.

6. Gaston Maurice, *Le parti radical* (Paris, 1928), 119.

7. Ibid.

8. Tony Revillon, *Camille Pelletan* (Paris, 1930), 45.

9. Ibid., 46.

10. Ibid., 44–47.

11. *Serbian Archives*, Belgrade, fund of Andra Nikolić, no. 10.

12. *Archives of the Serbian Academy of Sciences and Arts*, Belgrade, memoirs of Jovan Avakumović, no. 9287/III

13. Among them, the most famous were Dragiša Stanojević,
Jovan Zujović and later Jaša Prodanović.

14. *Archives du Ministere des affaires étrangères français*, CP
Serbie, 1882–1883, May 8, 1883.

15. Ibid., 1887–1888, December 25, 1888.

16. For more details about Svetozar Marković, his activities
and thoughts in English, see Woodford McClellan, *Svetozar Marković*

and the Origins of Balkan Socialism (Princeton: Princeton University Press, 1964).

SOME THOUGHTS ABOUT THE HISTORICAL DESTINY OF SERBS

Radovan Samardžić

The history of the Serbian people is marked by a continuous upward development. Such perseverance is not manifested among those nations which remained passive for long periods of time or faced the future under the guidance of poor leaders. In the course of centuries the most developed European nations produced a multi-layered society in which the upper classes determined the common issues. Particular upper-class feudal groups decided about the behavior and destiny of the rest of the population, being guided by their own interests. For that reason their indifference towards popular national feelings was all prevailing. The rise of the national spirit, or more precisely of national responsibility, was stipulated among the large population only by satisfying certain local interests and promoting hopes for a social transformation. Thus, the big European nations, although organized in their own states, were created later than the Serbian, in spite of the fact that the Serbs had been vassals and were divided under foreign rule and boundaries.

The Serbian nation emerged heavily burdened from the former state of the Nemanjids. The larger part of the nations was not an amorphous flock which became submissive to the Ottoman conqueror and which accepted without inner resistance the moulding of domestic spiritual life and identity, forged by the aliens. Some of these imposed laws, institutions, and customs as well as concepts of life and history, might have been accepted. However, although under strain and hardship, foreign influences were accommodated to the Serbian character and beliefs. The entity of the Serbian nation was jeopardized by the Turks, Greeks, and Catholics, but the core of the nation stubbornly resisted. It was protected from the intruders by genuine folklore and customs as well as by attempts to change the foreign influence by adjusting it to domestic trends.

The Serbs were not able and seemingly did not want to give up their medieval heritage. During the times of the Nemanjids the unity of the state, church, and people had been established. The extent to which this concord existed can be understood by comparing the heritage of the old Serbian civilization with the heritage of other European nations. Traces of a kind of specific spiritual life, initially inspired by Saint Sava, were implemented in the theological thought of Eastern Orthodoxy, in literary writing in native language, in forms and meanings of art, legal codes, and popular customs as well as individual activity of prominent personalities and representatives of the common people. The main characteristics, and therefore the main quality of such a spirituality, consisted of the omnipresent love for everything that is God's creation. It also expressed a gentle pride of individual identity and consensus in decision-making instead of class division. Overall, there was a common tendency to cultivate the heroic past and to share moments of pain, distress, and misery. Above all it echoed Christian ethics already in their developed and complex forms. In that regard the Serbs proved the correctness of the ideas of the founders of the romanticist movement, who asserted that the European nations formed their character and spirit already in the middle ages and kept them alive thereafter.

The depth of the impact of the Nemanjids, especially the endowment left by St. Sava to the Serbian people, was confirmed during the later times of subordination to foreign rule. The people preserved the spirit of St. Sava's faith in which was later founded the cult of the Kosovo battle's legacy. Many Serbs had been uprooted, converted to different religions, and incorporated in various nations. However, the Serbs had compensated the loss by demographic expansion, keeping alive and transmitting their consciousness, customs, and folklore to the peripheral parts of the nation. It manifested the process of ethnic equation among all Serbs, which will result in the modern period in joining the periphery to the national community. During centuries of foreign rule, the Serbs maintained their upward development in efforts and endeavors which stamped several historical epochs.

First. The Serbs recognized the masters in Constantinople, Venice or Vienna, but never abandoned the idea of their own lordship. The object of their cult was the sacred family of the Nemanjids to which was added the cult of Prince Lazar, the Kosovo martyr, promoted later to emperor in the popular tradition. The fact that Serbia was an empire created the desire to renew it, which became implanted in the minds of all Serbs. The imperial title was not attributed only to a universal autocrat: the Serbs assigned the title not only to medieval rulers but also to distinguished rebellious leaders in the later period. The word *car* [emperor] had a special meaning in the Serbian language.

As a part or the Ottoman empire the Serbs were very well aware, and thus behaved accordingly, that the sultan's Divan represents the Supreme Court. This institution was vested with the authority to appoint the Serbian Patriarch, selected among the Serbian archbishops, as well as to confirm the self-managing privileges afforded to the population in the realm of the empire. However, all this was an imposed vassal subordination which tended occasionally to be expressed in marginal and false sincerity. It was a kind of vassal mimicry on the part of the Serbs to cover their renegate attitude of which the Turks were well aware and the reason why the Turks attempted to destroy them.

In the Habsburg Monarchy the Serbs relied on commitments and agreements concluded with the Crown. In accordance with their own evaluation of peril, the Serbs expressed their loyalty to the emperor, even when it could expose them to the revenge and/or resentment among the neighboring opponents of Austria. Serbian attachment to the House of the Habsburgs expressed their hope to find in it a higher justice which was equally protective to all.

An unusual dualism emerged from this relationship. Just at the time when the Serbs were turning to Vienna for support—not only because they had to, but also because they became more and more included in the Western culture (after the migrations under Arsenije IV Jovanović, 1737–1739)—the idea of the Nemanja state was renewed and plans for the state resurrection were born. Appearing as a subject in history, the Serbs were for decades expecting their renewed state to be under the protectorship of an eternally lasting foreign empire. Gradually they moved more and more towards the solution of their question through total and final emancipation. Both the metropolitanate in Karlovci and the popular leaders in Turkey worked in favor of the final solution, especially along the troublesome border on the Southern banks of the Sava and the Danube, in the Pashalik of Belgrade. The Serbian movement caused a consternation in Europe, which already attributed the Southeastern confines to the sphere of European interests. The Serbian liberation was to be paid at the highest price.

The emergence of the two Serbian states—Serbia and Montenegro—in the nineteenth century questioned the hegemony of the great European powers and threatened the method they applied in international affairs. The establishment of three national Serbian dynasties—Petrović, Karageorgević, and Obrenović—disturbed the idyll of the German dynasties who took over the old and new thrones and dominated the political climate on the continent and the colonial world. The Serbian example became even more evident after the formation of new national states, Greece, Romania and Bulgaria, in which homeless German dynasts were installed as rulers in order to balance the presumed harmony of the great powers.

The Serbs inherited the concept of monarchy from the Middle Ages. It became part of their national creed which kept them alive through centuries: the Nemanja dynasty was considered sacred, its cult being the protector of the nation. The same spirit was predominant during centuries of foreign rule. In some regions, the population obtained certain self-governing privileges from the Turks. Small villages and local districts were administered by local leaders (*knez*), who were sometimes all subordinated to one supreme *knez*. Such an organization was known to have existed in Serbia at the end of the fifteenth century, and later in Slavonic and Walachia (Mala Vlaska) in the sixteenth century. Awarding his leadership in the First Serbian Uprising, the national assembly in Topola bestowed Karageorge with the title of the hereditary ruler (*Gospodar*) of Serbia. After the truce achieved with the Turks in 1817 Miloš Obrenović was proclaimed as the supreme *knez* (*bas-knez*), based on the tradition of village self-government. Later, it was up to Milos to transform this title into the real meaning of a ruler's attributes. The rise of the Obrenović dynasty on the level of European sovereigns, first as independent *knezes* and then kings of Serbia, meant the finale of a struggle for emancipation in the course of a bloody recapturing of every inch of the native soil.

Although the state of Montenegro shared the same path and destiny as Serbia, it achieved the same goal with less opposition, probably because Europe looked upon Montenegro as an exotic part of the continent, squeezed between mighty neighbors and separated from Serbia. Later, the liberating endeavors of Serbia and Montenegro, which ultimately brought about the collapse of two World Empires, provoked resentments in the Western world as well as in communist Russia, who turned against the united Yugoslav State. They contested the existence of Yugoslavia and the historical role played by Serbia and the Karageorgević dynasty, which they questioned and denied. The Serbs were to enter another epoch in their struggle for survival.

Second. Oral tradition, supported by various historical documents, confirms the fact that the best part of Serbian nobility perished in the battle of Kosovo. It was one of those medieval battles in which all was willfully put to risk in order either to win or to lose everything—the power, the land, and the people. During the following centuries, unlike other nations, the Serbs refused to comply with the reality imposed by historical development. On the contrary and according to the vertical trend in their history, the Serbs nurtured the idea of persistently moving up, trying to confirm their status, prestige, and material well being. New Serbian upper stratas, establishing their reputation and participation in popular affairs, obtained the recognition of the population. Like former members of the Nemanjid dynasty, these Serbs assumed during later difficult times the role of protectors of churches and monasteries as well as instigators of common public endeavors and noble deeds. The action of national leaders illuminated the path to the common people in its struggle for survival. The common men did not reject those who were of a better standing but strove to achieve it themselves. Certainly this was one of the reasons why the Serbian nation was formed early, before the end of the eighteenth century. The entity of its society originating from below was not checked and jeopardized by class confrontations, apparent among many other nations.

What happened then with the Serbs? Why did the Serbian people, describing their history in the form of epic poetry, accuse the former nobility of internecine squabbles, disloyalty and treason, yet still identified with their epoch and sang about heroes which the people itself produced?

The idea to renew the Serbian state, headed by its own nobility, originated soon after the Kosovo battle was over. Under the threat of further Ottoman penetration the Serbian nobility, in both its own territory and the Hungarian kingdom, stepped in as warriors, assembling their own people: knights and common plebeians. Under those circumstances the old customs and cults were reinforced and new ones originated. The self-consciousness of belonging to one ethnic community was inspired by St. Sava's legacy and the entity of the entire Serbian history. Involved in the chaotic events resulting from Turkish offensives, a good number of Serbian nobility perished in the wars in Hungary, were victims of local conflicts or disappeared moving somewhere abroad. However, new people emerged, with no name or origin, who obtained, in official documents, usually the name *Rac*. They distinguished themselves as warriors and diplomats, enrolled in Austrian, Transylvanian or Wallachian services. In the 1593–1606 wars they produced many prominent heroes such as: Deli Marko, Starina Novak and Djordje Rac. At the same time they experienced the greatest persecution and destruction. Their ascendancy was still maintained, in spite of challenges, because the Serbs in the Panonian plain represented people under arms, frequently changing leaders, and calling their military units *junaci* [heroes]. These were the circumstances when the Turks were defeated at Vienna in 1683. The Serbian warriors immediately took off and obtained high ranks and honors in both the Austrian and Russian armies. Again a new echelon of Serbian nobility appeared. A similar thing happened on the Adriatic coast where the Krajina Serbs, outlaws Haiduks and Uskoks waged a war with the Ottomans for years. They created their own concept of chivalry, decorated themselves and their horses with gold and built castles. They were ornamented with Venetian medals and bestowed with noble titles, leaving a strong memory of their achievements among the rest of the population.

A similar situation developed on the other side, where Muslim landlords (*begs*) fought for the sultan. They considered themselves nobles, built castles, and invited poets and bards to record their own heroic achievements. Interestingly enough, verses and songs were composed in the same language as were the fiddlers' songs about the Haiduks and Uskoks.

The success of individuals who had limited chances to prove themselves as warriors was obvious too. Generally speaking, this social group could be called aristocratic. They emerged among the old former nobility, hereditary *knezes*, popular leaders as well as prosperous businessmen. They established gradually a kind of patriciate. This process was not hindered even by wars which took place between 1683 and 1739 in Southeastern Europe. Thus, the Serbian people obtained as leaders prominent personalities who mirrored a general prosperity and opened the door for liberation. The advent of aristocracy meant the success of all. On the eve of the 1804 Serbian uprising in the Pashalick of Belgrade there already were people who distinguished themselves with authority and wealth. In order to deprive the people of its leadership the Turks started executing prominent leaders. A century later the Serbs produced an intellectual aristocracy. Professors Bogdan Popović and Slobodan Jovanović were among the best representatives of this elite.

The rise of individuals and social groups during five centuries manifested the constant vertical development of the Serbian nation. It inspired others too, giving the opportunity to strive ahead and prove the strength of energy hidden in the people. In fact, it responded to the inherited concept of the middle ages, the period of nobleness, legality and firm moral norms, combined with spirituality which bound them all together and continued to radiate. Waves of Western influences, which splashed the Serbian people introduced a confusion in the harmony of established values. The Serbs were unable, due to the general melee, to ever produce a conventional class system.

Third. The destiny of each individual is imbedded in his/her character. It is also true for the destiny of the nations, especially those which already achieved a certain level of anthropological development. At the end or the medieval period the Serbian nation consisted of its core, hardened under the Nemanjids, and scattered peripheral areas, a phenomenon known among other European nations. These peripheral areas experienced unequal development. In the Ottoman Empire they all lived together, including the core of the nation (to which the Serbian migrations and the extension of the Patriarchate of Peć significantly contributed). Some peripheral parts were converted to Islam or to Catholicism which, in due time, influenced changes of their character. These were mainly the people who stayed out of the regions covered by the Patriarchate of Peć. They preserved the archaic forms of language and spirit and, during the long time, either stayed attached to their ethnic community or complied with foreigners. The very core of the nation, highly challenged by the foreign occupator, carried the heavy burden of inherited legacy. Serbs were very proud people which contributed to difficulties in bearing the foreign yoke.

When a society, which in time becomes more and more patriarchal, takes over the heritage from the previous epoch, when ideas and spiritual life were more sophisticated, the new concepts must derive from a condensed codex of thoughts and behavior. The Serbian people became fully aware of moral and historical obligations. In the first place, it had undergone centuries of hardships without ever losing sight of its own role in history. There is no doubt that, encouraged by religious leaders, an uninterrupted flow of epic poetry was created. The singing of the bards was not merely entertainment, but the possibility to perceive all that had happened in the past and to learn a lesson from it. The poems reflected not only the historical consciousness but also the guidelines of moral behavior. This morale, if we take apart human cruelties present in every epic song, might to some extent surpass the ethical principles of contemporary European philosophers. At the same time the Serbian patriarchal society did not abandon the characteristics of St. Sava's spirituality. They determined the relationship with God, humble piety, concern for endowments, attitude towards family and off-springs, death and martyrdom for the faith. Although the Serbs occasionally experienced downfalls, they preserved the main qualities of a Christian people who emanated love for each living creature. Their espousal of the Kosovo message, which came out of their medieval spirituality, played a part in the deeply religious and philosophical idea that without death there is no resurrection and that without suffering and destruction there cannot be freedom, personal or national. Based on these concepts the Serbs became the nation of forgivers.

Once they were solidified in the core of their being, the Serbs condemned themselves to solitude and isolation. It was not easy to persist in the strict regime of a patriarchal society, with the requirements of democracy, unwritten laws, historical awareness, respect of elders and a strict social discipline. For that reason some Serbs abandoned their people and faith, feeling that they could live a freer life with less moral burdens and restrictions. One portion of this population would be nationally lost permanently, while the rest, the national core, became even more condensed. Finally, the Serbs entered the wars for liberation in 1912, overwhelmed with national and moral obligations which they accumulated over the centuries.

Such historical determination and the formation of a collective mentality distinguished the Serbs from other nations, particularly from the neighboring ones. Exceptions are usually not easily tolerated, especially when they are accentuated. This became even more apparent when the Serbs represented the advance guard of a religion that did not fit within the universal concept of another church. The ultimate animosity occurred when national and foreign leaders found in the Serbs an obstacle to the realization of their own programs. This animosity resulted from the different historical mentalities of the nations surrounding the Serbs.

(Translated from Serbo-Croatian by Bojana Hill.)

THE HISTORICAL DEMOGRAPHY OF THE OTTOMAN EMPIRE: PROBLEMS AND TASKS*

Maria Todorova and Nikolai Todorov

I. INTRODUCTION

Demographic studies of the Ottoman empire became significant during the second half of the nineteenth and the beginning of the twentieth centuries. This was a period when the Near Eastern interests of the large European powers and the aspirations of the newly liberated Balkan states over the partitioning of the Ottoman Balkan possessions mobilized all arguments in favor of one or another national cause. European and Balkan scholars developed a series of ethnographic maps. Many studies of the ethnic composition of the Ottoman population appeared, based on the rich concrete material from travelogues, taxation records and other Ottoman registers, parish registers and other sources. Gradually the modern census system appeared, resulting in a number of valuable demographic works on the territorial distribution, the movement and the ethnic composition of the population.

Political and national goals determined the direction of demographic research: it was primarily devoted to ethno-demography (general number of the separate nationalities, relationship between the various ethnic and religious groups, etc.). Population studies were also defined by the internal development of demography which influenced census-taking methods.

The search for new explanations for the complicated processes of the socio-economic and demographic development of the Ottoman Empire followed the general development of the historical discipline.

---

* This is an abridged variant of an article published as "Problemi i zadachi na istoricheskata demografiia na Osmanskata imperiia," in *Balkanistika* 2 (1987). A part of the material was read as a plenary report at the Fourth International Congress on the Socio-Economic History of Turkey, 1071–1920, held in Munich, 4–8 August 1986.

Until World War II historical population studies seldom employed demographic methods. The development of a demographic methodology since the late 1940s and early 1950s gave rise to a new discipline: historical demography.[1] The distinguishing factor in the development of historical demography in Western Europe was the type of sources as well as the specific methods employed.

The most important historical sources in the West are parish registers, which, since the sixteenth century, systematically reflect baptisms, marriages and deaths. Two fundamental methods are applicable to these types of sources—the so-called aggregative method, by which general calculations of birth, marriage, and death rates are made, and the method of family reconstitution.[2]

Without underestimating the decisive influence of various motives underlying the study of Ottoman historical demography, we want to emphasize the significance of the source base as determining the nature of Ottoman demographic studies. Accordingly we will dwell briefly upon the sources for the historical demgraphy of the Ottoman Empire.

II. SOURCES FOR THE HISTORY OF THE POPULATION OF THE OTTOMAN EMPIRE

Ottoman Sources

Scholars agree in general that Ottoman documentary material is the fundamental source for demographic studies; even its critics are forced to rely upon it if they do not want to fall into skeptical silence. The Ottoman statistical material is a direct product of (and bears all marks of) the centralized government of the Ottoman Empire. This explains at least two of its advantages—it is homogeneous and comprehensive for the entire Empire which makes comparative research possible. On the other hand, this explains at least one weakness (aside from the question of reliability which will be addressed below), namely that this material is a direct function of the strength and competency of the central administration. It is no accident that the Ottoman materials are most numerous for the second half of the fifteenth and during the sixteenth centuries, the zenith of the centralized Empire; and again during the nineteenth century, the modernizing and centralizing reform period. During the seventeenth to eighteenth centuries, a time of gradually intensifying decentralization and feudal anarchy, the statistical records are fewer in number and more irregularly compiled.

Most numerous are the registers of the fiscal administration. These are different types of *tahrir defterleri*, pertaining to all kinds of financial issues: regional taxation assessment, evaluation of land and other revenue sources, etc. Because of the purpose of these registers the question of their reliability and usability naturally arises. Above all it is necessary to emphasize that they cannot be used for statistical analysis in the same way as the data from contemporary censuses. For example, the richest sources—the tax records—do not represent the sum total of the population because they exclude different non-taxed segments of the male population, while women are left out altogether; they are influenced by accidental circumstances, most frequently dissimulation; and in most cases do not indicate the number of individuals taxed, but only the number of households. Despite this, and without exaggerating their significance, it must be stressed that they are an important source for the study of property relations and the social structure of the rural and urban population; of the form and size of the feudal rent; of the dissemination of monetary relations, and so forth. The amount and frequency of compilation of these records render them the only quantitative source for population movement and for ethnic/religious composition during the early centuries of Ottoman rule in the Balkans.[3]

The statistical materials from the nineteeth century are much better known and more widely used.[4] Beginning in 1831, several censuses, meant to cover the entire Muslim and Christian male population, were conducted for military and administrative purposes connected with the Tanzimst reforms. From the end of the 1860s *salname* [statistical annuals] were published, containing information from the general censuses conducted at different times in the separate provinces. From the 1880s censuses began to include women. These statistics became more accurate toward the end of the century, which, however, does not diminish the need to handle them cautiously. Most numerous are the materials from the beginning of the twentieth century.

European Sources

The European sources are primarily counts taken by various occupying powers in the Balkans. This category includes the assorted Venetian registers of the Peloponnesus, Dalmatia and the Ionian Islands.[5] Also important are the Russian assessment for various periods of the nineteenth century in Bulgaria, as well as French sources for Egypt in the beginning of the nineteeth century.[6]

Consular reports and diplomatic correspondence contain important, albeit often supplementary, information which, however, can be of primary importance for given periods and regions (such as for the Anatolian population during the second half of the nineteeth century). The data of travelers should also not be underestimated. In many cases they are the sole source material and substantial critical perusal of their contents makes them a valuable supplemlentary source.[7]

Ecclesiastical Sources

We will group together those sources deriving from the institutions of the local millets, above all those of the different churches. In contrast to the Catholic and the Protestant Church, the Greek Orthodox Church did not leave such a rich heritage of methodically kept and exhaustive registers. Despite the fact that this practice was not common and mandatory among the Greek Orthodox, records from baptisms, marriages and births sometimes existed for surveying purposes. As a whole, however, they are fragmentary and sporadic. In actuality, evidence of this sort is nearly nonexistent and the discovery of a massive statistical source systematically covering a more significant part of the Orthodox population is not deemed likely.[8]

During the second half of the nineteeth century and later, the Church, as an active participant in the national movements, organized the gathering of census data for the population within its jurisdiction. This data group includes the Constantinople Patriarchate, the Armenian Patriarchate, and the Bulgarian Exarchate. Because the Catholic population of the Ottoman Empire was under the jurisdiction of Rome, its documentation is of the type of the European parish registers.[9]

III. DEMOGRAPHIC PROCESSES

Total Number of the Population – Density and Territorial Distribution

Interest in the total number of the population of the Ottoman Empire increased immensely during the nineteenth century when the national liberation movements of the Balkan peoples made the question of the future state system of the Balkan population a central issue. Those powers mostly concerned with Balkan affairs, like Austria and Russia, made arrangements to compile population descriptions of the Balkan provinces. Also widely used were the reports of English,

French and other travelers and historians. Official Ottoman data also entered into circulation. Arguments based on the national affiliation of the population was used to support the territorial claims of the different liberation movements. Demographic data was gathered from assorted state organs, the church, communities, and individuals. The essence of these data is summmarized aptly by Felix Kanitz:

> If we add up the numbers, which patriotically minded Turks, Serbs, Bulgarians, Tsintsars, Albanians and Armenians claim to represent their size, then Turkey would represent a country with the greatest population density of all European states. However, it is authoritatively well known that this is not the case.[10]

The earliest to date, and comparatively the most complete data for the number of non-Muslim households in the Balkan peninsula are those from a *cizye* (poll tax collected from non-Muslims) register from 1489–1493 which is preserved in the Oriental Department of the National Library "Kiril i Metodii" in Sofia.[11] The data for 23 administrative districts cover practically the entire peninsula. 603,858 households (without the widows' households which number 43,018) are registered for 1491. This is not a definitive and complete figure. Comparing the data from 1490 and 1491 it is clear that the registration continues to reveal hidden households from the most remote corners of the administrative districts. In some cases this increase is from 4 to 12 percent even after the decline from those lost to death and conversion to Islam. Yet this number maximally approaches the probable total size of the non-Muslim population of the Balkans.

Chronologically, the next series of data are published by O. L. Barkan as summarized excerpts from the Istanbul Archives for 1520–1530.[12] They apply to *avariz-hanes*[13] and cover practically the entire population of the European provinces of the Ottoman Empire as delimited by three groups: non- Muslim, Muslim, and Jewish. The data for the 26 districts includes: 814,777 non-Muslim households, 186,952 Muslim households, and 4,134 Jewish households, a total of 1,005,863 households.

Various estimates of the Ottoman Empire's population have been made. Basing his calculations on the 1520–1530 figures and making several assumptions (5 persons as average household size, 6 per thousand annual growth, supposed numbers for unregistered and newly acquired population) Barkan arrives at the optimistic number of 30–35 million for 1600.[14] This figures is amended by F. Braudel at 22 to 26 million, while the *Atlas of World Population History* accepts the figure of 28 millions[15] It is obvious that once we step outside the limits of exact data, we enter into the attractive, but dangerous, area of hypotheses based on the construction of possible, but unverifiable population models.

With this we once again want to underscore the necessity of concrete local studies which rest upon a sound source base. During the period in question some regions underwent a population decline, while the increase of others fluctuated between 5 percent and 130 percent. Greatest was the rise of the cities, a result both of an influx of the village population toward the city and of a move of population from the small urban to the larger agglomerations.[16]

In spite of the uncertainty as to the number of the total population of the Ottoman Empire at the outset of the seventeeth century, there is no doubt about the general growth of the population during the sixteenth century.[17] Still, the question is open of whether we observe simply a significant population growth, or a "demographic explosions," the concept most often employed in the literature on the demographic development of the Ottoman Empire during the sixteenth century. This can be decided only after a meticulous study of the concrete character of the population rise: what part was the result of immigrations, what part a natural population growth, how much can be attributed to the settling of the nomadic population and the newly registered, etc.

The literature on the decline of the Ottoman Empire is immense. By analogy it has been accepted that the decline of the economy and of the external power of the Empire was automatically accompanied by a concomitant population decline. However, this widespread idea has not been proven by the existing sources, which for the seventeenth and eighteenth centuries are still few in number, and, as a whole, give an inaccurate representation of the population.

Several studies have been published for Anatolia addressing individual regions and concerned primarily with the late sixteenth and early seventeenth centuries. Based on these studies, it is possible to speak tentatively about a certain population decline by the end of the sixteenth century. This decline, however, varied regionally, and in some cases the data attest to the opposite process. As the only parameter which can be abstracted from the sources is the decrease in the number of taxpayers, it is difficult to decide whether we are witnessing a real natural population decline, or intensive population shifts, accompanied by an increase in the number of the unregistered population. In any case, it is proven that during this period substantial changes occurred which resulted in significant movements of the population to other regions, or to the cities, as well as in the appearance of "lost villages" in some regions, and even in the renomadizations of particular districts.[18]

An attempt, based on analysis of *cizye* registers, has been made to prove the decrease of the Balkan population during the seventeenth century, even to speek of a "demographic catastrophe."[19] This attempt has not been left unchallenged.[20] On the other hand, the eighteenth century remains a "dark age" as far as, among other reasons, its demographic information is concerned. The period of decentralization and separatism precluded all attempts of the central government to control entire aspects of the administration, including population issues. Conversely, the nineteenth century saw successful attempts at centralization and rationalization of the administration, known collectively as the Europeanizing reforms of the Tanzimat period.

For the time being the census of 1831 is accepted as being the first of the nineteenth century. According to this census the general male population was 3.7 million, but the real figure would be much higher considering that the census was not conducted in all areas. It seems that the most successful correction, made on the basis of the data from 1831 and supplemented with other information, is that which suggests a total population of around 18.5 million for the 1830s.[21] This number includes only territories in which the power of the Sultan was absolute. The tributaries of the Ottoman Empire (Walachia, Moldavia, Serbia) are excluded, as are the territories in the Arabian peninsula and North Africa. The population of these territories amounted to approximately 12 million.[22] Analysis of the data from the 1831 census is still inconclusive. Interesting and detailed demographic information can be expected from the over 20,000 individual registers that constitute the basis for the general census.[23]

The next census was conducted in 1844 and is known to us only from the work of Ubicini who evidently had access to the summary data.[24] The discovery and pubiication of the original data from this census is an important task. According to this census the total population of the Ottoman Empire, including all autonomous territories, exceeded 35 million. Compared with the numbers from the beginning of the 1830s this would give an average annual growth rate of about 10 per thousand, which for the nineteenth century is plausible and accepted by a number of researchers.

The first official publication of the total number of the Empire's population appeared in the *salname* of 1294 (1877–78). It was probably founded upon data from previous censuses, but updated with information about births and deaths, including those lost in the wars (the Balkan uprisings of 1875 and the Russo-Turkish War of 1877–78). Excluding data from Egypt, Tunis, the Danubian Principalities, Serbia and several other areas, as well as about the nomads and the military segment of the population, the *salname* places the general male population at more than 13 million.[25]

The next census was begun during 1881–82, conducted for most regions of the Empire until the end of the decade, and was completed in 1893. In this census women were counted for the first time and nomadic tribes were included; this was unconditionally the most complete and detailed census conducted in the Ottoman Empire. The total population figure is given at 17.4 million. A supplementary figure of approximately 3 million could be accepted to account for the regions with an incompletely conducted census. This gives a population of around 20.5 million in the territories under the direct power of the Ottoman government, which had been in a position to conduct the registration.[26] The last Ottoman census from 1905–06 gives a total population of about 20.8 million. Like the previous census, it reports on women and given the overall distribution of the population according to religious groups.[27]

It is not our goal here to reach a final assessment about the total number of the population of the Ottoman Empire. The idea was rather to give a general survey of the source base, as well as to alert to the possibility of multiple and often contradictory interpretations of the same data.

A question awaiting research is the density and territorial distribution of the population. This problem is directly dependent, on one hand, on the establishment of the total population size for the entire Empire and for individual regions, and on the other, on advances in historical geography. The data at our disposal attest to a low population density compared to the rest of Europe. By the mid-eighteenth century countries like Italy, the Netherlands, and Belgium had a population density of over 46 people/square kilometer; Great Britain, Spain and Central Europe had under 16–46p/km^2 and the whole of Southeastern Europe had under 15p/km^2.[28] In fact the population density in Rumelia (European Turkey) was 13.4 p./km^2 during the first half of the nineteenth century, while that for the entire Empire was 10.5p/km^2.[29]

Age and Sex Structure of the Population

The only data on age and gender, for the time being, are found in several of the nineteenth century censuses. The summary data for the Empire in 1894 give the following breakdown according to age: from a population of 26,106,068 people, 7,783,809 (29.8 percent) were in the 0–20 years of age bracket; 13,009,001 (49.8 percent)in the 20–50 age group; and 5,313,258 (20.4 percent) in the over 50 years of age segment.[30] Such an age structure indicates a stationary population.[31] There are some, though not significant, distinctions between the European, Anatolian, and Arabian provinces.

We have some earlier data from the 1860s from Northeastern Bulgaria when it was still part of the Ottoman Enlpire. The distribution of 2,360 individuals (1,709 urban and 651 village dwellers) shows that this population fell into the progressive model of population development. This is valid for all ethnic groups included in the registration—Bulgarians, Turks, Moldavians, Circassians, other Crimean emigrants, and to a lesser degree, the Cossacks.[32] A similar situation can be observed from the 1866 data (3,795 people) for three towns of the Danubian province as well as for 7 villages in the Plovdiv district from 1844 (628 Muslim males).[33]

Reconstruction of the age structure from the data of the *tahrir defterleri* by using regional model life tables merits attention.[34] However, this method can be successful only with larger populations because the inhabitants of one village or small town can have an atypical age structure.[35]

The sources attest to an interesting phenomenon: the general preponderance in the Balkans of male over female population. Data from 16 towns in the Danubian province reveal a sex ratio of 105, and data from Northeastern Bulgaria shows a sex ratio of 110. At the same time in Greece the sex ratio was 108, and in Serbia, 106.[36] General data for the Ottoman Empire in 1894 show a sex ratio of 118. Men predominated in 23 of the administrative regions, women in 12, and in one, Baghdad, their share was equal.[37] In many cases, especially in the Arab provinces, this evidently stemmed from female under-registration which took on huge proportions in some regions. Unstudied, but deserving attention, is the question of possible female infanticide. There were cases of incomplete registrations also for the male population, primarily young Muslims evading military recruitment.

The differences, however, cannot be explained only by the partial registration of women or by the hiding of the male population. This is especially true in the Balkans, where (except for the Greek census data), the reliability of both the Ottoman census in the Danubian province and the censuses of the nineteenth and early twentieth centuries of the independent Balkan States has been proven.[38] The predominance in the Balkans of males over females continued as a whole until the 1920s when, for the first time, a weak female preponderance was noticeable. Among the factors explaining male predominance the most essential are the high death rate of women during childbirth, and the overall high death rate which meant that the population did not attain the advanced ages at which women usually enjoy a biological superiority.[39]

Natural Flow of the Population: Fertility, Nuptiality, Mortality

Ottoman documentation does not provide material for the computation of birth and death rates. More precise data can be expected only from the Catholic parish registers, something which strongly raises their value, despite the fact that they are relevant for a limited population and restricted regions. The preliminary calculations based on the death registers of several Plovdiv Catholic villages for 1840–1872 show that of 1,409 registered deaths, 1,360 indicate the age of the deceased. A significant part, 585 (43 percent) fall into the category of infant mortality (0–1 year of age). These data also allow establishment of the seasonal fluctuations of mortality, the differential gender mortality, etc.

The study of the effects of natural disasters, epidemics, famines, and wars receives increasing attention. We already have at our disposal an excellent general work on the most dreadful epidemic—the plague in the Ottoman Empire from the early eighteenth to the mid-nineteenth centuries.[40] As a whole, despite geographic and temporal variations, the population of the Ottoman Empire during the eighteenth and the first half of the nineteenth centuries seems to have experienced a quantitative stagnation due to the plague. The analysis leaves the impression of a population of low density which was subject to unceasing plague attacks although these attacks did not have the devastating impact of the epidemics of the Middle Ages. The merit of these studies is that they usher into analysis a factor which had previously received insufficient attention, but which undoubtedly exercised a strong influence on the demography, economics, and subsequently on the politics of the Ottoman Empire. Similar investigations need to be made for cholera, smallpox, and other diseases.

A little more can be deduced about nuptiality as the nineteenth century Ottoman registers include information on marriages. In the 1960s the concept of the European marriage pattern was introduced, describing a phenomenon observed from the seventeenth century to World War II and confined to Western and Central Europe. This marriage pattern was characterized by late marriages and a significant proportion of celibate individuals. The rest of Europe and the world was distinguished by the "traditional" marriage pattern, characterized by early and almost universal marriage. In the "European" pattern the age at first marriage for women was higher than 24, and in the "traditional" it was lower than 21.[41]

An analysis of the age at marriage of Muslims and non-Nuslimls has been made on the basis of the reports on the urban population of three cities from Northern Bulgaria during the 1860s,[42] There is practically no difference between the two religious groups. The age at marriage for men and women of the two groups was 29 and 18.5 respectively. Although clearly being part of the traditional marriage pattern, the Bulgarian data have some specific traits; for example, the high age of marriage of urban men, which in some instances was higher than in Western Europe.

Celibacy was basically unknown, being a socially unacceptable, even reprehensible phenomenon. Practically all women and men married. Spousal age disparity shows that in over 62 percent of cases the husband was more than 10 years older than the wife. This large age difference is a phenomenon typical of the city and is connected with the specificity of the urban economy. On the other hand, the large age difference between spouses in a population cheracterized by a high death rate and low life expectancy should result in a diminished probability of women to marry. That this was not the case was due primarily to remarriage, defined already in the eighteenth century as *polygamia successiva.*

In this respect, comparison with a Muslim community in Anatolia is revealing. The analysis of data from the mid-nineteenth century shows that in spite of the demographic stress due to constant military recruits, diseases and migration, the population succeeded in reproducing itself. The explanation for this is found in the widespread practice of polygamy. In the framework of universal marriage and a long reproductive period for the men, the shortage of males was compensated by polygamy and the large age disparity between marital partners.[43] In contrast, among the Muslim population of Northeastern Bulgaria during the 1860s only one case of polygamy was established.

We permitted ourselves to dwell in more detail on these examples in order to show the importance of local studies. Only research of this nature can protect against hasty generalizations. Some authors, for example, maintain that there were significant differences in Muslim and non-Muslin fertility, stemming from specific economic and social conditions favoring the non-Muslims. It is asserted that after the 1830s the non-Muslim population increased at an average annual rate of 20 per thousand, while the Muslim population remained stationary and began to grow slowly only from the mid-nineteenth century.[44] Such a high growth rate for the non-Muslims is not only demographically impossible for this period, but the data from the statistical period of the Balkans (from the 1880s on) until the World War I which coincided with the demographic transition show that the average annual growth rate did not exceed 15 per thousand and reached the peak of 20 per thousand only during the 1920s after which it fell continuously.[45] The Muslim population also allegedly suffered from incomparably worse economic conditions and most of all from the separation of the male population due to military service. As we have seen, different mechanisms existed for the regulation of the population which adjusted to the various circumstances. Besides, the available data on the age-sex structure are unambiguously indicating the progressive development of all population groups independent of ethnic or religious affiliation. Moreover, without endeavoring to extrapolate this conclusion for other regions as well, the urban data indicate a higher death rate for female Christians.

Family and Household

The basic sources at our disposal are those of the Ottoman and other cadastres. To a lesser degree evidence from testaments can be useful. As noted above, the Ottoman Empire did not have at its disposal the invaluable wealth of information the church registers present. Accordingly, the technique of family reconstitution is, with minor exceptions, practically inapplicable for our regions. The available sources permit the analysis of "snap-shot" material which reflects a given historical movement, but does not allow tracing of the cyclical evolution of the family and its dynamics.

Several studies on the Balkan family and household are based on Ottoman material from the eighteenth and nineteenth centuries and on Venetian and Austrian enumerations from the seventeeth to the nineteenth centuries.[46] The Venetian registers reflect the overall male and female population, allowing tracing of the size and structure of the household during the earlier centuries of Ottoman rule. The Ottoman counts include only the male population, although in some cases women and children are counted in nineteenth century census data.

These studies cover a considerable part of the Balkans. The distribution of the household according to type and geographical location discloses the following picture: in the narrow Adriatic littoral simple family households with fewer than five persons per household were predominant. To the east, in the region of the Dinaric mountains between the Sava and Morava rivers, the large family household of the extended or multiple type prevailed, its average number differing regionally and temporally between seven and seventeen, We are intentionally using the concepts of extended and multiple family and avoiding the term *zadruga* because the existing sources do not allow the presence of the *zadruga* to be deduced only from quantitative data. Supplementary information about the relationships of ownership, production, and distribution are necessary to verify the existence of the *zadruga*.

To the east and to the south of this region the simple family household was pervasive. In the Peloponnesus the average household size hardly extended beyond four persons. For Northeastern Bulgaria the average household size varied from 4.4 for urban Christians to 4.9 for rural Muslims. In the central Balkans (the region of Plovdiv) in the mid-nineteenth century, the simple family household with an average number of around 5.4 was typical of the rural Muslim population.[47] An investigation of more than 50,000 individuals from the Plovdiv region during the 1870s reports an average of 5.007 members per household.[48]

Of great importance is the question of a possible continuity between the pre-Ottoman tradition and the Ottoman centuries. Researchers of Byzantine and Balkan agrarian relations demonstrated the existence of two forms of ownership and inheritance—individual and collective—and the presence of two forms of family organization—the individual family household and the family commune (the *zadruga*) without, however, categorically passing judgment on distribution or prevalence. Some investigations hold that in the first quarter of the fourteenth century the predominant share of households (up to 80 percent) were small, numbering 1–5 members.[49]

Special attention must be paid to the *zadruga*, which in a large portion of the literature is described as the most typical and widespread household form among the Balkan Slavs. However, as Phillip Mosely has justifiably noted

> The *zadruga*, or the communal multiple family, has long been recognized as one of the basic forms of social organization within the societies of Southeastern Europe, but it has usually been an object of romantic musings and patriotic theorizing rather than of precise investigation.[50]

As a whole, current materials on the family and household point to Southeastern Europe as part of the general Europeen area with a predominence of the simple end extended family types. The presence of multiple families and the *zadruga* in the Western Balkans is a unique trait, deserving in-depth research. However, it should not be treated as an obligatory phase of regional development which was set aside with only the rise of a market economy.[51]

As far as Anatolias concerned, the data for the Black Sea region demonstrates the presence of a significant contingent of extended families (more than 30 percent. The average size of the households is delineated as 6.5.[52]

Possible research in this field should focus on the type of economy, especially the relationship between crop-growing or stock-breeding agriculture and family and household size and structure. An interesting direction is the possible correlation between population density and household structure. Another promising area of research is the character of the taxation system in relation to different types of family structure,and the interesting question of what it actually reflects: social fact or meaning.

IV. THE STATE AND TASKS OF OTTOMAN
HISTORICAL DEMOGRAPHY

The goal of this section is not to give a comprehensive survey of the literature on the historical demography of the Ottoman Empire which includes several hundred works. To some extent such a bibliographic review has been accomplished for publications for 1940 to 1980.[53] It is imperative to compile a complete bibliography of the historical demography of the Ottoman Empire.[54] The goal here is to show several of the fundamental, most common characteristics of extant studies which also determine the basic conclusions drawn.

There has been no single general work on the historical demography of the Ottoman Empire. The bulk of the literature is comprised of articles which are usually important studies relying upon new source material and covering specific issues confined to restricted regions and periods. However, studies on general problems concerned with larger regions and longer periods have only gradually been accumulating. It is not accidental that the comparatively few conclusive monographs which have appeared were published during the 1970s–80s.[55]

The focus of scholarly study has been on the sixteenth and on the nineteenth centuries due both to the rich source base as well as to the political nature of these periods: the sixteenth century being the period of Ottoman might, and the nineteenth the period of the formation of the Balkan national states. Geographically, nearly half the works center on the Balkans with the remaining works concerned unequally with Anatolia, the Near East (Iraq, Syria, Lebanon, Palestine, and North Africa (Egypt, Algiers, Tunis, and Morocco). This has clearly influenced also the present work. In spite of the desire to give a generalized and uniform picture of the Ottoman Empire, the focus falls upon the Balkans due to the more abundant studies and the fact that the authors are better acquainted with that region. We endeavored, on the the basis of the extant literature, to reflect the level of knowledge attained on Anatolia. Due primarily to the unavailability of the literature, the Ottoman influence in North Africa and the Near East remains practically outside our synopsis.

This brief survey of the sources and nature of the research leads to several conclusions about the state and future development of historical demographic studies of the Ottoman Empire. An enormous quantity of sources lie untouched in archives. Because of this it is natural that a large portion of the publications represent editions of sources in documentary collections or as separate publications. The largest body of material and the one most suitable for statistical analysis is of Ottoman origin. These sources alone permit the inclusion of processes affecting the entire Empire, suggesting the use of the comparative method for analysis of data intrinsic to the whole Empire and for tracing the specific development of various regions.

Basic tasks to be carried out are the investigation and publication of the archival materials and a systematic approach to the demographic data. The experience to date shows that the publication *in extenso* of the Ottoman sources is a difficult and extremely time-consuniing process, which has affected unevenly different regions and periods. Attempts at extracting concrete data in a unified way in order to facilitate their systemization have not been entirely successful; therefore, a comprehensive program for systematic work is needed.

Speaking of a program, we should not expect it to include all registers. This can be a long-term task of several decades or more, which depends upon the competency and interest of many state authorities, most of all of those of Turkey, but also of those countries which comprised the Ottoman Empire. Specially trained personnel are also needed to work with the research material. What we have in mind is the creation of a pilot program which would focus on those provinces and periods heretofore not researched. It would result in compiling a necessary minimum of data for the Empire at large and establishing general guidelines and a working model of the basic demographic processes.

It is important to establish clearly the possibilities and limitation of the Ottoman sources. Their character does not permit a definitive analysis of demographic phenomena. In this regard we should conduct a series of studies on assorted provincial sources in order to establish generally accepted coefficients. At the same time, non-Ottoman source material should be made use of for comparative purposes, especially in regions where there were censuses taken and other population descriptions made for various goals.

Studies detailing terminological questions are of primary importance. The disclosure of the meaning of terms in their historical context is mandatory for the validation of demographic, and in general, of historical observations and deductions. A thesaurus of Ottoman demographic history would be invaluable. An impetus must be given for the investigation of *historical geography.* It is imperative to make a detailed study of the administrative divisions of towns and villages in order to undertake valid comparative studies. As demonstrated above, Ottoman historical demography is still at a stage in which emphasis on local research is necessary.

A circumstance complicating the study of ethnodemographic problems is the variegated ethnic composition of Ottoman society, characterized by intensive population movements and ethnic mixes. The nineteenth century saw the formation of national consciousness and national states, a process the Ottoman Empire was not able to either contain or survive. As part of this process national minorities were formed that did not receive rights or were suppressed by such discriminatory measures, that their speedy assimilation was induced.

We hope this article has once again demontrated the interconnected destiny of the inhabitants of the Ottoman Empire. After all, the demographic processes were commion for everyone. The history of the Ottoman Empire, especially of its socio-economic processes, must be examined not only as part of the history of contemporary Turkey, but as the history of all constituent peoples of the empire.

NOTES

1 .J. Dapâquier, *Introduction à la démographie historique* [Introduction to demographic history] (Paris, 1975) and *Pour le démographie historique* [On demographic history] (Paris, 1984); T. Hollingsworth, *Historical Demography* (London, 1969); D. K. Shelestov, *Demografiia: istoriia i sovremenost* [Demography: history and modernity] (Moscow, 1983).

2. L. Henry, *Techniques d'analyse en démographie historique* [Analytical techniques in demographic history] (Paris, 1980); A. E. Imhof, *Einführung in die historische Demographie* [Introduction to historical demography] (Munich, 1977).

3. See the numerous publications of Ottoman sources, for example the series of Turkish sources on Bulgarian history published in Sofia, Vol. 1 (1959) Series SV–SVI; Vol. 1 (1964); Vol. 2, (1966). See also *Turski dokumenti za istorijata na makedonskiot narod* [Turkish documents on the history of the Macedonian people] (Skopije, 1968–72); *Defteri i regjistrimit të sanzhakut te Shkrodes i vitit 1485* [Registers of the Shkrodra sandzhak in 1485] (Tiranë, 1974); and other single publications of sources.

4. K. Karpat, *Ottoman Population, 1830–1914* (Madison, WI, 1985); J. McCarthy, *The Arab World, Turkey and the Balkans (1878–1914): A handbook of historical statistics* (Boston, 1982).

5. V. Panagiotopoulos, *Plithismos kai oikismoi tis Peloponnisou, 13–18 aionas* [Population and settlements in the Peloponnesus, 13th-18th centuries] (Athens, 1985).

6. N. Todorov, "Ruski dokumenti za demografskoto sustoianie na chast ot iztochna Bulgariia prex 30-te godini na XIX v." [Russian documents on the demographic composition of Eastern Bulgaria in the 1930s], *Izvestiia na durzhavnite arkhivi* 13 (1967).

7. See the numerous statistical materials compiled from European authors and published by N. Mikhov in *Naselenieto na Turtsiia i Bulgariia prez XVIII–XIV v* [The population of Turkey and Bulgaria during the eighteenth-nineteenth centuries] 5 vols. (Sofia, 1915–68).

8. The Greek Orthodox Church in Budapest during the eighteenth-nineteenth centuries kept parish registers which might contain demo-

graphic information about the Orthodox Balkan merchant colony in
Hungary.

9. P. K. Medauvar, "Actes de baptême, mariage et sépulture en
Egypte (grec-catholique mélkite)," [Certificates of baptism, marriage
and burials in Egypt] (*Annales de démographie historique* (1972); I.
Hunyadi "Egyhazi anyakönyvezés a török vilagban: A Segedi példa,"
[Church registration in the Turkish period: the case of Sebed] *De-
mografia* 21:4 (1978). Parish registers from the Bulgarian Catholic
population have been analyzed in M. Todorova, *Balkan Family History and the European Pattern: Demographic Development in Ottoman Bulgaria* (forthcoming in 1992 from American University Press).

10. F. Kanitz, *Donau-Bulgarien und der Balkan: Historisch-
geographische Reisestudien aus den Jahren 1860–1879* [Danubanian
Bulgaria and the Balkans: historical-geographic travel notes from
the years 1860–79] Vols. 1–3 (Leipzig, 1875), cited in N. Todorov
Balkanskiiat grad XV–XIX vek [The Balkan city during the fifteenth-
nineteenth centuries], (Sofia, 1972), 305.

11. N. Todorov, *Za demografskoto sustoianie na Balkanskiia
poluostrov prez XV–XVI vek" [The demographic situation of the Balkan
peninsula during the fifteenth-sixteenth centuries], Godishnik na Filosofsko-
istoricheskiia fakultet 1959–1960*, 2. The full text of the register is
published in N. Todorov and A. Velkov, *Situation démograph- ique
de la péninsule balkanique du XVe-début du XVIe siècle* [The demographic situation of the Balkan peninsula in the fifteenth and early
sixteenth centuries] (Sofia, 1988).

12. O. L. Barkan, "Osmanli imparatorluğunda bir iskân ve kol-
onizasyon metodu olarak sürgünler," *Iktisat Fakültesi Mecmuasi* 15
(1953–54), 237.

13. Taxation unit for the collection of the tax *avariz*. In this
particular case the size of the *avariz-hane* and the size of the *cizye-
hane* of the 1490s is identical.

14. O. L. Barkan, "Tarihi demografi araştirmarlari ve Osmanli
tarihi," *Türkiyat Mecmuasi* 10, No. 11 (1953).

15. C. McEvedy and R. Jones, *Atlas of World Population History*
(London, 1980), 136–37.

16. See the works of O. L. Barkan: "Research on the Ottoman
Fiscal Surveys," *Studies in the Economic History of the Middle East
from the Rise of Islam to the Present Day* (London, 1970), 169; "Essai
sur les données statistiques des registres de recensement dans l'Empire
Ottoman au XVe-XVIe siècles," [Essay on the statistics of the census registers of the Ottoman Empire in the fifteenth-sixteenth cen-

turies] *Journal of the Economic and Social History of the Orient*, Vol. 1 (Leiden, 1957), 25; "Quelques observations sur l'organisation économique et sociale des villes ottomanes des XVIe et XVIIe siècles" [Some observations on the economic and social organization of Ottoman cities during the sixteenth-seventeenth centuries], *Recueils de la societé Jean Bodin*, Vol. 7 [Collections of the Jean Bodin Society] (Brussels, 1955), 292. Refer also to N. Todorov, "Po niakoi vuprosi na balkanskiia grad prez XV–XVI v" [Some questions on the Balkan city during the fifteenth-sixteenth centuries] *Istoricheski pregled* No. 1 (1962), 44–45. One concrete example of useful local research showing the increase in the urban and rural population of the administrative district of Evbeya during the fifteenth-sixteenth centuries is V Karidis D.,. M. Kiel, "Santzaki tou Epirou, 15–16 ai," [The Epyros sandzhak], *Ta Tetramina*, 28–29 (Amfissa, 1985).

17. M. Cook, *Population Pressure in Rural Anatolia, 1450–1600* (London, 1972); R. Jennings, "Urban population in Anatolia in the Sixteenth Century," *International Journal of Middle East Studies*, Vol. 7, No. 1 (1976); L. Erder and S. Faroqhi, "Population Rise and Fall in Anatolia, 1550–1620," *Middle Eastern Studies* 15:3 (1979); A. D. Novichev, "Naselenie Osmanskoi imperii v XV–XVI vv" [The population of the Ottoman Empire in the fifteenth-sixteenth centuries], *Vestnik Leningradskogo gosudarstvenn universiteogo. Seriia istorii iazyka i literatury* 14:3 (1976); M. Meier, "Osobennosti demograficheskikh protsessov v Osmanskoi imperii XV–XVI vv. i ikh sotsial'no-ekonomicheskie posledstviia" [Features of the demographic processes of the Ottoman Empire in the 15th and 16th centuries andtheir social and economic consequences], *Demograficheski protsessi na Balkanakh v srednie veka* [Demographic Processes in the Balkans during the Middle Ages] (Kalinin, 1984).

18. W. D. Hütteroth, *Ländliche Siedlungen im südlichen Inneranatolien in den letzten vierhundert Jahren* [rural settlements in southern Anatolia in the last 400 years] (Göttingen, 1968); X. de Planhol, "Geography, Politics and Nomandism in Anatolia," *International Social Sciences Journal* 11 (1959); M. Akdağ, "Celâli Isyanlar, 1530–1603," [The Dzhelyali Revolts] *Ankara Üniversitesi Dil ve Çoğrafya Fakültesi Yayinlari* (1963), 144; N. Tunçdilek, "Eskişehir bölgesinde yerlesme tarihine toplu bir bakis," *Istanbul Üniversitesi Iktisat [A look at the history settlements in the Eskişehir region] Fakültesi Mecmuasi* 15: 1–4 (1953–54).

19. B. McGowan, *Economic Life in the Ottoman Empire* (Cambridge, 1981).

20. M. Todorova, "Was There a Demographic Crisis in the Ottoman Empire in the Seventeenth Century?" *Études balkaniques* 12 (1988).

21. E. Z. Karal, *Osmanli imparatorluğunda ilk Nüfus Sayimi 1831* (Ankara, 1943). See also Karpat, *op. cit.* In the important statistical appendices to his book, which comprise more than half of the work, Karpat has published the data from various nineteenth century Ottoman censuses.

22. D. Panzac, *Le Peste dans l'Empire Ottoman, 1700–1850* [The Plague in the Ottoman Empire] (Louvain, 1985), 276–77.

23. They are preserved at the Istanbul Başvekâlet Arsivi.

24. A. Ubicini, *Lettres sur la Turquie*, Vols. 1–2 (Paris, 1853–54). There are some differences in the figures in the English edition: *Letters on Turkey* (London, 1856).

25. Karpat, 25 and 121.

26. Ibid., 33–34 and 122–151.

27. Ibid., 35 and 162–190.

28. *Atlas of World Population History*, 26; Todorov, "Za demografskoto sustoianie," 211–214.

29. Panzac, 176.

30. Karpat, 212–13.

31. According to the demographic classification the three age groups, 0–14, 15–49, and over 50 are distributed among a progressive population as 40:50:10, among a stationary as 25:50:25, and among a regressive as 20:50:30.

32. The explanation for the almost stationary structure among the Cossacks is that they were recent male settlers, most of whom came without women, and had not yet established families in their new place of residence.

33. Todorov, "Balkanskiiat grad," 344; M. Todorova, "Struktura na naselenieto, semeistvo i domakinstvo na Balkanite" [The structure of the population, family, and household in the Balkans] *Istoricheski pregled* 4 (1983), 90; T. Güran, *Structure économique et sociale d'une région de campagne dans l'Empire Ottoman vers le milieu du XIXe siécle* [The economic and social structure a rural region of the Ottoman Empire in the mid-nineteenth century] (Sofia, 1980), 55.

34. A. J. Coale and P. Demeny, *Regional Model Life Tables and Stable Populations* (Princeton, 1966); S. Ledermann, *Nouvelles tables types de mortalité* [New mortality tables] (Paris 1969); *Methods of Estimating Basic Demographic Measures from Incomplete Data* (New York, 1967).

35. L. Erder, "The Measurement of Preindustrial Population Changes: the Ottoman Empire from the Fifteenth to the Seventeenth Century," *Middle Eastern Studies* 11:3 (1975), 284–301.

36. Todorov, "Balkanskiiat grad," 312, 317, and 343–44; Todorova, *Structure*, 90–1.

37. Karpat, 211.

38. M. Todorova, *Balkan Family Structure*, 20–27.

39. The high female death rate during the reproductive period can be clearly demonstrated on the basis of the data from the censuses of the Danubian province during the 1860s. The growth pyramid for the urban Bulgarian population exhibits a "dip" in the curve for women between 20 and 50 years of age. It is interesting that this is nor registered in the growth pyramid of Muslim women; see Todorova, *Structure*, 91–2.

40. Panzac and the literature cited in his extensive bibliography.

41. J. Hanal, "European Mariage Patterns in Perspective," in D. V. Glass and D. E. C. Eversly, eds., *Population in History* (London, 1965).

42. Todorova, *Structure*.

43. J. McCarthy, "Age, Family and Migration in the 19th Century Black Sea Provinces of the Ottoman Empire," *International Journal of Middle East Studies* 10 (1979).

44. Karpat, 11.

45. *Demografiia na Bulgariia* [The demography of Bulgaria] (Sofia, 1974), 301.

46. T. Stoianovich, "Family and Household in the Western Bal- kans, 1500–1879," *Memorial Ömer Lütfi Barkan* (Paris, 1980); "Model and Mirror of the Premodern Balkan City," *Studia balcanica* 3 (1970), 103–05; see also the previously cited works of V. Panagiotopoulos, M. Todorova, and T. Güran.

47. Güran, 9–11.

48. These calculations were made by a British official in the Plovdiv consulate on 50,622 people from 50 villages, which constituted 10,110 households. The data were published in *House of Commons. Account and Papers* 92/44(1) (1877) and are cited by Karpat, p. 10.

49. A. P. Kazhdan, *Agrarniye otnosheniia v Vizantii v XIII-XIV vv* [Agrarian relationships in Byzantium during the Thirteenth-Fourteenth Centuries] (Moscow, 1952), 75; G. G. Litavrin, *Bolgariia i Vizantiia v XI-XII vv* [Bulgaria and Byzantium in the Eleventh-Twelfth Centuries] (Moscow, 1960), 65–66; D. Angelov, *Agrarnite otnosheniia v Severna i Sredna Makaedoniia prez XIV v* [Agrarian

relations in northern and central Macedonia in the fourteenth century] (Sofia, 1958), 96–97; N. Kondov, "Za purvichnata obshtestvena edinitsa pri selskoto naselenie v Srednovekovna Bulgariia," [The archetypal social unit among the village populations in Bulgaria during the Middle Ages], *Istoricheski pregled* 1 (1965).

50. Phillip Mosely, "The Distribution of the Zadruga within Southeastern Europe," in *The Zadruga: Essays by Phillip E. Mosely and Essays in His Honor*, Robert F. Byrnes, ed. (University of Notre Dame Press, 1976), 58.

51. For an extensive treatment of these problems, see M. Todorova, *Balkan Family Structure*.

52. McCarthy, *op. cit.*

53. D. Panzac, "La Population de l'empire ottoman et de ses marges du XVe au XIVe siècle: bibliogaphie (1941–1980) et bilan provisoire" [The population of the Ottoman Empire and its fringe territories in the fifteenth and during the sixteenth centuries: bibliography and preliminary assessment] *Revue de l'Occident Musulman et de la Méditerranée* 31 (1981).

54. The International Center for Information on Historical Sources for the Balkans and the Mediterranean (CIBAL) has begun preparation of a bibliography on Balkan demographic history.

55. See the previous citations for M. Cook, N. Todorov, S. Faroghi, V. Panagiotopoulos, K. Karpat, as well as J. McCarthy, *Muslims and Minorities. The Population of Ottoman Anatolia and the End of the Empire*, (New York and London, 1983).

THE FIRST SERBIAN ORGANIZATION IN
NORTH AMERICA
PAN-SLAVISM, REGIONALISM, AND SERBIANISM

V. Nicholas Vucinich

San Francisco was the first center of Serbian and Yugoslav social organization in the United States. The first organizations established by Serbian and other Yugoslav immigrants were the mutual-aid societies. The mutual-aid societies were formed in order to provide security for the immigrants far from their homes and families. They also served as centers for social and cultural life. It is out of the mutual-aid societies that most of the future Serbian institutions in America, such as churches, newspapers, and cultural and political organizations developed.

The first South Slavic mutual-aid society in America was organized in San Francisco on November 17, 1857. The Slavonic Illyric Mutual and Benevolent Society was founded by a small group of immigrants from the southern section of Dalmatia and the Adriatic islands. They were Croats from Dalmatia, and Serbs from Boka Kotorska. The object of this organization was stated to be,

> the promotion of social and intellectual intercourse among its members, and rendering of mutual assistance to sick and distressed members, and the internment of its deceased members.[1]

These would become the essential purposes of all Serbian and other Yugoslav mutual-aid societies that would follow this first one.

Originating from the same provinces along the Adriatic Coast it was natural that the earliest, and not yet numerous, Serb and Croat immigrants in the New World would band together to form mutual organizations. This process also reflected the pan-Slavic literary and political trends that dominated the intellectual atmosphere of Dalmatia during this part of the nineteenth century.[2]

In the 1860s the mutual-aid society was followed by the establishment of an Orthodox Church parish and a Slavonic reading room in San Francisco, both of them either Pan-Orthodox or Pan-Slavic in character. In Dalmatia reading rooms (*citaonice*) often served as local cells for political parties, and as institutions whereby means of dances, songs, music, discussions, and literary activities—national and political—consciousness was developed.

The Serbian-Greek-Russian Orthodox Church in San Francisco owed its beginnings, in part, to the presence of a number of ships from the Imperial Russian fleet that were harbored in San Francisco Bay during the American Civil War. Priests from the Russian ships that entered San Francisco Bay were responsible for baptizing the first Serbian-American children in California. One of the early children to be baptized in 1863 would go on to become the first American-born Serbian Orthodox priest and missionary, Archimandrite Sebastian Dabovich.[3]

The presence of the Russian fleet with Russian Orthodox priests, together with Russian government agents and a Serbian immigrant community resident in San Francisco, gave the impetus for the establishment of the Greek-Russian-Slavonic Orthodox Church and Benevolent Society. The society was founded in 1864 with an initial membership of fifteen: twelve Serbs, two Greeks, and one Roman Catholic from Dubrovnik.[4] As the name of the society indicates, the purpose of the organization was both religious and benevolent. The society grew and in 1867 the members drew up a Constitution, and registered formally at the San Francisco City Hall. It may seem as if the Serbs in San Francisco were too distant from their homeland for their activities to have any impact there, yet a copy of the Constitution of the Greek-Russian-Slavonic Orthodox Church and Benevolent Society was published in the *Srpsko Dalmatinski Magazin* of Zadar, Dalmatia in 1869.[5]

With the arrival of a Russian priest in San Francisco in 1868, an Orthodox Church parish was established in San Francisco. The first services were held in the home of a Serb, Peter Sekulovich. Later Russian Bishops arrived, a church was built, and in 1871 San Francisco became the Episcopal See for the Russian Orthodox Diocese of Aleuto-Alaska. A Serbian Orthodox priest from Montenegro arrived in San Francisco in the 1870s and briefly served at the Orthodox Church.[6] Most of the priests who served the Orthodox parish in San Francisco were Russian, and the parish was officially under Russian ecclesiastical jurisdiction. Archimandrite Sebastian Dabovich, who would later serve at this parish for some time, became head of the

Serbian Orthodox Mission in America under the jurisdiction of the Russian Orthodox Church.

The Orthodox Church in San Francisco long served Serbs scattered throughout the Far West. Serbs from towns as distant as Virginia City, Nevada, and Bisbee, Arizona, traveled to San Francisco, when travel and communications were slow in the nineteenth century, to baptize their children, marry, and bury their dead.[7]

The Orthodox Benevolent Society established an Orthodox Cemetery in San Francisco. This cemetery and many of the functions of the Orthodox Society were later taken over by the Serbian Benevolent Society. The Orthodox Benevolent Society continued to exist into the 1890s when it was disbanded due to financial difficulties, and the co-option of many of its activities by the Serbian Society. The Orthodox Church was pan-Orthodox and included Russians, Greeks, Syrians, and converted Eskimos and Aleuts among its parishioner. Yet by all indications the Serbs were the dominant element in the parish throughout the early years of existence.[8] In the 1890s and early 1900s there was much talk in the Serbian colony of San Francisco about the need for a separate Serbian Orthodox Church in the City, but for various reasons they did not accomplish this until after World War I.

The first purely Serbian Orthodox Church in North America was the St. Sava Serbian Orthodox Church which was built in the Mother Lode gold mining town of Jackson, California in 1894. This church was founded by Archimandrite Dabovich and the Serbian miners who resided in Jackson and neighboring towns in the foothills of the Sierra Nevada mountains. Donations for the construction of this church were received from Serbs living in towns throughout the Far West.[9]

The first distinctly Serbian institution in the New World was the Serbian-Montenegrin Literary and Benevolent Society of San Francisco, founded in 1880. This society still exists as the First Serbian Benevolent Society. The Serbian-Montenegrin Literary and Benevolent Society was organized with the goals of aiding the needy and sick, and through a reading room, spreading education. This first Serbian organization in America was founded by a half-dozen Serbs. At their first official meeting they were joined by two more of their compatriots. In the first year of its existence the Serbian-Montenegrin Literary and Benevolent Society numbered a total of twenty-seven members.[10]

Of the eight founding members of the society, six were from Boka Kotorska: Antonije Vukasovich, Krsto Gopcevich, Jovan Pavkovich,

Rade Begovich, and Jovan and Vladimir Jovovich. Djuro S. Martnovich was from Montenegro. Mihail Raskovich was from Vojvodi₁a,
a rarity in a colony that was made up of Serbs almost all of th℮m
from the Boka, Montenegro, and Hercegovina area.[11]

While the early cooperation between the Serbs and Croats in the
Slavonic organizations had reflected the Illyrian and pan-Slavic political and literary trends that were so prominent in Dalmatia before
1878, the establishment of separate Serbian and Croatian organizations in America after 1878 also reflected events that were taking
place in the homeland.

In 1869 an uprising took place in the Krivosije region of Boka
Kotorska over the Austrian administration's institution of a policy
of military conscription of the local Serbian population. The Serbs
there had been previously free of military obligations and possessed
the right to bear arms. The Krivosije uprising aroused the Serbs in
San Francisco, most of whom were natives of Boka Kotorska, and
divided them from the Croats, most of whom appear to have supported the Austrian authorities in the incident. The dispute over the
Krivosije uprising caused a great deal of dissension in the Slavonic
Illyric Mutual and Benevolent Society, and one of the San Francisco
Serbs, Luka V. Zenovich, became renowned among the local Serbs
for attacking a group of the pro-Austrian members of the Slavonic
Society and tearing their Austrian flags and banners.[12]

During the period of the Hercegovinian uprising and Eastern
Crisis of 1875–1878 the Serbs and Croats in San Francisco pulled
together, formed committees to aid the insurgents and refugees, and
even sent a few volunteers to the front.[13] Yet the subsequent Austro-
Hungarian occupation of the provinces of Bosnia and Hercegovina
in 1878 served to divide the Serbs and Croats in San Francisco, a
process that was also taking place in Dalmatia. In 1878 Serbia and
Montenegro won recognition of their independence from the great
powers at the Congress of Berlin. The Serbs in Dalmatia were forming
separate Serbian nationalist political parties and journals. The Serbs
in San Francisco were not far behind in duplicating these events taking
place in their distant homeland.

The period between 1878 and 1903, when Serbia was ruled by the
Obrenović dynasty, has been called "the era of Austrian supremacy
in Serbian affairs." Yet while the official government of Serbia bowed
to Austrian wishes in its foreign policy, Serbian nationalist organizations and political parties in Serbia, Vojvodina, Dalmatia, and Bosnia,

and Hercegovina advocated an aggressive and libertarian foreign policy. The liberal and nationalist trends among the Serbs had their origins in earlier liberal organizations like the United Serbian *Omladina*, and in the political thought of figures such as the leader of the Vojvodina liberals, Svetozar Miletić, and the young Serbian radical-socialist, Svetozer Marković.[14] Organizations like the *Omladina* had a strong influence on the Serbs in Dalmatia, Hercegovina, and Montenegro who began to form their own liberationist organizations in the 1870s.[15] Svetozar Miletić was a particularly revered figure among the San Francisco Serbs in the nineteenth century and in the early 1900s.[16]

Immediately after its founding the Serbian-Montenegrin Literary and Benevolent Society in San Francisco corresponded with the Serbian government, and received a reply and gift of books from the Minister of Education in Belgrade.[17] This began a tradition of correspondence with individuals and organizations in Serbia and other Serbian lands that lasted throughout the early history of the San Francisco society. Leading Serbian publications such as *Srpska Nezavisnost* in Belgrade, *Glas Crnogoraca* in Cetinje, and *Zastava* in Novi Sad reported on the activities of the Serbian-Montenegrin Society in San Francisco in the 1880s and 1890s.[18]

The Serbian-Montenegrin Literary and Benevolent Society in San Francisco bestowed honorary membership on the rulers and heirs to the thrones of Serbia and Montenegro in 1882. In the same year they sent honorary memberships to the Russian pan-Slavic leaders Ivan Aksakov and General Mikhail G. Cherniaev.[19] In later years they also bestowed this honor on Sava Bjelanović, the leader of the Serbs in Dalmatia, and editor of *Srpski List* (later *Srpski Glas*) of Zadar, and Jovan Sundečić a well known Serbian pan-Slavic poet from Dalmatia. The society's choice of figures to honor were another indication that Serbian nationalist and pan-Slavic currents found support among the Serbian immigrants in San Francisco.

Despite the fact that in its first quarter of a century nine-tenths of the members of the Serbian Montenegrin Society were natives of Austria-Hungary, the members refused any cooperation with Habsburg officials in San Francisco. In 1897 they declined the summons of the local Austro-Hungarian Consul that they take part in the 50th anniversary celebration of the reign of Emperor Francis Joseph. On the other hand, the Serbian-Montenegrin Literary and Benevolent Society honored the Czars of Russia, celebrated the anniversaries of the

Petrović dynasty in Montenegro, and the local Italian community's 20th anniversary of the liberation of Rome in 1890.[20]

With the increased immigration of Serbs to California beginning in the 1880s the Serbian-Montenegrin Society grew steadily, and when it celebrated its 25th anniversary in 1905 it numbered over 300 members in good standing.[21] The Serbian-Montenegrin Society sponsored parades, dances, and picnics. And in 1881 the society instituted a yearly celebration of St. Sava's Day, honoring the twelfth-century founder of the Serbian Orthodox Church. The society was also responsible for the organization of a Slavonic People's social club, and a Serbian Reading Room in the 1890s.[22]

In 1881, a similar Serbian-Montenegrin Benevolent Society was organized in Chicago. The San Francisco society corresponded with the society being formed in Chicago, and there is some indication at the initial stage of its organization that the Chicago Serbian Society was considered a branch of the San Francisco organization.[23] The Chicago society was reorganized in 1894 and still exists to this day.[24] The origins of the membership and nature of the activities of both societies were almost identical. The Serbian-Montenegrin Society in Chicago had its roots in a Serbian social club and patriotic organization that had been organized in Chicago, in 1878, at the close of the Bosnian-Hercegovinian Crisis and Serbian and Montenegrin Wars against the Ottomans. In 1892 a Serbian journal in Zagreb reported:

> Most of our Serbs are in the large and wealthy city of Chicago and in San Francisco, the major city of the state of California. In Chicago they have their Serbian Orthodox parish, their church and their priest by the name of Firmilian Dražić, a well-known Serb. In San Francisco Serbs are most numerous and they have their Serbian-Montenegrin Benevolent Society, which has its Serbian flag, its seal, its laws, and its Serbian celebrations and other institutions.[25]

Another Serbian benevolent society was established in the gold country in 1893. The Serbian Benevolent Society of Angels Camp, California, a town made famous by Mark Twain in, "The Celebrated Jumping Frog of Calaveras County," organized a number of branches in other areas, the first of which was founded in Jackson, California, at about the time the St. Sava Serbian Orthodox Church was built.[26] In the early 1900s the Serbian Benevolent Society in Angels Camp had three branches, in addition to the main lodge, and about 300 members by origin from Boka, Montenegro, Hercegovina, and Serbia.[27]

In 1903, the Serbian Benevolent Society of Angels Camp joined the Serbian Society *Jedinstvo*, the reorganized Serbian-Montenegrin Benevolent Society of Chicago, in one of the early Serbian national fraternal federations in the United States. The First Serbian Benevolent Federation (*Prvi Srpski Bratski Dobrotvorni Savez*) was sometimes known as the "Hercegovinian Federation" due to the large proportion of its members that originated from Hercegovina.[28] It was also called the "Chicago Federation." In 1902 the Serbian Society *Jedinstvo* [Unity] in Chicago corresponded with the Serbian-Montenegrin Literary and Benevolent Society of San Francisco, and asked them to join the newly emerging federation, but the San Francisco society refused.[29] In 1904 a branch of the Chicago Federation, and a direct branch of the Serbian Benevolent Society of Angels Camp was organized in San Francisco, the Serbian Benevolent Society *Zmaj*. The Serbian Benevolent Society *Zmaj* quickly grew to a size of close to 200 members, about two-thirds of whom were natives of Hercegovina.[30]

In the formative years of the Serbian organizations in America, the regional origins of the immigrants were extremely influential in determining their associational affiliates. In the Far West most of the immigrants were natives of Boka, Montenegro, and Hercegovina, regions that are close to one another geographically, enthnographically, and historically. Yet these regions were also the Serbian areas where tribal and clan relations were strongest and longest lasting. Regionalism even had the consequence of the establishment of separate Bokelian, Montenegrin, and Hercegovinian societies in some parts of the American West.[31] Where the formation of separate societies did not take place many of the immigrants fought within the societies for control on the basis of their regional origins.[32]

The Serbian-Montenegrin Literary and Benevolent Society of San Francisco had been founded primarily by immigrants from Boka Kotorska. In the first twenty-five years of its existence, the Serbs from Boka remained the dominant element in the society, although, throughout this period the number of members from Hercegovina kept growing. In the 1880s and 1890s two Hercegovinians were elected to terms as President of the Serbian-Montenegrin Literary and Benevolent Society. However the election for the board in 1894, when a Hercegovinian won, was reported to be very bitter, and characterized by a good deal of name calling and insults.[33] A Hercegovinian could not have won at this time solely on the basis of the Hercegovinian vote.

Other issues were also at hand, but regionalism did play a significant role in the disputes between the immigrants. When the Hercegovinian, Petar Vukanovich, won in 1894, the other Hercegovinians all gathered together to celebrate his victory.[34] The Serbian Benevolent Society *Zmaj* was largely Hercegovinian from its inception. Some of the members of *Zmaj* were also members of the Serbian-Montenegrin Literary and Benevolent Society. Other members of this society had been in California for years without joining the Serbian-Montenegrin Society.

In 1907, the national convention of the First Serbian Fraternal Benevolent Federation was held in Los Angeles. But in 1909, when this federation had reached a peak of about 4,000 members, the federation was disbanded, and a number of its branches joined the newly organized Federation of United Serbs—"Concord" (*Savez Sjedinjenih Srba-Sloga*). At this time, the Serbian Benevolent Society *Zmaj* of San Francisco merged with the Serbian-Montenegrin Literary and Benevolent Society.[35] After the merger the Serbian-Montenegrin Literary and Benevolent Society numbered over 600 members, the majority of whom were natives of Hercegovina.[36] One of the main causes for the decline of regionalism among the Serbs in America was Austria-Hungary's annexation of the provinces of Bosnia and Hercegovina in 1908. This event shocked and united the Serbian immigrants. It also made them forget many of their regional and clannish squabbles and disputes. The annexation provoked intense patriotic and nationalistic feelings in Serbia and the other South Slav lands, the echoes of which were heard among the immigrant Serbs in America. During the crisis of 1908 the Serbs came close to war with Austria-Hungary, and many of them now realized that an eventual conflict was probably inevitable. Patriotic, physical culture, and cultural organizations in the Serbian lands became centers of national agitation. Almost immediately similar organizations and branches of the organizations in Serbia were formed among the Serbs in the United States.

Aside from regionalism, conflicts among the Serbian immigrants in the San Francisco Bay Area were often based on personal jealousies, and on dynastic rivalries in Serbia and Montenegro.[37] A few Serbs from Serbia, and particularly Montenegro, fled to the United States due to their opposition to the governments in powers. Although Serbian nationalism and pan-Slavism appeared to be the dominant trend among the immigrants, underneath the surface were rivalries between and in opposition to the Petrović and Obrenović dynasties.

After the last Obrenović ruler was assassinated in 1903, and Petar Karadjordjević ascended to the throne, Serbia began to pursue an aggressive foreign policy and a democratic domestic policy. Serbia increasingly became a beacon for Serbs throughout the Serbian lands, as well as in the diaspora. This factor, together with the above mentioned annexation of Bosnia and Hercegovina and the rising tide of Serbian immigration to America, did much to accelerate the expansion of Serbian national organizations in the San Francisco Bay Area in the early part of the twentieth century.

At the turn of the century the first Serbian-American women's society was organized in San Francisco, and this organization was responsible for the establishment of the first Serbian school in America. After the San Francisco earthquake and fire in 1906 the Serbian school was discontinued since the disaster had dispersed the Serbian children all over the city.[38]

In 1902, a cultural, athletic, and social organization, the Serbian Club was founded in San Francisco. A number of similar Serbian Clubs were later organized in other colonies such as Fresno, California, and Butte, Montana. The San Francisco Serbian Club was always one of the leading organizations of its type in America.[39] This club would play a critically important role in the years of the Balkan Wars and World War I when it was transformed into the Serbian *Sokol* [Falcon] organization.

The dispersal of the San Francisco Serbian colony, following the earthquake and fire of 1906, brought about a substantial growth in the size of the Serbian community in Oakland. With this growth came the formation of two Serbian Benevolent Societies in the East Bay city, the Serbian Benevolent Society *Zora*, which was largely Hercegovinian and Bokelian, and the Serbian Benevolent Society *Zeta*, which was Montenegrin.

Earlier, in 1906, Serbian leaders in the San Francisco Bay Area had bemoaned the divisions in the local community, and called for the formation of a broader national, economic, and patriotic organization.[40] The result of these pleas was the formation of the Serbian National Fund in San Francisco, an organization that in its day was considered one of the most progressive organizations to be formed among the Serbs in America.[41] The Serbian National Fund of San Francisco was organized in 1907 on the eve of the Annexation Crisis. The Serbian National Fund was sponsored jointly by the Serbian Club, the Serbian-Montenegrin Literary and Benevolent Society, the

Serbian Benevolent Society *Zmaj* and other local Serbian organizations in the San Francisco Bay Area. The goal of the organization was to open schools and libraries, and support poorer Serbs in many regions of the Serbian homeland, particularly in the southern regions that still belonged to the Ottoman Empire. The Serbian National Fund sent thousands of dollars to the Circle of Serbian Sisters in Belgrade, Serbian schools in Macedonia, the *Privrednik* Society in Zagreb, *Prosveta* in Sarajevo, *Zora* in Dubrovnik, and the Serbian National Defense in Belgrade.[42] The intention of the founders of this organization was to have it serve as the central patriotic, cultural, and educational institution among the Serbs in America. The founders saw the need for an organization with much purer political-economic purposes than those stated by the Serbian mutual-aid societies.[43] For a number of reasons, including the inability of the Serbian National Fund to gain any significant following in the Eastern and Midwestern United States, the organization never quite fulfilled its goals.

Thus, in conclusion, the Serbian mutual-aid societies in the United States were the first and most important organizations from which stemmed all future religious, cultural, and political organizations. The Serbian communities in America, with their modest Serbian organizations, awakened Serbian national consciousness even where it had not previously existed. In the course of the development of these organizations, provincial allegiances became secondary to Serbian national unity.

NOTES

1. Anton Ssambuck, "Slavonic Mutual and Benevolent Society" in V. Meler, *The Slavonic Pioneers of California*, p. 38.

2. Rade Petrović, *Nacilonalno Pitanje*.

3. Eterovich, "First Serbian Pioneers," p. 48.

4. Eterovich, pp. 48–49.

5. *Srbsko-Dalmatinski Magazin*, XXVIII, 1869, pp. 192–196.

6. Sebastian Dabovich, "The Orthodox Church in California," *Russian Orthodox Messenger*, II, 1897–1898, 2.

7. *Sloboda*, 16 August 1893, p. 2. and *Srbin-Amerikanac*, 22 December, 1893.

8. *Sloboda*, 3 May L894 and *Srbin-Amerikanac*, 29 December 1894.

9. *Sloboda*, 14 June 1894.

10. Vladimir Popović, *Život i Rad Srpsko-Crnogorskog Liter-arnog i Dobrotvornox Drustva u San Francisku Prilikom 25 Godišnjice* (Oakland: Srpska Nezavisnost, 1905).

11. Ibid.

12. *Srbin-Amerikanac*, 25 August 1893, p. 1. *Sloboda*, 5 September 1893.

13. Petrović, "Djelovanje Dubrovackog Odbora za Pomaganje Hercegovackih Ustanika, 1875–1878," *Godisnjak Drustva Istoricara Bosne i Hercegovine*, Sarajevo, X, 1959, pp. 221–245.

14. Jovan Skerlić, *Omladina i Njena Knjizevnost, 1848–1871* (Beograd, 1906).

15. Kosta N. Milutinović, "Crna Gora i Primorje u Omaladin-skom Pokretu," *Istorijski Zapisi*, 6, knj. 9, January-February 1953, 1–46.

16. *Sloboda*, 17 February 1896.

17. Pero Slepcević, *Srbi u Americi: Beleske o niehovostanju radu i nacionalnog vrednosti* (Geneva, 1917), p. 43.

18. *Glas Crnogoraca*, XVII, 1888, 38, p. 3, *Srpska Nezavisnost*, 4, 1888, 65, p. 3, and *Zastava*, XXIX, 1894, 114, p. 2.

19. Slepčević, p. 43.

20. Popović, p. 28.

21. Slepčević, p. 43.

22. Branko Lazarević, "Jugoslovenske Potporne Organizacije u Americi," *Nova Evropa*, No. 1, 1921, p. 16.

23. P. Slepcević, *Srbi u Americi*, p. 44. see also *Srbin-Amerikanac*, 3 November 1893, p. 3. The article in *Srbin-Amerikanac* claims that the Chicago society was in fact a branch of the San Francisco society, and that in the first few years of its existence the two societies corresponded by mail and had the same finances. This relationship was said to last for only a year or two.

24. United Serbian Society, *100th Anniversary Booklet*, (Chicago: 17 October 1981).

25. Sima Lukin Lazić, "Nesto iz Amerike za Srpkinje," *Srborbran Illustrovani Kalendar* (Zagreb, 1983), pp. 89–92.

26. *Sloboda*, 22 June 1896, p. 2. The St. Sava Society in Jackson was organized with an initial membership of seventy.

27. *Sloboda*, 1 October 1903.

28. Slepčević, *Srbi u Americi*, p. 44.

29. Slepčević, *Srbi u Americi*, p. 45. See also Popović, *Život i Rad*.

30. Membership rolls of the Serbian Benevolent Society *Zmaj*, 1904–1909.

31. Slepčević, *Srbi u Americi*, pp. 50–52. In Montana separat· Bokelian, Montenegrin, and Hercegovinian organizations were forme i in the towns of Butte and Anaconda. The Butte, Montana, Serbi,.n colony was one of the largest in the West in the 1900s. It wa; a major center for Montenegrin and Hercegovinian social, benevolent, and political activities.

32. Djordjije D. Pejović, *Iseljavanje Crnogoraca u XIX Vijeka* (Titograd, 1962), p. 393.

33. *Srbin-Amerikanac*, 22 October and 22 December 1893.

34. *Srbin-Amerikanac*, 29 December 1893.

35. *Call*, 22 December 1909, 1, p. 7.

36. Slepčević, *Srbi u Americi*, p. 43.

37. *Srbin-Amerikanac*, 21 August 1896.

38. Bishop Firmilian, "Prve Parohijske Škole u Americi," *Kalendar Srpske Pravoslavne Crkve u Sjedinjenim Dr zavama i Kanade*, 1980, pp. 65–67. See also Slepčević, *Srbi u Americi*, pp. 66–67.

39. Slepčević, *Srbi u Americi*, p. 68.

40. "Udruzimo se," *Sloboda*, 13 March 1906, p. 1.

41. Slepčević, *Srbi u Americi*, p. 70. See also C. Pavić, "Srbi i Srpske Organizacije v Americi," *Ujedinjeno Srpstvo Kalendar* (1911), pp. 117–156.

42. Slepčević, p. 70.

43. Pavić, pp. 117–156.

PART IV

THE BALKANS AND EASTERN EUROPE IN THE TWENTIETH CENTURY

THE FAILURE OF BRITISH POLICY IN THE BALKANS IN THE WINTER OF 1914–1915 AND ITS IMPACT ON THE BRITISH WAR EFFORT

Lynn H. Curtright

By the end of 1914 the slaughter underway in the trenches of the Western Front had become obvious to the men who governed Great Britain. It was therefore natural that many of Britain's leaders should propose a return to Britain's traditional strategy of secondary operations in alternative theaters, especially those which could make use of British seapower and draw German troops away from the Western Front. In the last week of December three such schemes were addressed to Prime Minister Herbert Asquith. They came from Winston Churchill, the First Lord of the Admiralty, Colonel Maurice Hankey, the Secretary to the War Council, and David Lloyd George, Chancellor of the Exchequer.[1]

Churchill proposed a scheme taken from the secret files of the Admiralty. Making use of her great navy, Britain was to seize the German island of Borkum, invade Schleswig-Holstein, take the Kiel Canal, win over neutral Denmark, and open the Baltic to allow Russian troops to be transported from Russia and landed ninety miles from Berlin.[2] This scheme had the immediate support of the First Sea Lord, Lord John Fisher, who had been a participant in the initial drawing of the plan back in 1906.

Hankey proposed the employment of British naval and military power against the Turks, who had joined the war on the side of Germany and Austria. He suggested that, rather than attacking Germany directly, Germany could perhaps be struck most effectively and with the most lasting results through her allies, and particularly through Turkey. Hankey believed that an Allied campaign against the Turks would bring the previously hesitant Balkan neutrals to join in the Allied cause.

He summed up his argument:

> It is presumed that in a few months time we could, without
> endangering the position in France, devote three army corps
> . . . to a campaign in Turkey. . . . This force, in con-
> junction with Greece and Bulgaria, ought to be sufficient to
> capture Constantinople. . . . If Russia . . . could simultane-
> ously combine with Serbia and Romania in an advance into
> Hungary, the complete downfall of Austria-Hungary could
> simultaneously he secured.[3]

Lloyd George, for his part, proposed that an expeditionary force
be sent to the port of Salonika in Greece, where the Vardar River flows
from Serbia into the Aegean Sea. Through Salonika British troops
could most easily bolster Serbia and attack Austria. In addition, as
Hankey had, Lloyd George thought that the establishment of a British
presence in the region would ease pressure on Russia and bring at least
some of the neutral Balkan states to join in the Allied cause.

As the front that would develop would be much too lengthy for
the Austrians to hold, Lloyd George optimistically forecast that the
Germans would be compelled to either divert German armies from
other fronts or abandon Austria to its fate, leaving Germany open to
attack from the south.[4]

As Asquith considered the three proposals, alarming and significant news arrived from both the Balkans and Russia. Telegrams
from Serbia and Bulgaria predicted a renewed Austrian attack on
the Serbs, this time with the aid of German troops. It was believed
in Serbia that a force of 240,000 enemy troops was already massing
on the Austro-Serbian frontier.[5] More important in the minds of the
War Council, however, was a telegram from the British Ambassador
at Petrograd. He reported that the Turks were seriously threatening
the Russian forces in the Caucasus, and that the Grand Duke had
asked if it would be possible for Lord Horatio Kitchener, the Secretary of State for War, to arrange for

> a demonstration of some kind against the Turks elsewhere,
> either by naval or ground forces, and to spread reports which
> would cause the Turks, who he thought very liable to go off
> on a tangent, to withdraw some of the forces now acting in
> the Caucasus, and thus ease the position of Russia.[6]

In response to this urgent appeal, the Foreign Office telegraphed
to Petrograd on 3 January a promise to help the Russians by making
a demonstration of some kind against Turkey. The telegram was

actually drafted at the War Office by Kitchener himself. By that date the Turkish offensive was already collapsing, however, and the Turks were routed by the Russians on 4 January and forced to retreat. The Grand Duke failed, however, to inform London of this turn of events.[7]

Kitchener's fear of Russian collapse moved him to accept, at least partially, Hankey's proposed offensive against Turkey. He was not ready to divert British troops from the Western Front, however, nor was he willing to send yet-untried divisions to a new theater. He therefore wrote to Churchill, asking if there were any possibility of a naval action against Turkey that would prevent the Turks from sending more troops to the Caucasus. Kitchener added his own view that the only place that a demonstration might have an effect would be at the Dardanelles.[8] Churchill responded by telegraphing Vice Admiral Sackville Carden, the commander of the Anglo-French squadrons in the eastern Mediterranean, asking the question: "Do you consider the forcing of the Dardanelles by ships alone a practicable operation ?"[9]

Lord Fisher, meanwhile, had come to support Hankey's scheme over that of Churchill. He wrote to Churchill on 3 January detailing how, while the fleet forced the Dardanelles, British, Greek, and Bulgarian troops would move against Turkey, and the Serbians, Russians and Romanians would march on Austria-Hungary.[10]

Vice Admiral Carden's reply to Churchill's inquiry into the possibility of an all-naval attack at the Dardanelles arrived at the Admiralty on 5 January. In his telegram Carden cautiously reported that the Dardanelles might be forced by extended operations with a large number of ships.[11]

Churchill later claimed in *World Crisis* that he read Carden's telegram at a meeting of the War Council later that afternoon, and Martin Gilbert repeats this claim in his biography of the First Lord.[12] The War Council, however, held no meeting on that date. It was not until 7 January that the War Council met to consider the various alternative campaigns. On the day before the meeting Churchill telegraphed Carden requesting a detailed plan for an all-naval attack at the Dardanelles.[13]

The War Council met on 7 January to consider the proposed campaigns for 1915. But as long as the members of the Government disagreed as to which course to pursue and Field Marshal Sir John French, the commander-in-chief of the British Expeditionary Force in France, opposed all far-off operations, it remained doubtful whether any of the alternative theaters would be adopted. Kitchener criticized a proposal by French which called for the employment of fifty battalions of Territorials in an advance on Zeebrugge in Belgium. After long discussions, the War Council agreed to reject the plan, "as the advantages would not be commensurate with the heavy losses involved." The meeting would then turn to the consideration of the three alternative proposals. The War Council of 7 January dealt only with Churchill's proposed invasion of Schleswig-Holstein, however. After the briefest of discussions the War Council agreed to the plan in principle, subject to the feasibility of the scheme when worked out in detail. Consideration of the remaining proposals was left for the following day.[14]

The War Council of 8 January opened with Kitchener expressing his fear of a fresh German offensive in the west, but the meeting moved directly to the discussion of the proposed eastern operations. Lloyd George was the first to speak. Kitchener then read a letter from Sir John French which stated that Lloyd George's scheme was the least objectionable. Kitchener followed, however, by giving the results of a preliminary examination by the War Office which gave preference to Hankey's proposal for operations against Turkey, specifically, an attack at the Dardanelles. Kitchener expressed the opinion that 150,000 men would be sufficient to capture the Dardanelles but reserved final approval until completion of further studies. Hankey recorded, "Mr. Lloyd George expressed surprise at the lowness of this figure." Further consideration of proposed operations was left for the next meeting.[15]

Kitchener notified French on the following day of the War Council's decision against the Field Marshal's Zeebrugge scheme, and added:

> It was thought that, after another failure by Germany to force the lines of defense held by the French Army and yours, the military situation in France and Flanders might conceivably develop into one of stalemate. . . . In these circumstances it was considered desirable to find some other theater . . . where operations against the enemy might lead to more decisive results.[16]

To many in England this condition of stalemate was already obvious.

Sir John French arrived in London three days later to attend the War Council of 13 January. Because of the Field Marshal's presence, the first matter to be brought before the War Council was a re-examination of the Zeebrugge offensive. Kitchener agreed that all necessary arrangements should be made, but he argued that final decision should be postponed until February. The War Council then moved on to consider the proposed operations in Turkey and the Balkans. It was at this moment that Churchill broke the news that he had received from Vice Admiral Carden the previous day. Carden now claimed that by systematic destruction of the Dardanelles fortifications, the navy could make its way to Constantinople without the aid of troops. This prospect of reducing Turkey without the aid of ground forces swung the War Council to accepting the venture.[17] As the official military history of the Dardanelle's campaign states:

> Here was the suggestion of a captivating enterprise, which apparently required no troops, which apparently was approved by the Admiralty experts, and which called only for vessels surplus to naval requirements elsewhere.[18]

The War Council therefore concluded that the Admiralty should "prepare for a naval expedition in February to bombard and take the Gallipoli Peninsula, with Constantinople as its objective."

The discussion next turned to the Balkan scheme proposed by Lloyd George. In response to questioning by the Chancellor, French answered that complete success against the Germans in the western theater was possible but not probable. He further stated that, if the German lines in France could not be broken, it would then be desirable to seek other theaters, such as the Balkans. Churchill, however, again objected to the use of troops in southeastern Europe until he was satisfied that there was nothing they could do in the north. Lloyd George then repeated his earlier argument that steps should be taken, though not irrevocable ones, for a campaign in the Balkans. The War Council agreed and concluded, "that a Sub-Committee of the Committee of Imperial Defense be appointed to deal with this aspect of the situation."[19]

Lloyd George's proposed campaign in the Balkans appears to have gained a great deal of support in the week which followed. After a Cabinet meeting on of January, Asquith informed the king:

> The position of Servia in view of the imminent renewal of the Austrian attack with German cooperation was anxiously considered, the Cabinet being strongly of opinion that a collapse of Servian resistance would have a most damaging effect on the cause of the Allies.

He went on to state that all had agreed on the importance of bringing in Greece and Romania.[20]

Asquith wrote to Grey on the following day, "I think—and Kitchener agrees—that we ought to give up all our sideshows . . . if we can give effective help to Servia." He also asked the Foreign Secretary if it would be possible to send an urgent message to both Greece and Romania asking them to go to the aid of the Serbs.[21]

On 22 January Alexandre Millerand, the French minister of war who had come to London to discuss the deployment of Britain's new armies, dined at Kitchener's house along with Asquith, Edward Grey, Lloyd George, Churchill, and Lord Richard Haldane, the Lord Chancellor and former Secretary of State for War. The Prime Minister recorded in his diary later that night:

> Of course I put to him [Millerand] strongly the Balkan situation and the irreparable disaster which could be involved in the crushing of Serbia.

Asquith also noted that after dinner Lloyd George and Grey had pressed the point.[22] We should notice that this was the first mention of active support for the Salonika expedition on the part of the Foreign Secretary.

Negotiations between London and the Greeks, meanwhile, were pressed forward. On 23 January the Foreign office instructed Sir Francis Elliot, the British Minister at Athens, to deliver a communication to Prime Minister Eleutherios Venizelos of Greece which promised territorial gains on the coast of Asia Minor in return for Greek intervention.[23] Venizelos' official reply, dated 25 January, was given to Grey by the Greek minister at London on 27 January. The text specified the need to determine the attitudes of Bulgaria and Romania before Greece could intervene in the Allied cause. The reply alluded, however, to the effect which a small contingent of Entente troops would have on the attitude of the Bulgarians. The Greek minister said that if even 5,000 British troops were landed at Salonika it would assure that Bulgaria would not intervene on the side of the Central Powers.[24]

Elliot telegraphed from Athens on 27 January that he had met with Venizelos that morning and discussed the possible cooperation of Allied troops with the Greek Army. Elliot had suggested that with Entente troops it would not be necessary for Greece to await the entry of Romania into the war. Venizelos had disagreed, He maintained that Greece would require an agreement with the Romanians, concluded by formal treaty, that if Greece went to the assistance of Serbia and were attacked by Bulgaria, Romania could attack the latter. This assurance was in addition to his requiring two British or French army corps to cooperate with the Greek Army.[25]

On 28 January there was a meeting of the subcommittee which had been called for in the conclusions of the War Council of 13 January to determine where troops might best be employed in future. Kitchener chaired the meeting and opened by reading a staff examination which favored Salonika. After lengthy discussion it was agreed

> to ask the Prime Minister to assemble an immediate meeting of the War Council for the purpose of discussing whether instructions should not be sent to Sir John French informing him that the Zeebrugge offensive was not to be undertaken, and that the reinforcements intended to enable him to undertake this operation would not be sent.[26]

Asquith therefore called a meeting of the War Council for 6:30 that evening. Kitchener opened the meeting with a summary of the subcommittee's discussions. The War Council approved the sending of British troops to Salonika. But there remained the task of properly informing Greece, France, and Field Marshal French of their decision. The War Council decided that Churchill should visit the Field Marshal and Lloyd George should visit Paris right away, while Grey would be left to contact Venizelos at the appropriate time.[27]

French was the first to be informed of the proposed expedition, when Churchill visited him on 29 January. The Field Marshal considered the War Council's decision and on the following morning told Churchill that he absolutely opposed it. Churchill, unwilling to accept defeat, proposed a compromise. As French recorded on 30 January:

> We talked again before he left in the evening and he promised that in any case no change should be made in the program of sending the troops on the dates they were to arrive, but he told me that when they were in this country I should have to be prepared for the possibility of the Government ordering the divisions away . . .[28]

Lloyd George left for Paris on the morning of 1 February. Since Millerand's departure from London, nothing had been heard from Paris as to their reaction to the proposed campaign. Upon his return to London, Lloyd George wrote to Grey:

> When I first mentioned it to the [French] Minister of Finance

I found that Millerand had never repeated to his colleagues
that the suggestion of an expedition to Salonika had been
made to him while he was in England.[29]

Lloyd George told the same to his secretary, Frances Stevenson, and
to Lord Riddell, the liaison officer between the Government and the
press.[30] Hankey claimed in his own work, *The Supreme Command,
1914–1918*, that Millerand had never reported the Salonika proposal
to his government, and historians have accepted this view.[31] Yet the
French sources disagree. Raymond Poincaré, the president of the
republic, recorded in his diary on 26 January that Millerand had told
the cabinet that day of the British plan to send a division to the aid
of Serbia, and Aristide Briand, the minister of justice, recorded the
same.[32]

When Lloyd George first met with Poincaré on the morning of
3 February, he put forth the British plan to send troops to Salonika.
Poincaré responded that the French Government had earlier considered a military expedition of about 400,000 men, French and British,
to Salonika as a diversion to lessen German pressure elsewhere. The
objections of Field Marshal Joseph Joffre, however, had killed the
proposal.[33]

The French government met on the following morning to discuss
the plan. They approved in principle that an army corps should be
sent to Salonika for the purpose of assisting Serbia, and that it ought
to be made up of one British and one French division. It was agreed,
however, that the French contingent could not be spared during the
coming three weeks as a German attack in France was anticipated
during that period. But they concurred that preparations for the
expedition should be made immediately so that troops might be sent
the moment they could be spared. The council further agreed that as
long a Britain sent the promised four divisions to France, they had no
objections to her sending an army corps to Salonika at once, though
they would prefer that France be represented in the expeditionary
force if Joffre could spare the troops for that purpose.[34]

Lloyd George took the opportunity, on his way home from Paris,
to visit the headquarters of Sir John French. In the very long letter
which the Chancellor addressed to Grey upon his return to England,
he reported that the Field Marshal was at first hostile to the idea of
an expeditionary force being sent to the Balkans, "not in principle,
but on the ground that he could not spare the troops." French had
asked to be invited to the next meeting of the War Council in order

to discuss the project. Lloyd George urged in his letter to the Foreign Secretary that the Prime Minister invite the Field Marshal.[35] French wrote to Kitchener after the meeting with Lloyd George, however, that he did not agree with the proposed operation. He argued,

> I find it very difficult to understand why the appearance of British and French soldiers in this part of the world should have so great an influence, and, unless something very decisive in that way will be gained by such a move, it appears to me to be a strategical mistake.[36]

At the time of Lloyd George's return from Paris, he was not the only member of the Cabinet to be urging quick action in the Balkans. Churchill, for his part, wrote to Asquith on 7 February:

> More than three weeks ago you told me of the vital importance of Servia. Since then nothing has been done, and nothing of the slightest reality is being done. Time is passing. You may not yet feel the import of the projectile. But it has already left the gun and is travelling along its road towards you. Three weeks hence you, Kitchener, Grey will all be facing a disastrous situation in the Balkans. . . . It will be beyond your power to retrieve it . . . unless we are prepared to run a risk and play a stake, the Balkan situation is finished totally for us.[37]

Back in Paris, meanwhile, Poincaré noted momentous news in his diary on 7 February. He wrote:

> Millerand has seen Joffre again and has told him of our decision in regard to an expedition to Serbia; the Generalissimo has allowed himself to be won over.[38]

Theophile Delcasse, the foreign minister of France, and Jules Cambon, the French ambassador to Britain, met with Grey, Asquith, Kitchener, and Churchill at Grey's house in London on 8 February. Delcasse did not, as Lloyd George had feared, prove uncooperative. It was agreed at their meeting that the situation in Serbia was urgent and that she should be promised two divisions, one French and one British, to be sent to Salonika as soon as possible.[39]

With the expedition to Salonika approved by the French, therefore, the War Council of 9 February was assembled for the sole purpose of discussing the Balkan operations. Grey opened the meeting with a report of his conversations with Delcasse. As a result of their discussion, he said, a telegram had been sent to Petrograd asking if Russia would be willing to join in the expedition, contributing a third division. The Russian reply, he said, had been that no infantry troops were available but that she would send a thousand Cossacks.

Grey also reported Delcasse's full agreement that the British and French should each send a division to Salonika. Kitchener then said that the troops would be so placed as to prevent Bulgaria from attacking Greece once the Greeks had gone to the aid of Serbia. He still hoped to put the main burden of saving Serbia on Greece. He proposed that the Twenty-Ninth Division, the last remaining regular division in England, be sent to Salonika.

Asquith reminded his colleagues of the political importance of the Salonika expedition and explained how the proposed diversion would bring in Greece and Romania, and neutralize Bulgaria. Haldane added that Germany would be forced to transfer troops to that theater, and French agreed that the effect would be almost decisive if those results were achieved.

As the discussion drew to a close, Grey proposed to send a telegram to Sir Francis Elliot at Athens to be presented to the Greek government. He suggested the following:

> Every obligation of honor and interest makes it necessary
> that Greece should go to the assistance of Serbia. In order
> to enable them to do so effectively and to secure their com-
> munications, Great Britain, France and Russia each propose
> to send a division to Salonica.[40]

The proposed telegram would ask Greece to go to the aid of Serbia while the Entente Powers would merely guard Greek communications. Greece would also be asked to declare herself at once, and prior to the dispatch of Allied troops. Churchill therefore argued that he thought it unlikely that the proposed terms would be sufficient to induce the Greeks to take part in the war. He was overruled, however. Grey telegraphed the proposed communication to Athens that evening.[41]

Important and disconcerting news arrived from Athens on 10 February. Elliot telegraphed in response to Grey's communication:

> I fear that if the matter is put as an intention to send French
> and British troops to Salonica, it will give great offence.[42]

He referred the Foreign Secretary to his earlier telegram of 27 January in which he had reported:

While recognizing moral effect upon Bulgaria of presence of the British and French troops, he [Venizelos] did not think that it would be a sufficient guarantee against Bulgarian attack on Greek flank, which would be disastrous.[43]

That same telegram had stated that Venizelos would only be satisfied by a formal treaty with Romania. That treaty would have to specify that if Greece went to the aid of Serbia and were attacked by Bulgaria, Romania would attack the latter. Elliot now suggested how the Greek Prime Minister, whom he knew so well, should be approached is Grey truly wanted to save the situation in the Balkans. Elliot argued along the same lines as Churchill had at the War Council. Elliot proposed that Greece should be allowed to follow the Allied lead rather than be told to take the lead herself. Greece would consent to the use of Salonika as a base for Allied assistance to Serbia. Allied assistance to Serbia would, in turn, have a great effect on the attitudes of Romania and Bulgaria, as it would on the king and army of Greece. The permitted use of Salonika by the Allies, moreover, might well bring the Central Powers to declare war on Greece, thereby solving the matter in the Allies' favor without further ado.[44]

But once again Grey ignored sound advice, closing his mind to any scheme that failed to guarantee in advance the active participation of the Greek army within Serbia, and he would promise no more than protection of Greek communications in return. He therefore telegraphed to Elliot on 11 February:

> The proposal is made on the assumption that Greece, by every obligation of honor and interest, must send help to Serbia in a very short time. Unless Greece is prepared to do this, there can be no question of British and French troops being sent to operate alone without participation of Greece. . . . Matter is urgent, and you should submit it to Venizelos directly your French colleague is instructed, and let us have a reply.[45]

Elliot could not have been but greatly distressed by the finality of Grey's reply. It is never easy to be an ambassador in disagreement with the Foreign Secretary, but Elliot had worked long and hard for a goal that seemed finally within grasp, a goal that was about to be thrown away by a superior who was refusing to listen to his representative's sound advice.

When Elliot's French colleague received his instructions on 15

February, the two western ministers presented Grey's communication of 9 February to Venizelos. As Elliot had predicted in his telegram of 10 February, and as Churchill had foreseen at the War Council of 9 February, the Greek Prime Minister rejected the terms of the communication as insufficient to secure the safety of his country. Elliot telegraphed London that Venizelos had rejected the initiative "at once without referring to the King or the General Staff." The Prime Minister had, Elliot stated:

> again used language reported in my telegram No. 54 of 27th January, and said cooperation of Greece was out of the question unless Romania joined, not only by attacking Austria in Transylvania, but in conjunction with the Greek forces.

Venizelos had told Elliot that he considered the presence of the British and French divisions to be entirely insufficient to protect the Greek flank from the Bulgarians, and he had protested that for Greece to join Serbia under such conditions would be suicide.[46]

Elliot's blaming of Grey for this fiasco can be seen in a second telegram of that day to the Foreign Secretary. He reported that Venizelos had told the Serbian minister at Athens that he had informed the king of the Allies' *demarche* and of his reply. The Serbian minister had followed by asking, Elliot recounted, as to "what Venizelos would have said if we had only asked for the free passage for French and British troops," precisely the approach that Elliot had pressed on Grey. "His Excellency [Venizelos] replied," Elliot reported, "That would have been a different matter, (see my telegram No. 1 Private and Secret, of 10th February)." In frustration Elliot concluded, "It might still be worth trying, but I am no longer so sure of a favorable answer."[47] Elliot had diplomatically told his boss, "I told you so!"

Those historians who have criticized Grey on this matter have done so by condemning the communication as ill-timed, as suggested by Hankey in *The Supreme Command*. Hankey wrote that the naval bombardment of the Dardanelles forts was to begin on 15 February, the day of the Allied demarche at Athens, but the operations were delayed until 19 February. He added, "The French Minister at Athens appears to have received his instructions on the 15th, and on that day the message was presented, unaccompanied by the hoped-for news of the naval attack." Hankey therefore concluded: "In the circumstances Venizelos absolutely declined to entertain the idea of

Greek intervention without the collaboration of Romania."[48] But, as we have seen, neither at the War Council nor in the Foreign Office correspendence with Elliot had the two moves been timed to coincide. Elliot had been told by Grey on 9 February, and again on 11 February, to make the communication as soon as his French colleague was similarly instructed, which, presumably, could have been before 15 February. And the Government had known since 10 February that the naval attack would not begin on 15 February.[49] Indeed, Venizelos was well aware of the coming Dardanelles operations. He could easily have delayed his answer, and delayed bringing the matter to King Constantine, until the bombardment had commenced. But he did not. He rejected the communication immediately and without consulting the King.

Yet blame for the failure of the *demarche* must lie with Grey, not for his poor timing, but for his refusal to heed the sound advice of his subordinate at the scene. The resulting consequence of the failure of the approach to Greece is summed up well in the official military history of the Dardanelles campaign, which states, "So the Salonika project had to be dropped, and attention at last became focused on the chances at the Dardanelles."[50]

On the following day, 16 February, the War Council approved the sending of the Twenty-Ninth Division to the Dardanelles.[51] The cancellation of the Salonika expedition had left the Twenty-Ninth Division available for employment in conjunction with the naval attack at the Straits, an operation whose popularity from the start had been based on the assumption that it could be done by ships alone. Gone now, however, were the arguments that no troops could be diverted from the western front. As Churchill later wrote in *World Crisis*:

> Under these influences in less than two months the naval attack, with its lack of certainty but with its limited costs and risks, became subsidiary, and in its place there arose a military development of great magnitude.[52]

Kirchener told the War Council of 19 February that he had changed his mind and that he wished to substitute the Australians and New Zealanders in Egypt for the Twenty-Ninth Division at the Dardanelles.[53] His aversion to sending out the Twenty-Ninth caused the postponement of the plan until he finally relented on 10 March.[54] But the die was cast. The approval of the Salonika expedition proved that British troops could be spared from the Western Front.

Grey's handling of the *demarche* at Athens led to its failure. That failure forced the abandonment of the proposed Salonika expedition. And the abandonment of the Salonika expedition left the Twenty-Ninth Division for use in conjunction with the naval attack at the Dardanelles. One failure was to lead to yet another and far more costly failure. The result was the ill-fated Gallipoli expedition, an expedition which proved to be one of the greatest fiascoes in the history of British arms.

Britain and France only resurrected the plan for a Salonika expedition at the very end of September 1915, when it had become clear the Bulgaria had actively joined with the Central Powers and that a combined German, Austro-Hungarian, and Bulgarian invasion of Serbia was imminent.

By the time the first British and French troops disembarked at Salonika on 5 October 1915, it would be far too late to save Serbia or create an effective Balkan front. Not until September 1918 would Allied forces, who had been sitting in Salonika for almost three years, press northward to play their part in the collapse of the Central Powers.

NOTES

1. Background to this topic, and a more detailed examination of what follows, can be found in the author's *Muddle, Indecision and Setback: British Policy and the Balkan States, August 1914 to the Inception of the Dardanelles Campaign* (Thessaloniki, 1986).

2. Martin Gilbert, ed., *Winston S. Churchill: Companion* (London, 1972), III, pt. I, 343–345: Churchill memorandum, 29 December 1914.

3. [Public Record Office] CAB[inet Records] 37/122/194: Hankey memorandum, 28 December 1914.

4. CAB 34/1/2: Lloyd George memorandum, 1 January 1914.

5. [Public Record Office] F[oreign] O[ffice Records] 371/1/1902 (88480/38540): Sophia (No. 221), 30 December 1914; and FO 371/2249 (1323/1323): Nish (No. 5), 4 January 1915.

6. Gilbert, *Companion*, III, pt. I, 359–360: Petrograd, 1 January 1915.

7. C. F. Aspinall-Oglander, *Military Operations: Gallipoli* (London, 1965), I, 52–53; and Arthur Marder, *From Dreadnought to Scapa Flow: The Royal Navy in the Fisher Era, 1904–1919* (London, 1965), II, 203–204.

8. Gilbert, *Companion*, III, pt. I, 360–361: Kitchener to Churchill, 2 January 1915.

9. Ibid., 367: Churchill to Carden, 3 January 1915.

10. Winston S. Churchill, *The World Crisis* (New York, 1931), 327–328: Fisher to Churchill, 3 January 1915.

11. Aspinall-Oglander, *Military Operations: Gallipoli*, I, 55: Carden to Churchill, 5 January 1915.

12. Churchill, *World Crisis*, 330; and Martin Gilbert, Winston S. Churchill (Boston, 1971), III, 237.

13. Gilbert, *Companion*, III, pt. I, 381: Churchill to Carden, 6 January 1915.

14. CAB 22/1/6: War Council minutes, 7 January 1915.

15. CAB 22/1/7: War Council minutes, 8 January 1915.

16. Ibid.: appendix, Kitchener to French, 9 January 1915.

17. CAB 22/1/S: War Council minutes, 13 January 1915.

18. Aspinall-Oglander, Gallipoli. I, 58.

19. CAB 22/1/8: War Council minutes, 13 January 1915.

20. CAB 41/32/2: Asquith to the King, 21 January 1915.

21. FO 800/1OO: Asquith to Grey, 21 January 1915.

22. H. H. Asquith, *Memories and Reflections, 1852–1927* (Boston, 1932), II, 68–69: diary extract, 22 January 1915.

23. FO 371/2242 (8487/214): to Athens (No. 24), 23 January 1915.

24. FO 371/2242 (11221/214); to Athens (despatch no. 9), 27 January 1915.

25. FO 371/2242 (10474/214): Athens (No. 54), 27 January 1915.

26. CAB 22/1/10: War Council minutes, 28 January 1915, 4:00 P.M.

27. CAB 22/1/11: War Council minutes, 28 January 1915, 6:30 P.M.

28. Gerald French, *The Life of Field-Marshal Sir John French, First Earl of Ypres* (London, 1931), 275–276: John French diary extract, 30 January 1915.

29. [House of Lords Record Office] L[loyd] G[eorge] P[apers] C/4/14/25: Lloyd George to Grey, 7 February 1915.

30. Frances Stevenson, *Lloyd George, a Diary*, A. J. P. Taylor, ed. (New York, 1971), 27 29: diary extract, 8 February 1915; and Lord Riddell, War Diary, 1914–1918 (London, n.d.), 59–62: diary extract, 7 February 1915.

31. Maurice Hankey, *The Supreme Command, 1914–1918* (London, 1961), I, 277.

32. Raymond Poincaré, *The Memoirs of Raymond Poincaré*, translated by George Arthur (Garden City, 1931), IV, 19–20: diary extract, 26 January 1915; and George Suarez, *Briand sa vie, sa oeuvre avec son journal* (Paris, 1939), III, 92: Briand diary extract, 26 January 1915.

33. FO 800/172: Bertie papers, 3 February 1915.

34. FO 800/172: Bertie papers, 4 February 1915; and Poincaré, *Memoirs*, IV, 29–30: diary extract, 4 February 1915.

35. LGP C/4/14/25: Lloyd George to Grey, 7 February 1915.

36. George Arthur, *The Life of Kitchener* (London, 1920), III, 108n.: French to Kitchener, 6 February 1915.

37. Gilbert, *Companion*, III, pt. I, 495–496: Churchill to Asquith, 7 February 1915.

38. Poincaré, *Memoirs*, IV, 31: diary extract, 7 February 1915.

39. Asquith, *Memories and Reflections*, II, 72–73: diary extract, 8 February 1915.

40. CAB 22/1/12: War Council minutes, 9 February 1915.

41. Ibid.; and FO371/2242 (15596/214): to Athens (No. 1), 9 February 1915.

42. SO 371/2242 (15890/214): Athens (No. 1), 10 February 1915.

43. FO 371/2242 (10474/214): Athens (No. 4) 27 January 1915.

44. FO 371/2242 (15890/214): Athens (No. 1), 10 February 1915.

45. FO 371/2242 (15890/114): to Athens, (No. 2), 11 February 1915.

46. FO 371/2242 (17907/214): Athens (No. 2), 1 February 1915.

47. FO 371/1242 (17993/214): Athens (No. 3), 15 February 1915.

48. Hankey, *Supreme Command*, I, 278–279.

49. Asquith, *Memories and Reflections*, II, 74: diary extract, 10 February 1915.

50. Aspinall-Oglander, *Gallipoli*, I, 66–67.

51. CAB 22/1/13: War Council minutes, 16 February 1915.

52. Churchill, *World Crisis*, 364.

53. CAB 22/1/14: War Council minutes, 19 February 1915.

54. CAB 22/1/18: War Council minutes, 10 March 1915.

MY DIPLOMATIC ASSIGNMENT IN BELGRADE

Alex N. Dragnich

My assignment as United States Cultural Attaché in the American Embassy in Belgrade in 1947 was to be the beginning of a long and interesting association with that city. It proved to be the place of many lasting friendships. It was my first on-the-spot study of a communist system in action. It was to be the center of my research into Serbian and Yugoslav history and politics. It was the city to which I returned many times over several decades.

In the pages that follow, I shall limit myself to the years of my diplomatic service—November 1947 to May 1950. Moreover, I can reflect on only a few highlights since I kept no diary of those years. I should note, however, that a few related references to my experiences from those years are the result of information gleaned during subsequent visits to Belgrade.

Upon our arrival, my wife Adele and three small children (Alix aged one, Paul three and George one) were faced with many problems: locating a place to live, finding my place in the Embassy structure, seeking contacts with Yugoslavs—official and unofficial—and related matters.

Once in Belgrade, the most urgent question was finding a place to live, and the Yugoslav authorities were not inclined to help American diplomats in this or in other respects. Before our arrival, the Embassy had asked that we be permitted to occupy the residence of a departing U. S. diplomat, but the Yugoslav foreign office reported that the house had already been assigned to a Yugoslav official. All housing was under government control, and if a diplomat arranged to rent a place from a private person, he or she could not occupy it without foreign office approval.

The first night or two we spent in the Hotel Moscow. After that for a few weeks we had a small apartment in an Embassy building used mainly by a U. S. military team known as the Graves Registration Unit, whose task was to locate the graves of American airmen who had perished in missions over Yugoslav territory so that the remains

could be returned to the United States. The building had a military
mess where we took our meals. This arrangement was particularly
difficult for Adele in trying to take care of three small children, but
soon we found a reasonably comfortable house, with a good walled-in
yard in which the children were to spend many happy days in the
next two and one-half years.

Getting the house, however, was not easy. One of the Embassy
drivers told me that a friend wanted to rent his house to us, and he
arranged a discrete night meeting to see the house. The rent seemed
high but we were willing to pay it. However, the owner (much later
we were to find out that he had merely leased the building) insisted
on payment only in dollars, which was against Yugoslav law. The
next day, I talked with Ambassador Cannon, and he authorized the
finance officer to sell me U. S. currency to pay my first three months
rent. At a secret meeting the next day—I had to be careful that I
was not followed—I gave the money to the owner.

There was still the problem of getting Foreign Office approval.
Embassy officers had told me of several instances where a diplomat
had found housing for rent, but when Foreign Office approval was
requested, the diplomat was told that the house in question was no
longer available. The Yugoslav authorities had taken such houses for
some of their people. Ironically, diplomats were finding housing for
Yugoslav Communist officials! One of the Embassy officers, assistant
military attaché Jack Twombly, advised me to arrange with the owner
to have us move in with his family and have him register us with
the precinct housing office, which was legal. After that, the owner
would move out. As it turned out, the owner's mother ended up
staying with us for a month. We were registered and moved in. Given
our name, I suspect that the local housing office was not aware that
we were diplomats. A few days after we moved in, the Embassy
requested Foreign Office approval, which was given, but not without
an expression of displeasure at the way we had arranged it.

Getting food was not easy. Some basic staples, such as bread and
meat, were picked up by Embassy drivers at the store for diplomats
and delivered to us. We do not know what they may have picked up
and kept for themselves. There was some reason to suspect that some
choice cuts of meat never made it to the house. The local peasant
market had some things (mainly vegetables, eggs, and fruits in season,
and dairy products). We did not use the local dairy products because
in prewar years Yugoslavia had the highest incidence of tuberculosis
in Europe. The Embassy had a few provisions. Unfortunately for us,

the administrative officer had traded most of the powdered milk to another embassy for French wine. Soon after our arrival, we opened an account with Pierce and Pierce of Boston, from which we ordered many grocery items.

During our stay in Belgrade, our children had only powdered milk to drink. In order to make it more palatable, Adele mixed in chocolate syrup. When we were back in the U. S., our dentist proclaimed that our children's teeth were the worst that he had seen. Many years later Adele learned that chocolate in milk destroys much of the calcium.

Fortunately, we enjoyed reasonable good health during our days in Belgrade. Aside from colds and flu, we were not ill. Our son Paul's tonsils were terribly enlarged and he had difficulty in breathing. Because medical services in Belgrade left much to be desired, we decided that Adele should take him to the U. S. Army Hospital in Trieste. The Embassy made the necessary arrangements. Adele and Paul (not yet four) took the eighteen-hour train ride to Trieste, but when they got there the army doctors refused to do anything but emergency surgery, because of a number of polio cases that had occurred.

When they got back, we sought advice concerning local doctors. We made an appointment with one who was highly recommended. He was willing to do the operation, but because medicine had been nationalized he did not have ether for the limited practice he could do in his apartment after his seven to ten hours in a government clinic. We got a can of ether from the Embassy nurse and took Paul to the doctor about 4 P. M. one afternoon. The doctor took us to a small room next to his kitchen. He put Paul in the lap of a teenager sitting in what looked like a dental chair, and told us to sit outside.

In a few minutes (I do not believe it was more than five), he brought Paul out and put him in our laps: fully conscious. He had given Paul a whiff of ether and quickly removed the tonsils. We took Paul home in a car and in a couple of days everything was well. It was a clean tonsillectomy.

Later, in mid-summer 1949, we had a polio scare in Belgrade. A young foreign service officer in our Embassy contracted bulbar polio and died within a short time. No other Americans were afflicted. Beyond a few months, future rental payments could not be made in dollars but in local currency. Subsequently, we learned that our landlords (they had some agricultural acreage) used their resources to open a resort hotel on the Dalmatian coast, only to have it taken over by the government in a nationalization drive in early 1948. They lost everything, even personal clothing that was in some of the rooms.

Both brothers spent time in jail, and the mother was held several months without any charges being made against her. The younger brother was not immediately apprehended (he came to collect the rent several times), and agents, posing as postal employees with a package for him, tried to learn his whereabouts from me, but I "could not" help them. To this day, I do not know what crimes they were charged with having committed.

During orientation sessions in Washington, prior to my departure, I was given information as to what my job was to be. When I asked who my superior would be in the Information and Cultural Section of the Embassy, I was told: "You are it." The Congress had cut the budget sharply (the State Department and the U. S. Information Service—hereafter referred to as USIS—had separate budgets at that time), so that when I arrived I did not have even a secretary. Fortunately, the Embassy had four recently-arrived secretaries and Ambassador Cavendish Cannon assigned one of them, Evelyn Blickensderfer, to me. Subsequently she had a successful career in cultural affairs work, and I would like to think that I helped to launch her on that career. USIS was located in a separate building about one-half mile from the Embassy. To assist me in carrying out information and cultural activites, I had ten local employees. As Yugoslav citizens none of them could have a security clearance. As a matter of fact, I was told that I should regard all of them as willing or unwilling informers.

This was a tense time for all of us, but especially for our local employees. Relations between two countries could hardly have been worse. The previous year the Yugoslavs had shot down two U. S. military planes that had strayed over Yugoslav air space. Following strong U. S. government protests, the Tito regime asked the Embassy to close down USIS. When it was permitted to re-open it was with the proviso that our news bulletin go only to an approved list of government offices, to diplomats, and to foreign newsmen. Moreover, nothing in USIS output for Yugoslavs would be critical of Yugoslavia or its regime. It should be kept in mind that at that time many U. S. publications, especially the news magazines, frequently had anti-communist items in them, some specifically referring to Yugoslavia or its patron, the Soviet Union. At one time I found an insert on world affairs in the magazine *Chemical Engineering* that blasted the Soviet Union and its satellites.

Sensing that our local employees were under a good deal of pressure, I brought them together in my office one afternoon and told them that I was aware of their situation. Moreover, I said that they were not in a position to learn any secrets, and therefore if questioned, "tell them all they want to know."

The next morning I was in the office early, as was my custom, and the only employee who was there was the woman who typed the mimeograph copy of our news bulletin, which had been transmitted via radio during the night. She approached me, and said:

> Mr. Dragnich, with respect to what you said yesterday, I can't start informing. If I did, there would be follow-ups. I might be caught not remembering everything and would be accused of withholding information deliberately. Moreover, at some point I would be asked to do things that I could not do.

Subsequently, after returning to university teaching, I learned how true was her latter statement. One of our employees who succeeded in getting to Israel, later recounted how he had been asked by the secret police, among other things, to steal typewriters from our offices at night. But I am getting way ahead of the story.

To get to work and to social functions, we had to rely on Embassy vehicles and/or our own cars. When my 1947 Ford arrived and was removed from the wooden van (the van made for a play house in the backyard), a designated Embassy employee (local) who had cleared the car through customs, obtained the needed diplomatic license. The license numbers for Western diplomats were in the 100 series. The Soviet camp diplomats had license numbers in the 1 to 99 series. The administrative officer, Robert Clifford, had instructed the Embassy employee to get him license number 33, the year of his Princeton class. The Employee succeeded, but subsequently was instructed by the authorities to get the license plates back, but Clifford would have none of it and told the employee to tell the authorities to go to hell.

Automobile traffic in Belgrade in those days was virtually limited to official Yugoslav and diplomatic vehicles. There were no traffic lights. At the major intersections stood a traffic officer to whom one signaled the desired direction—one toot on the horn for straight ahead, two for right, three for left, and a repeated three toots for a U-turn—followed by his signal to proceed. The city streets were also used by horse and ox-drawn vehicles.

Even with the sparse traffic there were accidents. One night an American soldier assigned to the military attaché's office drove his jeep into a peasant cart and killed the occupant. He was tried and sentenced to eight years in prison. Since he was not a diplomat, the Embassy could do nothing to help him. However, he was released soon after the Stalin-Tito break.

On another night, the Canadian Chargé, a man named Branscombe, hit and killed a Yugoslav Army officer. Since he had diplomatic immunity, the severest possible penalty under international law was to be asked to go home. In this case, however, the Yugoslav authorities asked him not to drive anymore, but to hire a driver.

Because of the strained relations between our two governments, contacts with Yugoslav agencies were limited and those with private Yugoslav citizens risky for them.

Designated Yugoslav officials came to the USIS library frequently, mainly to consult technical literature not available to them elsewhere in Yugoslavia. Some other readers also came, but with trepidation.

On Sundays a Russian émigré employee of ours by the name of Zukov, who was well-versed in music, put on recorded music concerts in the USIS library. These were very popular and a great many young people flocked to them. This irked the authorities, and those agents took a number of the concertgoers into custody. They were questioned and some even held overnight, Some parents came to see me personally and begged me to discontinue the concerts. In any event, the secret police tactics soon reduced our audiences to near zero. We complained to Yugoslav officials who gave us no satisfaction.

The Voice of America (VOA) radio broadcasts to Yugoslavia (as to other countries) were designed to provide listeners with information about U. S. government policies as well as general news. The head of VOA at one time was Charles Thayer, who visited us. He was especially desirous of getting news of certain happenings in Yugoslavia that could be broadcast by VOA as a way of demonstrating to the Yugoslav public that VOA knew what was snowfall. As luck would have it, a week or so later there was a huge snowfall that snarled Belgrade traffic (some 12 inches). As instructed, I immediately dispatched a restricted cable (all cables being signed by the Ambassador), reporting on the snowfall.

The cable caused a certain amount of consternation in the State Department because it was the last cable out of Belgrade before radio traffic was interrupted between Washington and Belgrade. Officers in the Department speculated about what the Ambassador was trying to tell them with that cable about the large snowfall. I listened to VOA broadcasts to Yugoslavia for two nights, but there was nothing about the snowfall!

One interesting aspect of my position was that of facilitating the work of American newsmen, which I welcomed. Among these, the ones I remember best are: syndicated columnist Joseph Alsop; Hamilton Fish Armstrong of Foreign Affairs; Homer Bigert and Gaston Coblentz of the *Herald Tribune*; Cecil Brown, radio commentator; John Boettiger (FDR's son-in-law) of the Seattle Post Intelligencer; Osgood Caruthers of the Associated Press; Edward Korry of United Press; William Nichols of *This Week Magazine*; Cyrus Sulzberger and Meyer Handler of the *New York Times*. After my return to university life, I kept in touch with several of them for a time, notably Alsop, Armstrong, Brown, Caruthers, Korry, and Sulzberger.

During my tour in Belgrade, I had a few brief encounters with Lawrence Durrell, then Press Officer in the British Embassy, and later a world-recognized novelist. Aside from our related professional contacts, we exchanged dinners. His wife at that time was a striking Egyptian woman. He had written some poetry, but I had no idea that he was to become a prolific writer.

Totally unrelated to my work were associations with relatives, mainly uncles and an aunt, as well as some cousins. Most of them I had met on my first trip to Yugoslavia as a graduate student in 1939.

My aunt (Vida Kontich, mother's sister) lived in Belgrade. Earlier she had lived in Montenegro. Her husband died sometime in the 1920s (I believe that he was a World War I veteran), and she was having difficulty rearing her four children. She was able to meet King Alexander on one of his trips to Montenegro and to tell him of her plight. Subsequently, he arranged for her to get a pension. At some point she moved to Belgrade and three sons and daughter became Communists. I met them in 1939, but I did not at that time know of their political affiliation.

Ironically enough, I received a letter from her daughter, Danica, just before we left for Belgrade. In it she had high praise for the Tito regime, and added that if she ever wanted to visit another country it would be only the Soviet Union.

Some weeks after our arrival in Belgrade, we wanted to phone them, but they did not have a phone. Noting their address (near the railway station), and knowing that everything was rationed, Adele and I paid them a surprise visit one evening, taking along some basic provisions. My aunt, cousin Dragisa and his wife, and cousin Danica and her husband with two small children were all living in the same crowded apartment. Some of them were sick in bed. Aunt Vida said she was glad to see me, but she was not pleased that I was with the American Embassy. It was obvious that Danica's children were malnourished, with pronounced bow legs. Soon thereafter we sent for cod-liver oil and a few other items which we gave to Danica. Many years later she was to tell us, "You saved my children."

That same evening, Aunt Vida told me that the Chetniks had killed her two older sons. Their brother Dragisa was captured by the Germans and taken to a camp in Norway, and Danica spent the war years in Belgrade and was able to deliver some food and medicines to the Communist-led Partisans.

Months later, I found out from Jovo Jovanović, a Communist from Montenegro who knew the family, that the two brothers were in the Partisan movement and were shot by the Communists for an alleged embezzlement of party funds. By the time I confronted Aunt Vida with this information, she had a framed letter from Tito, hung on the wall, that her two sons were innocent and expressed regret that this tragic mistake was made.

In the late 1960s and early 1970s, I saw Danica several times (her mother had died in the meantime). Danica and her husband were living more comfortably (later they had an apartment in a better section of Belgrade). Nevertheless, Danica had aged fast and was not well. She told me how she had worked in the hope that everyone would have a better life, and expected others to work for the same goal, but she discovered that members of the new ruling class liked to live well but did not want to soil their hands. "As you can see," she said in a saddened voice, "Communism is no good." On another occasion, she opined, "Disillusionment is a terrible disease."

At another time, she told of a conversation she had had with her daughter, who asked about life before the war: "How much money did you make? What could you buy with it?," etc. When her mother answered, the daughter asked rhetorically: "Why then did you spit on all that?!" Danica had no answer.

During our stay in Belgrade we had visits from my three uncles (Dad's brothers Peter and Mihailo and Mother's brother Jovan Knezevich). Uncle Peter visited us several times, usually bringing a smoked ham and some plum brandy (*slivovica*). My Uncle Frank had died in 1940 and his widow was killed by the Italians in 1942, when she ran toward her house, which had been set on fire by them, presumably in an effort to put the fire out. Their two young children, Milorad and Cveta, who were then six and four, were saved by Mihailo and his family. After the war they were reared by Uncle Peter and his wife, who had no children of their own.

When World War II broke out, Uncle Peter was living near Peć on land that had been given to him as a veteran of World War I. Sensing that this area would no doubt be occupied by the Bulgarians, he drove his few sheep to Montenegro where he had grown up and where his two brothers lived. He soon became involved in the guerrilla resistance, which at that time was not divided into Chetnik and Partisan forces. Uncle Peter told me that when he and his friends noticed that respected men were disappearing one after another, they suspected that this was the work of Communists. The result was that they spent the war years in Chetnik ranks. Immediately after the end of the war, he and other Chetniks were captured by Partisan units, and he was allowed to return to his home. Younger Chetniks "were not so lucky," he said, implying that they were killed.

Uncle Peter lived out his life helping his wife rear his deceased brother's children, Milorad and Cveta. Both Milorad and Cveta visited us in Belgrade. They were then in their early teens. Before leaving Belgrade, we approached Yugoslav authorities unofficially about letting us bring them to the U. S., but we were told to forget it. Subsequently both became members of the Communist Party. Cveta came to Belgrade and became a medical technician and married there. They were blessed with two attractive girls. Her husband, however, lost out on a promising military career because his brother was suspected of being pro-Stalin at the time of the Stalin-Tito break in 1948. Milorad first taught school near Peć, which is in the province of Kosovo, and later became a local party secretary. Many years later he came to see me on one of my research trips to Belgrade. At that time, I asked him how he got along with the Albanians there. "I get along fine with them," he answered, "but I always carry a revolver." In the 1970s, he and his family settled in Belgrade in order to escape persecution by the Albanian majority in Kosovo, to which countless Serbs had been subjected.

Uncle Peter brought his wife to visit us at least once. Another time she came with either Milorad or Cveta, I believe the latter. She had never been to a real city before, and modern conveniences were strange to her—bathtub, flush toilet, refrigerator. She followed Adele all over the house, and after she had watched her brush her teeth, she took the toothbrush and tried it. We took her for a ride through Belgrade, after which she remarked that Belgrade must be the most beautiful city in the world. To top things off, we once sent her home via plane to Skoplje, where she had to change to a bus.

Dad's brother Mihailo also visited us, as did Mother's brother

Jovan, but I do not remember much of their visits.

One of the most interesting of my experiences in Belgrade was the Stalin-Tito break of June 1948. I played a small role in the Embassy's prediction that a break was likely. Soon after my arrival in Belgrade, Ambassador Cannon (whom I had met in the State Department during the war) told me that he would appreciate help in political reporting. He was aware that I knew Serbo-Croatian and might be in a position to pick up information. Two young foreign service officers who were on the S.S. *America* with us on the way to Belgrade, Norman Stines and Charles Stefan, had picked up bits and pieces of intelligence (e.g. withdrawal from Yugoslavia of Soviet advisers) that indicated some trouble between Moscow and Belgrade. They went to R. Borden Reams (counsellor of embassy), who had arrived in March. He also called me in to discuss the subject.

Perhaps the most telling piece of information about Moscow-Belgrade differences came from Yugoslavia's foreign affairs planned conference on navigation of the Danube which could not be held in Belgrade because Yugoslavia did not have the needed facilities. Thereupon the minister of foreign affairs called in the ambassadors of the involved states, and told them that the judgment that Yugoslavia did not have the needed facilities was his idea, "with which my government does not agree."

After a little more discussion, the now famous cable was dispatched to the State Department. Ambassador Cannon was at a meeting in Rome, along with Bill Leonhart, at that time the Ambassador's more senior political reporter. Hence the cable was signed by Reams as Chargé.

A copy of the cable had gone to our Moscow Embassy, which reported to the State Department that they did not have information to support the Belgrade cable. Officers in the Department in Washington were skeptical, and were convinced that the new arrivals in Belgrade had gone off the deep end.

After Ambassador Cannon and Leonhart returned, they too expressed skepticism in a meeting of officers in the Ambassador's office.

A few days later, most of us on the staff escorted the Ambassador to the airport. He had been named to head the U. S. delegation to the conference on Danube navigation (now to be held in Belgrade), and was to be briefed in Washington. According to Reams, the last thing that the Ambassador said to him before departure was: "Bob, I think you better start hedging on that telegram." To which Reams responded, "No, Mr. Ambassador, I believe it."

As it turned out, the plane on which the Ambassador was flying had stopped for refueling (I believe in the Azores) when news from the Cominform meeting in Bucharest broke, detailing Tito's alleged misdeeds and proclaiming Yugoslavia's expulsion from the Cominform.

I attended some of the public sessions of the Danubian Conference. Andrei Vishinsky represented the Soviet Union and Ana Pauker Romania. We saw both of them at a reception given by the Yugoslavs one evening.

About ten persons (men and women) accompanied the Ambassador from Washington as members of the U. S. delegation. Counsellor Reams suggested that we plan a party for them with some Yugoslav flavor. I got in touch with Jovo Jovanović at Putnik and a party was arranged for one Sunday at a winery about twenty miles from Belgrade. Before, during, and after a noon meal there was a good deal of drinking. The wine tasting in the afternoon proved devastating. Upon coming out of the cool cellars we were hit by the hot July sun. Nearly everyone stretched out on the grass outside to sleep off the hangovers. Everyone got home safely that evening, but too late for the party hosted by the Ambassador. The only members of the delegation who arrived at the Ambassador's were two men who had missed the ride to the winery.

At a reception the next evening, hosted by another American, the Ambassador, who had learned from Mrs. Reams that Adele and I had not been invited to his party, apologized to me, saying that he thought that his wife would invite us and she thought that he would invite us. A little later, he apologized to Adele, and she replied, "That's all right, Mr. Ambassador." With a twinkle in his eye, he asked, "But would you have come?" Somewhat disingenuously, she replied, "Of course, Mr. Ambassador."

One man whom I saw a great deal in the days after the Stalin-Tito break was Jovo Jovanović, mentioned above. He was one of the first Yugoslav citizens that I met after my arrival in Belgrade. He was then secretary of the soon to be defunct press club. More important, I subsequently had reason to believe that he was a secret police operative who was especially charged to keep track of my activities. His cover was a position with the travel agency Putnik. I went to see him a few times, mostly to complain of harassment of young people who came to the USIS recorded music concerts.

During one of our discussions, he asked me if $10,000 was a lot of money in America. I replied that it was. I interpreted this as a feeler to see if I could be bought. He must have sensed that the way I changed the subject left him no reason to come back to the subject, and he never did. A time or two we invited him to join us in a family picnic and he accepted. At one of them, he said that if we would give him George (then two years old), he would make a good Communist of him. After I interpreted, Adele told him, "You come with us and George will make a good American out of you." There was no response.

On the day after the news of the Cominform Resolution, I met Jovo on the street. He was very friendly and eager to talk. He gave me the clear impression that he supported Tito's position. In subsequent meetings he often used the expression, "Tito and the Party are one and the same." He reiterated this statement in one all night discussion with Counsellor Reams at our house, when I acted as interpreter.

About a month after the break, Jovo came to my office, the first time he had done that. After a brief exchange of pleasantries, he said: "As I have told you in the past, Tito and the Party are one and the same." And after a brief pause, he added, "and therein lies the tragedy." Surprised, I replied: "Come now, Jovo, you are just trying to provoke me. I know you are a strong Titoist." "No," he retorted, "I believe that Stalin is right."

A few weeks later, he disappeared, along with some recordings he borrowed from USIS. I learned from a mutual acquaintance that he had been arrested. Later I found out that he was sent to that most horrible camp for Cominformists on *Goli Otok* (Naked Isle) in the Adriatic. Many years later, after he had been released, I met him on the street in Belgrade. We exchanged a few words and parted. He seemed to be a broken man. Now I wish that I had tried to set up a meeting for an extended discussion. Perhaps he would have been disinclined, knowing that the secret police was interested in my presence in Yugoslavia.

Even after the break with Moscow, Yugoslavia was trying to prove its loyalty to Marxism-Leninism. A few weeks before the split, the regime extended its nationalization by taking over small businesses, even including used book stores. In foreign policy, too, Yugoslavia was basically following the Soviet lead.

One example of the latter were nation-wide demonstrations against colonialism on July 4, 1949. A few days earlier, on my way to and from work, I noticed extensive preparations at a large street intersection (*Autokomanda*) near our house. There was a flag-draped platform and colorful streamers attached to light or telephone poles. Since July 4th was a holiday, I was home. As I went out for a walk, I noticed a good deal of activity in the adjoining street. When I investigated, there were groups of people who were being directed by leaders to line up in formation. They were carrying banners with slogans and flags. Soon they marched to the above-mentioned intersection, where they heard speeches from party leaders.

The next day's newspapers carried stories and pictures of "spontaneous demonstrations against colonialism," held in various parts of the country.

About mid-way through my assignment in Belgrade, one of the local employees told me of a trial next day of a group of young men (nearly ten) who had allegedly conspired to overthrow the Tito regime. The next morning I was in the court room. Those in the dock were young men except for one man who said that he was forty-two. The latter pleaded guilty and implicated the rest. All but two or three pleaded *not* guilty. There was no news of the trial in the local press until after the second day of the trial, after the Voice of America had already broadcast the information I had cabled. The news in the local press was not accurate, however, in that it reported that *all* of the accused had pleaded guilty.

Another interesting event was my visit to a session of the Yugoslav parliament in May 1949. At a diplomatic reception I approached the Chief of Protocol of the Yugoslav foreign office, a Dr. Smodlaka, telling him of my desire to witness a meeting of parliament then in session, particularly because of my political science background. He responded favorably, but said he thought that the session had adjourned that day. The session was indeed a brief one, lasting less than two days.

I watched the papers closely for notice of a new session, and when I saw one I immediately called Smodlaka. He sent me a ticket for entrance to the visitors' gallery. I witnessed all of the sittings of that particular session, stretching over three and one-half days, but with fewer than nine hours in actual sittings.

About half of the time was consumed in two long speeches. Nevertheless, eight laws were passed, no amendments proposed, no bills except those put forth by the government, no dissent, no long debates. All bills passed by unanimous vote. No bill took more than five minutes to pass. The one nationalizing the drug stores took even less time.

One chance aquaintance with a Yugoslav citizen before we departed for Belgrade led to my loyalty being brought into question. Early in 1947, Graduate Dean Wilbur White of Western Reserve University introduced me to a Dr. Madjarek, a recent arrival from Zagreb under a Rockefeller Foundation grant that enabled him to spend a year at the medical school. He had fought with the Partisans and was a strong supporter of the Tito government. He gave me the names of a couple of his friends in Belgrade, who he said could help us in getting responsible household help. Because of the tense situation we found in Belgrade, I thought it best not to try to get in touch with his friends.

Since we badly needed certain things that could not be bought in Belgrade, I made a train trip to Trieste about two months after our arrival. On my way back, I stopped in Zagreb to see Dr. Madjarek, who by this time had returned from Cleveland. I told him of our difficulties with the authorities. He replied that he was sorry. Moreover, he said that he realized that relations between our two countries had worsened since his departure for the United States.

In May 1948, Adele and I were invited to join third secretary William Leonhart and his wife, together with security officer Jack Pedigo, on a circular trip that took us south as far as Skoplje and then west over the mountains of Montenegro to Dubrovnik, returning by way of Mostar and Sarajevo. Leonhart and Pedigo had proposed the trip to Counsellor Reams, who said ok, but since I knew the language they should take me along. As it turned out, I also ended up getting help on hotel arrangements through Jovo Jovanović at Putnik.

The part of the trip that triggered the matter of my loyalty was our last stop—Sarajevo. After checking in at the Hotel Europa, we took a stroll along several streets. Pedigo noticed that we were being followed, and suggested that after we turned the next corner we get into the nearest doorway, which we did. When the agents following us turned the corner and could not see us, they stopped dead in their tracks, at which time we burst out in uproarious laughter, much to the chagrin of the agents.

That evening we were having dinner in the hotel restaurant when in comes Dr. Madjarek, who had been transferred to Sarajevo. I believe that I knew of his transfer but I did not have an address. During the afternoon, his wife had recognized me while we were on our stroll and told her husband. He reasoned that if indeed we were in town, we could be only at the Europa, so he came looking for us.

I introduced him to the Leonharts and to Pedigo. I thought that I had done something useful in that they would have an opportunity to talk with an intellectual supporter of the regime. During the prolonged discussion, Leonhart and Pedigo were critical of the communist system, among other things reporting on our being followed that afternoon. Madjarek, for his part, reported that while in Cleveland, the FBI had kept track of his movements. I did not get involved in the conversation; I saw no point in repeating my complaints that I had earlier made to Madjarek in Zagreb.

Much later, after both Leonhart and Pedigo had been transferred to other posts, I learned that after our return from Sarajevo, Leonhart and Pedigo had gone to Reams, telling him that in Sarajevo, Dr. Madjarek had been critical of the United States and that neither Dragnich nor his wife had said anything in defense. This cast doubt on our loyalty, they said. Reams told them to forget it. I have reason to believe, however, that Pedigo reported the matter to the security people in the State Department, since he had his own communication link, separate from the Embassy pouch or code room. But I cannot be sure of this.

At about that time, the Ambassador had instructions to take me off the USIS payroll and to put me on the Embassy one while a full FBI field investigation was to be made of my background. This was in response to language in the Congressional appropriations bill for the USIS program, requiring that all USIS personnel have a full field FBI investigation. At the time, I saw my transfer to the Embassy payroll as compliance with Congressional direction, pending my special clearance, so perhaps Pedigo and Leonhart had little or nothing to do with it.

They did not, I am sure, refrain from talking about the Sarajevo incident, because there was (I learned later) a good deal of talk among the Embassy staff that I was being investigated. Even American newsmen in Belgrade knew.

Some time later, my clearance came through and I was again put on the USIS payroll. Moreover, a few months later I was promoted to the position of Public Affairs Officer, with a good increase in salary.

This needs a further note, because after I had returned to university teaching and writing, I was to learn that I was regarded as a security risk, not because of alleged pro-communist sympathies, but the precise opposite—I had become a critic of the Tito regime, which the United States was helping.

Vanderbilt had begun a program to help less developed countries. I was asked to lecture in the program, which I did. Since U. S. government money was involved, all of us in the program had to fill out brief security clearance forms. Long after the program was history, I was called in by Chancellor Branscomb, who had brought me to Vanderbilt, and asked what did I know about my being a security risk.

I told Branscomb about the Sarajevo incident, and expressed my desire that he investigate. He took the matter up with top State Department official, I believe the Under Secretary, who told him that I had been cleared. Upon inquiry with the visiting economist who had headed the Vanderbilt program, I learned that the negative information about me stemmed from my criticism of U. S. policy of assisting Tito.

I also learned from a friend in CIA that after Ambassador George V. Allen had returned to Washington, he was asked, at a debriefing session at which my friend was present what he thought of Dragnich's views on Yugoslavia. Ambassador Allen replied that they did not square with his assessment or that of the Embassy staff. It was evident to me that someone at that meeting had taken it upon himself to put in a negative note in my file.

Subsequently, I took the matter up personally with Ambassador Allen, then an assistant secretary of state. I told him of the report of his debriefing, and my assumption that someone who had heard him had put negative information in my file. His response: "By God, if they are putting such information in the security files, I am going to hit the ceiling!" He promised to look into the matter, and later informed Branscomb that I was not a security risk. He must have been right, because in subsequent years I had security clearances as professor at the Naval War College and as a consultant to the Defense Department.

I served under Ambassador Allen only a few months (January to May 1950). One event stands out in my memory—his official presentation of his credentials as Ambassador. He took me along as interpreter. In the days before he was to present his credentials, Counsellor Reams told him of the procedures as outlined by the Yugoslav foreign office. One of his first acts was to review an honor guard, and to address them with: *Smrt Fašismu!* [Death to Fascism], and the honor guard would answer: *Sloboda Narodu!* [Freedom to the People]. Ambassador Allen clearly did not like this part of the ceremony, telling us beforehand that he would also like to say *Smrt Comunismu* but he accepted the inevitable.

My service under Ambassador Cavendish Cannon lasted a little over two years. He was a friendly career foreign service officer with whom I had a few conversations when he was in the State Department during World War II. He was also an accomplished concert pianist—I heard him play the piano at more than one embassy reception. He also played at our house.

After he welcomed me to the Embassy, he first instructed me to be very cautious at USIS, so as not to give the Yugoslavs an excuse to close it down. Second, he wanted me to help in political reporting by passing on any significant information I might pick up. At the same time, he said that I should be careful so as not to get local citizens in trouble. Word had come to him that if he should by chance meet someone he knew on the street, the greatest favor he could do for him was to pass him by as if he did not recognize him.

Ambassador Cannon was of pioneer Mormon stock. His wife was of Austrian-English background and a Roman Catholic, to which faith he converted. Physically, she towered over him. Among Embassy personnel the general impression was that she did not like Americans. Moreover, she was viewed as a "battle axe," a characteristic to which the Ambassador lent credence.

At a party in our house he told several of us about an incident between them in years past. They were walking through a park in Vienna during which they got into an argument. At one moment he spotted some flowers on the hillside and dropped back to pick a few as a peace offering. Not noticing his actions, she walked on. Just as he was catching up to her, he heard her say, "and furthermore. . ." As he ended this story, he led us in a bit of uncomfortable laughter.

One event that particularly stands out in my memory was the reception at the Ambassador's residence on July 4, 1949. It is customary for American ambassadors to host receptions on the Fourth of July, and this one was rather special. It was a year after the Yugoslav break with Moscow, and Yugoslav officials had begun coming to U. S. social functions. There were two or three cabinet ministers and some lesser officials at this one.

The reception was for late afternoon and early evening (five to eight as best as I can recall). The weather was perfect. Most of the guests were milling around the spacious outside garden areas, eating and drinking. Sometime during the party, the Ambassador told some of us that since Mrs. Cannon was not feeling well, he would appreciate it if we encouraged people to leave before the scheduled end of the reception, so that they would not linger. Much to the embarrassment of the Americans present, Mr. Cannon began turning off the garden lights promptly at eight. For the next few days, this was the major topic of conversation among many in Belgrade.

In January 1950, Cannon was replaced by Ambassador George

V. Allen, whom I have mentioned above. In the summer of 1951, I met Ambassador Cannon in the corridors of the State Department. After an exchange of greetings, I asked about Mrs. Cannon. "She is ok," he replied, "but recently she was bitten by her little poodle. We were afraid of rabies," he continued with a chuckle, "and you know, two days later the dog died."

Speaking of ambassadors, I knew that our Constitution provides that the President appoints ambassadors, but I noticed that while all of the cables and other communications from the Embassy carried the Ambassador's signature, all of them were addressed to the Secretary of State. I once discussed this with Counsellor Reams and pointed to the seeming incongruity. I asked if ambassadors ever reported directly to the President. His response: "Some have tried it, but we soon cut their throats." One who reported directly to the President, he said, was John G. Winant, when he was Ambassador in London.

Incidentally, Reams sought to convince Adele and me that I should follow a career in the foreign service. I had a reserve appointment, but Reams assured me that a lateral transfer to the career foreign service would not present a great difficulty, and he wanted to set the process in motion. While this was an interesting opportunity, Adele and I concluded that in rearing our three young children, we preferred to have them grow up in American society, with the attributes that we experienced—the local drug store, the movie house, and all the rest. Moreover, wanted. Nevertheless, my diplomatic experiences had been interesting, enlightening, and satisfying. I learned a lot that was helpful in the pursuit of my career in academia.

GERMAN POLITICAL POLICY IN ALBANIA
1943–44

Bernd J. Fischer

The Italian collapse in August 1943 required the Germans to occupy not only the Italian peninsula but also that territory in the Balkans which the Italians had either taken by force of arms or had been given by Hitler. This action strained an already overburdened German military which could not spare the number of troops required for an effective occupation. As a result, the Germans were forced to develop and carry out a policy heavily dependent upon indigenous political and military resources. While this policy was applied elsewhere in the Balkans, its implementation in Albania, in its four stages, serves as an example of the extraordinary degree of flexibility the Germans were forced to accept, as well as the limitations of such a program. The policy, which the wartime U. S. Office of Strategic Services described as being applied with "imagination, skill, and vigor," experienced some success but ultimately failed.[1]

The policy itself was broadly laid out by the German foreign minister, Joachim von Ribbentrop, in a telegram to his ambassador in Rome at the end of August 1943. Ribbentrop speculated that Italy might soon vacate Albania leaving Germany with a new burden, the protection of the Adriatic coast and the Straits of Otranto. He suggested that this protection might best be handled with the construction of an independent yet friendly government, which would create a stable political system and a reliable security force; such action would free German troops entirely or at least lighten their load by having Albanians maintain order. Ribbentrop suggested that the German consul general in Albania, Martin Schliep, locate "statesman-like people," a few of which incorrectly identified, who might carry out this role for the Germans. The foreign minister did not foresee the numerous obstacles involved in the initial introduction of such policy.[2]

The question of obtaining reasonable intelligence on internal Albanian conditions constituted the first hurdle in implementing Ribbentrop's rough sketch, a question that plagued the Germans during their entire period of occupation in Albania. As evidenced by Ribbentrop's error-filled telegram, the Germans were almost entirely ignorant of Albanian conditions. Indeed the German foreign minister complained that the information with which he had to work, particularly the records from the German consul general, were often contradictory.[3]

This lack of information upon which to develop effective policy can be attributed to a number of considerations including German concerns about Italian sensibilities. After the Italian occupation of Albania in April 1939, Count Ciano, the Italian foreign minister, and his staff were continually concerned about further German moves into Albania, Their concern stemmed from the good reputation enjoyed by the Germans because of the positive impression made by Austro-Hungarian troops in World War I.[4] In order to assuage Italian fears, Berlin scrupulously avoided collecting data on Albania, something which they clearly regretted after the German invasion of Albania in September of 1943.

Other factors included the inability of Martin Schliep to gather accurate information, the problem of language, hindered this gathering process. Even at the height of the German occupation in 1944, there were never more than ten Germans in Albania who spoke Albanian.[5] Another part of the problem, however, came from German carelessness. Throughout the 1940s, a certain Major von Scheiger, who not only spoke Albanian but had lived there for twenty years and had become acquainted with many of the major Albanian political figures, worked for the foreign mininisty in Berlin. Scheiger was not consulted until Ribbentrop commanded his presence on September 3, 1943. Scheiger was immediately sent to Mitroviza, the German zone of Kosovo, to test the water and make contact with Albanian leaders.[6] During the same week, Ribbentrop appointed the former mayor of Vienna—and the *Sonderbeauftrager des AA für den Süd-Ost*—Hermann Neubacher, as his personal representative for Albania. Neubacher, then, was responsible for the coordination of this new policy—all in all these major actions were the extent of German political preparation for their occupation of Albania.

The invasion itself procceded without serious difficulty on September 9, one day after the capitulation of Marshal Badolgio who had replaced Mussolini. Three divisions of the XXI A.K. quickly overran Albania, Montenegro, and northern Greece encountering little or no resistance from either the more than eight Italian divisions in Albania (90,000 of whom were captured) or from the already existing Albanian resistance groups. The German aims had carefully and seemingly effectively, covered the country with leaflets announcing that they had come to Albania to protect the Albanians from the enemy and from communism. The leaflets reassured the Albanians that nothing would endanger Albanian independence from Italy "who robbed you and has betrayed us," and Albanian youths were complemented for their struggle against fascist Italy.[7] The Germans declared that they wished only the best for Albania within its ethnic frontiers, a reference to Albania's enlarged geographic frontiers for which German action was responsible. The Albanians needed only to preserve discipline and aid in the defense of the coast against Allied invasion.

Based on the success of their operation, German commanders encouraged Neubacher, who arrived in Tirana on September 10 accompanied by some 200 people, to believe that he would rapidly gain the support of a significant cross section of Albanian politicians with whom he could build a broadly based anti-communist regime. This task proved more difficult than expected and constituted the second initial obstacle to the introduction of Germany's unique pacification policy in Albania, an obstacle that can be traced hack to the lack of an understanding of conditions and realities in Albania.

Neubacher's arrival signalled the beginning of the first phase of German policy, the aim of which was the construction of a government apparatus. This required genuine collaboration, something which proved to be more difficult to obtain than Neubacher had expected. The most important early setback concerned Albania's traditional elite—rather than welcoming the Germans with open arms as had been anticipated, they viewed the German occupation with considerable skepticism. It is true that Germans had a good reputation and that the disciplined German troops had an overall good effect; but it was widely assumed, even by resistance leaders like Enver Hoxha, that an Allied invasion was imminent. This assumption can be attributed to the success of British propaganda disseminated by the BBC and a network of agents who had been infiltrated into Albania in April 1943. Hesitance on the part of the traditional elite can be further explained by the fact that few of them made good ideological partners for the Germans. Unlike Romania, Hungary and Croatia, Albania produced few people fanatically attached to the Nazi "new order."

The exceptions to this rule were the Albanians of the province of Kosovo, in what was once Yugoslavia, who, in 1941, were awarded to Italian Albania by the Germans after the destruction of Yugoslavia. (During the war Kosovo was known as "new Albania.") Neubacher reported to Ribbentrop that these people would stand and fall with Germany because of Allied promises to return Kosovo to a reconstructed Yugoslavia. We went on to note that the Kosovars constituted the racially purest and politically and militarily most united elements among the Albanians and that they could be useful in the occupation of a large part of Albania.[8] Cooperation between the Germans and the Kosovars began immediately. Before Neubacher reached Tirana, Xhafer Deva, a prominent Kosovar had visited Belgrade to see Neubacher. Consequently, Deva accepted the interior ministry in the occupation government that was being formed.

The politicians of "Old" Albania turned out to be much more difficult to attract. Neubacher's solution was to apply Ribbentrop's policy with determination. He pushed the Albanians for a hasty declaration of independence and insisted that Germany observe this independence whenever possible. To achieve these goals Neubacher encouraged the formation of a national committee made up of representatives of new Albania, including Deva, and as many old Albanian politicians as possible. By September 14 this committee of some twenty-two people was in place but it suffered from two distinct disadvantages. First, it included only a few minor politicians from old Albania, and second, its deliberations proceeded very slowly. Neubacher stepped in and threatened a full military occupation unless the work of the committee was quickened.

Under the leadership of the Kosovar Bedri Pejani, the committee responded by instructing a six-man provisional government under Ibrahim Bicaku, a landowner from Elbasan, and after checking the wording with Neubacher, proclaimed Albanian independence and neutrality. To accompany this move Neubacher insisted on living up to the forms of independence. The local press was virtually free from censorship and was permitted to publish Allied communiqués.[9] Even Reichsführer Heinrich Himmler was temporarily prevented from creating an Albanian Waffen SS division because of its incompatibility with the notion of an independent Albania. Further, the Germans prudently refrained from encouraging the construction of any fascist organizations, and for propaganda purposes even refused to use exfascists in the puppet governments. Berlin had created the unique situation of a German Occupation without any signs of fascism.

The Germans were also able to take full advantage of Allied blunders, the most serious of which was allowing Victor Emmanuel III to continue referring to himself as King of Albania until the beginning of December 1943. The Albanians themselves had denied him of the crown six weeks earlier while at the same time revoking the law providing that Albania was automatically at war with all states at war with Italy. All of this was done with the good will and encouragement of the Germans. The Allies had allowed themselves to be put in a position where an admitted wrong to a small nation had been righted with German cooperation.[10] Other unfortunate errors in political warfare included the failure to make clear statements about the status of southern Albania and Kosovo, the failure to mention the Albanian guerrillas when praising the Greeks and Yugoslavs, the dropping of leaflets over Albania in Greek and Serbo-Croatian, and confusion at the BBC concerning the difference between the nationalists and the partisans.[11]

Further, the Germans were quick to take full advantage of nationalist feelings towards Kosovo. First, the Germans emphasized that it was their action which destroyed Yugoslavia and facilitated the return of Kosovo to Albania in 1941. Then the Germans encouraged the construction, on September 16, 1943, of the Second Congress of the league of Prizren (in Kosovo) which announced that the people of Kosovo desired to be officially united with the remainder of Albania. By this move, the Germans created the impression that only now, with the coming of the Germans, would the real union of Kosovo with Albania be achieved. The former union proclaimed by Italy was dismissed as a simple act of colonialist annexation.[12]

As hopes for an Allied invasion receded and as the Germans were able to demonstrate their military might in the first actions against the resistance, many Albanians who had been content to sit on the fence began to accept the Germans simply as a reality. By the middle of October the German strategy was beginning to work; non-communist nationalist elements from old Albania began coming around. Neubacher hoped to reinforce this trend in three ways: through renewed attention to Albanian sensibilities, increased references to Albania's ethnic frontiers, and extended use of threats and bribes.

On October 16 the national assembly, for which the committee

had conducted very limited elections on October 1, finally met. Some
150 deputies attended, although more than half represented Kosovo
and the northern Albanian mountain areas dominated by Geg tribes,
areas where many local people really had cooperated with the Italians. Southern Albania, where the two largest resistance groups were
centered—the noncommunist nationalists, called *Balli Kombetar*, or
BK, and the communist dominated LNC or partisans—was weakly
represented. Still, the national assembly went a long way toward legitimizing the German occupation. With Lef Nosi, a supporter of
the BK, as president, the assembly rapidly moved to construct the
basis of a new regime; it dissolved the union of the Albanian with
the Italian crown, it revoked many laws passed after April 7, 1939.
It reaffirmed the decrees of September 1, 1928, which had declared
Albania a monarchy, and announced that for the duration of the war,
Albania was to be governed by a regency.

Finally, the assembly chose the council of regency headed by
Mehdi Frasheri, an elderly Bektashi liberal and former prime minister under Zog; he had been arrested by the Italians and then courted
by Neubacher as crucial to the success of German policy. Frasheri
was joined by three politicians of national reputation. American OSS
documents, referring to a Tirana radio report of October 20, suggest that each had refused to serve but were forced by the assembly.
German documents and Neubacher's memoirs make no mention of
this incident and claim that Frasheri had offered to head a government himself. In light of these assertions, the American claim seems
suspect.[13] Real collaboration had been achieved.

On November 6, Berlin announced that the regents and the national assembly (which carried on as a modified parliament) had
formed a new Albanian government. Rexhep Mitrovica, who was
attached to the BK, was prime minister and Xhafer Deva minister of
the interior. Both were from Kosovo but other ministers represented
Old Albania. Indeed, many Albanian national groups were represented including prewar influential politicians, the Catholic clergy,
the Kosovars, and the Geg tribes in the north.

The support which this new government had among the people
can only be conjectured. Mehdi Frasheri was undoubtedly very popular because of his political past as well as because of some of his
actions as regent. He and his colleagues refrained from the more in-
gratiating attempts at fawning on military masters. While Frasheri
thanked Hitler for Albanian independence, he also delivered a New

Year's message which explained that his social reforms would be based on "democratic principles that eliminate all dictatorships." Here we have a public official under German occupation who in the official press declares his unquestioned support for democracy and his equally unflagging opposition to dictatorship, a situation that must have been unique in Europe and lent Frasheri considerable credibility.[14]

The Second League of Prizren held the sympathy of the majority of new Albania, and most of those in northern Albania at least tolerated the regime in Tirana. Although difficult to substantiate, Berhard Kuhmel, a German scholar, has argued that it would be reasonable to suggest that this first Albanian government under the Germans was received favorably by 25–30 percent of the people, leaving 30–35 percent neutral and 40 percent in opposition.[15]

This level of support was not ideal for the Germans, but Neubacher could be pleased as his policy seemed to be working, at least slowly. With this government in place, Neubacher initiated phase two. He hoped to encourage the government to assume direct control of the state and build up forces to oppose the partisans.

This phase proved to be even more difficult than the first one. As Mitrovica suggested in his first address at the national assembly, four-and-one-half years of Italian domination had left anarchy and chaos in Albania. The pre-1939 state apparatus was destroyed. To suppress every sign of Albanian independence, the Italians had destroyed the army, the gendarmerie, the police, the foreign ministry; they had changed the flag, altered personal greetings, renamed cities, and even reassigned family names. To reestablish the state, Mitrovica set down a very ambitious plan which included gaining foreign recognition, reorganizing the economy, introducing effective agrarian reform programs and, as a major Albanian and German priority, creating a military force. None of this program worked very well, and here we see some of the limitations of Germany's pacification policy.

Several factors account for these failures—yet German miscalculations and mistakes must head the list. The experiment during the second phase failed partially because of the absence of government legitimacy. The government had hoped to remedy the problem by gaining some foreign recognition, but it was hindered in doing so by German obstructionism. Neubacher refused to allow Frasheri to request relations with the Swiss and the Turks. The only regime willing to recognize the Albanian one, the Ustashi regime in Zagreb, was prevented from doing so by Neubacher, who was afraid of offending the sensibilities of the Serbs.

The efforts of the government to deal with the economic problems were also complicated by German policy; indeed German policy was responsible for the creation of most of these difficulties. Despite some well-meaning efforts on the part of Neubacher to build domestic support for the regime by stabilizing the economy, the German presence proved to be nothing short of an unmitigated disaster for the Albanians. Although German officials denied responsibility, the presence of some 36,000 Germans in Albania resulted in a rapid increase in prices as well as a shortage of goods. The situation became serious enough to create famine conditions in southern Albania by the spring of 1944.[16] While conditions never became quite as bad as those in Greece, Mitovica's effectiveness was slowly hampered by the desperate economic conditions.

In a closely related matter, the much publicized agrarian reform—which the government declared itself committed to implementing—basically remained on paper. This is not surprising since the government was constructed of men who had little to gain by such a program. The Germans had attached themselves to the traditional elite, the large landowners and beys, those people who were the natural enemies of the communists and had something in common with the Germans themselves, linguistically and culturally. The Germans, by tieing themselves to the narrow European-educated elite, denied themselves a knowledge of the needs of the average Albanian. The Germans created in Albania a German ghetto and spawned an atmosphere of the "ugly German," similar to what the Americans would create in southeast Asia in the 1960s.

The most profound failure for both German policy and the Mitrovica government, however, was the inability to create useful Albanian security forces, which would not only have legitimized the government but would also have unburdened the Germans. German strategy here was multifaceted and included arming and using some nationalists bands, creating and maintaining an Albanian army and gendarmerie corps, and creating an SS division in Kosovo. The German military set aside 14,000 rifles and 425 machine guns, most of which was actually turned over to selected nationalists and volunteers from Kosovo. The original enthusiasm for using these units quickly died, however, when it became clear that not only were they of questionable value militarily but in many cases they did much to alienate the population as a result of brutality and a penchant for plunder.[17]

Fitzthum, the SS chief in Albania, and Fehn, the commander of the XXI AK, were placed in charge of the second part of the plan, the construction of a army and gendarmerie. After considerable reassessment it was decided, in April 1944, that any more than 8,250 troops for the army and 2,400 for the gendarmerie was unrealistic. Even this proved to be very optimistic and many fewer men were enlisted. The problems included a lack of instructors, a lack of Albanian officers and non-coms, and a disastrous recruitment program. Finally, those Albanian soldiers who successfully completed the program proved to be highly unreliable. After the operation turned into a fiasco, Fitzthum wrote angrily to Himmler that one battalion dissolved after being attacked by a few planes and the rest simply disappeared.[18]

The last attempt to use the Albanians as support troops was Fitzthum's notion of creating an Albanian Waffen SS division under direct German command. This idea had originally been vetoed by the foreign ministry because of its incompatibility with the notion of an independent Albania; but by February 1944, because of increasing pressure on the Germans. Hitler gave Himmler his personal approval for the creation of the SS Skenderbeg Division. The division was to consist of approximately 1,500 prisoners of war, natives of Kosovo who had served in the Yugoslav army, remnants of the failed Albanian army and gendarmerie, volunteers from both old and new Albania. and draftees. The area of operation was to include Kosova, part of Macedonia and part of Mitrovica. The division was used against the partisans and fared somewhat better than had the gendarmerie and Albanian army. It proved to be the government's and the German's most useful tool, although its success, too, was limited.

The Germans on the spot blamed all of these failures on the Albanians themselves. The German commander of the SS Skenderbeg Division, General Schmidthuber, explained his failure by suggesting that the Albanians had not developed culturally since the time of Skenderbeg in the fifteenth century. They had evolved no concept of "state" or "nation," indeed they had vegetated. The military leaders of the XXI AK came to the same conclusions, blaming a lack of nation-state traditions and the impetuosity of the Balkan temperament. General Fitzthum interpreted everything in racial terms and suggested that the main problem was the officer crisis since it was not only worthless but filled with pederasts. Since none of these character flaws was attributed to the partisan resistance, we can only assume that the Germans were desperate to find excuses for their own failure.[19]

The high hopes for the creation of effective security, then, were not realized. This certainly constituted the most serious failure for both parties since it made Albanian sovereignty look like a facade and exposed the Germans for what they were, an army of occupation. The more Albanian sovereignty looked like a facade, the more collaborationist politicians lost their hold on the people. The more many lost their hold on the people, the more successful partisan appeals were and the stronger the partisans became.

By the beginning of 1944 these failures had significantly hampered the government's effectiveness and forced the Germans to re-examine their strategy. While they hoped to stay within the bounds of their original policy as laid down by Ribbentrop, a broadening of indigenous support was required—specifically, a broadening of the government even if questionable elements were included. Neubacher targeted elements of the *Balli Kombetar*, who while they had declared themselves uninterested in a confrontation with the Germans, continued to maintain a significant distance. This constituted the beginning of the third phase.

The timing for this move was propitious in that the Germans had just completed a successful winter campaign against the partisans which impressed the variows noncommunist groups. Much of the *Balli Kombetar*, which had remained aloof, was finally convinced to throw in its lot with the Germans. First, the *Balli Kombetar* informed on partisan activities, receiving funds and buying weapons from both the collaborationist government and the Germans. Ultimately the *Balli Kombetar* policed and administered large sections of the country for both.[20] By the beginning of February 1944, British liaison officers reported that it was becoming increasingly difficult for the partisans to attack the Germans since they were being screened by the *Balli Kombetar* and that these forces had become a normal part of any German force.[21]

The *Balli Kombetar* support for the Germans cannot, however, be explained as an ideological shift. The organization had no illusions about a German victory and it never disavowed its support for a democratic regime built on broad social and economic reform. The move was a calculated tactical one with which the *Balli Kombetar* hoped to achieve two goals. First, the organization hoped to avoid reprisals, thereby increasing its political stock, since many of the strongest *Balli Kombetar* centers were in towns and exposed districts of the coastal plain, areas under strict German control. Second, the *Balli Kombetar* hoped to increase its weapons stock and preserve its strength for the inevitable showdown with the partisans once the Germans had left. Accordingly, at the end of January, three members of the *Balli Kombetar* joined the Mitrovica cabinet.

This move had the effect of temporarily staying the government's slide into chaos. This was clearly in the German interest but negative aspects quickly became apparent. The Germans were not fooled by *Balli Kombetar*'s strategy and knew that their move had not been motivated by any sense of loyalty. Many *Balli Kombetar* members were clearly pro-Allied and if given too much power, they could easily threaten German interests. The Germans were put in an awkward spot. They needed *Balli Kombetar* adherence to the failing government but they could not give them enough authority to have them make any difference. Even more importantly, and clearly not foreseen by the *Balli Kombetar*, their collaboration ultimately had the effect of compromising them in the eyes of the people, thereby strengthening the partisans. By the summer, as a result of collaboration, the *Balli Kombetar* ceased to be a serious contender for power in Albania. The more groups the Germans attracted, the stranger the partisans became, a lesson learned too late.

By the summer the Germans concluded that a further broadening of the base of its support was necessary. In July the Mitrovica government had become almost completely ineffectual. Its work had been paralyzed since May under the same pressure which had required the integration of the *Balli Kombetar*. This time Frasheri decided that a greater change was needed and for this he looked to the Zogists and the independent northern tribal leaders who in the fall of 1943 would not have considered dealing with the collaborationists or the Germans. Now with the rapidly increasing power of the partisans, collaboration was no longer out of the question.[22] The negotiations were drawn out because of German hesitation about the inclusion of Zogists who were considered pro-British and unreliable, the same hesitations, although stronger, which the Germans had about the *Balli Kombetar*. The Germans actually rejected Frasheri's first suggestion on the integration of the Zogist. But when the Germans became aware of the extensive British attempts to build resistance unity and witnessed the rapid growth of partisan strength, their objections slowly withered.

The Zogist leader Abaz Kupi suggested Fiqri Dine as prime minister. The Germans objected but nevertheless realized that the Mitrovica government had lost all credibility. The Germans complained that, added to the many problems already mentioned, the most pro-German elements in the government were succumbing to corruption. Deta, the minister of interior, was accused of releasing captured communists for money. As with the other charges, then, this further broadening of the government was forced on the Germans.[23]

So despite misgivings, the integration of the Zogists into the government became unavoidable, The Germans were assured by Frasheri that the Zogists would create no difficulty for a German withdrawal, indeed they would cover it. At the end of May, then, Mitrovica resigned and after considerable political intrigue and a partisan move into northern Albania, Dine became prime minister of a cabinet composed of Zogists, *Balli Kombetar* supporters, northern chieftains who had supported the Italians, and of course, Kosovars.

The government hoped to use the Germans against the partisans, and the Germans simply hoped to hold on a little longer. The original concert of creating a state supported by the population had been replaced by one of basic survival by whatever means possible. The Germans were also able to hold on despite the continued shrinking of support for their puppet regimes. As a result they achieved at least some of their goals. The Dine government, on the other hand, did not. Dine hoped to convince the Germans to give him weapons and supplies. He was given some trucks and some bread for Kupi but denied the tanks and equipment for which he had asked. Schliep set down the German attitude towards Kuri. He was to be considered an enemy but he was to be used whenever possible. It is probably that Kuri finally received some light weapons and ammunition.[24]

But none of this was enough, the partisan influence continued to grow. In a desperate effort to survive, Dine attempted to convince the Allies that his government was neutralist but without success. The Zogist gamble had failed; the government became as ineffective as the previous one with fewer than 10 percent of its officials reporting for work by the middle of August.[25] With Romania and Bulgaria out of the war by August 26, the situation seemed hopeless. On August 28, after only forty days in office, the Dine government resigned.

Dine's fall initiated the last phase of German occupation policy. He was succeeded by Ibrahim Bicaku who had headed the provisional government in 1943. Bicaku, however, was never more than a figurehead. Julian Amery, one of the British officers in Albania during the war, tells us that the only remaining evidence of political activity was the German minister's daily game of ping-pong with Bicaku.[26] With the fall of Dine, the Germans essentially gave up their attempt at the pacification of Albania by the Albanians and assumed direct control, initiating a policy of more severe military expansion and terror. This new policy was carried out primarily by Fitzthum who assumed control of the German military in Albania on September 1. He remained the most significant German influence in Albania until the complete withdrawal of German troops on November 29, 1944.

German policy in Albania failed, although this failure was not unqualified. The first priority had been to hold Albania with a small number of troops. Not only was the German military able to do this, but during the course of 1944 more troops were transferred out than replaced. The German army was able to withdraw from Albania with moderate losses. The Germans also succeeded in playing Albanian groups against each other thereby hindering resistance. It is clear that without the aid of the German nationalists in the north, the German escape route might have been blocked. None of this would have been possible had Ribbentrop's policies not been implemented. At this late stage of the war, the mere survival of a German military force must be considered something of a success.

Still if the central point was the pacification of the country through the construction of an independent regime with prestige and its own military authority with which to fight the opposition, then the Germans fell far short of their goals. The Mitrovica government gained a degree of acceptance and was certainly taken more seriously than under the Italians, although the Dine and Bicaku governments failed to excert anything more than regional influence. None of the regimes under German control were able to construct military forces effective enough to challenge the partisans. Instead, a long series of German military operations extending scarce military resources were required. This is what the Germans had hoped to avoid.

NOTES

1. National Archives, Washington, DC, United States Department of State, Office of Strategic Services, (hereafter USDS., OSS) Research and Analysis Branch, Survey of Albania, December 20, 1943, No. 1475.

2. National Archives, Washington DC, Captured German Records (hereafter Captured German Records), roll T120, 340, Auswartigess

Amt, Nr. 1250, 21 August 1943, Ribbentrop, Wolfsschanze.

3. Captured German Records, roll T120, 340, Auswartiges Amt, Nr. 1250, 21 August 1943, Ribbentrop and Captured German Records, roll T501, 258, p. 622, OKW report.

4. Herman Neubacher, *Sonderauftrag Südost, 1940–1945, Bericht eines fliegended Diplomaten* (Göttingen: Musterschmidt Velag, 1956), p. 108 and Gerrhard Kuhmel, *Deutschland und Albanien 1943–1944, Die Auswirkungen der Besetzung auf die innenpolitische Entwicklung des Landes* (Ruhr-Universität Bochum: Unpublished Doctoral Dissertation, 1981), p. 80 and Captured German Records, roll T120 313, Auswartiges Amt, Office of the State Secretary, 13 September 1940, Nr. 652, Pannowitz.

5. Captured German Records, roll T 501, 258, p. 622, OKW report.

6. Captured German Records, roll T120, 340, Auswartiges Amt, Nr. 4193, 23 August 1943, Schliep to Ribbentrop and Kuhmel, *Deutschland und Albanien*, p. 128.

7. USDS, OSS, Research and Analysis Branch, Survey of Albania, December 20, 1943, Nr. 1475 and Laun Omari, *The People's Revolution in Albania and the Question of State Power* (Tirana: "8 Nentori" Publishing House, 1986), p. 50.

8. Captured German Records, roll T120, 340 Auswartiges Amt, Nr. 942, 12 September 1943, Neubacher.

9. USDS, OSS, Research and Analysis Branch, German Military Government over Europe, Albania, December 1, 1944, Nr. 2500.1.

10. Great Britain, Public Records Office, Foreign Office (hereafter FO) 371/43550 R7779/39/G90 Bawker to Howard May 9, 1944.

11. Great Britain, Public Record Office, [Foreign Office] FO 371/43550 (R7779/39/G90): 9 May 1944 and FO 371/33108 (R8/70/184/980): 21 December 1942.

12. Omari, *The People's Revolution in Albania and the Question of State Power*, p. 50.

13. USDS, OSS, Research and Analysis Branch, Survey of Albania, December 20, 1943, No. 1475.

14. Great Britain, Public Record Office, FO 371/43550 R7779/39/G90 Bawker to Howard, May 9, 1944.

15. Kuhmel, *Deutschland und Albanien*, p. 448.

16. Ibid., p. 345.

17. Ibid., p. 220.

18. Ibid., pp. 303–305.

19. Ibid., p. 205.

20. *Captured German Records*, roll T120, 340, AA Office of the State Secretary, Belgarde, Neubacher, Nr. 227, February 1, 1944 and Great Britain, Public Record Office, FO 371/43549 R277/39/G90 SOE, January 6, 1944 and FO 371/48079 R4145/46/G90 February 23, 1945.

21. Great Britain, Public Record Office, FO 371/43549 R 1718/39/G90 January 22, 1944 and FO 371/43549 R7167/39/G90 February 7, 1944.

22. Captured German Records, roll T120, 340, Auswartiges Amt, Nr. 321, 20 May 1944, Schliep.

23. Kuhmel, *Deutschland und Albanie*, p. 373.

24. Ibid., pp. 391–392.

25. Captured German Records, roll T501, 258, p. 16, OKW report.

26. Julian Amery, *Sons of the Eagle* (London: Macmillan Press, 1948), p. 270.

THE "TAKEOVER" IN THE HISTORIC PERSPECTIVE

Stephen Fischer-Galati

The "revolutionary" events of 1989 and the corollary repudiation of communism have led many students of East European developments since the "Takeover" to reinterpret the history and political culture of the countries of Eastern Europe. The dominant view would make us believe that the "Takeover" itself and the ensuing communist period were an aberration from the democratic traditions and politics of Eastern Europe. Of course, the definition of democratic traditions and concepts varies considerably in function of political ideologies and interests of the exponents of such theories.

Speakers for "bourgeois democracy" extol the activities and philosophies of liberal bourgeois, socialist, and peasant political parties even though the achievements and constituencies of those organizations do not necessarily correspond to the image created by their contemporary champions. The more vocal spokesmen for "populist democracy" reject the claims of bourgeois democratic forces as distorted and self-serving; instead, they suggest that "fascism" or variations thereof were in consort with the political culture of the masses and that the authoritarian leaders identified with those ideologies represented the *vox populi*. The reformist communists, in turn, still proclaim the essentially democratic character of original Leninism and do not deviate from the tenet that pure Leninists have always been the true exponents of the people's democratic goals, the standard bearers of "people's democracy."

This *reductio ad absurdum* of historic realities by all users—in fact, misusers—of the term "democracy" as reflective of the political culture and traditions of Eastern Europe needs to be clarified as we try to place the "Takeover" and its aftermath in the proper historic context of the twentieth century. And that will be attempted in the pages that follow.

Casting aside, for the moment, all definitions of democracy that deny individual rights, human and political, that reject the individual's rights to liberty and property and pluralistic participation in the

determination of the political order, we may well ask to what extent
was "bourgeois democracy" representative of the political culture and
experience of the peoples of Eastern Europe at the end of World War
II. We may also question the corollary claims of anti-fascist and anti-
communist leaders that they were the true representatives of their
peoples' interests at that time. Caution must be exercised since,
axiomatically, all leaders who sought recognition by the victorious
Allies had to have been identified with the "struggle for liberation
from facism" and, preferably, with a long-standing commitment to
"democracy."

It is fair to say that at least in a few countries of Eastern Europe,
those in which urbanism and bourgeois capitalism had created conditions for meaningful participatory democracy, such as Czechoslovakia
and, to a lesser extent and largely on regional bases, also Hungary,
Romania, Poland, and Yugoslavia, liberal, peasant, social democratic,
and socialist parties had sought, and on occasion, commanded the political allegiance of significant segments of the population. It is also
fair to say that most of these political organizations were generally
uncooperative with totalitarian forces, fascist or communist, during
the interwar and war years. To say, however, that they were representative of the interests of their constituencies and of their political
culture, that they overtly opposed the authoritarian regimes of Hungary's Horthy, of the Poland of the colonels, of the royal dictators
of Bulgaria, Romania, and Yugoslavia or, perhaps more significantly,
first the "fascists" and later in the war, the communists would be less
than accurate.

It has been argued, of course, that the primary function of political organizations in the developing societies that had to adapt to
the world that emerged from and after the dissolution of the European imperial order of the Habsburgs, Romanovs, Germans, and Ottoman Turks was the political education of the masses. Participatory
democracy with guaranteed human, property, and political rights, as
imposed by the Western Allies, was by-and-large a novel experience
for the majority of the peoples of Eastern Europe accustomed, as they
were, to paternalistic, divinely-ordained and religiously-sanctioned,
socio-political orders. Moreover, since the dissolution of the empires
was legitimized by the principle of national self-determination, which
the Allies regarded as entirely compatible with the "democratic" aspirations of the inhabitants of the succession states, nationalism and
democracy were deemed prerequisites for the successful entry of East-

ern Europe in the community of a peace-loving and prosperous continent. Given the absurdity—based on either cynicism or ignorance or
both—of these assumptions advocated by Woodrow Wilson and his
fellow peacemakers, the "historic" and the nascent political organizations committed, or paying lip-service, to democratic principles were
faced with well-nigh impossible tasks and, more often than not, with
losing battles.

We need not recapitulate the political history of the interwar
years. Suffice it to say that in general nationalism proved to be incompatible with bourgeois democracy and that non- or anti-democratic
forces were readily able to exploit that contradiction, and other objective conditions, that mitigated against successful democratization of
the succession states. Unpopular view as it may be, the historic fact is
that the largely illiterate peasant masses that comprised the great majority of the population of Eastern Europe at the end of World War
I had virtually no acquaintance with democratic means of political
expression or, for that matter, any meaningful interest in politics as
such. The peasantry's primary concern was the securing of the land
received through agrarian reforms or through redefinition of property rights in the new Eastern Europe of greater or smaller national
states. Identification of the peasants' interest with political organizations, primarily peasant parties, was evident in most East European
countries—most notably in Bulgaria; but whether that identification
superseded the traditional allegiance to the paternalistic monarchy
and church is questionable. The historic experience would tend to indicate that the effectiveness of peasant parties was limited whenever
crown and church were in opposition to or non-supportive of their
plans or programs. Moreover, the leadership of the peasant parties
incorporated elements not necessarily recognized by the peasants as
"one of their own"—urban intellectuals, nationalist businessmen, and
in certain instances even liberal Jews—which mitigated against the
ability of the parties to gain the unequivocal allegiance of the peasantry, to consolidate the gains secured by the peasantry at the end of
the war and, above all, to prevent the "splitism" which weakened the
peasantry's potential political power and strengthened that of non-
or anti-democratic forces.

Inasmuch as traditional conservative elements sought to prevent
"peasant democracy" and, as such, to at least limit the effectiveness of peasant organizations, the political dynamics of the interwar
years focussed, directly or indirectly, on controlling and directing the

politicization of the process of adaptation of rural societies to the urbanization and industrialization of the succession states.

The modernization of East European societies to which all leaders had committed themselves, *volens nolens*, at the end of the war and corollary migration from village to town did entail rapid urban industrial development. This dual process resulted, as is generally known, in disaffection primarily by the young who settled in urban centers either as workers, in generally primitive industrial or commercial establishments, or as students. The disaffection was enhanced in most East European countries by the multi-ethnic character of urban settlements and, particularly, by ownership of commercial and industrial enterprises by Jews, not to mention the disproportionate Jewish presence in educational institutions. The ensuing exacerbation of xenophobia and anti-Semitism—never alien in Eastern Europe for that matter—was exploited by nationalists, by influential conservative groups in the military and clerical establishments, as well as by the monarchies. The fact that Bolshevism was identified with Judaism, especially in Hungary, Poland, and Romania, and viewed as a threat to the interests of the inhabitants of the new nation states, the presumed "Judeo-Bolshevik" threat was used as an instrument for discrediting the peasant parties, generally labeled as leftist, as well as other political organizations—socialist, social-democratic and, of course, communist—which presumably were unable to combat the "enemy" with the required vigor.

The task of discrediting political organizations concerned, at least nominally, with problems related to the working class was much simpler than that of compromising the peasant parties. Most communist organizations were virtually dismantled, if not always legally dissolved, following the Béla Kun fiasco, the unsuccessful rebellions sponsored by Moscow in Bessarabia, the Soviet-Polish war, the assassination of Stamboliski, to mention but a few of communist actions deemed threatening to the political and socio-economic interests of leaders and citizens alike. Socialists and social-democrats were generally self-styled bourgeois and intellectual spokesmen for the interests of a largely apolitical labor force which did not necessarily identify its own interests with those of its urban, white collar, champions. Through invocation of the Judeo-communist threat and promises, more often than actual measures, designed at least to placate if not "buy off" the working class and the usually weak trade unions, the conservative political parties with the support of conservative ruling establishments and of military religious leaders were, as a rule, able to contain strikes and labor demonstrations even during the years of the Great Depression. However, such actions by the "left" were almost invariably exploited for legitimizing consolidation of autocratic power by "defenders" of the nation and national interests. They were also exploited by the radical "right."

It may well be asked then whether pluralistic—even if "controlled" or "guided"—democracy was ever regarded as a desirable formula for governance of the succession states by elites and masses alike. The evidence would speak against acceptance of the traditional answers which would blame the failure of democracy on the irresponsible attitudes and actions of overly partisan, radical organizations and leaders of the "left" and, even more so of the "right," and of their external sponsors or supporters—the Russian Bolsheviks and, respectively, the Italian Fascists and German Nazis.

The fact is that radical political orgnaizations of the right or of the left were opposed to political pluralism. However, with few exceptions, for most of the interwar period the radical communist left had virtually no constituency and its political activities, within and outside the parliamentary framework, could not jeopardize the security of any succession state and, as such, justify the abandonment of the democratic experiment. Such influence as could be and, occasionally, was exerted by Moscow and the Comintern was largely negated by the heavily Jewish leadership that could be, and mostly was, readily discredited and persecuted in the name of national and nationalist interests. The radical right, which emerged as a force in East European politics in the late twenties and early 1930s, had greater power but such power as it had was also subject to direction from the conservative ruling elites.

The radical right did enjoy significant support among the peasantry and working class in part because many of its members, youths of peasant or proletarian origin, could identify with the masses. This was particularly true of such organizations as the Romanian Iron Guard or the Hungarian Arrow Cross whose populism and anti-urbanism were expressed primarily through virulent and violent anti-Semitism. Their actions and ideologies, such as they were, appealed also to much of the petty bourgeoisie and, at least in the early stages, to conservative political groups that preferred not to be expressly identified with overtly anti-democratic and anti-Semitic actions. Most notable in this respect was the support provided to the radical right by "clerico-fascists" and like opponents of political pluralism and "democratic experiments" in general. While it is true that power reverted to the radical right only after the massive intervention by Nazi Germany and Fascist Italy in the internal affairs of the countries of Eastern Europe it is also true that conservative political forces, through skillful exploitation of the inroads made by the radical right, managed to gain either outright control of the political order of the succession states or, at least, to erode the initial commitment to pluralistic, democratic politics and witness the decline and eventual collapse of liberal or moderate governments in the thirties. And it should be noted that these processes of "de-democratization" were in full swing even before Mussolini or Hitler could be held responsible for the "collapse of democracy" in Eastern Europe.

It is undeniable that Fascist Italy and Nazi Germany were supportive of the radical right and also that rightist politicians were more often than not sympathetic toward the aims and policies of the Axis. It would be fallacious, however, to assume that the radical right and its organizations were creatures of Mussolini or Hitler. Rather, Iron Guardists, clerico-fascists, and similar groups expressed views compatible with nationalist ideologies held dear by most conservative politicians and by a significant proportion of the inhabitants of the succession states. For indeed, nationalism was the *lingua franca* of irredentists and anti-revisionists, of anti-Semites and anti-communists. That Hitler, Mussolini, and Stalin, each in their own way, exploited and encouraged irredentism for the attainment of their own revisionist and imperialist goals is unquestionable but that exploitation was possible only because conditions for "divide and conquer" were ripe in the 1930s. Under the prevailing "objective conditions" the several moderate and democratically-inclined political parties that were in power throughout most of the interwar years in Czechosolvakia and occasionally, if briefly, other countries of Eastern Europe could never establish strong enough a political base and develop a devoted constituency to resist the anti-democratic, separatist, extremist, anti-communist, and other negative forces that led, gradually, to the establishment of dictatorships or authoritarian regimes. The internal forces opposing democracy were, generally, acting if not with the formal consent of the population at least without meaningful opposition. The fact that the anti-democratic forces succeeded in their goals does not, however suggest that they were unequivocally supportive of Hitler's and Mussolini's. And that was so because the Axis was ready to undermine its supporters and sympathizers in the succession states whenever it suited the Führer's or Duce's interests. Yet, this apparent contradiction does not imply, as has so often been suggested, that democracy failed in interwar Eastern Europe because of external pressures which caused the adoption of or support for anti-democratic attitudes and measures by political organizations and by people at large which would not have occurred under different international circumstances. Rather, it failed or, more correctly, failed to take root because the preconditions for pluralistic democracy were almost uniformly missing in the historic experience and political and cultural values, traditions, and mentalities of the majority of the peoples of the succession states and of the ruling elites.

Under the circumstances, questions related to the destruction of actual or potential democratic values, practices, experiences, and aspirations of the peoples of Eastern Europe by the communists in the "Takeover" at the end of World War II seem worthy of reconsideration and reassessment.

The prevalent contemporary view is that the peoples of Eastern Europe, no matter what their attitudes toward the Nazi penetration, conquest, or domination of their countries, were generally united, toward the end of the war, in their massive opposition to totalitarianism and committed to the restoration of the democracy which generally eluded them in the interwar years. Moreover, a significant majority of the same people who had identified the Soviet Union as a "liberating" force from "fascism" that would allow them to to achieve democratic goals, realized by 1944 that "liberation" to Stalin meant only the substitution of one dictatorship for another. Whether the majority of the population also realized that "people's democracy" had little, if anything, in common with Western democracy or, for that matter, that communist rule would be the least compatible with the historic traditions and political culture of Eastern Europe and, as such, the least desirable alternative to any form of governance experienced during the interwar and wartime years is, however, uncertain. What is certain is that the majority of political leaders and organizations that emerged toward the end of World War II were not committed to democracy as much as to anti-communism; that, in fact, their democratic tendencies and pronounciamentos generally represented a disclaimer of their presumably involuntary "cooperative" attitudes toward wartime regimes. There were, of course, exceptions particularly among the so-called "governments in exile," but, perhaps cynically, the democratic commitments of those governments assumed exaggerated proportions as the likelihood of their ever assuming power vanished after the nefarious agreements between the Western allies and the Soviet Union. It should not be forgotten that "collaborationists" with the Axis were rather numerous even before the outbreak of the war in Hungary, Yugoslavia, Albania, Romania and even Czechoslovakia and that their number increased markedly during the war itself. The *Ustasha*, Marshal Antonescu, Father Hlinka and others have been condemned for their wartime activities but surely they did not lack in actual or tacit support from other political leaders and, for that matter, even from a significant part of the population. Also of interest is the fact that the "resistance" forces, be they "democratic" or overtly "anti-fascist," were generally "fighting facism" not in a western, democratic, sense but usually in defense of "nationalism" or in support of the "struggle for liberation" from fascism through the military and political efforts of the "democratic" Soviet Union. That the pro-Soviet, if not necessarily communist-sponsored and directed, "resistance" fighters were able to dupe the population when the defeat of Nazi Germany seemed inevitable after the collapse of Mussolini and Soviet victories in the post-Stalingrad period, is not surprising given the misleading legitimation of "anti-fascist" activities by men such as Tito or the Greek communists, the cynical manipulations of Stalin and, in their own way, those of Roosevelt and Churchill. But lest we forget, few of the East European political leaders who could champion democracy by the end of the war had voiced more than token opposition to the ruling wartime regimes even in the waning stages of the conflict. Whether their failure to do so was prompted by the great risks involved in opposing totalitarian regimes acting under Nazi orders, or in consort with Hitler's Germany, or whether it was based on realization of the inevitability of Soviet domination of Eastern Europe and of the likely realities of such domination, is unclear. It would appear, however, as if the threat of communism and Soviet retaliation against all political groups other than those subservient to Stalin was deemed to be more fatal to their existence than acquiescence to non-communist totalitarian or authoritarian rule. The corollary question of whether "closet" democrats would have been more active in the late stages of the war had their secretive or indirect contacts with Britain and the United States met with encouragement as regards the dangers of communist liberation, is also difficult to answer. It is reasonable to assume, however, that the naive or cynical responses of the British and Americans dampened any realistic hopes for avoidance of the substitution of a communist for a "fascist" dictatorship at the end of the war. Because of the unwillingness of the United States and England to unmask the presumed "democratic" intentions of the Soviet Union, the potentially, and few actual, democratic political groups had to opt for cooperation with the communist-led "resistance" and "liberating" forces in the forlorn hope that the United States, at least, would prevent outright Soviet takeovers and resultant Stalinist dictatorships in postwar Eastern Europe. There was, indeed, Hobson's choice: was it more important to discredit the compromised regimes and participate in pseudo-democratization in the hope of communist moderation or was it best to abstain from any participation in communist infiltrated or dominated political coalitions while promoting democratic ideals? As it is known, few indeed were those political leaders who chose the latter alternative but, in truth, even the number who chose the former was quite limited.

The question may rightly be asked then whether abstinence or opportunism were the most realistic approaches given the "objective conditions" prevailing at the end of World War II? If a communist takeover was inevitable, as the vast majority of political leaders and politically-conscious population surmised, the only hope was reliance on Western actions designed to moderate Stalin's aims and methods. To actively counter the communists was an option for the foolhardy, or politicians in exile, since the communist-dominated organizations championing "people's democracy" as a reward for victory over "fascism" were sufficiently persuasive, at least initially, to appeal to the politically naive or indifferent masses as exponents of the "glorious Soviet armies" were reinforcing the "democratic, anti-fascist" forces in a manner that cast doubts about the trustworthiness of the propaganda did not, per se, exclude for the gullible the possibility of moderation in the "Takeover." It was only after the "democratic fronts" became more and more exposed as instruments of Soviet policy and of Stalin's true goals, as the leadership of these organizations became more and more infiltrated by alien elements, mostly Jews and foreigners, when the role of the "liberating" Soviet armed forces and Soviet political advisers and representatives became all-the-more evident, that reality began to awaken and impress the masses. Nevertheless, even then political leaders of "historic parties," who in one way or another cooperated in or tolerated the "democratization" of Eastern Europe orchestrated and conducted by the Soviet Union, were willing to seek further compromises as long as the communists limited their definition of "fascists" and sought, at least pro forma, cooperation with those who could be identified with the traditional interests of the people. The convergence of the communist claims of representing the "workers and working peasantry" with those of other presumed representatives of the workers' and peasants' interests, the socialists and agrarians, respectively, still deluded those segments of the population that were traditionally anti-urban and anti-bourgeois capitalist and, as such, accepting collaboration of socialist and agrarian leaders with communists as a feasible, if not necessarily normal, relationship. The fact is that "democracy," in the western pluralistic and participatory sense, was not much of an issue for the majority of the peoples of Eastern Europe as soon as that political alternative became utopian after the end of the war. However, the true nature of "people's democracy" was realistically faced only by a small number of politically-conscious individuals who, unlike the majority of their compatriots, understood the significance of "salami tactics" and the total cynicism and indifference of the Western Allies to the gradual and inevitable conquest of Eastern Europe by Stalin and fellow communists. Individual details may have differed in terms of specific geopolitical and internal conditions but, in fact, the differences between Tito's tactics and success and those of Dimitrov, Ana Pauker, Rákosi, and even Gottwald were in essence the same. Without the support of the Western Allies— in fact with their acquiescence of gradual communist takeovers—the few democratic forces present in wartime and early postwar Eastern Europe could under no circumstances secure a lasting foothold in the Stalinist regimes imposed or supported by the Soviet Union.

Yet, in our opinion, the takeovers should not necessarily be viewed as a confrontation between "democracy" and "totalitarianism," as a communist destruction of actual or potential democratic forces. To assume that the defeat of "fascism" was due to the opposition of the peoples of Eastern Europe to totalitarianism which resulted, after years of experience under the "fascist heel," in an awareness of the merits of democracy, if not necessarily in a revival of alleged democratic sentiments and practices stifled by totalitarianism, is an exaggeration at best and a cynical propaganda ploy at worst. The native "fascist" dictatorships were generally accepted, albeit more with resignation than enthusiasm, throughout most of Eastern Europe. The defeat of the Axis was welcomed as it meant the end of a cruel war. "Liberation from Facism" would have aroused enthusiasm had it been carried out by the democratic forces of the Western allies; however, it aroused suspicions, and often fears, as the democratic liberating forces were those of the Soviet Union. But even those liberators would have been acceptable, or at least tolerable, had the communist-dominated "democratic" leaders been selective in implementation of their plans by insuring their compatibility with prevailing political cultures and traditions. However, the gradual desecration of religion and religious institutions, the attack on private property rights, the elevation to power of Jews and "Moscovites" unidentified with national cultures and traditions, failed to compensate for the "reforms" that eliminated the political power of the bourgeoisie and urban and rural "capitalists." And, ultimately the presence of "liberating" Soviet armed forces combined with the ruthless exploitations of the "Soviet Bloc" by the Soviet Union and its satraps led to the resurgence of two fundamental or deepening elements of the political culture of Eastern Europe—anti-communism and nationalism.

Anti-communism was an option available only to Eastern European political leades in exile and to the ethnic diasporas. Anti-communism was not, however, necessarily equated with or identified with democratic revulsion against totalitarianism. In fact, except when such identification was required by the political environment of the host country or stemmed from genuine conviction that democracy was the answer to the problems of postwar Eastern Europe, anti-communist activities were directed and orchestrated by conservative, authoritarian, and quite frequently "neo-fascist" politicians. Nationalism, however, was adopted by nearly all anti-communists who held the "Bolsheviks" responsible for the desecration of national historic and cultural traditions, for conquering by force and illegitimate means the national states of Eastern Europe and establishing the "evil empire." The political goal of the governments, national committees and other political organizations in exile and of most of the politically conscious and concerned members of the diasporas became defined as a "crusade for freedom" from communism for the satellites of the Soviet Union. The essential incompatibility between historic nationalism and communism and Western bourgeois democracy was often deliberately ignored by the sponsors of "liberating" movements—mostly the United States—who, shortly after the total communist takeover of Eastern Europe, equated the crusade for freedom with liberation of "captive nations" yearning for western democracy. That incompatibility, however, was known to and capitalized upon by nondemocratic leaders of liberation movements, mostly in Western Europe. Aware as they were of the general absence of democratic traditions and of the paternalistic, authoritarian, and conservative political culture common to Eastern Europe, they rightly claimed that anti-communism does not imply democratic sentiments and goals but rather replacement of the heathen, Judeo-communist, dictatorships by conservative, authoritarian, nationalist regimes.

The new rulers of Eastern Europe including, of course, Stalin himself also realized from an early date that limited identification of communism with nationalism was politically expedient not only to counter external propaganda but also, and primarily, to allow them to assume the role of executors of the peoples' historic interests and of the national historic traditions. The obvious falsifications of the aim of the people, defined as the struggle for the attainment of socialism, did not erase the anti-communism of the inhabitants of the Soviet bloc. Nor did, for this matter, the redefinition of historic nationalism as "socialist patriotism" correspond to the historic truth. However, the coopting of nationalism and the enunciation of the doctrine of "national roads to socialism" relieved, at least partially, the anti-Soviet sentiments of the East Europeans.

The efficacy of making nationalism an essential element of the political dialogue and platforms of all parties concerned with Eastern Europe is questionable; what is important, however, is that the common denominator—nationalism—was considered an integral and indispensable part of the political culture and historic traditions of Eastern Europe. Gradually too, all parties made "democracy" an integral part of the political dialogue and platforms albeit in incompatible definitions and utilizations of the term. The communists never deviated from the premise that they were the trustees and fulfillers of the people's "democratic" goals as evidenced, inter alia, in the retention of the term "people's democracy" for identification of the nature and status of such countries as Hungary, Poland, and Bulgaria. Other Eastern European countries, such as Romania and Czechoslovakia, which deleted "people's democracy" in favor of "socialist republic" merely regarded "socialist" as a more perfect "democracy" on the assumption that communism itself was ultimate expression of the peoples' historic "democratic" goals. It is worthy to note that even in 1989 reformist communists did not necessarily reject that definition of "democracy"; they merely admitted to errors in the formulation and implementation of policies by dogmatic interpreters of Marxism-

Leninism.

It is, however, more important to note that even after the "revolutions" of 1989 the establishment of western bourgeois democracy has been neither a *sine qua non* nor a realistic goal for the majority of the inhabitants of Hungary, Poland and other countries of Eastern Europe. Few indeed are those in Eastern Europe, or for that matter even in the West, who believe in the likelihood of genuine democratization, at least in the near future. The chances of developing meaningful political organizations that could participate in determining a democratic course for one or another country appears to be limited. The destruction of the moderate liberal urban bourgeoisie and of the petty rural bourgeoise, and of the political parties identified with or representative of their interests, would require a lengthy restructuring of the socio-economic and political orders. Besides, the world economic conditions, as different as they are now from what they were before World War II, would virtually—at least in the near term—preclude the establishment of viable "bourgeois capitalist" and corollary "bourgeois democratic" systems. Economic and social changes do not require, in the view of the majority of East Europeans, coincidence of political orders; of greater importance is the restoration of human and property rights. Those rights need not be those granted by the American constitution or, for that matter, by the first and fifth amendments to that unique document; they do, however, encompass the right to free practice of religion, the right to private property and unhindered disposition thereof, the right to free association and expression. Political paternalism by a benevolent bureaucratic state would be acceptable as long as the abusive elements which characterized the monolythic communist police states of Eastern Europe will not recur.

This perception is incorporated in the political platforms of non- or pseudo-democratic opponents of communism who advocate the restoration of property and religious rights, however not in conformity with formulae devised by western bourgeois democrats and their East European adherents and counterparts but with what they consider to be the historic legacy of pre-communist Eastern Europe—"Orthodoxy, Autocracy, Nationality." The neo-Slavophiles or, rather, the "neo-Fascists" are persuaded that the political culture of the majority of the peoples of Eastern Europe is rooted in religion, paternalism, and the quest for independence within a national state ruled by the ethnic majority for the benefit of that majority and that those who are not "one of us" from a religious, national, and cultural stand-point could only hope for toleration. In other words, the alternative to "national socialism" of the communist variety is not western social-ism or democracy but "national socialism" of a "populist democratic" variety. The fact that these views appear to be popular with a large number of anti-communist émigrés, with much of the diaspora, and apparently also with significant segments of the peoples of Eastern Europe itself one may well wonder whether conventional interpreta-tions of the significance of the "Takeover" in the history of Eastern Europe are not questionable at best.

To summarize our views: the "Takeover" was inevitable and suc-cessful not because it was compatible with the desiderata of the peo-ples and political leaders of Eastern Europe but because of the lack of alternatives available at the end of World War II. The internal demo-cratic forces were weak not only because they were de facto obliterated during the war but also because, with few exceptions, they never had broadly based constituencies or, for that matter, extensive support from the people. The rejection of "fascism" was not necessarily the result of an explosion of democratic sentiments by the East Euro-peans which had to be hidden during the war; it was, in many cases, a necessity to avoid a greater evil, heathen Bolshevism, and to secure the support of the Western Allies in the fact of the Soviet threat. The actions of the Allies which facilitated the takeover, with cynical disre-gard of the consequences of that expansion of Soviet power, rendered any democratic resolution of the fate of postwar Eastern Europe im-possible. The Russians were *"bon pour l'Orient"* and *"l'Orient"* was good for the Russians. While the Western attitude was character-istic and hardly based on cognizance of factors other than strategic and geopolitical, the fact is that the political culture and historic ex-perience of most of Eastern Europe was not incompatible with that of pre-communist Russia. Russian intervention in "wars of national independence" and in World War I, for instance, and resultant occu-pations of parts of Eastern Europe were often viewed as advantageous and congruent with national interests; in fact, more often than not, Russia was the "Big Brother." This is to say that had Stalin kept the promises made to his wartime allies and had he been true to his own propaganda, "liberation" and the ensuing takeover would not have been regarded as a disaster either by the West or by East Europeans themselves. But Stalin's totalitarianism differed greatly from the tra-ditional authoritarian, paternalistic, nationalistic political patterns prevalent in Eastern Europe, that his "orthodoxy, autocracy, nationality" was incompatible with that of the "liberated" countries. The takeover destroyed the traditional conservative forces—church, aristocracy, bourgeoise, and peasantry—by means far more brutal than any known in modern times. His, and his satraps' in Eastern Europe, was the wrong orthodoxy, autocracy, and nationality and, despite cosmetic efforts at seeking identification of the communist order and state with the precommunist and historic political cultural traditions, communism of the Stalinist variety remained unacceptable. The collapse of communism then does not necessarily entail acceptance of bourgeois democracy as an ideology and system representative of or even compatible with the political cultural traditions of the "developing" East European national, and nationalist, states of the twentieth century. There are other alternatives.

POUR LA FRANCE:
FRENCH INTELLIGENCE AND THE MONTENEGRIN GOVERNMENT-IN-EXILE, 1916–1921

Kim Frančev

For the hapless state of Montenegro, the history of the events of 1916 to 1921 have been obscured by an incomplete record, and the mishandling of those records that did survive. We will never know the exact events surrounding the capitulation of the Montenegrin government in 1918, and King Nikola himself left no apologia. In addition, many of the papers left by the government-in-exile were destroyed during the Austrian occupation and afterward. Much of the work of the government-in-exile was carried on underground, and therefore, the record of its activities is somewhat obscure. Nonetheless, the archives which survived most intact in regard to the Montenegrins are those of the French Foreign Office and the French military. Fortunately, then, for Montenegrin historiography, the French, in the fulsome recording of their punctilious spying activities, have filled in many gaps.

At the outbreak of World War I, Montenegro, a small and backward kingdom of some 400,000 souls, with a state treasury of less than 89 cents per capita, had been ruled for the past five decades by its seventy-eight year-old poet-warrior, Nikola Petrović-Njegoš.

Despite the severe poverty of his country, King Nikola had nonetheless managed to marry his prodigious family throughout the European noble houses. Queen Jelena of Italy was Nikola's eldest living daughter, two other daughters had married Russian granddukes, and Danilo, the crown prince had married a Mecklenberg-Strelitz of the German royal family. Additionally, the Russian czar, always desiring a foothold in the Adriatic, provided a large annual stipend, favoring Montengro as the protector of South Slav unity. Support from the Russians is said to have caused King Nikola to remark whenever apropos, "The Russians and us 60,450,000 strong!"

French intelligence activities in Montenegro began as early as the first official consulate to the country—seated initially in Dubrovik in 1880. At first, the entire diplomatic corps consisted of a *charge d'affaires*, a secretary, and an interpreter. There was a military attaché who was also accredited to Serbia and Romania. For the next sixteen years, this tiny mission attempted to keep its finger on the pulse of Montenegrin affairs from Dubrovnik, a task made more difficult by the fact that that city was controlled by Austria-Hungary. To bridge this gap the French employed the services of one of their countrymen, a physician named Fevrier, who lived in Cetinje. However, in 1888 Fevrier angered Nikola by publicly criticizing him, and was forced to leave Cetinje. With Fevrier's departure, the French lost their contact in Montenegro.

At the urging of August Gerard, the French *charge d'affaires*, the French diplomatic mission was finally moved to Cetinje, although it was not opened until June of 1896. Even so, the French consuls continued to spend most of their time in the considerably more agreeable Dubrovnik than in Cetinje, until 1910, when a French consular residence was constructed in Cetinje.[1]

Although French policy toward Montenegro warmed considerably in the years preceding World War I, the French diplomatic corps, which reported the daily events in Cetinje, were not admirers of the Montenegrin dynasty. Delaroche-Vernet, the French consul in Cetinje, maintained an abiding distrust of King Nikola and much of the royal court. French official dealings with the Montenegrin royal family and government were cordial and correct, but the dispatches reaching the *Quai d'Orsay* were filled with ironical asides and innuendo, which in one way or another colored the official French attitude toward Montenegro.

Although Montenegro quickly seconded Serbia in its ill-conceived war against Austria, less than two years into the war, the Montenegrins were forced to capitulate. Although no more beaten militarily than the Serbian Army, which was slowly retreating through the Montenegrin highlands, the Montenegrins suffered from a total lack of supplies, and they were, in fact, deliberately denied Allied aid. France, the dominant ally of Montenegro, had early on determined, albeit secretly, to support Serbia in the realization of its war aims, which included the annexation of Montengro. In January of 1916, with the Austrians at their door, Nikola and the Montenegrin Government determined to flee the kingdom and seek refuge in an allied country.

Between 1916 and 1921, France was home to the Montenegrin

royal family and the remnants of the government that had chosen to follow the King into exile. The French expected that in due time King Nikola would install his government on Corfu, where he could oversee the remnants of his troops, while the Queen and her daughters would remain in Lyon, because of its proximity to Italy. However, in February of 1916, Nikola advised Delaroche-Vernet that he wanted his residence at Bordeaux.

The presence of the Montenegrin government in Bordeaux presented a security problem for the French, since King Nikola had attempted to use the good offices of Spain, as a neutral country, to formulate peace terms with Austria. In the same month, Austria asked the Spanish ambassador in Vienna if Spain would act as a *parvenir* with Nikola and his ministers for negotiating a peace. The Austrians wanted Nikola's formal consent to the peace, as well as his authorization to the remaining ministers in Cetinje to act on his behalf. Although the French, at this point, took scant interest in the details of any capitulation, they did fear that Nikola would somehow use Spain as an intermediary to conduct independent diplomacy with Austria. Despite all efforts on the part of both the Spanish and Montenegrin governments to persuade the Allies otherwise, Spain was prevented from acting openly as an envoy.[2]

No sooner had the Montenegrin Government established itself in France, than the French began their surveillance. They tapped the telegraph between Lyon and Nice, where Prince Danilo and his wife—no strangers to the Cote d'Azur—rented a villa, and cultivated spies among the growing émigré community. The Minister of Interior kept a record of even the most banal activities of the royal entourage and the government-in-exile, to which Delaroche-Vernet often added his own colorful, if frequently obtuse, observations.

Serbian Prime Minister Nikola Pašić and his coterie were eager to add their own disinformation to the record. The reports sent by Deloroche-Vernet were often commenced with the words, "from a source secret but sure," which more often than not referred to a disaffected Montenegrin or Serbian informer with a personal axe to grind. For example, according to Petar Plemanac, one of Delaroche-Vernet's Serbian informers, a certain member of the Montenegrin government was not only the lover of Princess Ksenija, but an Austrian agent. Moreover, the Popović brothers, also prominent in Montenegrin affairs, reportedly were involved in "the dangerous world of international business." The Serbian informants advised that Princess

Ksenija should be carefully watched, as she exerted more influence than anyone over her father, and was regarded as a notorious intriguer. Danilo's wife, thc Princess of Mecklenberg, on the other hand, was considered a "loyal" Montenegrin, and French intelligence claimed that only she cried at the taking of Mt. Lovcen when Montenegro fell.

Miloš Živković, Nikola's personal secretary, was accused in a Serbian intelligence report to the French of being not only Austrophile but also a homosexual. Živoković was, in fact, a Serb born in Croatia who claimed Montenegrin nationality. He had been educated in Zagreb and later worked in Belgrade on the staffs of several Serbian publications before becoming editor of *Glas Crnogorca*, the official organ of the Montenegrin Gouernment. According to Montenegrin sources, Živković became a Montenegrin citizen in 1912, and had followed the government into exile. Months after thc accusations against Živković, which had been made by a rival Montenegrin émigré in Belgrade, the French Interior Ministry retracted its claims, saying that despite all investigations, Živković seemed to be exactly what he and Nikola's government claimed. Nonetheless, he remained under the careful eye of the French police.[3]

The French were aided in their surveillance by Delaroche-Vernet and his family, who installed themselves in Merignac, near Bordeaux, along with a Madame Garnier, who operated the Montenegrin postal bureau and telegraph station. The consulate, at 307bis Boulevard de Cauderon, employed one Montenegrin as an interpretor and translator. Its other "collaborators," as Delaroche-Vernet referred to them—all members of the Montenegrin consulate in France—were, in his words, "conscious of their patriotic role."[4]

The French intelligence network reached deep into the Montenegrin Government and even into the court itself. Since 1916, Montenegro had maintained a consulate on the Boulevard Berthier in Paris under the direction of Louis Brunet, a former French deputy, who had been a member of the High Council and Consultive Committee for the Colonies. During the Balkan Wars, he was an intermediary in supplying arms to Montenegro and had become a confidant of King Nikola. Brunet, who was also involved in several Montenegrin financial affairs, made an ideal informant for the French.[5]

Early in 1917, Brunet was appointed Secretary General of the Ministry of Foreign Affairs for the government-in-exile. Soon thereafter, he arranged with the French to have Commander Pierre Letang, ex-chief of the 91st Territorial Infantry Division, to become *marechal* of the Montenegrin court and *aide-de-camp* to King Nikola. Letang, then a depot chief at Rouen, was a long-time friend of the Montenegrin court.[6]

In anticipation of a brighter future, and at the urging of the French, Nikola moved the seat of the government from its damp and uncomfortable quarters at Merignac to the royal residence on the Boulevard Victor Hugo in Neuilly, outside Paris. Here, of course, the Montenegrins could be kept under even better surveillance. In Neuilly, French agents joined the newly formed Franco-Montenegrin Committee for Economic Studies and promoted a future economic development of Montenegro to the benefit of France; they also reported regularly to the *Quai*.[7]

In early December 1916, Louis Brunet was fired suddenly by Nikola. Brunet claimed that it was Ksenija's doing, but, in any case, it is likely that Nikola was finally convinced of Brunet's role as a key informer for the French. Brunet attempted to prove his innocence by claiming that the rest of the consulate had resigned in protest.[8]

It became increasingly difficult and less fruitful to spy on the Montenegrin Government and court more and more isolated behind the walls of its massive residence in Neuilly. As a result, the French concentrated their efforts on the small Montenegrin communities abroad, especially those in Geneva and Lausanne. The French Foreign Ministry felt sure that there was some kind of nefarious Montenegrin triangle between King Nikola and the government-in-exile in Paris, Prince Danilo in the south of France, and Lazar Mijušković, the former president of the Montenegrin Council, in Geneva. The French knew that there was an attempt by Austria during the summer of 1917 to attract the Serbs and Montenegrins into a federation with Bulgaria. Mijušković was suspected of being the scheme's Montenegrin connection in Switzerland. However, this was denied by Mijušković's friends, and some of the French as well, whose informants and diplomatic corps believed Mijušković to be loyal to the Allied cause. Nonetheless, many French officials continued tn suspect him of involvement in Austria's plans, and the "problem Mijušković" remained an enigma. According to a report from the Ministry of War to the Foreign Ministry, Mijušković was involved in a scheme to form a South Slav state under the auspices of Austria. However, as the War Ministry noted, the problem was a complex one for Austria since it was not possible for the scheme to be considered openly without angering Germany, one sf the countries whose hegemony the new union was designed to contain.[9]

According to the *Deutsches Tageszeitung* of January 5, 1917, there were open negotiations between the Austrians and the Montenegrins in Switzerland, at which Mijuskovic was present, on the subject of the creation of a South Slav state. Although Mijuškovic vehemently denied the reports, the French believed that he was involved in secret plans. They cited a meeting which had taken place at Mijuškovic's apartment in Geneva, during which he, Pavle Popovic, Dusan Gregovic and several other prominent Montenegrin businessmen discussed the future of Montenegro in the event of an Austrian victory. They reportedly discussed the partitioning of Serbia among Austria, Bulgaria, and Montenegro. The new Montenegrin kingdom, in this event, would be under the sovereignty of Prince Mirko, King Nikola's second eldest son, who had remained in Montenegro with his army after the capitulation.[10]

According to the same report, it was Pavle Popovic who was the liaison between the Austrian Government and this secret Montenegrin committee. Mico Popovic, Pavle's father, who remained in Cetinje, had been the confidant of Nikola and for many years shared in the machinations of the Montenegrin regime. Jovo Popovic, Pavle's brother, who was interned in an Austrian concentration camp, was purported to complete the triangle of communication which eventually lead back to Nikola in Paris. However, of the Montenegrins in the Swiss community, only Mijuškovic and Popovic were accused of negotiating directly with the Central Powers.

Dušan Gregovic was the former Montenegrin minister of the interior. He lived at the Hotel Beau Rivage in Geneva, where he spent the majority of his time playing cards, and, according to French sources, had not taken direct part in any negotiations with the Austrians. Typical of the Montenegrin community there, Gregovic was considered unambitious and apolitical even by the Serbs.

Despite the reports of French intelligence officers and the accusations of émigrés against the Montenegrins in Switzerland, there was no hard evidence to link Mijuškovic or Popovic to direct dealings with the Central Powers. The Swiss Montenegrins tended to be in favor of unification with Serbia, and were not partisan to King Nikola. They supported him only as a hedge against the "radicals" in the Montenegrin Committee for National Union, which also championed union with Serbia. When one of his exile cabinets failed, Nikola tried to induce Mijušković and Gregović to return to Paris and form a new government, but they both refused. Thereafter, both the Montenegrin Committee for National Union (MCNU) and French intelligence reported numerous meetings between Prince Danilo and Mijušković. As a result, the Prince's purported Austrophile leanings were inferred to Mijušković. Mijušković and other adversaries of the MCNU did form the Montenegrin Economic Association and the Montenegrin Society for People's Law, which openly attacked both Serbia and the MCNU.[11]

During the summer of 1917, Mijusković wrote a lengthy letter to the French Foreign Office in which he denied personal responsibility for the capitulation of Montenegro, and accused the French and British consuls of encouraging Nikola to demand a separate peace. Louis Brunet, who received a copy of Mijušković's official rejoinder and the counteraccusations of the MCNU, agreed with the French foreign Ministry that while they were sympathetic to Misusković's description of events, and regarded them to be generally accurate, they decided that political necessity determined that the story not be revealed because it placed France and the Allies in a particularly bad light.

In October of 1920, the royal family moved to Cap d'Antibes, where Nikola's daughters Milica and Anastasia and their husbands, the Granddukes Peter and Nikola Nikolaevich, had resided since leaving the Crimea in 1917. By this time, French agents spied on King Nikola by riding their bicycles close behind him as he took his daily walks. They reported that the King suffered increasingly from mental and physical depression.[12]

By the end of 1920, the Montenegrin treasury was bankrupt and the government-in-exile had ceased to exist. When the constituent assembly of the government of the Kingdom of Serbs, Croats, and Slovenes voted Montenegro into the union, Delaroche-Vernet informed King Nikola that his functions on behalf of the French had come to an end.[13]

French intelligence efforts, thorough as they were in the Montenegrin case, uncovered little information of real value of its own government. Throughout the period, the French remained confused about the "Swiss connection," and consistently misinterpreted the intentions of the Montenegrin underground movement. Nikola, as frail as his position, continued to toy with the French, who could not compete with the consistent disinformation campaign that he waged almost to the end of his life. As Delaroche-Vernet remarked, *"L'ombre de l'ombre humaine existe et fail de l'ombre!"* ["The shadow of the human shadow has come alive and cast its own shadow!"].[14]

NOTES

1. Dimitrije Dimo-Vujović, "The Montenegro et la Troisième Republique," in *Le Montenegro dans les Relations Internationales,* 123–124.

2. France, Archives de la Ministere des Affaires Étrangères (AME), Vol. 324, 2/11/1916: Spanish Minister of Foreign Affairs to French Ambassador in Madrid.

3. AMAE, Vol. 324, 108–109, 2/16/1916: Note of Minister of the Interior (MI) to Minister of Foreign Affairs (MFA); Vol. 325, 1/17/1917: Note of MFA to MI; Ibid., 1/24/1917: Letter of Tomanović to Vernet.

4. AMAE, Vol. 324, 3/25/1916: Letter of Brunet to MFA.

5. AMAE, Vol. 329, 11/17/1917: MI to MFA.

6. AMAE, Vol. 324, 2/20/1916: Brunet to Briand.

7. Telegram #97527 A. R. Chef du Service des Renseignements Generaux to Prefet de Police, Paris.

8. AMAE, Vol. 328, 12/5/1916: Note #62, Vernet to File; ibid., 2/7/1916: Letter of Brunet to Margerie.

9. France, Archives de la Ministere de la Guerre (AMG), Box 7 N 1587, #294: Report of Capt. Raspail to Minister of War.

10. Ibid.

11. Dimo-Vujović, *Ujedinjenie Crne Gore i Srbije,* 270.

12. AMAE, Z Europe, Vol. II, 181–182, 12/14/1920 and 12/15/1920, telegrams #560 and #562: Fontenay to MFA.

13. Ibid., 12/28/1920: Vernet to MFA.

14. Ibid.

THE HUNGARIAN FINANCIAL COLLAPSE, 1945–46

Remi Nadeau

Early in 1945, when the Red Army occupied Hungary, there was a story in Budapest of a storekeeper who found Russian soldiers loading his wares on a truck. He ran out into the street shouting, "Patrol!" to call for the Red Army military police. One of the looters then stepped forward, smiling, and announced, "I am the patrol."[1]

The story was symbolic of the relationship between the Soviet Union and Hungary after World War II. Legally, the Hungarian armistice agreement allowed the Russians $200 million in war reparations, and the Potsdam agreement allowed them to seize German assets. These vaguely worded concessions were interpreted by the Soviets into outrageous proportions. The value of materials taken to satisfy reparations was established unilaterally by the Russians and therefore at extremely low figures, so that reparations payments were doubled or tripled, according to Stephen Kertesz and estimated by Ferenc Nagy to be three to five times the allowed figure. German assets were made to include assets previously owned by Hungarians but seized by the Germans, and were interpreted to include debts owed by Hungarians to Germans (and now owed to Russia). In addition, the reparations agreement forced on the Hungarian Government by the Soviets called for interest of 5 percent per month (60 percent per year) on late payment of reparations—an odd twist in which a Communist Government played Shylock. This forced Hungary to extreme measures to keep up payments. Ferenc Nagy, a cabinet member at this time, later wrote:

> In the second half of 1945 Hungary was able to pay only
> by dismantling her factories and sending a certain number
> of cattle. Even so, this made up less than a third of the
> required amount. The period of reparations indebtedness
> and economic slavery was beginning.[2]

But the legal demands, imposed unmercifully, were only part of the problem. Stephen Kertesz, a Hungarian official from 1945 to 1947, adds more:

> Besides carrying the legal burden of the armistice obliga-
> tions, Hungary suffered through illegal seizure and large-
> scale looting. The notion of "war booty" was interpreted
> most extensively. Valuable machines, and in numerous in-
> stances whole plants, were dismantled and removed to the
> Soviet Union. Grains and other victuals were seized in huge
> quantities. Almost one-half of the livestock was taken out
> of the country. Safe deposit boxes were forced open and
> their contents removed. Whether the property was private
> or public did not make any difference. Private homes, pub-
> lic warehouses, stores, government agencies, and banks all
> received the same treatment. Legations of neutral powers,
> such as Switzerland, Sweden, or Turkey were not spared.[3]

This inhuman draft on the Hungarian economy came on top of
the wholesale removals by the retreating Germans and Hungarian
Nazis, and the massive destruction of war. Nagy reported that in
Budapest alone, 54 percent of households and 84 percent of buildings
were destroyed or damaged.

From the beginning the Soviets held economic control, which in
turn became a weapon in achieving political control. Some of the
money seized from Hungarian banks was turned over to the Communist Party. Economic thumb-screwing was used to wring political concessions. When the Moscow Communist, Zoltan Vas, became
Mayor of Budapest in 1945, he asked the Red Army for food. The
generous Russians sent him 180 carloads of grain, thousands of head
of livestock, and several carloads of sugar. This was part of the farm
produce previously seized in Hungary by the Red Army. The Communist Party took credit, of course, for winning this largesse from the
Soviets. The so-called "food loan" was later demanded back by the
Russians.[4]

Early in 1945 the Soviets began pushing for an economic treaty
with Hungary. In August two Hungarian cabinet members, Antal
Ban and Erno Gero, traveled to Moscow with powers to negotiate
a fifteen-month barter agreement valued at about $30 million. But
the Soviets also presented a much larger, five-year agreement that
had never been discussed by leaders in Hungary. This provided for
joint Soviet-Hungarian "economic development" in Hungarian industry, mining, aviation, shipping, trade, and agriculture. Among other

things it would create stock companies jointly owned by Hungary and the Soviet Union on a 50–50 basis in operating such industries as iron and steel, aluminum, petroleum, electric power, chemicals, banking, air and motor transport, and Danube River navigation.

In sum, the second agreement unveiled in Moscow injected Soviet control into the entire Hungarian economy. When Antal Ban, a Social Democrat, flew back from Moscow to Budapest for authorization to sign the new proposal, Nagy exclaimed, "We mustn't give such authorization under any circumstances." But Gero, a Muscovite Communist, had remained behind in Moscow; acting on wider authorization that had been given unwittingly by Prime Minister Bela Miklos, he signed the treaty in "preliminary" form, along with the smaller agreement, on August 27, 1945.

For three months the issue was debated in Budapest. Some leaders could see that the agreement handed over the Hungarian economy to Soviet control. Nagy asked whether the United States or Britain were interested in such an agreement, but they declined. The Soviets applied pressure by warning that if their agreement were rejected they would remove to Russia all the rest of the industrial equipment that had been awarded to them as German assets at Potsdam. Promised relaxation of certain reparations payments in the form of food might also be canceled.

Meanwhile, Marxist members of the cabinet pressed Miklos to bring the issue before the council. Smallholder Party members declared they would withdraw from the cabinet if the economic agreement were signed.

Early in October the President of the National Council, which was the body ratifying international agreements, called on American and British representatives in Budapest. If Hungary refused to sign, would their governments support it? The British wired London for an answer. The American representative, H. F. Arthur Schoenfeld, replied that he hoped Hungary "would do its best always to facilitate harmonious cooperation among the Allies," and therefore that the issue "could be formulated in a manner not involving request for support from the U. S. against the Soviet Union." However, despite this negative answer, he asked Washington for instructions.

On October 11 Prime Minister Miklos sent Schoenfeld a copy of the proposed agreement. The issue, he added, was coming before the cabinet, and if it were approved,

I will seek to postpone final acceptance of the agreement

until such time as on the basis of the international agreements, namely Yalta and San Francisco, it will be possible for the British and American Governments to give adequate expression to their position.[5]

Schoenfeld wired the text to Secretary of State James P. Byrnes, who at first advised against any direct answer, then took up the issue with Moscow. In a cautiously worded note, he hoped the Soviets would recognize that major economic agreements should await a peace treaty and should include all of the Big Three powers. The British sent a similar note and also proposed the issue for the ACC agenda in Budapest. On October 31 Andrei Vishinsky rejected the American note, and the Soviets in Budapest continued pressing the Hungarian Government for the economic agreement.

Meanwhile, the Hungarian cabinet had taken up the economic agreement on October 12. At a stormy meeting in which the minister of defense walked out in a huff, the ministers approved the agreement with two amendments. As Istvan Balogh told the others, "it would be too hazardous to raise the suspicions of the Soviet Union by delaying the ratification."[6]

While the Hungarian Government delayed final ratification by the National High Council, the Americans and British continued to press Moscow. In particular, the Western Allies wanted assurance that the proposed economic agreement did not grant monopolistic Soviet control of the Hungarian economy to the exclusion of other nations, especially since the U. S. and Britain had most favored nations treaties with Hungary dating to the 1920s.

The Soviets gave assurance that the agreement was not exclusive. In this case, said the U. S., the Soviets would have no objection to revealing the text (the Western Allies already had texts given them simultaneously by Miklos, but could not say so for fear of compromising him). The Soviets refused to show the text, and the issue went round again.

But on December 20, 1945, the contest ended when the Hungarian National High Council ratified the agreement. It did so without change, except to note separately that "this agreement by no means impedes the Hungarian State to conclude economic or commercial agreements of any kind with other states." Clearly the statement was made to please the Americans and British, but since the Soviet Union had not stipulated this in the agreement, the point was made gratuitously by the Hungarian Government, without the force of a treaty obligation.

Having urged the Western Allies to oppose the treaty and thus support its own resistance, the Hungarian Government now ratified the treaty anyway and threw a sop to one of the American objections. The spectacle showed how far the Soviets had intimidated Budapest, even though a national election had just installed a legitimate democratic government.

In fact, the treaty did operate to bring Hungary's economy entirely within the Soviet orbit. It also enabled the Soviets to accelerate their exploitation of Hungarian resources. As it turned out, each of the so-called 50–50 companies was headed by a Soviet citizen. The Danubian navigation firm gave rise to another wry Hungarian joke: "This is a fifty-fifty company. The Soviets can navigate the river up and down, and the Hungarians can navigate it across."[7]

To Janos Gyongyosi, the Hungarian Foreign Minister, a Soviet official gave assurance that "ratification would clear the way for active assistance by the USSR to the present economic distress."

Distress was, in fact, an understatement. Drafts on the food supply to support the Red Army and the Allied Control Commission (ACC) had cut so deeply into agricultural output that by December many Hungarians were again near starvation. In Budapest, food rationing provided each person with an average of 560 calories per day. Between looting, "war booty," reparations, and seizure of "German" assets, the Soviets had nearly dismantled Hungarian industry. At the same time, urged by the Soviets, the Marxist-led unions in Budapest demanded and won large pay increases. With the economy flattened, it was almost impossible to levy or collect taxes.

By November 1945 the national income was approximately half the pre-war level. Factory production was 35 percent of the pre-war volume. Reparations payments and support for the Red Army together took 31 percent of the national income. In the month of December 1945, two-thirds of the Hungarian Government's budget was used for armistice obligations. As the president of the Hungarian National Bank reported confidentially to the American and British missions in Budapest:

> The industrial goods to be delivered as reparations, the industrial exports necessary to obtain the raw materials for their manufacture, and the investments needed to get reparations production started up, if taken altogether amount to very nearly the total value of the production of industry.[8]

In fact, industry was rapidly being nationalized under pressure from the Marxist parties, yet there were almost no Government funds to pay the workers. Without factory output, goods could not be created and sold to generate funds or earn international currency.

At first the answer seemed obvious: create more money. The Soviets had, in fact, already begun the process by adding 4 billion pengos to the existing money supply of 11 billion pengos in the spring of 1945. Then they lent the Government part of the Hungarian bank notes seized by the Red Army from various banks and businesses. Although the bank note printing press had been taken by the Germans, the Government found another and began turning out a wealth of pengo notes.

As soon as the public realized that this flood of paper money had no backing in gold or other resources, prices began to rise. As prices rose people rushed to spend money before it lost more value, thus driving prices still higher. The inflation thus created was probably the most spectacular in world history—much faster and higher than the German inflation in 1923. On April 1, 1945, the black market value of one dollar was 250 pengos—an increase of over 1,000 percent—and still rising. On one morning the pengo was worth 22 percent of its pre-war value. By evening, after people had been paid their wages and had gone to the market, the pengo was worth only 8 percent. One result of this fantastic inflation was that the value of assets was utterly destroyed and with it the substance of all Hungarian families. The middle class was virtually wiped out as an economic force. According to Schoenfeld, "the Finance Minister lived in fear of a breakdown of the currency printing press which financed 95 percent of the budget . . ."

Reporting to Secretary of State Byrnes, Schoenfeld concluded,

I believe present trends will lead to economic chaos, large-scale starvation, and civil unrest by the end of January or latest mid-February. . . . Such developments would liquidate present government and recent progress of democracy in Hungary."[9]

On December 4, the Soviet Economic Adviser to the ACC summoned the Hungarian Finance Minister, Ferenc Gordon, to report on the nation's inflation crisis. Gordon then wrote a report on Hungary's financial and economic situation. At the ACC offices he handed a Russian translation to the Soviet official and an English version to a

British representative who happened to be present. Angrily, the Russian said the meeting had nothing to do with inflation, and handed the report back to Gordon without reading it. So did the British official.

Gordon took the opportunity to state, however, that

> continuation of the present situation will bring complete collapse within a few weeks for which he could not accept responsibility and therefore he had to request early ACC consideration of Hungary's economic problems.

The Russian replied that he "would discuss the problem with him soon." The episode typified the entire situation at that time: Hungarian desperation, Soviet indifference, and Western Allied passivity. Next day Gordon called on Schoenfeld to describe the meeting and offer a warning. He could only conclude that the Soviet Union "was deliberately engineering complete economic collapse knowing that it would be followed by revolution." Faulting the Americans and British for their "passive role," he said "there could no longer be doubt as to the course of events if Anglo-Americans did not act soon." Schoenfeld himself warned Byrnes that world opinion may "place partial responsibility for this course of events on lack of aggressive American policy . . ." He proposed instructing General Key to raise the Hungarian economic crisis in the ACC.[10] A week later Dean Acheson, Undersecretary of State, wired back his agreement.

Gordon's report had, in fact, proposed a three-power commission to examine Hungary's financial and economic plight and recommend actions. Taking up this idea, the U. S. began pressing for a tripartite effort to save the Hungarian economy. It was brought up in the ACC in Budapest and in the Council of Foreign Ministers then meeting in Moscow.

But the Soviets rejected the idea, saying the economy was the "province of the Hungarian Government." The most that was permitted by Kliment Voroshilov, Chairman of the ACC, was distress relief from the United Nations Relief and Rehabilitation Agency (UNRRA), which the Hungarian Government had repeatedly requested since mid-October. The ACC agreed on the need for UNRRA help on December 28; the UNRRA central committee authorized it informally on January 8, 1946, approved it finally on February 4, sent relief goods in May.

But otherwise the situation remained the same. Because of his

November report on the Hungarian financial crisis, the president of the Hungarian National Bank was removed from his bank position and from the Hungarian peace treaty delegation on orders from Voroshilov.[11] Two Finance Ministers were forced to resign or left in protest of the Soviet economic policy.

"Voroshilov," according to Schoenfeld, "does not countenance discussion of Soviet policies which are throttling the Hungarian goose that lays the eggs because those policies are deliberate."[12]

By February 1946 Schoenfeld was virtually pleading with Byrnes for the U. S. to forget three-power action on the Hungarian economy, which the Soviets consistently blocked, and instead to give direct, unilateral aid. Specifically, he urged that the U. S. grant credits for purchase of surplus American Army equipment in Europe, especially badly needed trucks. The Communists, he wrote on February 9, argue that:

> Western Powers including America are disinterested in this country's welfare and that therefore Hungary's survival depends only on Soviet good will. Those resisting exclusive Soviet orientation of Hungarian economy cannot effectively refute Communist allegation as long as alleged American policy of aloofness continues.

On the same day, Ference Nagy, who had become Prime Minister, sent a written plea to Schoenfeld for other assistance. The retreating Nazis had carried off many millions in Hungarian property. Much of it had been captured by the American Army in Austria and Germany.

"The restitution of these properties," wrote Nagy, "would be more urgent even than any help or relief from abroad."
And he added:

> The peasant and the working classes together with the intelligentsia, who are almost literally in want of their everyday bread, are sacrificing, so to speak, their last strength to ensure the future of the country, but we feel that all our sacrifices are in vain if the Government of the United States does not grant us its help by fulfilling our request.

In Washington the Hungarian Legation's Economic Adviser, Alexander Szasz, went to the State Department's Division of Investment and Economic Development on February 15. Describing his country's economic plight under Russian occupation and reparations demands, he asked for a loan or credits from the Export-Import Bank. His plea was rejected.

On the same day Schoenfeld made a last appeal to Byrnes. "Hungary's financial deterioration is now proceeding at runaway pace," he wrote. During the week prices more than doubled. And he added:

> Time is rapidly and inevitably approaching when Hungarian currency will cease entirely to be acceptable as medium of exchange. All economic activity will then stop except that which can be transacted on barter basis.

Hungary, he continued, needed a stretchout in reparations payments, reduced demands from the Red Army, foreign aid, and emergency food and medical supplies. The Soviets were not helping and were blocking help from other sources. Schoenfeld then added:

> Unwillingness of USSR to facilitate rehabilitation of Hungary at this time and its contribution to country's economic disintegration is palpably part of Soviet strategy of economic penetration of Hungary which has been in process since last summer and is now in full swing.

And finally:

> It is increasingly evident that USSR through successive and individually tentative steps bids fair to advance steadily in this area and elsewhere in Europe much as Nazi Germany advanced through the late thirties. During 1945 Hungary lay in the front line; it is already becoming a Soviet interior area. It may be expected that in relatively short time Hungary will become an economic colony of USSR from which western trade will be excluded.[13]

At this barrage of logic, Byrnes at last acted. On February 21, 1946, the State Department announced the U. S. was advancing a $10 million credit to Hungary for purchasing surplus army equipment in Europe. In Budapest the democratic press and Hungarians in general were jubilant. "Americans would certainly not lend money to a country and then permit it to go Communist," was a common reaction. The Communists, in turn, spread rumors that Hungary would have to give up all interest in its assets in the American zone in return for "worn-out" American trucks. Voroshilov told General Key that the Americans could not really think the Hungarian financial conditions were so bad if they were willing to risk being repaid the $10 million.

Over the next five months the U. S. increased the credit advance to $25 million. At the same time the Americans launched a diplomatic offensive. George Kennan, the chargé d'affairs in Moscow, fired a sharp note to Molotov on March 2, 1946. All proposals of the U. S. to rescue Hungary from disaster has been rejected by the Soviets, he wrote. The U. S. had been kept in the dark about Soviet plans for Hungary's economic future. By now Hungary was on the verge of "complete economic and financial collapse."

> It is clear that this situation is due in a very considerable degree to the over-burdening of the country with reparations and requisitions, to the maintenance of very large occupying forces, to the interference of the occupying authorities in economic matters, and to the failure of those authorities to take energetic measures to combat inflation and other undesirable economic tendencies.

The U. S., he went on, could not stand by and allow this to happen. Then, referring to America's plan for "a broad program of international economic collaboration," he seemed to imply that this would include some type of benefit to the Soviet Union. Then came his clincher:

> But it is self-evident that no nation can claim the benefits of broad international collaboration in the economic field unless it is willing to recognize corresponding obligations in its own international dealings. . . . The United States will necessarily have to be guided by this fact in formulating its economic policies.

With that he requested that the Big Three representatives in Hungary meet to devise a plan to rescue and rehabilitate Hungary. After a seven week's delay, Andrei Vishinsky responded. Soviet occupation and reparations "do not and cannot exercise any serious influence on the economic situation of the country." Hungary was behind in its reparation payments. Deliveries of grain to the occupation troops were relatively small. "There has been no interference by the occupation authorities in Hungary's economic affairs."

On the contrary,

> one of the main reasons for the difficult economic situation in Hungary at the present time is the fact that a large quantity of Hungarian property and valuables continues to this day to remain in the American Zone of occupation. . . .

The Government of the U. S. has thus far given the Hungarian Government no reply to its repeated communications requesting the return of this property.

As for a tripartite "plan for the economic reconstruction of Hungary," such a plan "falls within the competence of the Hungarian Government."[14]

Thus the big-power impasse remained. Meanwhile, leaders of the Hungarian Government had begun a round of visits to Moscow, Washington, and London. In Moscow, Stalin displayed his usual charm to foreign visitors. He extended the term of reparations payments from six to eight years. He granted other requests. He disavowed any intent to interfere with Hungary's domestic affairs. On the Transylvania issue, Molotov urged that this was an issue that could be negotiated between Hungary and Romania. Ferenc Nagy returned from Moscow encouraged. To Schoenfeld he confided his "strong conviction that he now had a free hand to manage his Government."[15]

Schoenfeld thought otherwise. By May 2 he was writing Byrnes that, in the few weeks since returning from Moscow, Nagy had made "frequent expression of deviation to Soviet Hungarian collaboration . . ." When Ference Gordon, Hungarian Finance Minister, asked for a $10 million loan from the Export-Import Bank, Schoenfeld opposed it as being too late to save Hungary. Such help might have been effective in February, he wrote Byrnes, but by now,

> Hungary is virtually a Soviet economic colony in the hands of a Communist minority whose principal objective appears to be collaboration with Russia.

In fact, he added,

> unilateral American assistance would make relatively little contribution to Hungary's rehabilitation because Soviet-imposed economic burdens would neutralize its beneficial effects.

Moreover, he warned,

> key Hungarian officials in control of country's economy would not hesitate to divert American aid to benefit of USSR at expense of their own country.

And finally,

> Hungary's rehabilitation and its adherence to UN objectives are now principally a Soviet matter and must be treated as

an element in overall American-Soviet relations.[16]

The bitterness of Schoenfeld's telegram, following his year-long pleas for American support to Hungary, bears the stamp of a subtle "I-told-you-so" message. In Paris at the time, Byrnes favored granting the loan, but it was killed in Washington by Acheson and William L. Clayton, Assistant Secretary of State for Economic Affairs, together with the heads of the Export-Import Bank.[17] In Paris the U. S. Economic Counselor to the U. S. Embassy broke the news to Gordon on May 9. At a previously arranged luncheon with Gordon afterward, the atmosphere was, as the American put it, "funereal."

In a last plea for American support, Nagy and other top Hungarian leaders including the Communist leader, Matyas Rakosi, visited Washington in June 1946. There they met with Byrnes, Acheson, the House Foreign Affairs Committee and President Truman. At a working meeting on June 12 with John D. Hickerson, Deputy Director of European Affairs, Foreign Minister Gyongyosi and the Hungarians outlined their country's desperate economic crisis and asked, one by one, for the return of stolen goods located in the American zones, increased UNRRA aid, an Export-Import Bank loan, and an increase in the $10 million credit already given to purchase surplus property. One by one Hickerson found excuses why the requests could not be granted. When in desperation the Hungarians hoped they could "pursue a Western orientation," Hickerson in a triumph of naiveté answered that their orientation "should not be exclusively Western, but rather Western, Eastern, Northern and Southern."

But the shock of the Hungarians turned to exhilaration after two meetings with Acheson. On June 14 he told them the U. S. would return the $32 million in gold and the Hungarian property now in the American zones and would consider increasing the credits for surplus property.

Before the jubilant Hungarians left Washington, they held a press conference. They were taken aback by some of the brassy questions.

"Mr. Premier," asked a young woman reporter, "would you tell us who robbed more from Hungary, the Germans or the Russians?"

While Rakosi squirmed in his chair, Nagy took a long breath and answered:

"A difference between the two must be recognized. The Germans and the Nazis robbed; the Russians took it as booty."[18]

After stopping in London and Paris, where the Hungarians made a last fruitless effort to secure a fairer settlement of the Transylvania question, they returned to Budapest. They found the economic crisis at the stage of panic.

The Government's printing presses were running round the clock to produce currency fast enough to keep up with inflation. The value of the pengo was increasing not just by the week or day, but by the minute. The number of colors in the currency was reduced to speed the printing, then even the numbers identifying each bill were eliminated to save still another step. The bills were printed in astronomical figures—quadrillions of pengos, then quintillions. The impact on the public was seen in the experience of one Budapest University professor, a distinguished scientist with an international reputation. By May 1946 his weekly pay was two billion pengos, and he rushed immediately to spend it before it lost more value. He paid 600 million pengos for a week's worth of school lunches. The monthly gas bill was two billion pengos, while electricity was 600 million. The price of a newspaper or a streetcar ride was 100 million pengos. A pound of flour was two billion pengos, one egg was 360 million. Along with everyone else, the professor and his family were reduced to barter, trading silver, furniture, linen and the professor's books.

Nagy himself was impacted with the rest, Inflation reduced his salary to the equivalent of two dollars a month. He and his family only survived through food received from relatives in the country. As he described the situation in Budapest:

> Scholars were trading priceless bindings for a loaf of bread or two or three eggs; fathers bartered their overcoats for food for their children. The gold of the wedding ring bought a few days' groceries for a household. Nationally prominent professional men were hiring out as day laborers in exchange for food for their families. Yes, a bag of flour brought half a dozen Persian rugs at street corners.[19]

By July 7, as Schoenfeld reported,

> The latest pengo note is one quintillion and new denominations are being printed daily. In fact, the economic structure can be said to have collapsed.

Gold and the American dollar had become the media of exchange, even though it was forbidden to own dollars. Stores and even restaurants set up small scales for weighing gold. Robbery was, of course, rampant. A professor in a quiet suburb was burglarized five times in one year. On the streets, police confiscated any dollars they found on people, and were strongly suspected of keeping most of the money for themselves. Not only the economy, but society itself, was in chaos.

On July 23 the new U.S. Ambassador to Moscow, General Walter Bedell Smith, gave a second U. S. note to Molotov in answer to Vishinsky's response to Kennan the previous April. In it he refuted Vishinsky's contentions one by one. The Soviet impact on Hungary's economy was enormous—one-half of Hungarian manufacturing for reparations and other requirements, 80 to 90 percent of heavy industry. The Red Army was requisitioning foodstuffs as late as April—how can this be reconciled with Vishinsky's statement that "the Soviet Command in Hungary has neither carried out nor is carrying out any requisitions?" Regarding the gold and property in the American zone, these were being returned to Hungary. And Smith quoted from the concluding paragraphs of Gordon's report (which Voroshilov had prohibited the Hungarians from giving to the Americans) in advocating a tripartite solution to Hungary's problems.

Three days later the Soviets replied, denying the American allegations.[20] Nothing came of the diplomatic crossfire, but the Hungarian economic frenzy whirled to a climax.

As early as mid-June, the Hungarian delegation had told their American hosts in Washington that they planned to stabilize the currency with creation of a new monetary unit on August 1, 1946. Delivery of the $32 million in gold by that time would provide the support needed to make the new denomination, the forint, credible.

On August 1 the Government established the new currency, with one forint equaling 400 quintillion pengos. Though six days late, the train bearing the Hungarian gold arrived in Budapest from Frankfurt on August 6. Possibly to guard against its seizure by the Soviets, the gold was transferred to the Hungarian Government in public ceremonies attended by wide publicity. Receiving the gold for the Hungarian National Bank were Prime Minister Nagy and Finance Minister Gordon. Delivering for the Americans were Schoenfeld and General George H. Weems, the U.S. representative on the ACC. Schoenfeld's statement released to the press called attention to the latest American note to the Soviets and took credit for this American

> initiative in harmony with the declaration made by the heads of the Allied governments at the Crimea Conference to bring about concerted action among the Allied governments with a view to the improvement and stabilization of the Hungarian economic position.[21]

The delivery of the gold was undoubtedly the factor enabling the forint to be accepted by the Hungarian public. It was the most important single act of the United States in support of the Hungarian nation, and together with the return of property it was, in the words of Stephen Kertesz, "the greatest outside help Hungary had received since the war." Had the gold never been carried off by the Germans and remained in Hungary in 1945, according to Kertesz, "the Red Army would have seized it as war booty, according to its consistent practice."[22]

In concluding his press statement, Schoenfeld referred to the American goal "that the Hungarian economy may be promptly restored so that it may take its place in the economy of Europe and the world." Yet the Americans had forgotten one factor. In pegging the new forint to other international currencies, the Smallholders had proposed 17 forints to the dollar. The Communists argued that the dollar was worth but seven forints. After repeated haranguing, the cabinet set the exchange rate at 11.7 forints to the dollar—a level that in Nagy's opinion "would make the establishment of trade between the United States and Hungary impossible."[23]

However, this soon became more or less academic. In 1947 a Communist coup d'etat forced Nagy to flee the country, while other top political figures were arrested. By 1948 Hungary was a complete Soviet satellite. The American return of gold and property had halted the financial collapse, and in the process had benefited not only the Hungarian people but also the subsequent Communist government and its Soviet rulers.

NOTES

1. Louis Mark, Jr. "The View from Hungary," in *Witnesses to the Origins of the Cold War*, Thomas T. Hammond, ed. (Seattle, 1982), p. 187

2. Ferenc Nagy, *The Struggle behind the Iron Curtain* (New York, 1948), p. 126.

3. Stephen D. Kertesz, *Diplomacy in a Whirlpool: Hungary between Nazi Germany and Soviet Russia* (Indiana: Notre Dame, 1953), p. 153.

4. Nagy, p. 124.

5. *Foreign Relations of the United States (FRUS)*, 1945, Vol. 4, pp. 880–888.

6. Kertesz, p. 259. The excerpts from the Council of Ministers minutes on October 12, 1945, are on pp. 255–260.

7. Mark, p. 200; U.S. Congress, 83rd Congress, 2nd Session. House Investigation, "Communist Takeover and Occupation of Hungary," Fifth Interim Report of Hearings before the Sub-committee on Hungary of the Select Committee on Communist Aggression, Washington, 1954, testimony of Dr. Nicholas Nyaradi, p. 227.

8. Kertesz, p. 252–254: "Memorandum of the Hungarian National Bank on Hungary's Reparations, prepared for the confidential information of the British and United States missions in Budapest." November 24, 1945, by Arthur Karasz, President of the Hungarian National Bank.

9. *FRUS*, 1945, Vol. 4, p. 919

10. Ibid, p. 917–920.

11. Mark, p. 198; Kertesz, p. 158.

12. *FRUS*, 1945, Vol. 4, p. 918n.

13. Ibid, 1946, Vol. 6, pp. 259–260.

14. Ibid, pp. 265–267, 285–387.

15. Nagy, pp. 204–214; FRUS, 1946, Vol 6, pp. 280–282.

16. *FRUS*, 1946, Vol. 6, p. 293–294.

17. Ibid., p. 295.

18. The Washington visit is drawn from *FRUS*, 1946, Vol. 6, pp. 306–316, and from Nagy, pp. 226–230.

19. Bess, Demaree. "Our Agents Behind the Iron Curtain," in *Saturday Evening Post*, August 24, 1946, p. 19.

20. U. S. Congress, 81st Congress, 1st Session. House Committee on Foreign Affairs. Report: "The Strategy and Tactics of World Communism." Washington, 1948, pp. 14–21.

21. United States, *Department of State Bulletin*, August 18, 1946, p. 335. "Gold Returned to Hungarian National Bank: Statement by American Minister to Hungary."

22. Kertesz, pp. 155 and 224.

23. Nagy, p. 257.

EDUCATION, ASSOCIATION, ACTIVISM: BULGARIAN WOMEN OF THE NATIONAL REVIVAL INTELLIGENTSIA (1850s–1870s)

Linda L. Nelson

The process of social transformation in the modern western world has often been conceptualized by scholars in terms of the public and overtly political, a conceptualization which, in light of the prevalence of social organization based on gender sphere separation of the public (male) world from the private (female) world, largely excluded consideration of women's roles in the process. Yet, women have not been mute objects of social processes, but have functioned in both the private and public spheres as agents of social change. Even as women were confined to the private sphere and viewed as bearers of tradition, they effected social change through the reshaping and transmission of culture in oral, written, and material forms.[1] The extension of women's actions in the public sphere frequently took the form of a synthesis of traditional and new roles and values and was justified in terms of serving a broader social cause. This model is applicable to Bulgarian women of the 1850s–70s, whose advances into public life took place within the context of a new socio-cultural system which emerged from the Bulgarian national movement, the *Vuzrazhdane* [National Revival]. This new system produced a class of educated women who formed women's associations to function as forums for educational, benevolent, and patriotic work in support of the national cause.

The Nature and Institutions of the Bulgarian National Revival

The national movement in Bulgaria was part of the wave of nationalism sweeping the Balkans during the nineteenth century. In the peasant societies of the Balkans, nationalism was first manifested in the form of national awareness arising from "instinctive affiliation" with the ethnic group, and reached a second stage of development during the 1840s–70s in the form of "historical nationalism," inspired by romanticism and marked by a scholarly and political revival of the past and a desire to destroy the status quo. Originating among members of the more developed Balkan Diaspora throughout Europe, historical nationalism spread to the peripheral, then interior, areas of the Balkans, becoming articulated in specific national programs.[2]

The Bulgarian national program developed as the culmination of the National Revival Era, a period of significant social, political and economic change dating from the seventeenth century. This epoch was characterized by the transformation of economic relations from a feudal to a capitalist base, the rise of a bourgeois class, the establishment of secular Bulgarian education, and the evolution of distinctive Bulgarian culture.[3] By the mid-nineteenth century nationalist aspirations resulted in movements for cultural/spiritual independence from Hellenistic hegemony and political independence from the Ottoman Empire. These aspirations were satisfied by the establishment of an independent Bulgarian Orthodox Church in 1870, and the creation of on independent Bulgarian state in the outcome of the Russo-Turkish War of 1877–78.

The revival process gave rise to a new class—the National Revival intelligentsia—a thin, upper layer of educated Bulgarians, dominant in national, cultural, and social life during the eighteenth and nineteenth centuries, most numerous during the 1870s. Out of a population of approximately 4.5 million in the latter decades of the *Vuzrazhdane*, some 10,000 Bulgarians were registered in historical documents as teachers, clerics, artists, students, doctors, soldiers, journalists, and others involved in national, cultural, and political development. Although constituting only 1.5 percent of the total population, the intelligentsia made significant contributions to the national cause, disproportionate to their numbers. This is especially true of women; the number of women identified as belonging to the intelligentsia is 659, or 6.8 percent of the total researched group, of which approximately half were active in the 1850s through the 1870s.[4]

The key to entry into the ranks of the intelligentsia was education. From the 1830s, a central part of the National Revival was the establishment of a Bulgarian system of education aimed at transforming the largely illiterate peasant society into a modern, educated society, capable of constructing an independent state. These secular, modern schools were crucial to the development of culture and politics in the late stages of the National Revival, creating a new socio-political consciousness and providing a structure for social organization and a forum for national and international contacts. By the time of the Liberation, more than 2,000 schools had been established, functioning not only as educational institutions, but also as cultural and political institutions.[5]

This complex of functions was found in all significant institutions of the late National Revival: the Orthodox Church, the émigré periodical press, teachers' associations, student clubs, revolutionary organizations, *chitalishta* [reading clubs], and *zhenski druzhestva* [women's associations]. With the exception of the revolutionary groups, these associations were legal bodies in the eyes of the Ottoman authorities, legitimated by a series of Ottoman reforms dating from the late eighteenth century extending limited autonomy to subject populations in the form of socio-political institutions at the community level.[6] By the mid-nineteenth century Bulgarian communities had the right to make decisions in church, administrative, fiscal, cultural, and educational matters.[7] This limited autonomy provided a material base for the development of national consciousness and the expression of national aspirations in specifically Bulgarian social and cultural institutions which created a nascent state infrastructure. Male participation in the infrastructure was significant not only in administrative bodies, but in the *chitalishta*. Dating from 1856 these clubs functioned as civic centers, community libraries, cultural clubs. and frequently as centers of revolutionary activity.[8] Corresponding women's associations arose a year later, evolving to play a central role in the extension and validation of women's roles in society. The origins of the women's associations are directly linked to the new interest in women's advancement and expanded educational opportunities.

The "Woman Question" in Bulgaria

Prompted by the extension of secular, public education to women in 1840–41, the "woman question" became a prominent aspect of National Revival discourse of the 1850s–70s. Arguments for changes in women's status and roles were made in publications of the émigré Bulgarian periodical press in which a relatively large number of articles were devoted to women's issues. The first to present the "woman question" was Petko Rachev Slaveikov, an eminent publicist. It is not incidental that the first spokesperson for women's advancement was a male, given the patriarchal social conventions which empowered men to speak for women and to mediate women's relations with the broader society. The point of departure for articles supporting expansion of women's educational opportunities and public roles tended to be the contemporary condition of Bulgarian women.

An 1868 article in *Makedoniia* laments the low status of Bulgarian women whom Slaueikov describes as being in:

> a miserable position and humiliating situation . . . in comparison with men in social life . . . accustomed to and hardened to that position the long suffering woman takes it as a natural one for her, as lawful and virtuous, and as if it is the best for her, often enclosed at home from her youth, poor thing. The woman comes to thoughts that the world is limited—to where she sees the skies, touches the summits of the hills which surround the place of her birth, and all her ways lead to nowhere but to the field and the vineyards and to the *horo* [traditional dance] and the village and to the public bath, and to the church. . . . What knowledge can she acquire from there and to what development could she reach when she goes to the church for nothing else but to meet and chat with her peers, her "friends in prison."[9]

The traditional role of the Bulgarian woman was extremely limited, circumscribed by the general low level of development of the patriarchal, peasant society, an ascetic Christian outlook and five centuries of Ottoman domination. This mixture of tradition, patriarchal structures, religion, and political oppression had limited acceptable spheres for women to the home, church, and marketplace, and the public baths.[10] Gender sphere separation and role restrictions were pervasive: urban women were not permitted to leave home alone, in church women sat separately from the men, women were forbidden to look at a strange man outside the home, village women ate at separate tables, and social gatherings of the higher levels of society in urban areas were often marked by gender separate spheres of activity.[11] In these conditions, the greatest injustice to women, according to Slaveikov, was the neglect of women's education and elevation because of "despotic prejudices." Therefore a task was set forth for *Makedoniia* to

> inform the readers in detail . . . of impediments to the advancement and well being of a people, that of the neglect of the intellectual development of women who are half of the numbers of any people and of all mankind.[12]

Issues taken up by *Makedoniia* and other periodicals included female education and upbringing, general advice for women, purpose of women in society, women's associations, and women's rights, with the emphasis on the destiny, education, and upbringing of Bulgarian girls.

This questioning of traditional roles combined with the ideology of the National Revival, rooted in the recovery and celebration of traditional culture as the prerequisite for national liberation, functioned to create the climate for reconstruction of women's roles based upon the extension of women's traditional roles in the public sphere and justified in terms of women's contributions to the national cause.[13] These new roles were mediated by males, institutionalized and sanctioned by establishment of women's associations, and based on a synthesis of the traditional and the progressive which informed the education and activism of Bulgarian women. These trends can be understood in terms of two aspects of role theory: the extent to which women's roles are gender defined and the necessity for mediation between tradition and progress. Because social roles are products "of shared expectations and positive and negative sanctions" changes in expectations and sanctions are necessary as new roles evolve from changing social conditions.[14] Given the historically limited position of women changes in their status require strong justification and validation through adjustment of social expectations and sanctions—accomplished in Bulgaria through the mediums of education and women's associations. The first women to be educated had formed a kind of "passive" intelligentsia, lacking a forum for application of their knowledge and skills. The associations functioned to transform passivity to activism, providing a sphere for the application, extension, and transmission of knowledge and skills through educational, benevolent, and patriotic activity.

The Women's Associations: A Synthesis of Tradition and Modernity

The functions and ideology of the women's groups are evident in their organizational names which refer both to traditional values and progressive goals.[15] The most frequently occurring names referred to the maternal role, education, and benevolent work: *Maichina grizha* [mother's care] (5); *Maichina liubov* [motherly love] (2); *Maichina dluzhnost* [motherly responsibility] (1); Maika [mother] (1); *Vuzpitana maika* [The well-bred mother] (1); *Razvitie* [development] (3); *Prosveta* [enlightenment] (2); *Prosveshtenie* [education, enlightenment]

(1); *Samorazvitie* [self-development] (1); *Uchenoliubie* [love of learning] (1); *Dobrodetel* [benevolence] (2); *Blagodetel* [benefactor] (1); *Blagotvoritelno zhensko obshtestvo* [women's charitable association] (1); *Bulgarsko blagodetelno zhensko druzhestvo* [Bulgarian benevolent women's association] *Milosurdie* [charity] (1); *Dobrodetelno zhensko druzhestuo* [benevolent women's group] (1). Others referred to feelings and emotions: *Nadezhda* [hope] (4); *Radost* [joy, happiness] (1); *Viara, nadezhda i liubov* [faith, hope and love] (1). These names might be read as references to nationalist sentiment ond aspirations, or or as allusions to the advancement of women. Direct indications of rising nationalist consciousness among women were evident in only two groups: *Rodoliubie* [patriotism, love of homeland] and *Vuzrazhdane* [revival, renaissance] also called *Bulgarska Zora* [Bulgarian dawn]. The name of *Suglasie* [agreement, consent, accord] found in three groups suggests group solidarity, common goals, and could be read in terms of a sense of national unity, and, perhaps, a sense of sisterhood. Only one reference is found to the housewife's role: *Stupanka (Stopanka* [housewife, hostess, landlady, owner, proprietress—the broader sense of household manager] (1). While local and regional socio-political conditions determined specific activities of the *zhenski druzhestva*, their primary goal was the education and enlightenment of females, with work also undertaken in the spheres of benevolent work and in support of the national cause.

The establishment of the first association reflects the convention of male mediation as well as the tendency for progressive developments to originate on the periphery. In 1857 the *Dobrodetelno zhensko druzhestvo* [Women's Benevolent Association] was founded in Lom, a Danubian town in northeastern Bulgaria, at the initiative of Krustiu Stoianov Pishurka, a local teacher, founder and president of the *chitalishte*, and one of the first Bulgarian directors and actors.[16] The idea of a women's association arose from Pishurka's theatrical group in which women were limited to behind-the-scenes participation by the constraints of social conventions.[17] Seeking to destroy the prejudice against women on stage as well as the general prejudice against women, Pishurka gathered a group of the most enlightened women in the area, including his wife Angelina Krusteva (a teacher), his sisters and sister-in-law, in an association to consider the question of education and general enlightenment (*prosveta*) for females. The group was soon joined by many of the wives of Pishurka's former students. Pishurka's goal of uniting women with the theater and the *chitalishte* did not come to fruition due to his arrest for anti-Ottoman activity, but the women's association endured and concentrated on the goal of providing for the education and spiritual growth of young women.[18]

The publicity and approval given the Lom group in the periodical press set the stage for the spread of women's associations which numbered approximately fifty by 1878. Most were established from the mid-60s to early 70s, arising first in border areas and larger towns. Although the theatrical component of the Lom group was unusual, the male organizational initiative was not. Many of the associations were founded at the suggestion of, or with strong support of men who were social, political, or cultural activists, usually members of the *chitalishta*. The usual forum for initiating the associations was not the theater, but the churches or the *chitalishta*.[19]

In 1869, the peak year of the establishment of women's organizations, Petko Slaveikov hailed the *zhenski druzhestva* as the "most pleasant and valuable fruit of our time," clear evidence of the strength of spiritual advancement, which

> can and will have to be the most favorable and most natural partners, co-workers and followers of the *chitalishta* in the great matter of our advancement.[20]

Certainly the associations were the most significant means for Bulgarian women to attain advancement.

The source material for the associations indicates a membership of 500 to 1,500 women, suggesting that participation was not limited to those who can be documented as members of the intelligentsia.[21] For the documented members the primary determinants of membership appear to have been kinship and education. The women involved in the groups, especially in leadership roles, tended to be wives and daughters, or, less often, mothers, of the male intelligentsia reflecting the tendency of the intelligentsia as a whole tended to come from families where the father was educated and the mother illiterate, but children of both sexes educated.[22] The number of members in the groups varied according to the size of the town or village, economic status of the inhabitants, and the attitude toward the education of women.[23] The associations had a genuinely democratic character, being open to all women regardless of age, social standing, faith, nationality or marital status.[24] A few groups were founded only for young, unmarried women, mainly students, as counterparts to the numerous male student associations. Although many activists were unmarried or widows, a number of married women also participated although there are some reports of women dropping their membership at marriage.[25]

While the groups were often established at male initiative or with strong male support, the governing boards consisted of women who functioned as presidents, vice presidents, treasurers, secretaries, and general board members. In fact, article 11 of the charter of the Koprivshtitsa group *"Blagoveshtenie"* stated that the board members "had to be women."[26] Functioning as board members gave many women political and administrative skills as well as the opportunity to have contacts with other socio-political institutions.

The groups were funded by dues, donations, and proceeds from lotteries. The Iambol group *Vuzpitana Maika* set dues at around 20 Turkish lira and received donations from 10 male and 24 female donors, the men giving a total of 203.5 Turkish lira, and the women 773. Three types of dues were issued: regular dues, dues of the founding members, and auxiliary fees for specific functions. The local *chitalishta* donated a subscription to a leading newspaper and other sources of funding came from Bulgarian émigrés, money lent out for interest, and church funds from fees for weddings and baptisms. In all regions there was a strong degree of cooperation among the town councils, church boards, *chitalishta*, schools, and women's associations, although the degree of support for women's groups and schools varied in response to local attitudes concerning the education of women.[27] However, community relations with the women's groups were facilitated by the pre-existing communal nature of Bulgarian society and the relatively small size of Bulgarian villages and towns. The *druzhestva* holidays, which were their founding days or corresponding religious holidays, were celebrated with programs in which the entire community participated in such activities as student presentations, lectures, and fundraising.[28]

The strongest support for the *zhenski druzhestva* tended to come from the *chitalishta* with their charters and functions taken as models for the women's groups, although in a few instances the women's associations pre-existed the *chitalishta*.[29] A range of relations appears to have existed between the *chitalishta* and *zhenski druzhestva*. While some sources maintain that the *chitalishta* were purely male preserves, others maintain that women were involved with the *chitalishta* in a number of ways. The fact that women contributed financially to the *chitalishta* is documented in the periodical press, as well as records of the *chitalishta* and *druzhestuva*. Other ways in which women are reported to have participated in the *chitalishta* range from being responsible for housekeeping functions, to assisting in activities, to attending and giving lectures. There are some reports of women attending meetings and, in rare instances, becoming full members.[30] The classic account of the *chitalishta* authored by Stilian Chilingirov, mentions women as members only in the post-Liberation period, but discusses their pre-Liberation affiliation in various ways. Referring to women's donations, Chilingirov notes that "the women were not limited only to their generosity," but "worked for their own self-education . . . gathering in the *chitalishta*." This is a specific reference to the Biala Cherkva *chitalishta* where the women established a separate room for girls who were being "educated together with the young men." This is indicative of a way in which girls' schools and *zhenski druzhestva* were started as well as suggesting that fluid relationships existed between the *chitalishta* and women. There is evidence of men and women participating equally in benevolent societies, such as one in Gabrovo which pre-existed the *chitaiishte*. In several locations, the women's associations were reported to be more active and enduring than the *chitalishta* because the women were more willing to work.[31] The Iambol women's association is said to have been called a *zhensko chitalishte* due to the scope of its enlightenment activity. Its members reportedly "advanced to the threshold" of the *chitalishte*, in order to take books from its library, listen to lectures, and even to deliver lectures.[32]

In other instances there appears to have been a stricter separation of women from the *chitalishta*. Ironically, the evidence here comes from a well-educated and well-connected woman, Rada Kirkovich, who was the daughter of the first woman to teach girls in Koprivshtitsa, Ivana Gerova, and the niece of Naiden Gerov, an active member of the Bulgarian intelligentsia who served as the Vice Consul to the Russian Embassy in Plovdiv. Gerov's connections permitted Kirkovich to be the first Bulgarian women to receive a higher education in Russia where she graduated from the Kiev gymnasium in 1866.[33] Upon her return to Bulgaria she became a teacher in Plovdiv and, according to her memoirs, was epecially interested in the lectures and discussions at the *chitalishte*, but "never dared" to go in consideration of her reputation as a teacher, knowing she was under the surveillance of all the parents, but confined herself to following affairs of the *chitalishte* by asking questions of her uncle.[34]

While a variety of relationships and various degrees of cooperation existed between the *chitalishta* and the *zhenski druzhehtva*, as well as the *druzhestva* and other community groups, an emphasis on education was common to all the socio-cultural institutions of the late National Revival. The main work of the women's associationss was the support of education, especially the founding and maintenance of girls' schools.

Education and Englightenment

The charters of the women's associations articulated the education of females as their fundamental purpose as evident in the charter of the Turnovo *Zhenska Obshtina* [Women's Society] which stated that the group:

> will have as its primary mission the establishment of a women's fund to gather donations. And when the capital is collected . . . to establish a girls' school and to support a respected and worthy female teacher who is able to teach the girls what is necessary for us here . . . and, God willing, to have the funds for the society to open girls' schools in the villages near Turnovo.[35]

In a similar vein, the charter of the women's benevolent group *Stupanka* in Ruse states that its primary purpose was to provide the female sex with "the broader and more complex education necessary for the time" through the opening of a girls' school and the extension of literacy in the Bulgarian language to girls and women.[36] The teaching of the Bulgarian language was vital to the National Revival in general, especially to the new education, as means of instilling national consciousness and pride with which to counter foreign influences.

Nearly all the associations opened or supported girls' schools, taking an active part in administration, hiring and support of teachers, and assessment of learning through public examinations. The Gabrovo group *Maichina grizha* established and supported a girls' school with five classes, the first higher classes for girls; contributed to the girls' pension at Stara Zagora, supporting three students from Gabrovo there; sponsored weekly lectures given by teachers and medical doctors; and provided financial support to the male gymnasium.[37] In Iambol the *Vuzpitana maika* group opened a girl's school, sponsored lectures, aided poor students of both sexes, and sent students to Russia and Romania.[38] The Turnovo group, one of the most active in the educational sphere, established a Sunday school for illiterate girls and women, and helped sustain the class school with material needs and payment of teachers.[39] In Lovech, the president of the association *Blagodetel*, Anna Predich, gave lectures on Sundays for the parents of her students.[40] Members of the women's associations visited the schools on a regular basis and formed committees to oversee the schools.[41] Other typical educational work included the establishment of association reading rooms, supplied primarily with newspapers from the Bulgarian periodical press, as well as international newspapers, magazines and books, and the holding of literary discussion groups. The typical way of stocking the libraries was through subscriptions donated by the *chitalishta* or individuals.[42] Overall, the groups aided both sexes in obtaining education and were central to the establishment of a Bulgarian educational system in the pre-Liberation period.

The attitudes toward education of females and the content of female education indicate the transitional nature of Bulgarian society in the latter stages of the *Vuzrazhdane*. Three viewpoints toward education of females have been delineated. The idea that men and women were equal and had to have equal education was radical for the times, and held by only the most educated and enlightened revival leaders such as Petko Slaveikov, Liuben Karavelov, and Marin Drinov.[43] At the opposite end of the spectrum was the idea that education of women should be strictly limited to that needed for family life. The prevailing argument was that education should be based on predestination of women, that is, it was a mistake for women to try to be anything other than what God had determined them to be, i.e. wives and mothers, but education could be useful in fulfilling these roles. This argument was articulated at the first meeting of the women's association in Kalofer by one of the association founders, Eka Karamnikova, After noting that men had advanced in Bulgaria, but women had not, and pointing out the better position of women in the "educated world," she defined the role of women:

> The woman brings abundance and happiness into her home; she has to be the source of well-being. . . . In this lies the main part of the lofty predestination of woman; these are the primary and ideal woman's responsibilities and only through them can the woman reach equality with the man, although in a different manner, useful to society in which she lives and from which she came.

Education of females should then be undertaken in consideration of domestic roles and for the tasks of becoming "acquainted with the demands of our faith . . . and to preserve the specific characteristics of a people."[44] Therefore the content of education became gender determined.

Predestination for women meant service in the domestic sphere; or "what is necessary for us here" in the terms of the Turnovo charter. Many girls received only a primary education, lasting three to five years, heavily informed by domestic considerations. Primary curriculums were composed of rudimentary academic subjects, with emphasis on religious and moral instruction, and needlework. A typical education would begin with basic literacy skills and proceed to religious history, arithmetic, Bulgarian language and grammar, geography, Bulgarian and general history and Church Slavonic. The charter of the Bulgarian girls' school in Svishtov, founded in 1872, exemplified the general attitude toward education, stating that the curriculum of the first class would be "exclusively rudimentary learning and needlework" with courses in religion, reading, basic math, geography, needlework and basic knitting, Courses offered at the second level, while advanced in academic content, had a definite domestic intention as well:

> physics . . . with attention to domestic life . . . drawing, with attention to natural history, maps, and women's work . . . technology, with special attention to various domestic remedies and useful dishes with an eye toward economical cooking; in that manner to make soap, starch, sugar . . . various beverages and other things . . . needlework, in order to be accomplished in all women's work and production of clothing.[45]

A major step in the development of female education came with the establishment of class schools stemming from a higher general state of economic development, foreign influences, especially Russian, the encouragement of the press, and the support of the women's associations. Dating from 1856 and numbering twenty by 1878, the class schools afforded women higher education in academic subjects, sometimes offering courses in foreign languages and sciences, but still including needlework. A major advance came with the institution of pedogogical courses in the class schools of Gabrovo, Stara Zagora, and Shumen in the late 1860s and early 70s. While the initial justification for education of women was preparation for enlightened motherhood, it became accepted that the purpose of class schools was the preparation of teachers, although in some it was possible to study only needlework.[46]

The emphasis on traditional female skills and values is evident also in the charter of the Koprivshtitsa association, *Blagoveshtenie*, which included the goals of providing for the "success, advancement, and refinement of all domestic needlework" and of supporting a teacher capable of instructing girls in the "sewing and designing of all types of needlework needed in the local community." While some criticism was made of the domestic nature of girls' education, domestic skills, especially needlework, nevertheless had personal and social utility.[47]

The social utility of needlework skills came not only from supplying clothing and other goods for the Bulgarian population, but also from its use by the associations as a means of fundraising for benevolent causes and the support of schools, an application of personal, traditional skills for progressive social ends. The most highly publicized and praised needlework exhibit and lottery was the one held in Constantinople in 1873.

Traditional women's skills provided a path to economic independence for some women, as evident in the career of Anka Aleksandrova of Iambol, a teacher and active member of the local women's association, who, after the death of her husband, opened a sewing school for poor girls in 1872. Her school served to free the young women from financial dependence, and introduced European styles in Bulgaria because Aleksandrova patterned her clothes on those of Greek women in Burgas (a Black Sea port) and of women who worked at the Iambol rail station and received foreign clothing via that avenue.[48] Aleksandrova exemplifies a Bulgarian women between tradition and modernity, using and transmitting traditional female skills and culture, while carving out new spheres of social activity for women.

Like Aleksandrova, many of the women active in the associations and in promotion of social change were, or had been, teachers. Young Bulgarian women were trained for this in the class schools (similar to middle schools), supported by their families or their towns. Most teachers, both male and female, came from small villages, from the middle and lower layers of the merchant and craft classes.[49] Women comprised 11.1 percent of all Bulgarian teachers during the nineteenth centuries. The majority of educated women became teachers or worked in other cultural fields such as translation, and other literary or artistic endeavors.[50]

Bulgarian teachers had to be extremely dedicated in light of the poor conditions under which they worked. According to one teacher, Raina Popgeorgieva Futekova (Raina Kniaginia), conditions for teachers were generally difficult, and male teachers received higher salaries than female teachers who often accepted salary cuts in order to help support other female teachers. Nevertheless, Futekova said "the school was for us a second necessity after our daily bread, for which reason we worked and labored for it with unusual, feverish speed so that in recent years the whole of work was given to it.[51] Her attitude here is one of not only devotion, but of traditional female selflessness in face of a range of difficulties confronting female and male teachers alike: internal struggles in administrations, divided feeling in the population about teachers and education, reaction of the conservative press and the *chorbadzhi*, the conservative upper class elements who opposed the revolutionary nature of education, and various efforts of the Ottoman authorities to close schools and persecute teachers.[52] The women (and men) teachers often lived in poverty, facing prejudice from those unwilling to break with traditional attitudes.

Benevolent and Patriotic Work in Peace and War

Before the anti-Ottomon uprising of April 1876 benevolent work of the *zhenski druzhestva* primarily took the form of aid to poor women and children. Some gruups were established solely for benevolent and civic purposes, such as two founded by Bulgarian émigrés in Romania. The Bolgrad *Blagotvoritelno zhensko obshtestvo* [Women's Charitable Organization] was created to help those in need of material or other aid, and the Braila group gave its entire capital to build a Bulgarian church in 1873 and then disbanded.[53]

The 1876 April Uprising opened the final and most violent stage of the Bulgarian national movement and changed the nature of benevolent and patriotic work. Although a failure as revolt, the April Uprising became a major issue in European diplomacy because of the atrocities committed by the Ottomans in the suppression of the uprising. These atrocities, which resulted in the deaths of some twelve to fifteen thousand Bulgarians, became widely publicized throughout Europe as the "Bulgarian Horrors."[54] The events of the uprising and the ensuing Russo-Turkish War of 1877–78 transformed the entire Bulgarian society, engulfing men, women, and children alike in a national catastrophe in which Ottoman reprisals took the form of beatings, rapes, torture, and mass killings. The multi-faceted role of women in the national liberation movement reached a new stage in response to these conditions.

Benevolent work increased, often becoming the only activity of the associations or sparking the establishment of new groups, such as those established in Braila in the summer of 1876. These groups gave aid to the sick and wounded of Serbia and Bulgaria, worked to ransom women and children taken as slaves, and established connections with all philanthropic associations in Europe from which they received a great deal of moral and material support.[55] Many associations within Bulgaria ceased other activities in order to support the national cause. The Gabrovo association gathered food and dress, sheltered victims of the uprising, opened a hospital in which its members worked, and provided food for orphans and refugees.[56] In Turnovo a new group, *Milosurdie*, was founded in August 1877 in response to the destruction of Stara Zagova. The first actions of the groups were the aiding of refugees from Stara Zagora with money, food, and clothing. The group later provided nurses and aides for hospitals and private homes which provided care for sick and injured Russian and Bulgarian soldiers.[57] These actions were typical of many of the associations after April 1876 and throughout the Russo-Turkish War of 1877–78. In Plovdiv the *Maichina grizha* association worked to distribute foreign aid from Britain and Russia. Their efforts were supported by a British philanthropist, Lady Strangford, and the mothers of two Russian generals, Skobelev and Stolypin, as well as by the Russian Beneficent Society run by General Stolypin.[58]

Women, both members and non-members of the *zhenski druzhestva*, participated in the uprisings and war in a variety of independent and collective ways, some of which reflect traditional categories of female patriotism, that is, support services, and in other ways which brought them into the center of the armed conflict. Their means of participation included: sewing banners and uniforms for revolutionary detachments, teaching revolutionary songs to children, caring for refugees and orphans, establishing and supporting hospitals, working as nurses, feeding and housing Russian soldiers, divulging informotion about Ottoman troops, publicizing the Bulgarian cause, engaging in forms of passive protest, such as refusing to divulge information to Ottoman authorities, and active protest in the form of demonstrations, hiding revolutionaries, acting as couriers for the revolutionary committees, casting bullets, hiding Bulgarian prisoners, and arranging prison escapes. Women were subject to arrest and punishment not only for their own actions in support of the anti-Ottoman struggle, but also for those of their husbands and sons.[59]

Bulgarian Women on the Eve of Liberation: The Transformation of Women's Consciousness and Roles

By the eve of the 1878 liberation new roles had been carved out for Bulgarian women. While not affecting the entire female population, the extension of education to women and their expanded participation in society created a new consciousness and a model for post-Liberotion development. The best measure of changes in women's roles is contained in the women's associations. While affirming women's roles as preservers of traditional culture and national identity, the educational and public nature of the associations placed women in new roles, enhancing their social status and contributing to the cultural advancement of the Bulgarian people. The primary goal of female enlightenment was addressed through educational activities including support of girls' schools and Sunday schools for illiterate adults, and dissemination of articles on the status of women. These educational activities were largely abandoned in the face of the dislocations created by the 1876 April Uprising; some groups disbanded, while others engaged in benevolent work to aid victims ot the Uprising and ensuing Russo-Turkish War. In the post-Liberation period women's associations were revived with their educational activities extended to work for professional education for women, and a new emphasis on defense of women's rights and interests, as well as an increase in benevolent activity.[60] *Zhenski druzhestva* have existed in various forms, determined by contemporory socio-political conditions, throughout the twentieth century.[61]

The ultimate significance of the *zhenski druzhestva* of the National Revival Era is evident in both the private and public spheres. Membership provided opportunities for a move outside the traditional spheres of the home, church, and marketplace; development and application of social, political, and communications skills; a forum in which to acquire and share knowledge; and fostered development of a nascent feminist sense of sisterhood. The socio-political significance of the associations was reflected in expressions of nationalist sentiment; interaction among associations as well as with male groups which encouraged the breakdown of gender separate spheres; support for the national liberation and church movements; civic and political work; and in the training of post-liberation social activists, educators, and professionals. Connections with international women's movements and Slavic committees and knowledge of the status of women in other countries demonstrate awareness of gender specific issues which transcend nationality.[62]

While the members' experiences varied according to social, economic, and political conditions, many sources reveal the joy felt by women from receiving education and having the companionship of groups of women. There was generous reciprocity among teachers and members of the women's associations who traveled to other areas to study the foundation and programs of other schools and associations.[63] The extant literature indicates that a strong communal sense among women and a desire to work for the benefit of other females existed. However, the accomplishments of women are usually downplayed by women themselves. Although a personal sense of satisfaction is often expressed, the memoirs of activist women do not reveal a strong sense of their contributions to society.

While overall the women's associations constituted a progressive move in terms of elevating women's status, some limitations should be kept in mind. The organizations did center around traditional female values and roles, albeit using these values and roles, wittingly or unwittingly, for progressive ends.

The origins of the groups as associations essentially in the service of the "state" raise the question of their potential to form alternatives to traditional, patriarchal institutions, to serve the female individual. Nevertheless, the women's associations were a vital and dynamic part of the National Revival movement during the 1850s–70s, a major contributor to the process of modernization and liberation.

NOTES

1. Barbara Alpern Engel, "Transformation versus Tradition," in *Russia's Women,* Barbara Evans Clement, Barbara Alpern Engel, and Christine D. Worobec, eds. (Berkeley and Los Angeles: University of California Press, 1991), 135–147.

2. See Dimiitrije Djordjević, "National Factors in Nineteenth Century Balkan Revolutions," in *War and Society in East Central Europe,* Vol. 1, Bela K. Kiraly and Gunther E. Rothenberg, eds. (Brooklyn, NY: Brooklyn College Studies on Society in Change, 1979), 197–213.

3. Nikolai Genchey, *Bulgarsko Vuzrazhdane* [The Bulgarian National Revival] (Sofia, 1988), 9–14. Nationalistic, economic, and armed resistance to the Ottoman occupier took place throughout the five centuries of Ottoman domination, but intensified in the nineteenth century due to the stage of socio-economic development and the internal decline of the Ottoman Empire.

4. Rumiana Avamova, *et al.*, *Bulgarskata vuzrozhdenska inteligentsiia* [The Bulgarian National Revival Intelligentsia], comps. Nikolai Genchev and Krasimira Daskalova (Sofia, 1988), 5–7. Hereafter cited as *Bulgarskata vuzrozhdenska inteligentsiia.*

5. Angel Dimitrov, *Uchilishteto, progresut i natsionalnata revoliutsiia: bulgarsko uchilishte prez Vuzrazhdaneto* [The school, progress, and national revolution: Bulgarian schools during the National Revival] (Sofia, 1987), 266–270.

6. The most significant of these are the Firman of 1773, the Hatti-Sherif of 1839 which started the Tanzimat reform period, and the Hatti-Humayun of 1856. See Roderic H. Davison, *Reform in the Ottman Empire, 1856–1876* (Princeton, NJ: Princeton University Press, 1963).

7. Khristo Khristov, "Obshtinite i bulgarskoto natsialno vuzrazhdane" [Communities and the Bulgarian National Revival] in *Bulgariia 1300 godini* [Bulgaria 1300 years], Stoian Genchev, Rumiana Radkova, and Nikolai Zhechev, eds. (Sofia, 1981), 271–288.

8. I have preserved the Bulgarian terms *chit- alishte* (singular)/*chitalishta* (plural) due to the lack of English equivalents. For development of the *chitalishta* see Stiliian Chilingirov, *Bulgarski chitalishta predi Osvobozhdenieto* [Bulgarian *chitalishta* before the Liberation] (Sofia, 1930).

9. "Edna duma" [A Word], *Makedoniia*, III, 2 (1868).

10. Alexandra Pundeva-Voinikova, *Bulgarkata prez epokhata na Vuzrazhdaneto* [The Bulgarian Woman during the National Revival Era], (Sofia, 1940), 6–9, and Nadia Velcheva, *Bulgarkata prez vekovete* [The Bulgarian Woman over the Centuries] (Sofia, 1983), 13–20. A detailed picture of the status of women can be drawn from folklore. It should be noted, as Pundeva-Voinikova points out, that publicists may have portrayed the condition of Bulgarian women as worse than it actually was in order to spur changes, 15.

11. Velcheva, 10–12 & 20; Rada Kirkovich, *Spomeni* [Memoirs] (Sofia, 1927), 39–43.

12. "Edna duma."

13. Such arguments were not unique to National Revival Bulgaria. Arguments for advancement of women have often been made on the basis of applying women's traditional functions to the public sphere. This "social utility" argument was used in early America where extension of education to women was justified in terms of "republican motherhood," producing educated mothers to raise educated children in the service of the nation. Other analogies are found in the women's reform and charitable groups of nineteenth century America. The status and roles of both American and European women were of considerable interest to the Bulgarian intelligentsia and were the subject of articles in the Bulgarian periodical press.

14. Mark K. Bauman, "Introduction" (to articles on role theory), *American Jewish History*, Vol. LXXlX, No. 1 (Autumn 1989), 5–10.

15. Listing of associations by names and locations: *Blagodetel* (Lovech); *Blagotvoritelno zhensko obshtestvo* – Bolgrad; *Blagoveshtenie* – Koprivshtitsa; *Bulgarsko blagodetelno zhensko druzhestvo* – Lom; *Evridiki* – Greek association in Plovdiv; *Kitka* – Panaguirishte; *Maichina dluzhnost* – Sliven; *Maichina grizha* – Gabrovo, Stara Zagora, Vratsa, Plovdiv, Razgrad; *Maichina liubov* – Kiustendil, Gorna Oriakhovitsa; *Maika* – Sofia; *Milosurdie* – Lom; *Nadezhda* – Bratsgovo, Panagiurishte, Svishtov, Tulcha; *Prosveshtenie* – Kalofer; *Prosveta* – Gorna 0riakhovitsa, Pazardzhik; *Radost* – Turnovo; *Razvitie* – Iambol, Svishtov, Pleven; *Rodoliubie* – Shumen; *Samorazvitie* – Kazanluk; *Stupanka* (Stopanka) – Ruse; *Suglasie* — Elena, Svishtov, Plovdiv; *Uchenoliubie* – Nevrokop; *Viara, nadezhda i liubov* – Chirpan; *Vuzpitana maika* – Iambol; *Vuzrazhdane* (or *Bulgarska zora*) – Solun.

16. *Bulgarskata vuzrozhdenska inteligentsiia*, 533–534.

17. The first Bulgarian women reported to have appeared on state was Matilda Popovich, who played in the opera "Pokrustbane na Bulgarite" in Braila, Romania, in May 1868. In light of the low stage of development of Bulgarian society, it is not suprising that the first Bulgarian woman to appear on stage did so in Romania. See Veneta Dacheva, *Iz istoriiata ne zhsenkoto dvizhenie Iambolski okrug, 1871–1971* [From the history of the woman's association in the Iambol District] (Iambol, 1971), 22.

18. *Bulgarski zhenski suiuz po sluchai 30–godishninata ot negovoto osnovavane 1901–1931 godina* [The Bulgarian women's union on the 30th anniversary of its establishment] (Sofia, 1931), 88–89; Echka Ivanova-Damianova, "Zhenskoto dvizhenie v Lom" [The women's movement in Lom] (Sofia, 1961), 189; Liubomir Iordanov, "Narodnopolezno

delo" [Work for the public good], *Zhenata dnes* (November 1987), 23.

19. Boika Vasileva, "Bulgarski zhenski organizatsii prez Vuzrazhdaneto" [Bulgarian women's organizations during the Vuzrazhdane] in *Godishnik na Sofiiskiia Universitet. Istoricheski fakultet* [Sofia University, Annual of the History Faculty] (Sofia, 1980), 268.

20. "Zhenski druzhestva u nas" [Women's Associations Among Us], *Makedoniia*, III 39 (August 13, 1869). The press covered all areas of activity of the groups, issued pleas for donations, and published articles on the social value of the groups, generally heralding them as institutions which would hasten intellectual development among the people. While some opposition to the associations can be assumed to have existed, it is not evident in the press, possibly because opponents of women's associations did not attempt to put their objections in print, or could not find a paper which would print them.

21. No complete archives of association records have survived. Evidence is found in archives of individual activists, records of the *chitalishta*, church records, memoir literature, and the periodical press.

22. *Bulgarskata vuzrozhdenska inteligentsiia* 6–8. The specific education of females accelerated and was articulated in conjunction with the spread of the women's associations. Some 3,702 persons, or 45.9 percent of the documented intelligentsia are shown to have received primary education, although it is considered, despite lack of evidence, that some 6,000 others were educated. Secondary education was received by 1,178 persons, or 32.1 percent of the subjects, and higher education by only 600, or 15 percent of the research subjects.

23. Vasileva, 270.

24. *Makedoniia*, IV, 16 (January 13, 1870).

25. Narodna Biblioteka Kiril i Metodii – Bulgarski Istoricheski Arkhiv [National Library Kiril and Metodii – Bulgarian Historical Archive], III, 819. Hereafter cited as NBKM-BIA.

26. NBKM Staropechaten otdel [Early Publications Section], No. 1456. Hereafter cited as HBKM-SO.

27. Vasileva, 270–273, 286.

28. Ibid., 271.

29. *Makedoniia*, IV, 54 (May 28, 1870). Slaveikov comments here on the existence of a *zhensko druzhestvo*, but the absence of a *chitaliste* in Pazardzhik.

30. L. Voivodova-Shokova, "Uchastieto na zhenata v zhivota na chitalishtata" [The role of the woman in the *chitalishta*] in *90 godini v kulturna sluzhba na naroda* [90 years in cultural service of the people]

(Sofia, 1946), 48–66.

31. Chilingirov, 178–79, 217, 222, 229, 243, 447.

32. Dacheva, p. 15.

33. Rada Gugova Kirkovich (1848–1941) also studied at the school of Countess Levashava from 1860–85. In addition to teaching, she was a translator of Russian textbooks. Her mother, Ivana Dobrivich Gerova (n.d.) taught in Koprivshtitsa from 1850–1861. Gerova's brother, Naiden, (1823–1900) received higher education in Russia and served as the Russian counsul in Plovdiv from 1857–77. *Bulgarskata vuzrozhdenska inteligentsiia*, 154–155, 332.

34. Kirkovich, 2–43.

35. Charter of the Turnovo Women's Association, first published in *Makedoniia* in Constantinople in 1870; reproduced in Virzhiniia Paskalava, *Bulgarkata prez Vuzrazhdaneto* [The Bulgarian Woman during the National Revival] (Sofia, 1984), 312–315.

36. Ibid., 316–317.

37. *Bulgarski zhenski suiuz*, 98; Zdravka Vodenicharova, and Nevena Popova, *Sto godini ot osnovavaneto na purvite druzhestva na zhenite v Bulgariia* [100 years since the founding of the association for women in Bulgaria] (Sofia, 1957), 31.

38. Dacheva, 15–17.

39. *Bulgarski zhenski suiuz*, 100.

40. *100 godini zhensko dvizhenie v Plevenski okrug* [100 years of the women's movement in the Pleven region] (Pleven, 1956), 7.

41. Vasileva, 275.

42. Dacheva, 15–16.

43. Petko Racho Slaveikov (1834–1879), a revolutionary ideologist and publicist; Marin Stoianov Drinov (1838–1906), an eminent activist in many cultural spheres. See *Bulgarskata vuzrozhdenska inteligentsiia*, 595–598, 312–314, & 227.

44. The text of Karamnikova's speech was published in *Makedoniia*, IV, 15 (January 10, 1870); see also Pundeva-Voinikova, 51–53, 107, 116; and Paskaleva, 78. Elizaveta Ivanova Goranova Karmanikova (1849–1920) was one of the Bulgarian women educated abroad. She studied first in Romania, and received her pedagogical training in Prague.

45. NBKM–SO, No. 1450.

46. Paskaleva, 97 & 103, and K. Vuzvuzova, "Poiava i razvitie na devicheskite uchilishta," [Appearance and development of girls'

schools] in *Istoriia na obrazovanite i pedagogicheskata misul v Bulgariia* [History of education and pedagogical thought in Bulgaria] (Sofia, 1975).

47. Paskaleva, 157–158, 321. The emphasis on needlework was not unique to Bulgaria; needlework was a highly valued skill at the time throughout Europe and in the United States and was part of the curriculum in many schools.

48. Manner of dress was a controversial issue among Bulgarian women; the women's associations and the periodical press frequently confronted the issue of foreign influence in clothing styles. While traditional dress gradually gave way to a new urban style, patterned on West European fashion, some traditional elements were maintained and incorporated into new styles. The European influence became intense in the 1860s among urban dwellers, functioning as an indicator of social status, while villagers tended to retain traditional dress. See: Paskaleva, 199, and Velcheva, 22.

49. Dimitrov, 230.

50. *Bulgarskata vuzrozhdenska inteligentsia*, p. 10.

51. *Raina Kniaginia, Avtobiografiia, dokumenti i materiali* [Raina Kniaginia: autobiography, documents, and materials], pp. 17–25. Female teachers received about half or less than half of the salary of male teachers. Paskaleva, 83.

52. Opponents of education in Kiustendil succeeded in closing the local school and banishing the teacher in 1866; in 1875 a proclamation against the young woman teacher was posted in the streets of Karlovo. Paskaleva, 84. Turkish opposition to Bulgarian schools is discussed in *Raina Kniaginia*.

53. Paskaleva, 195; Vassileva, 291.

54. Barbara Jelavich, *History of the Balkans*, Vol. 1 (Cambridge: Cambridge University Press, 1983), 347–348

55. *Arkhiv na Naiden Gerov, 1857–76* [Archive of Naiden Gerov], Vol. I, 43–44; Vasileva, 194 & 291; *Nova Bulgariia* I:11 (13 July 1876).

56. NBKM–BIA, Fond 584, 617–618; Vodenicharova and Popova, 98–99.

57. Paskaleva, 175, 272–273.

58. Nevana Manalova, "Uchastieto na bulgarkata prez Vuzrazhdane na Plovdiv," [The role of the Bulgarian women during the National Revival in Plovdiv] in *Iubileen sbornik po sluchai 50-te godini na Plovdivska devicheska gimaziia* [Jubilee collection on the occasion of the 50th anniversary of the Plovdiv girl's gymnasium] (Plovdiv,

1934), 292.

59. Paskaleva, 240–272; Vodenicharova and Popova, 22. Some of the banners and uniforms are on display at the National History Museum in Sofia.

60. Vodenicharova, *Bulgarski zhenski suiuz*, 85–86.

61. The fate of women's associations is an open question at this writing. During December 1989 splinter groups of the communist Bulgarian women's committees formed, but the current socio-economic conditions have apparently rendered them ineffective. At the present it is difficult to obtain accurate information on conditions in Bulgaria.

62. This is a point on which I differ with Bulgarian historiography which denies connection with the world women's and feminist movements, viewing the associations in a specific national context; see *Bulgarski zhenski suiuz* which states that the *zhenski druzhestva* "are purely ours," (85), and Paskaleva who denies feminist intentions, stressing the uniquely Bulgarian nature of the groups. (201–203).

63. Pundeva-Voinikova, 94.

DIE BOSNIAKEN KOMMEN!:
THE BOSNIAN-HERCEGOVINIAN FORMATIONS
OF THE AUSTRO-HUNGARIAN ARMY, 1914–1918

Richard B. Spence

The Balkans is a region virtually synonymous with ethnic diversity and conflict. Perhaps no sub-region better exemplifies these qualities than Bosnia-Hercegovina. Since its conquest by the Ottoman Turks in the fifteenth century, the area has been home to three related, but very distinct, ethnic-cultural groups—Orthodox Christian Serbs, Muslim Serbs (or Serbo-Croats), and Roman Catholic Croats. Although these groups share a common language, their religious affiliations gave each a distinct cultural orientation complete with different, and often conflicting, attitudes and values.

Although Bosnia and Hercegovina were historically distinct, by the late nineteenth century they were regarded, practically speaking, as a single entity. For the sake of brevity thus, unless specifically differentiated, "Bosnia" and "Bosnian" will be used to identify both the provinces and their inhabitants.

By the decision of the Berlin Congress of 1878, Bosnia-Hercegovina, although still technically under Ottoman rule, was to be occupied and administered by the Austro-Hungarian Empire. This situation persisted until 1908, when the Habsburgs unilaterally annexed the provinces, provoking an international crisis. In fact, from the beginning of their occupation, Habsburg authorities behaved and acted on the assumption that they had come to stay.[1] One of the most obvious manifestations of this attitude was the conscription of Bosnians into the Austro-Hungarian armed forces and the formation of special Bosnian-Hercegovinian units as integral parts of the Austro-Hungarian Army.

The manpower of these formations reflected the ethnic diversity of the provinces. In 1914 Bosnia-Hercegovina had a population of just about 2,000,000, of which 43 percent (roughly 850,000) were Orthodox Christian Serbs, 32 percent (650,000) Serbo-Croat-speaking

Muslims, and 22 percent Roman Catholic Croats.[2] The remainder consisted of some 10,000 Jews, Gypsies, and Habsburg civil and military administrative personnel of various nationalities.

Although numerically the largest element, the Serbs generally occupied the bottom of the socio-economic ladder. Historically neglected and oppressed under Ottoman rule, the Serb population had fared little better under the Habsburgs whose policies and officials tended to favor the Muslims and Catholics. In particular, the semi-feudal *kmet* system was preserved which kept much of the Orthodox peasantry in economic bondage to their Muslim landlord, or *Aga*.[3] While official policy became more conciliatory towards the Serbs after 1903, on the eve of World War I the prevailing opinion among Habsburg civil and military authorities was that the Serbs of Bosnia-Hercegovina could not be counted as loyal subjects. In the decade preceding the war, Pan-Serbian sympathies were fanned by the aggressive propaganda of the Karadjordjević regime in Belgrade and, to a lesser degree, by Montenegro.

But the Serb population of the provinces was divided into regional sub-groups manifesting varying attitudes. Eastern Bosnia and Hercegovina, roughly those areas east of the Bosna and Neretva Rivers, were, by simple proximity, the most affected by nationalist agitation. By 1914 it was probably correct to assume that most of these areas' Orthodox inhabitants were "devoted to the Greater Serbian idea."[4] Pro-Serbian nationalist organizations such as *Mlada Bosna* and *Narodna Odbrana* were well established in this area, and as early as 1906, Austrian authorities had uncovered hidden arms caches intended to support terrorism and armed rebellion.[5]

In the eyes of the Habsburg Army, however, the Serbs of eastern Hercegovina were the most suspect.[6] This was due not only to the Pan-Serb agitation emanating from Montenegro, but also the traditional hostility of the Orthodox mountain clans to governmental authority, be it Ottoman or Austrian. In fact, the embers of armed insurgency had never been stamped out completely in the rugged border districts.[7] During the Balkan Wars of 1912–1913, many Hercegovinian Serbs deserted army and gendarmerie units to enlist in Montenegrian service, a tendency that reappeared in 1914.[8]

Separated from their eastern brethren by a belt of Muslim and Croat settlement, the Serbs of western Bosnia presented a slightly different case. Separatist propaganda had not been so intense in these areas and the Orthodox inhabitants had strong communal and economic links with the Serb populations of the Lika and Krajina districts of Croatia and Dalmatia, regions with a long history of loyal service to the Habsburgs.

As the only ethnic groups unique to Bosnia, the Muslims believed that the term Bosniak properly referred to them alone. For centuries they had been the favored group under Ottoman rule, and by the twentieth century Muslims still comprised more than 90 percent of the land-owning *Agas*.[9] Following the Austrian occupation in 1878, Muslim chieftains were the soul of indigenous resistance and led an armed rebellion that took much time, blood and treasure to suppress. This fighting spirit earned the respect of the Austrian military and undoubtedly stimulated the desire to incorporate such manpower in the ranks of the Emperor's *Wehrmacht*. Moreover it convinced men such as Benjamin Kallay, Imperial overseer for Bosnia-Hercegovina (1882–1903), that Muslim support was the key to governing the territory and so initiated a policy of favoritism and appeasement.[10] Despite this support, Bosnian Muslims steadily lost ground between 1878 and 1914. Due to several factors, including large-scale emigration to Turkey, the Muslim population dropped from almost 39 percent in 1879 to less than 33 percent in 1910.[11] Reluctant to embrace "Western" education and technology they lagged behind the Christian groups in literacy and economic development and in political organization.[12] This meant that few Muslims had the interest or skills to rise in a modern military establishment. But the Muslims did come to see the Habsburg Empire as their protection against absorption by Serbia, something many felt would mean their cultural, if not physical, extinction. As a result, the high command in Vienna viewed the Muslim Bosniaks as solidly loyal to the Empire, a fact that made them the key element in the Bosnian military formations.[13]

Although they were the smallest element in the population, the Croats had close communal and political ties to the Catholic populations of Dalmatia and Croatia-Slavonia, and military authorities considered them *Habsburgtreu* no less than the Muslims.[14] As with the Muslims, this was largely because Croats saw the Empire as the best guarantor of their existing privileges and the best hope for their aspirations. The Bosnian Croat political establishment generally favored the union of Bosnia-Hercegovina with Dalmatia and Slavonia to form a third autonomous unit of the Empire, one in which Croats would compose the dominant element.[15] In addition, many Croats had been alienated by the threatening tactics of pro-Serbian separatists. In eastern and central Bosnia, Catholic communities were frequent targets of terrorism and intimidation, and Croats responded with anti-Serb demonstrations.[16] Because of their generally higher educational levels, Catholic soldiers also formed a disproportionately high percentage of NCOs and junior officers (50 and 60 percent, respectively) in the Bosnian units and would dominate staff and clerical positions.

Like the empire it served, the Austro-Hungarian Army was a rather complex and confusing institution in which the Bosnian-Hercegovinian (*Bosnisch-Herzegowinische*, abbreviated bh) formations were one of the more peculiar elements. The recruitment and organization of the main imperial army was shaped by the 1867 *Ausgleich* between the Empire of Austria and the Kingdom of Hungary which sought to "equalize" the status of the two states under a limited imperial framework. In military terms this meant that out of each annual call-up of conscripts, two-thirds went into units of the Common or Imperial (KuK) Army and the remaining third to formations of the Landwehr (KK) or Honvéd (KU), the respective Home Guard armies of Austria and Hungary.

Bosnia, however, lay outside this arrangement, and all its manpower served in the Common forces. Having completed active service, non-Bosnian soldiers subsequently passed through two reservist classes, Reserves and Landsturm. Those eligible men who had not received active training were organized in a general Ersatz Reserve. But again, this system did not apply to Bosnia-Hercegovina. Instead, Bosnian reservists passed through ranks of lst, 2nd, and 3rd Reserve, the last category also fulfilling the functions of the Ersatz.[17] Militarily, at least, Bosnia did constitute an autonomous "third element" in the Habsburg Empire.

The organization of regular Bosnian-Hercegovinian military units began in the later 1880s and by 1906 there were four *Bosnisch-Herzegowinische Infanterie Regimenter* (bh.IR) and an independent Bosnian *Feldjäger* battalion (bh.FJB). Each regiment had four battalions plus support units with a total mobilized strength of just over 4,000 officers and men.[18] The FJ battalion was about 1,200 strong. In addition to its field units, each regiment also had a depot or *Ersatz* battalion (EB) stationed in the regimental district to process new recruits and supply the frontline formations with replacements. The EBs also became a dumping ground for men deemed unsuitable for service at the front, be it for medical or political reasons. The FJ battalion had an *Ersatz* company (EK).

Although the Bosnian formations were new units, recruited from peoples without a tradition of service to the Empire, and many of them of questionable reliability, from thebeginning they were intended to be a *corps d'elite*.[19] The model for their formation were the Tirolen Kaiserjager (TKJ) Regiments, and like the Tiroleans, Bosnian troops enjoyed a number of special characteristics. Bosnian units were distinguished from all other formations by their uniform. In contrast to the billed cloth field cap that was standard issue in the rest of the Habsburg *Wehrmacht*, Bosnians wore a grey fez with a grey tassle (the parade or dress fez was red). The oriental flavor was further accentuated by their trousers which fastened tightly around the calves while being wide-cut above the knee in the Turkish style. In fact, these were the same pants issued to Habsburg artillery troops and the the Tiroleans, but unlike these, the Bosnians wore no gaiters or other leggings. Finally, the Bosnian formations even received their own march, "*Die Bosniaken Kommen,*" penned, with some appropriately "Turkish" airs, by Eduard Wagnes.[20]

The blatantly Ottoman character of the Bosnian uniform was not just for show, but was an obvious indication of the deference accorded Muslim sensibilities. Nevertheless there is no real evidence that Christian soldiers objected to the attire. On the other hand, ethnic-religious differences were a frequent source of misunderstanding and trouble. Both Serbs and Muslims were better disposed towards Croats than each other, another factor that made Croats preferable for command positions. But ethnic clashes were inevitable. In one instance a Serb NCO ordered a Muslim soldier to "March out, you swine!" Taking offense, the latter shot the Serb in the shoulder.[21] But in the main inter-ethnic relations, while seldom warm, were usually correct.

Each of the Bosnian units drew recruits from a distinct regimental district, and, thus, each represented a slightly different spectrum of ethnic groups. The 1st Regiment was depoted in Sarajevo and drew its manpower from central and southeastern Bosnia, highly diverse regions. The ethnic mix was roughly 40 percent Serb, 40 percent Muslim, and less than 20 percent Croat. Bh.IR2, depot Banja Luka, covered western Bosnia and had the smallest proportion of Croats and Muslims, its manpower being at least 60 percent Serb. The 3rd Regiment, depot Tuzla, covered northeastern Bosnia and contained the largest concentration of Muslims, some 50 percent, but relatively few Croats. The 4th regimental district, depot Mostar, corresponded to Hercegovina. It had the largest proportion of Croats, again about 50 percent, and no more than 20 percent Muslims. The bh.FJB, headquartered in Sarajevo, took its recruits from all four districts. It should also be noted that 4–7 percent of each regiment's personnel was non-Bosnia-Hercegovinian, most of them Germans, Czechs, and Poles who made up the senior officers, commissary and technical troops.[22]

At the outbreak of war in 1914, the bulk of the Bosnian units were stationed outside their territory as peacetime garrisons. Only the 3rd Battalion of each regiment remained at the home depot. The other three were deployed as follows: bh.IR1, Wiener-Neustadt; bh.IR2, Graz; bh.IR3, Trieste; bh.IR4, Bruck an der Leitha. Thus, mobilization found the Bosnian troops widely dispersed.

A war against Serbia, of course, raised the painful question of loyalty among Orthodox Bosnian soldiers. Habsburg officials, most prominently Bosnia's military governor (Landschef) Gen. Oskar Potiorek, now commander of all forces on the Serbian Front, feared a mass uprising of Serbs and demanded that Orthodox personnel be stripped from Bosnian formations before they were returned to the Balkan theater.[23] This move was approved by the high command, but actual implementation was left to the discretion of unit commanders. The command staff of the KuK III Corps in Graz, to which most of bh.IR2 was attached, shared Potiorek's concerns. On the order of the Corps' commander, most Serb soldiers were separated into ad hoc labor companies and the remaining Muslims and Croats, along with a minority of "reliable" Serbs, were combined into two battalions.[24] Likewise, the battalions of bh.IR3 in Budapest saw most of their Serbs transferred to Ersatz formations. To compensate this loss, the regiment received a battalion of Serbs from the upper Danube, troops considered untouched by anti-Habsburg propaganda.[25] The 1st Regiment in Wien also sent most of its Serbs to labor service and was reinforced with a composite battalion of Germans. Interestingly, bh.IR4, whose Orthodox Hercegovinians had been regarded as the least reliable, lost the fewest men, only some twenty per company (about 300 soldiers) being sent to labor duties in Upper Austria. This was due to the personal intercession of the Regiment's commander, Major M. Sešić, who was confident that most of his Serbs were trustworthy.[26]

The net result of these reductions was that the Serb component in the Bosnian formations was reduced by about 40 percent. Only in bh.IR2 did Serbs remain a plurality, while in Regiments 1 and 3 and the FJB they were reduced to some 25 percent of the total manpower.

These changes in the field units, it should be noted, were carried out in the absence of overt seditious or mutinous behavior on the part of the Serbs, probably due, in part, to the fact that most of them were isolated from their native soil and its influences. But in the Ersatz battalions the situation was quite different. From simple accessibility these units had long been the focus of anti-Habsburg agitation and, owing to the restriction of Serbs in the field units, they were filled disproportionately with Serbs. Unrest among the latter was muted but obvious. Serbian propaganda circulated freely, many of the men affected a kind of passive disobedience, and there were clashes with Muslim and Croat recruits. In November 1914 Potiorek ordered the dissolution of the existing Ersatz formations. In EBs 1 and 2 all Serbs, about 65 percent of the manpower, were shipped-off to build fortifications along the Danube. New battalions were formed on the basis of the remaining Croat and Muslim personnel. EBs 3 and 4, most of whose recruits were Croat or Muslim, lost only about a third.[27] EB 4, however, saw many Serbs desert and flee to Montenegro, a problem that continued in the months following. As a result, the battalion was eventually relocated to Knittelfeld in Styria.[28] By 1917 all of the Bosnian *Ersatz* formations would be moved to other regions.

Despite the disaffection of many Serb soldiers, evidenced by a steadily high desertion rate, the battle-worthiness of Muslims and Croats earned Bosnian formations a good reputation in combat. The existing units were expanded and new formations raised as the war continued. By late 1917 each of the original four regiments had raised 9–10 battalions, exclusive of temporary *Marsch* (field replacement) or reserve battalions. Several of these battalions were attached to other formations or operated as independent units. Feldjäger battalions grew from one to eight. A 5th Regiment appeared in 1916 formed from two battalions of the 1st Regiment (1st and 9th, or 1/1, 1/9) and bh.FJB 5.

In the autumn of 1917, a general army reorganization reduced regimental establishments from four to three battalions, and the battalions so released, plus bh.FJBs 6–8, were combined to form Regiments 6-8. Bh.IR 6 was formed from two supernumary battalions of bh.IR2 and bh.FJB 6 and the other two new regiments were similarly composed of elements from bh.IRs 3 and 4 and bh.FJBs 7 and

8.　Seven Bosnian battalions continued to operate as independent (*selbständige*) units. Three other battalions (1/6, 2/6, 3/8) were combined with two companies from bh.FJB5 and elements of the Common 103rd Regiment to form the *Kombiniertes Orient-Korps*.[29] This formation, composed almost entirely of Muslim troops, was intended as Austria-Hungary's contribution to the Palestine Front but ended the war in Italy.

In addition to the above, a paramilitary battalion of Bosnian gendarmerie was also raised, and Bosnian personnel supplied most of the manpower for the 6th *Grenzjager* Battalion and several static *Festungs* (fortress) battalions.[30] Moreover, Bosnian manpower, primarily Serb, was used to build thirteen *Etappen* (lines-of-communication) battalions.[31] Finally, although not part of the regular armed forces, some 20,000 Bosnians, predominantly Muslims and Croats, served in the *Schützkorps*, a kind of local militia whose primary function was the intimidation of the Orthodox population.[32]

The operational histories of the Bosnian formations during the war is generally a very distinguished one, despite a constant problem of disaffection and desertion among the Serb component. The latter meant that Muslim and Croat soldiers were compelled to play a disproportionate role in combat and bore a disproportionate share of casualties (see below), but this should not be interpreted to mean that Serbs were wholly unreliable or lacked bravery. The majority of Bosnian Serbs performed their duties adequately and many fought every bit as hard as their Muslim and Catholic comrades. Those that did not were simply obedient to different loyalties.

Bosnian units fought on all fronts and earned a reputation for bravery and tenacity second to none. Tough in defense, they were perhaps even more valuable as offensive shock troops, and they displayed particular skill in night attacks.[33] Complete operational histories for each unit cannot be given here, but the following examples will suffice to present a general portrait of their performance and behavior.

Parts of all four regiments participated in the campaign against Serbia in 1914, although only bh.IR3 participated as a complete unit. This campaign, which ended in a humiliating defeat of Habsburg arms, was marked by brutality and atrocities on both sides, and it surely constituted a supreme test of the loyalty of Bosnian troops. But the only significant defections took place in the 3rd Battalion, bh.IR2 during the final retreat of the Austrian forces. The battalion commander, a Colonel Coudenhove, reported that many of his

Serb soldiers, mostly wounded and stragglers, gave themselves up to their Serbian brethren. His Muslims and Croats, however, remained full of fight and their losses were almost entirely "dead and seriously wounded."[34]

In the opening campaign against Russia, bh.IRs 1, 2, and 4 played conspicuous roles and suffered heavy losses. By January 1915 the regimental commands were forced to call for the return of Serbs previously detached to labor service. At this time, for instance, bh.IR1 had 2,900 men in its ranks of which only 450 were Muslims and some 200 Croats. During 6–8 January, nearly 200 Serbs deserted to the enemy, and the 1st Battalion subsequently was removed from the frontlines to prevent further desertion.[35] Similar incidents occurred in bh.IRs 2 and 4 and in the former these led to the dismissal of five Serb officers and the return of several hundred Serbs to the labor units.[36] Similarly the Bosnian 6th *Marsch* battalion, which arrived at the front in late February, was composed almost entirely of Serbs who were deemed "completely unreliable" by frontline commanders.[37] Despite such problems, Bosnian formations successfully resisted several Russian attacks in this period and even conducted successful attacks. Between May and September 1915 bh.IR2 was involved in constant offensive operations during which it lost 4,400 men and earned several unit citations.[38] In these months Bosnian troops were frequently used as "stiffening" or as watchdogs attached to less reliable formations. One example is the pairing of bh.IR1 with the mostly Czech IR 35 in the fall of 1915.[39]

By 1916, however, most Bosnian units were withdrawn from the Russian Front, only bh.IRs 1 and 2 remaining by August. At about the same time, a new bh.IR5 was formed and thrown into the fight against Romania. This regiment, teamed with the Croatian 33rd *Honved* (*Domobrani*) Regiment, distinguished itself in fighting for the Oituz Pass.[40]

By 1916, however, most of the Bosnian formations—Regiments 2 and 4 and eight independent battalions—were concentrated on the Italian Front. Yugoslavs generally mistrusted Italian aspirations in the Balkans, and as a result Serbs fought with greater reliability on this front.[41] On 7 June 1916, for example, bh.IR2 stormed the key position of Monte Meletta on the Asiago sector. In doing so the regiment outfought four battalions of crack Alpini troops and repelled repeated counterattacks while surrounded on three sides. The victory cost the regiment half its strength, but earned it divisional and army citations and each man in its lst battalion received a 500 crown reward for bravery.[42] However, when bh.IR2 later withdrew from the Meletta, many Serbs took the opportunity to surrender to the Italians.[43]

Bosnian units also distinguished themselves in the bitter trench warfare on the Isonzo sector. In September 1916 a night counterattack by bh.FJB 6 threw the Italians off hard-won positions on Monte Hermada. Bh.FJB 4 also displayed great energy in counterattacks and in fierce fighting on the Biansizza Plateau reduced its strength from some 700 to a mere 164 officers and men.[44]

In late 1917 bh.IRs 1, 2, and 4 were combined under the command of the 55th Division which became the closest equivalent to a Bosnian Division in the entire war. These troops played a key role in the attack that smashed the Italian front at Caporetto in October. On 4 November the 4th battalion of bh.IR4 captured the railway bridge at Cornino, and bh.IR2 secured a bridgehead on the west side of the Tagliamento, thus ensuring that the-Italians could not rally behind the river.[45] Even the Germans, who usually had little good to say about the performance of Austrian troops, praised the Bosnians.[46] In the final months of the war, Bosnian troops fought in the bloody struggle for the Monte Grappa and acted as shock troops, with some success, in the Habsburg Army's abortive Piave offensive in June 1918.[47] All eight Bosnian regiments participated in these final attacks. On 16 June, for instance, bh.IR4 stormed Monte Solarola in the Grappa sector and held it for eight days against constant counterattacks.[48]

Although the general morale of the Austro-Hungarian forces rapidly disintegrated in the wake of this failed offensive, even in the last days many of the Bosnian formations preserved some military effectiveness. As the Army retreated from Italy in the autumn of 1918, elements of bh.IRs 1 and 2 formed a rear guard in their sectors and conducted several successful counterattacks against the pursuing Italians.[49]

In the last year of the war Austria-Hungary was gripped by a deepening internal crisis which manifested itself in mass protests, strikes, and mutinous uprisings in both army and navy. War-weariness and hunger were the direct causes of this unrest, but long-simmering nationalist resentments and the none-too-distant example of revolutionary Russia also played their parts. To man this "inner front" the Habsburg military was compelled to employ many of its Ersatz formations in police duties, designated *Assistenztruppen*, and even to detach entire divisions from the frontlines. But the deployment of forces in the interior created its own difficulties.

As mentioned above, the dubious political climate in Bosnia prompted the Army to relocate the indigenous Ersatz units. Nevertheless in 1918 many of the Bosnian Ersatz formations were still found suitable for Assistenz duties on the inner front outside their home territory. By January 1918 bh.EBs 1 and 3 had taken up quarters around Budapest where they kept an eye on the restive workers of Csepel and other trouble spots. In April, however, bh.EB1 was disbanded and its remaining personnel and responsibilities taken over by bh.EB3 which remained in the Budapest area until the end of the war, although one company was diverted to Sopron in the last weeks. The beginning of 1918 found bh.EB2 deployed in Lebring, Styria, south of Graz. In June it moved to Bohemia, first to Pilsen and in October to the Prague area where its companies were used against strikers. Bh.EB4 was relocated to Györ and remained there throughout most of the following year. In September, however, its remaining three companies were split up, one going to Szombathely and the others to Vienna.

The *Ersatz* companies of the bh.FJ battalions were initially redeployed in southern Hungary in the Pecs-Siklos-Villany area. By June only bh.EKs 1, 2, and 7 were still active in Assistenz roles. Bh.EK7, actually enlarged to an EB of two companies, stayed at Siklos until October when it transferred to Pecs to quell rebellious miners. Of the two other units, bh.EK2, also expanded to a two company battalion, went in May to the Styrian town of Judenburg where it helped suppress a mutiny of Slovene troops. Other Bosnians, from an unidentified unit, crushed a rebellion by Slovak troops in Serbia and even served as executioners for the ringleaders. Finally, bh.EK1 relocated to Mahrisch-Ostrav and remained there to the end of hostilities.

But not all Bosnian soldiers were so reliable. In mid-February, a Marsch company of bh.FJB 8 joined Croat troops in a mutiny aboard a train on its way to Belgrade.[50] At the beginning of February, mass mutiny erupted in the main Austro-Hungarian fleet anchored in Cattaro Bay. Several army units, including the 7th Battalion of bh.IR4, were moved against the mutineers. The 4/7 was mostly Croat, but then so were the largest part of the rebellious sailors. The Battalion's commander reported that his men openly sympathized with the mutineers and he did not think they could be relied on to take hostile action against them.[51] Most of these Bosnians (actually Hercegovinians) were transferred to Sinj where they were to be employed in agricultural work. Here, in late February, they went "on strike," and many fled into the countryside to join the growing bands of armed deserters, the so-called Green Cadres (*Zeleni Kadr*).[52]

The Green Cadres were a phenomenon not only in Bosnia, but also in the neighboring regions of Slavonia and Dalmatia. By the end of 1918 these deserter bands, many well-armed, may have numbered 100,000 and dominated much of the countryside.[53] Combining Yugoslav nationalism with quasi-Bolshevik revolutionism, the Cadres attracted mostly Serbs, but also many Croats. They became so powerful in the eastern border regions of Bosnia and Hercegovina that they effectively prevented the conscription of men from these areas during the last months of the war.

The Bosnian-Hercegovinian units of the Habsburg Army provide an important example of both the efficacy and ineffectiveness of nationalism among Yugoslav groups in this critical period. Nationalist agitation certainly worked to alienate the sympathies of much of the Serb population and undermined the effectiveness of Bosnian units. Yet there were never any mass rebellions by Serbs and most, actively or passively, served the Habsburgs effectively. On the other hand, it was anti-Serbian as much as pro-Habsburg sentiments that motivated Muslims and Croats to give their all in the fighting.

In the course of World War I, some 325,000 Bosnians and Hercegovinians were called to arms in defense of the Austro-Hungarian Empire. The great majority of these men served in the combatant regiments and battalions. Bh.IR2, for example, saw 38,000 men pass through its ranks, although its field strength was never more than 4,000 and usually much less.[54] By the end of 1917, 34,106 Bosnian soldiers had been killed, and by the conclusion of the war this number probably reached 40,000.[55] In addition, approximately 115,000 were wounded, 54,000 made prisoner and 16,000 missing—a total casualty rate of some 56 percent. Given that some 14,000 of the prisoners died in captivity and that most of the missing were actually dead, the total number of war-related fatalities probably exceeded 60,000.

Based on battlefield casualties, Wilhelm Winckler later compiled an military death rate for Bosnia of 1.91 percent of the total population.[56] On the face of it, Bosnia's loss rate was comparatively low relative to other areas of the Empire, the Tirol, Moravia, and the Slovene districts, for instance, where military deaths often exceeded 3 percent or 4 percent of the population. But the overall figure for Bosnia disguises widely unequal losses for the three ethnic groups:

	% Gen. Pop.	% Tot.Losses	% Pop. Dead
Serbs	43%	23%	1.1%
Croats	23%	27%	2.3%
Muslims	33%	50%	3.3%

While Croat losses are roughly equal to their share of the general population, Serb and Muslim losses show an almost inverse ratio. This seems to confirm that Muslims were called upon to take up the slack caused by the unreliability of the Serbs.

This disparity is a reflection of national and political sympathies compounded by official military policy. From the outset of the war, Serb disaffection led Habsburg authorities to limit their numbers and role in the Bosnian-Hercegovinian units. As the war continued even some of the Bosnian Croats became questionable, and their higher educational levels also removed a larger proportion of them from the deadly frontlines. The Muslims, therefore, were reliable and expendable cannon-fodder and were used accordingly.

The Bosnian-Hercegovinian formations vanished with the end of the Habsburg Empire. The new state of Yugoslavia inherited the territory of these units but, for its own political imperatives, did not seek to continue its military traditions. However, during World War II the German Army and the Ustasa regime in Croatia tried to resurrect something of the old Bosnian units and several such formations were formed to serve the Axis cause, most prominently the 13th *Handschar* and 23rd *Kama* SS Divisions. Nor has the distinct character of Bosnia disappeared under more that forty years of Communist rule. As this is written the Yugoslav state is disintegrating and Bosnia-Hercegovina has declared its independence while poised on the brink of civil war. Could the future see an independent Bosnia and a resurrection of a distinctly Bosnian army? If recent history has reminded us of nothing else, it is that anything is possible.

NOTES

1. Hamidija Kapidžić, "Austro-ungarska politika u Bosni i Hercegovini i jugoslavensko pitanje za vrijeme prvog svejtskog rata," in *Godisnjak istoriskog društva Bosne i Hercegovine,* God. IX (Sarajevo, 1957–58), 7–55.

2. The census of 1910 counted 1,931,802 inhabitants. Auguste Gauvain, *La Question Yougoslave* (Paris, 1918), 27. See also Kriegs-

jarchiv (KA) Wien, Nachlass Sammlung. B/800 #278, Rudolf Kiszling, MS, "Das Volkerbild der ehëm. Öst.- ung. Monarchie," 82; Peter Urbanitsch, Adam Wandruszka, *et al.*, *Die Habsburger Monarchie, 1848–1918*, Band III (Vienna, 1980), 666.

3. Ibid. There were some 900,000 kmets. Serbs composed 75 percent, Croats 21.35 percent, and Muslims 3.63 percent.

4. KA, Nachlass Sammlung, B/726 #1, Robert Nowak, MS, "Die Klammer des Reiches, Das Verhalten der elf Nationalitäten Öst.-ung., 1914–1916," 197, 297. In 1914 the military governor of Bosnia, General Oskar Potiorek, reported that at least 60 percent of the city's Serb population was blatantly "anti-Austrian."

5. Nowak, 183–184.

6. Ibid., 334.

7. Ibid., 191, 196.

8. Ibid., 197, 202.

9. D. A. Dyker, "The Ethnic Muslims of Bosnia–Some Basic Socio-Economic Data," *Slavonic and East European Review*, Vol. 50, 119 (1972), 238–256. Of 10,437 landlords with tenents, 9,537 were muslims. See also Rudolf Kiszling, *Die Kroaten* (Graz, 1956), 3.

10. Kiszling, *Kroaten*, 73, 83. Bosnia-Hercogovina was administered he a special bureau of the Imperial Ministry of Finance with the Imperial finance minister, Kallay to 1903 and afterward Stephan Burian, as its head. Kallay was not opposed to some appeasement of the Serbs and, in one gesture, sanctioned the rreation of Church schools for Orthodox children. Burian adopted a more favorable policy towards Serbs, partly in response to increased Pan-Serb agitation. See also Nowak. 184 and Hugo Hantsch, *Geschichte Österreichs, 1648–1918*, Vol. 2 (Graz, 1962), 482–483.

11. Dyker, 240.

12. Signe Klein, "Freiherr Sarkotić von Lorčen: die Zeit seiner Verwaltung in Bosnien-Hercegogina von 1914 bis 1918" (Ph.D. dissertation, Universität Wien, 1969), 30.

13. Nowak, 197 and "Das bosnisch-herzegowinische Infanterie Regiment Nr. 2 in Weltkrieg 1914–1918," (bh.IR2), Brosch #1304, *Bundesministerium für Landesverteidigung* (Vienna, 1969), 5–9.

14. Nowak, 251, 333 and Deutsche Gesellschaft für Wehrpolitik und Wehrwissenschaften Zweigstelle, *Das Volkerbild der Ehemaligen Öst.-ung. Monarchie* (Vienna, 1944), 83–84; Edmund von Glaise-Horstenau, ed., *Österreich-Ungarns Letzter Kreig* (ÖULK), Vol. I (Vienna, 1931),

15. Nowak, 202. Bosnian Croats actually enjoyed more political liberties than their co-religionists in Hungary and Dalmatia.

16. Nowak, 184, 223, 297. Following the assassination of Franz Ferdinand in June 1914, Croats and Muslims in Sarajevo joined forces in an anti-Serb pogrom.

17. J. S. Lucas, *Austro-Hungarian Infantry, 1914–1918* (London, 1973), 12,

18. Lucas, 26, 29–30.

19. Ibid.

20. This march is recorded on "Berühmte Marschmusik," Fiesta Records, #1838, New York.

21. Rudolf Kiszling, "Die militärischen Beziehungen der Kroaten und Nordserben zu die Deutschen," *Südostdeutsche Vierteljahresblatter*, #1 (1960), 22.

22. KA, Erganzungsheft #9 zum Werke Österreich-Ungarns Letzter Krieg, Oberst a.D. Max Ehnl (comp.), *Die öst.-ung. Landmacht nach Aufbau, Gleidurung, Friedengarnison, Einteilung und nationaler Zussamensetzung im Sommer 1914* (Vienna, 1934).

23. Nowak, 247–252.

24. Ibid., 333.

25. Ibid., 334.

26. Ibid.

27. Ibid., 336.

28. Lucas. 105, Nowak, 197.

29. Bh.IR2, 33, and Richard Georg Plaschka with Horst Haselstein and Arnold Suppan, *Innerer Front: Militarassistenz, Widerstand, und Umsturz der Donau Monarchie, 1918* (IF), (Munich, 1974), 352. The commander of the Orient-Korps was a Colonel Bošnjaković.

30. The Grenzjäger formations were sometimes referred to as *Bosnisch-Herzegowinische Grenzjäger*, but only the 6th battalion contained native troops, the others being German, Magyar, and Czech. These battalions were the outgrowth of six independent companies formed to police the Bosnian-Hercegovinian frontiers. Thr 6th battalion also contained Croat troops of the 16th Common Regiment (*Bjelovar*). Most of the *Festungs* battalions were formed as local garrisons against a Serbian invasion in 1915. Most of their manpower was later absorbed into the *Feldjäger* battalions. See Plaschka, IF, 334, Lucas, 105; KA Ergänzungsheft #9.

31. Lucas, 29.

32. Klein, 68–70. See also Vladimir Dedijer. *et al. A History of Yugoslavia* (New York, 1974), 494.

33. ÖULK, VII, 604.

34. Bh.IR2, 30.

35. KA, AOK, Op.#6l5l, "Bh.JR 1 und 2." K.u.K. 11 Korpskmdo, Op. #1247/1, 9 January 1915.

36. KA, AOK, Op. #6151,"Bh.JRI 1 und 2." K.u.K. 6 ITD Kmdo, Op. #211/8, 4 January l915; AOK Op. #72O7, "Bildung bh. Mannschaft, 15 February 1915; AOK Op. #73l6,"Agitation bei Ersatztruppen," 11 February 1915.

37. KA, AOK, Op. #7470, "bh. Mannschaft bei der 5. Armee," 24 February 1915.

38. Bh.IR2, 20–24.

39. OULK, IV, 501.

40. Kiszling, Kroaten, 103; Bh.IR2, 32.

41. KA, AOK, Op. #13225, K. K. Landespräsidium für Krain, #3605/Mob. "Haltungder Sudslawen gegenüber Italien," 6 July 1915.

42. KA, 3. Armeekmdo, Pras. #59906/VI, Feldpost #239, 4 August 1916. BH.IR2, 44–45; OULK, VI, 289.

43. ÖULK, VI, 672.

44. Fritz Weber, *Isonzo 1916* (Vienna, 1927), 98; Hans Fritz, *Bosniak* (Waldhofen a.d. Ybbs, 1931),

45. Bh.IR2, 52.

46. Ernest Bauer, *Glanz und Tragik der Kroaten* (Vienna, 1969), 93.

47. Bh.IR2, 58; OULK, VII, 698.

48. ÜLK, VII, 259.

49. ÖULK, VII, 695.

50. Plaschka, IF, 156.

51. R. G. Plaschka, *Cattaro-Prag: Kriegsmarine und Heer. Öst-ung. in Feuer der Aufstandbewegungen von 1 Feb. und 28 Okt. 1918* (Vienna, 1969), 189.

52. Plaschka, IF, 156–157.

53. Klein, 229; Plaschka, IF, 79, 76; OULK, 45.

54. Bh.IR2, 8, 9.

55. Wilhelm Winckler, *Die Totenverluste der Öst.-ung. Monarchie nach Nationalitaten,* (Vienna, 1919), Tabelle I.

56. Ibid.

THE ROLE OF THE YUGOSLAV COMMITTEE IN THE FORMATION OF YUGOSLAVIA

Gale Stokes

The breakup of Austria-Hungary in the name of national self-determination brought about the creation of an equally multi-national new state, Yugoslavia.[1] It is paradoxical that the idea of Yugoslavism, emphasizing as it did the subordination of historical peoples to an ideal of brotherly unity, should have triumphed at a moment of nationalist exaltation, especially since Yugoslavism was popular only among the youth and a few intellectuals at the outbreak of World War I. This outcome may lie attributed, at least in part, to the activities of a group of politicians and intellectuals from the Habsburg lands who escaped into Western Europe at the beginning of the war and organized themselves into a political action group called the Yugoslav Committee. By 1917 this committee had become a quasi-independent body with a headquarters in London and private financial support. Members of the committee held close connections with the French and British governments and with emigrants who supported the committee in the United States, and they even had some influence on American policy.[2] In 1917 the committee reached an agreement with the Serbian government that a new Yugoslav state would be founded after the war, so that when separate peace talks with Austria-Hungary failed for the last time in 1918 when the committee was in position to push for the complete dismemberment of that ancient state. When the war ended, the committee's efforts had helped create an atmosphere in which the establishment of a Yugoslav state became not only an acceptable policy for the Allies, but a desirable post-war goal.

The Yugoslav Committee, therefore, has with justice been considered an important element in the history of the formation of Yugoslavia.[3] It would perhaps be an exaggeration to say that without this committee no Yugoslavia would have emerged, but its significance is unquestionable. And yet, there is another side to the story, a more ominous side whose history is still being written, because the Kingdom of the Serbs, Croats and Slovenes did not turn out to be the sort of state the Yugoslav Committee had hoped.

Frustrated by German and Hungarian domination in the Habsburg Monarchy, the Croatian and Slovenian members of the Yugoslav Committee had sought to create a state in which no people would dominate or feel dominated. Aware of the dangers of imbalance in a multi-national state, Croatian and Slovenian émigrés insisted throughout World War I that post-war Yugoslavia would have to be a fusion of peoples, an equal partnership or organic union, not a Slavic-Habsburg Empire in which certain national groups were favored. Despite their understanding of this danger, their insistence that it must not happen and their work to avoid it, committee members could not prevent the creation of a Yugoslavia that was dominated by Serbs. The costs of this failure were incalculable. Politics in interwar Yugoslavia never functioned normally because the only real issue was the national one. Hitler's easy success in 1941 was partially attributable to widespread disaffection with Belgrade, and the victory of Tito's partisans during World War II was in important measure the result of the promise to put into practice the ideal of equality among the Yugoslav peoples.

Problems of the Yugoslav Committee

The history of the Yugoslav Committee, then, is one of many important successes and one fundamental failure. The purpose of this article is not to enumerate or praise the successes, which has been done often enough, but to analyze the failure. The basic reason the Yugoslav Committee did not find it possible to create the state of equal peoples it sought was that the committee only worked within the limitations of its situation and never transcended them, so that in the end its success was limited as well. To achieve the equitable Yugoslavia it desired, the committee would have had to overcome four liabilities: its émigré nature; its vulnerability to Serbian initiatives; the incompatibility of its territorial aims with Italian aspirations; and its Croatian, even Dalmatian, composition.

The émigré nature of the Committee was its most obvious and problematical feature. Just before and just after the beginning of actual warfare in 1914, several prominent Croatian politicians from Dalmatia succeeded either in leaving the Habsburg lands or in not returning. Ante Trumbić, Frano Supilo, and Ivan Mestrović established a nucleus around which later émigrés could gather. But no matter how well balanced this nucleus strove to become by additions from inside Croatia and Slovenia, no matter how much support it could generate among South Slavic immigrants in the new world, and no matter how favorably inclined friendly individuals close to allied governments became, the committee remained an émigré organization, unrecognized by the law of any state, and without official sanction to represent the people for whom it claimed to speak. In the early stages of the war this did not matter. The committee could conduct its propaganda easily enough as a private interest group. But later, its only hope of influencing the character of the new Yugoslav state was to be formally recognized by the Great Powers as the legal representative of an allied people. To succeed the Yugoslav Committee needed the acquiescence of the two allied powers already interested in South Slavic lands, Serbia, and Italy.

The small likelihood that Serbia would permit the Yugoslav Committee to achieve legal status was implicit in the assumptions under which its Premier, Nikola Pašić, helped the committee form itself in 1914 and 1915. Serbia's immediate fear in 1914, besides collapse, was that an early peace would be signed before it could formulate comprehensive war aims.[4] Very early, therefore, the Serbs laid out a maximum program calling for the creation of a large South Slavic state. On September 21, 1914, Pašić formally suggested borders for a post-war state that stretched well into Habsburg lands, split Istria with Italy, and claimed all of Dalmatia. These proposed borders conflicted with Italian ambitions in the Adriatic and would necessitate the destruction of the Habsburg Empire.[5]

The Establishment of the Yugoslav Committee

At the same time, the Dalmatian émigrés in Italy had begun to discuss their situation. They concluded that the best hope for the future of Croatia and Slovenia lay in the creation of a new Slavic state on the Adriatic. This state would have to include Serbia, so that it could act as a Slavic barrier to German penetration into the Balkans, but more importantly it would provide a chance for Croatia and Slovenia to become independent of Austrian and Hungarian domination. These conclusions led to specific goals that were remarkably similar to those of Pašić: dismemberment of the Habsburg Empire, and acquisition of lands on the Adriatic. Already in October, Frano

Supilo was in France trying to interest French politicians in adopting the destruction of Austria-Hungary as a war aim.

When Pašić heard of Supilo's campaign in France and realized that Serbian and Croatian goals coincided, he quickly grasped that the Croatian émigrés, who had excellent contacts, could be helpful in popularizing Serbian war aims in Western Europe. Accordingly, he sent two special emissaries to Italy to offer the émigrés financial support in their common effort. On November 22, 1914, these representatives concluded an agreement with Ante Trumbić in Florence to establish a Yugoslav Committee consisting of leading émigré politicians of the three major South Slavic peoples. The purpose of the committee would be "to assist in the creation of a united Yugoslav (possibly Serbo-Croatian) state by informing leading circles and by publicity activity."[6] As this wording indicated, the committee was to assist Serbia through a propaganda effort. As far as Pašić was concerned, this was the extent of its purpose and authority.[7]

Pašić unquestionably sought the creation of a Yugoslav state.[8] The position papers worked out for him in the fall of 1914 demonstrate this, as does the Niš Declaration of December 7, 1914, by which the wartime Serbian government committed itself to a Yugoslav goal.[9] But quite naturally, Pašić did not think of Serbia as merely a partner of the other South Slavs in the struggle to create this new state. He thought of Serbia as a liberator. Since he considered the Macedonians and Montenegrins as Serbs that should be united with the motherland, he had no thought of allowing them any special status. The Croats and Slovenes were clearly not Serbs, so he was willing to allow them their national symbols, alphabet, religion, and even their traditional political organs. But the new Yugoslavia was not going to be an amalgam of these peoples. It was going to be a state in which the victorious Serbs would grant their new acquisitions equal rights as Serbs or as associated peoples. Pašić's supporters found this prospect emotionally satisfying, but they also had a good legal argument, since Serbia was recognized as an independent state and therefore could expand legitimately without a revolutionary European settlement.[10]

Worries of Croats and Slovenes

The Croats and Slovenes did not find the idea of liberation by the Serbs a congenial prospect. The example of Macedonia worried them. When Serbia seized Macedonia from Turkey and Bulgaria in the two Balkan wars, it did not extend normal constitutional rights to the newly acquired territory, even though it insisted that the Macedonians fulfill the regular obligations of citizens, including taxation and conscription. The Croatian émigrés in Italy who agreed to propagandize for a Yugoslav state had no desire for Croatia to become another Macedonia.[11] They were willing to begin cooperating, even if at first the Yugoslav Committee was subordinate to the Serbian government, because they believed there could be no Yugoslavia without Serbia. But they firmly believed that the logic of events would eventually transform the Yugoslav Committee into an equal partner.

Doubtful of Serbian intentions but assured of Serbian financial support, the committee members began to work. They laid plans for Yugoslav legions composed of volunteers from allied prisoner of war camps, invited politicians from Croatia proper and from Slovenia to join the emigration, and sent their representative to America, where he met with an enthusiastic welcome. But fearing that their interest in the Adriatic would spark a reaction from Italian nationalists, they did not make the committee's work public.

As one of the primary organizers and most prominent figures of the Yugoslav Committee, Frano Supilo spent the early months of 1915 attempting to work out a clearer understanding with Serbia and the Allies of what Croatia's future might be.[12] In the early spring this effort took him to Niš, the wartime capital of Serbia, where he found it very difficult to discover from Pašić what sort of terms the Croats could expect if they were to unite with Serbia. From Aleksandar Belić's semi-official *Srbija i južnoslovensko pitanje [Serbia and the South Slav Question]*, he learned that the Serbs believed no special contract was needed. Belić claimed that Serbs and Croats were simply the same people with two names, so that any sort of autonomy that divided them would go against the national consciousness.[13] The dangers for the less numerous Croats of uniting with the Serbs before achieving agreement on the terms of unification were obvious to Supilo, but he was not able to find much sympathy for his point of view.

Reaction to Treaty of London

Unsuccessful in Niš, Supilo travelled on to Petersburg to seek assurances from the Tsarist government. Instead of assurances he found disaster. Late in March, Sergei Sazonov, Russian Foreign Minister, let slip to Supilo that the Allies were about to promise Italy

Dalmatia in return for her declaration of war. Supilo immediately informed both Pašić and Trumbić of this finding, but despite a month of frenzied activity by all three men, they were not able to head off the debacle. On April 26, 1915, Italy and the Allies signed the Treaty of London, by which lands claimed by the Yugoslavs on the Adriatic were assigned to Italy.[14] Stunned by this provocation, on April 30 Trumbić hastily assembled Croatian and Slovenian émigrés in Paris and brought the Yugoslav Committee out into the open. Designating London as its headquarters and electing Trumbić president, the new public committee sent a delegation the very next day to Delcassé to complain about the concessions to Italy, and within a few days it produced a policy memorandum setting out aims that directly conflicted with Italian goals.

Territorially, the committee's memorandum of May 1915 went beyond Pašić's memo of September 21.[15] Besides Dalmatia, it claimed for the Yugoslavs all of Istria, Gorica, and Koruska, allowing to the Italians less territorial gain in the case of victory over Austria than Austria herself had offered as a reward for staying neutral. This emphasis on Slovenian and Croatian claims in the Adriatic was only natural for the Yugoslav Committee, since its composition was heavily Croatian, and its leadership Dalmatian. Just as the Serbs considered Macedonia inviolate, and the Italians came to see the Treaty of London as unchangeable, so the committee became intransigent concerning lands to which it was emotionally attached.

The committee's obduracy cannot be considered solely a matter of principle, such as self-determination, or nationality, although this is no doubt how many saw it. On occasion, for example, members of the Yugoslav Committee suggested that Serbia give up part of Macedonia and concentrate on creating an outlet to the sea. This position was fully comparable to the Serbian view that Macedonia was untouchable, but compromises on the Adriatic might be possible. And, just as Serbia gave up too little too late in Macedonia to prevent Bulgaria from attacking her, so eventually Trumbić conceded too little too late on the Adriatic to obtain Italian support. From the first moments of the committee's public existence this strong Adriatic orientation hindered the evolution of a realistic policy.

Yugoslav Committee's Restraints

By the time the Yugoslav Committee began the public phase of its work in May 1915, then, the restraints within which it worked for the rest of the war were established. It was an émigré committee with a special interest in the Adriatic question and Dalmatia, it was an uneasy junior partner of Serbia, and it was in conflict with Italy. Its goal, beyond the day-to-day demands and programs, was the creation, with Serbia, of an equitable Yugoslav state on the ruins of the Habsburg Empire.

This requirement that a Yugoslavia could exist only if Austria-Hungary ceased to exist had an important effect on the work of the committee. Until the spring of 1918 the likelihood that the Allies would seek the breakup of Austria-Hungary was small. The remoteness of the possibility of a Yugoslav state meant that committee members felt only the relatively light pressure of working out ideal plans, not the inexorable urgency associated with immediate and actual possibilities. With so much else uncertain, there seemed to be no compelling reason to break with Serbia even though the committee was not achieving equality, or to accommodate Italian wishes in the Adriatic, even though Italy continued to oppose Yugoslav aspirations there. In 1916 and 1917, therefore, the committee took two crucial steps that confirmed its original relationship to Serbia, thereby helping to ensure that the committee would not achieve its ultimate goal.

By 1916 relations between the Serbian government and the Yugoslav Committee had become strained. In trying to convince Bulgaria to enter the war against the Central Powers, the Allies had made Serbia several territorial offers to compensate for proposed concessions in Macedonia in favor of the Bulgarians. Quite naturally, when rumors of these possibilities leaked out, the Croats and Slovenes felt that they were being callously parcelled out, not treated as peoples with their own aspirations. At one point, in an effort to work out a solution, Supilo endorsed a compromise suggestion made by Sir Edward Grey that Bosnia and Hercegovina, Southern Dalmatia, Slavonia, and Croatia be allowed to choose their future by plebiscite after the war. This formula only worsened the situation. The Serbian government interpreted it to mean that Supilo was preparing the ground for the creation of an independent Croatia, while members of the Yugoslav Committee objected that Supilo had made this important compromise without consulting them. Supilo responded vigorously.[16] He hoped, he said, that successful prosecution of the war would produce a state that would be the "harmonious product of all our national strengths, a fusion of spirits, traditions, and hopes." But for this to happen, Serbia would have to undertake fundamental political, constitutional, and cultural reforms that would prevent what he called a Serbo-Orthodox exclusivism from destroying Yugoslav unity. If Serbia did not change, Supilo warned, unification would have to await a more opportune moment. In the meantime, in the absence of reform, all those Yugoslav lands in which a majority of people wanted to be united with Croatia should be granted that desire.

Supilo's outright threat to seek a separate Croatian state did not achieve the support of the Yugoslav Committee. Naturally, the Serbian members of the committee, as informal representatives of the government, opposed it, but so did the Slovenes. One of Supilo's blind spots was that he thought of Slovenes much in the same way that he complained Serbs thought of Croats. He considered Zagreb the center of Croatian-Slovenian activity, and did not understand that the Slovenes found this offensive. Naturally, therefore, he could not count on their support of his Croatian-centered idea. Even some Croats opposed Supilo. Still, at a plenary meeting of the committee in February 1916, the crisis was patched over. The committee formally reaffirmed its commitment to a broad unification, but placed many of Supilo's views in a policy memorandum to the French government on March 13. This was only a temporary solution, however.

Worsening of the Serbian Situation

The situation of the Serbian government changed dramatically for the worse by 1916. Thoroughly defeated by the Austrians under German leadership and hounded by the Bulgarians from the south, the Serbian army conducted a heroic but costly retreat through the winter of 1915–16 that took it finally to the island of Corfu. In the spring of 1916 Pašić was bearing the political consequences of this defeat, threatened on the one side by the machinations of Regent Alexander Karadjordević, and on the other by disloyalty of an important segment of the military under the leadership of Colonel Dimitrijević-Apis.[17] In an effort to improve his fortunes at home by success abroad, Pašić travelled to Paris, London, and Petrograd in May 1916. Under great pressure, not certain of the outcome of the war, and none too confident of the purposes of the Croatian emigration, Pašić stated in an interview to the Russian press that he was ready to recognize Italy's predominant interest in the Adriatic.

Pašić's statement outraged the Yugoslav Committee, particularly Supilo, for whom it simply demonstrated the impossibility of trusting the Serbs to protect Croatian and Slovenian interests.[18] Supilo demanded the Yugoslav Committee break its relations with Serbia. But, once again, an emergency session of the full committee did not agree.[19] Harmony with Serbia was considered so vital that the committee simply asked its president, Trumbić, to speak privately with Pašić. To restrain Supilo from using his great personal influence to promote a break with Serbia, the committee prohibited any member from making personal contacts and statements without approval from Trumbić. Supilo responded to this gag rule by resigning from the committee, leaving it firmly under Trumbić's leadership until the end of the war.[20]

Supilo had accurately assessed the underlying attitude of Pašić and his government. Not only was Pašić a superb politician, a magician of appearance and nuance, and a dogged pursuer of personal power, he also was a true representative of the faith of all Serbian politicians in Serbia's destiny as the liberator of the Balkans. Supilo grasped that in something as basic as the structure of a future Yugoslavia, Pašić could never yield, either politically or temperamentally. Some others saw this, but none were hard-headed enough to follow the logic of the realization to its unpalatable conclusion: a break with Serbia. So Supilo was isolated, and despite its doubts, the committee tied itself even closer to Serbia.

The Corfu Agreement

A year later, conclusion of the Corfu Agareement seemed to indicate that the decision of 1916 had been correct. This agreement, which was achieved by lengthy and difficult negotiations between the representatives of the Yugoslav Committee and the Serbian government, was signed by Pašić and Trumbić on July 20, 1917.[21] It called for the creation of a democratic, constitutional Kingdom of Serbs, Croats, and Slovenes under the Karadjordjević dynasty in which the cultural and religious rights of all three peoples would be preserved. A constitutional assembly to be held after liberation would determine the internal organization of the state.

The two signatories interpreted the Corfu Declaration quite differently. The Yugoslav Committee believed it had achieved basic agreement with Serbia. Even Supilo's pessimism was momentarily overcome. Despite the failure of the conferees to agree on the organization of the new state, it seemed that a great step forward for Yugoslavism had been achieved, and many still hold that this was the case. Today, however, one may doubt that this positive interpretation is the whole truth. Pašić did not come to the negotiations because of any desire to plan for the future Yugoslav state. He called for discussions only under severe pressure, and after the agreement had been signed, he ignored it except as a device for silencing those who accused him of ignoring the committee. Internally, Pašić's government was under attack for accepting Regent Alexander's scheme to rid the army of disloyal elements. By this plan Colonel Dimitrijević-Apis and his closest collaborators had been condemned to death for treason and attempted assassination. There is considerable doubt that these charges could have been sustained in a fair trial, but no doubt whatsoever that Apis and his organization, "Union or Death," were a center of independent power that had disrupted Serbian public life for years. "Union or Death" had been involved in the assassination of Franz Ferdinand and its machinations had resulted in the fall of Pašić's government in June 1914. The basic question was who would be the final authority in Serbia, the Prince, that army, or the government. Because of his opposition to Pašić, Apis had close links with the opposition parties. Therefore, when Pašić decided to go along with the Regent's plan to remove Apis he lost the support of these parties, with whom he had been allied in a coalition government since 1914.[22] Apis's trial also hurt Serbian regard abroad, since it was represented by Pašić's enemies not as an effort to establish the authority of the civilian government but as an act of political revenge.

Pašić faced other uncertainties. In May 1917, the South Slavic political parties remaining inside Austria-Hungary proclaimed their desire for unification "under the sceptre of the Habsburg-Lorraine dynasty."[23] This May Declaration, as it became known, hinted that the new Emperor Charles might be on the verge of forestalling Serbian gains by granting the Croats and Slovenes some sort of autonomy within the empire. Rumors of peace feelers further indicated that Serbian war aims might be in danger. Furthermore, Pašić was worried that the Yugoslav Committee, which he still considered simply an arm of Serbian propaganda, was slipping away from him. Not only did the committee constantly have its own views on affairs, but by 1917 it had become financially independent due to the generous support of the emigrant community in South America.

Rapprochement with the Yugoslav Committee would have a positive effect on all these problems. It would provide an antidote to the bad press Pašić was receiving abroad over the Apis case by pleasing the foreign supporters of the committee; it would mollify the opposition, which tended to favor accommodation; it would reaffirm Serbian claims to represent the Habsburg South Slavs in spite of the May Declaration; and it would draw the committee into closer cooperation with Serbia.

Having called for the meeting to serve these clear short-term ends, Pašić almost ignored the agreement after it was made. Before the ink on his signature was dry, he left Corfu to attend the conference on Balkan problems being held at Versailles. Rather than present the agreement officially to the Powers, as the Yugoslav Committee hoped, he contented himself with belatedly and reluctantly making it known to them only orally.

In a way, of course, the standard interpretation of the Corfu Agreement as a positive step for Yugoslavism is correct. The agreement put both the Serbian government and the Yugoslav Committee on record as pursuing the same broad goal. But unfortunately for the Yugoslav Committee, it was not realized at the time, nor has it been clearly seen since, that the agreement was also a masterful diplomatic success for Pašić.[24] In return for acceptance of the Karadjordjević dynasty, with its clear implication of Serbian continuity, Pašić agreed to the principles of democracy, civil rights, and constitutionalism. This was not any sort of concession for him, since all of these were features of pre-war Serbia and matched well the policy he had enunciated in 1914. Beyond that, however, Pašić conceded nothing. He did not change his view that Serbia should be the liberating power, nor did he make any agreement that would hinder his ability to organize the state after the war. In a typically brilliant maneuver, he achieved several short-term goals while putting the committee in his debt by giving it something it wanted, all the time retaining full initiative for himself in those things he considered most important. Without giving up anything fundamental, he severely limited the Yugoslav Committee's freedom of action by linking it more closely to Serbia than it had ever been before.

Italian-Yugoslav Differences

Committed now to cooperating with Serbia in the creation of a new state rather than going it alone, as Supilo had suggested, Trumbić had reason to hope in 1918 that progress in modifying Italian policy might also be possible. The solid rock of that policy was foreign minister Sidney Sonnino.[25] Sonnino had negotiated Italy's entrance into the Great War in return for South Tirol, Trentino, Istria, and central

Dalmatia with its islands. Sonnino considered the acquisitions in the north the final stage of Italian unification, and those on the Adriatic necessary for Italian security. Since the treaty also provided that the Great Powers could eventually assign some of the Adriatic lands to Slavic states, he believed that the treaty was a "working formula" from which all could profit.[26] He was wrong. The Slavs saw the treaty only as a threat to their unification, not as a starting point for negotiations. Nonetheless, from the moment Sonnino secretly negotiated the treaty until his death in 1922 he resolutely held out for every last inch of territory promised him. As a result, even though some influential Italians favored a modified policy of cooperation with the South Slavs, Italian foreign policy remained until the end of the war extremely hostile to both Serbia and the Yugoslav Committee.

Late in 1917 English supporters of the Yugoslav cause began trying to do something about the deep differences between the Italians and the Yugoslavs.[27] Several meetings ensued, including one between Trumbić and the head of the Italian government, Vittorio Orlando. The eventual outcome was the Torre-Trumbić agreement of March 1918.[28] Andrea Torre was the chairman of an *ad hoc* committee of the Italian parliament that was trying to organize a public meeting of the leaders of the Habsburg nationalities in exile for propaganda purposes. He had come to London to get the agreement of the Yugoslav Committee that was needed if the meeting was to be held. Trumbić was not enthusiastic. He refused to discuss border issues with Torre, and by insisting that the Italians renounce the Treaty of London he pushed their discussions to an impasse. Only when Henry Wickham Steed, foreign editor of *The Times* and a staunch supporter of Yugoslavism, frankly told Trumbić that his attitude would forfeit the support of Steed and his friends did Trumbić consent at the last minute to a statement of rather general principles. The Yugoslavs recognized the legitimacy of Italy's policy of national unity and the Italians recognized the Yugoslav goals of unification and independence. No specific territories were mentioned because "national unity" for the Italians included the same lands the Yugoslavs meant when they used the term "independence." Accordingly, and just as impossibly, it was agreed that territorial disputes would be decided after the war on the basis of the principle of nationality but in a way that would not injure the vital interests of either people. Rather than deciding anything, the Torre-Trumbić agreement simply recognized the two parties had incompatible goals: "nationality" for the Yugoslavs, and "vital interests" for the Italians.

But this was enough, and the Congress of Oppressed Nationalities was duly held in Rome in April 1918, bringing together not only the Yugoslavs, but Poles, Czechs, and Romanians as well. Orlando, along with other Italians more or less sympathetic to the South Slavs, attended the two-day meeting, but the intense feelings and rivalries precluded meaningful negotiations. The only communiqué adopted by the congress was simply a verbatim rendering of the Torre-Trumbić agreement.

Despite the superficial nature of this accomplishment, it appeared to many that the Pact of Rome, as it was called, implied that the Italians were willing to renounce Dalmatia and the Yugoslavs Trieste and Istria. For this reason it created considerable enthusiasm among the subject nationalities and was a great propaganda success. Leo Valiani has even gone so far as to say that the congress "represented a mortal blow to Austria-Hungary."[29] But for the Yugoslav Committee the ratification of the Pact of Rome was the Italian counterpart of the Corfu Declaration, with Sonnino playing the part of Pašić. Just as Pašić had drawn the committee more closely to Serbia by concessions that did not forfeit his own initiative, so Sonnino allowed the Pact of Rome to achieve a propaganda success for the Italians without budging an inch on the Treaty of London. Sonnino did not approve of Torre's initiatives except in so far as they might help an Italian propaganda effort, did not attend the Rome Congress, and did not turn away from his obsession with the Treaty of London. Having committed himself to cooperation with the obdurate Pašić in 1916 and 1917, Trumbić committed himself to finding a compromise with the unyielding Sonnino in 1918.

These commitments proved to be the committee's downfall. When the war began to draw to a close, Trumbić realized ever more clearly that unless the committee could achieve formal recognition as the representative of the Habsburg South Slavs it would not be able to influence the shape of the post-war state. The last few months of the war were taken up with this fruitless task. None of the Powers would recognize the committee, even though they recognized the Czechoslovak National Committee and expressed increasing sympathy with the Yugoslav aims, unless Serbia and Italy also agreed. Agreement with Italy meant agreement with Sonnino, who continued to ignore the South Slavs and to consider the Treaty of London inviolate. The last possibility of a modification of his position occurred in August 1918, when Leonida Bissolati, the socialist Minister without portfolio, convinced Orlando to call the first full meeting of the Italian cabinet in two years to discuss foreign policy. One of his main motives was to achieve a more balanced Italian policy toward the Yugoslavs. The importance of this opportunity was so obvious that for the first time Trumbić was moved to modify the committee's maximum territorial claims, originally established in reaction to the London Treaty in 1915. But when his compromise offer fell far short of total acceptance of the London Treaty, Bissolati could only get the cabinet to agree to an official statement recognizing the existence of "the movement of the Yugoslav peoples."[30]

This result was not encouraging, but it was enough to make it seem that progress was being made. It was not. The Italian government did not publish its mild statement, which fell far short of recognition, until September 25, and more importantly, Sonnino did not change. He intended to occupy the Yugoslav lands promised Italy by the Treaty of London as enemy territory. Recognition of the Yugoslav Committee would make those lands friendly territory, preventing their occupation. The futility of the committee's campaign received its final confirmation at the meeting of the Supreme Allied War Council at Versailles on November 1, at which time the Italians easily brushed aside the Yugoslav demands for recognition and received permission to occupy territory up to the line of the 1915 agreement.

Pašić too was intransigent. Responding to a request from Trumbić that Serbia support formal recognition of the committee, he claimed that the Serbs, Croats, and Slovenes were already adequately represented by the Serbian government, and that it would be a mistake to have two centers of power. This policy took enormous personal strength on Pašić's part. He was ruling without a majority in a rump parliament. An intense opposition criticized his every move, and most of this opposition favored an accommodation with the Yugoslav Committee. His potential friends in the West, both in France and England, were becoming estranged by his unwillingness to negotiate. Robert W. Seton-Watson, England's foremost authority on Eastern Europe, publicly attacked him, and when he visited London, in early October 1918, British Foreign Minister Balfour warned him in person that no positive outcome for the Yugoslavs could be expected if he continued his adamant attitude.[31] And yet he stood firm against recognition.

By the end of October, as the Central Powers neared collapse, a new element entered the picture. Throughout the war the politicians who had remained in Austria-Hungary had been constrained to follow policies that were more or less loyal to the crown. But this did not prevent some of them from expressing their desire for unification and recognition, as the May Declaration demonstrated. In the difficult year of 1918, those parties that were inclined toward the creation of a larger Yugoslavia gained in strength. When it was obvious that the days of the monarchy were numbered, intense activity by these parties led to the creation in Zagreb of a government of the Serbs, Croats, and Slovenes in the Habsburg lands on October 29, 1918. With the formal approval of the Croatian Sabor and shortly of Emperor Charles himself, the *narodno vijeće*, as this government was styled, proclaimed itself sovereign. Immediately its president, the Slovene Anton Korošec, set off to Geneva to seek recognition from the Allies and to establish relations with the Serbian government and Yugoslav Committee. Korošec immediately contacted both Pašić and Trumbić, and when he learned that the Allies were meeting in Versailles during the first few days of November to discuss armistice terms for Austria, he designated the Yugoslav Committee in the person of Trumbić as the official representative there of the *narodno vijeće*.

The Yugoslavs were not able to influence the Versailles meetings, but the Allied powers did recognize that something had to be done about the existence of two, now three, groups that claimed to represent portions of the Yugoslav peoples. The French government in particular summarily directed Pašić to meet with Trumbić and settle their differences. Accordingly, these two met in Paris on November 4. On Korošec's invitation, however, they immediately adjourned to Geneva to attempt to achieve agreement to the composition of a joint government as demanded by the Allies. The Serbian opposition was also represented at this meeting, which took place from November 6 to 9.[32]

Geneva Agreement Creates Dual Govenment

Trumbić appeared to have the strongest hand at Geneva, since the Serbian opposition parties opposed Pašić's intransigence, as did Korošec. Pašić realized that he would have to come to a distasteful compromise, and on November 9, 1918, he signed the Geneva Agreement, even though it did not accord with his views. By this compromise, put forward by Trumbić, a dual government reminiscent of the Dual Monarchy it was in part replacing would be formed. This new government would regulate the joint activities of the South Slavs, but the *narodno vijeće* and the Serbian government each would retain sovereignty over their own local affairs. The members of the joint government would take their oaths to their own sovereigns, Alexander Karadjordjević in the case of the Serbs, and the *narodno vijeće* in the case of the Habsburg Slavs. A more lasting constitutional arrangement would be worked out later.

This agreement, had it lasted, meant unification on the equal basis the Yugoslav Committee had sought. It appeared that Trumbić and the Yugoslav Committee had succeeded. But once again, and for the last time, appearances were deceiving. When Pašić first notified his government on Corfu of his signature, Stojan Protić, his closest political associate, accepted the decision. But the next day, November 10, Pašić sent a telegram to Protić in which he broadly hinted that if the Regent wished another sort of arrangement he could accept the government's resignation. On November 11, Protić changed his mind and repudiated the Geneva Agreement. The government resigned. Within a few days Pašić destroyed the support of the Yugoslav Committee among Serbs by asking the political parties that had opposed him for so long to join in a coalition government. Accepting the opportunity to participate in the making of a new Serbia, these parties lost much of their interest in the Yugoslav Committee, and the Geneva Agreement was forgotten.

Meanwhile, support of the committee was being undermined in Zagreb as well. Prince Alexander did not favor the Geneva Agreement since it did not require all of the persons in the new state to take an oath of allegiance to him. This obviously influenced Protić's rejection. But another important reason for Plotić's step was that he discovered on November 10 that the balance of forces in the *narodno vijeće* was shifting away from the Yugoslav Committee. The main South Slavic political force in the Habsburg Monarchy for the decade preceding 1918 had been the Serbo-Croatian Coalition. Although originally founded by men such as Supilo and Trumbić, during World War I it had remained passive toward the efforts of others to bring forth a new Yugoslav state. Only with difficulty and at the last minute was the Coalition enticed into the *narodno vijeće*. Its acceptance of the national program was considered the final step that would insure the creation of a new Yugosiavia. However, when the Coalition entered the *narodno vijeće* it immediately became the dominant force and its leader, Svetozar Pribićević, the strongest figure. Pribićević was a Serb who favored unification along the lines suggested by Pašić and Protić, not those favored by Korošec and Trumbić. Fortuitously, Protić had received word on this favorable situation on November 10 from Prince Alexander, who was not in Corfu, but in Belgrade, having entered the Serbian capital only the day before with his victorious army. Protić was able to repudiate the Geneva Agreement in the knowledge that the *narodno vijeće* was likely to do so also eventually, under Pribicević's leadership. In fact, on November 25, this is just what happened.

In November the rapidly changing course of events moved completely out of the control of the Yugoslav Committee. The Serbian army occupied Belgrade on November 1. By November 13 a military representative of the high command was in Zagreb, encouraging Pribićević. By the end of the month the *narodno vijeće*, without consulting Trumbić or Korošeć, decided to join Serbia immediately and without conditions. On December 1, 1918, Alexander received the petitioners of the *narodno vijeće*, as well as representatives of other bodies from Montenegro, Bosnia and Hercegovina, and the Vojvodina, and announced the formation of the new Kingdom of the Serbs, Croats, and Slovenes.[33] The Croats and Slovenes had done just what Supilo had feared in 1915 and what Pašić all alone had hoped they would do: they had agreed to unification with Serbia without first working out the terms.

Evaluation of Yugoslav Committee's Role

There is probably only one way the Yugoslav Committee could have improved upon this result. If the Yugoslav Committee had understood how accurately Pašić represented the deep feeling of most Serbs that Serbia should be the liberator of the South Slavs, its only course of action would have been to break with Serbia. If the committee had appreciated the impossibility of agreeing with Sonnino on any terms less than full acceptance of the Treaty of London, its only solution would have been to accept that treaty. But these were impossible choices. Not only did the Serbian government have its representatives on the Yugoslav Committee, but even among the Croats there was no agreement that Pašić's way was wrong. The Slovenes could not accept Supilo's proposal to break with Serbia because Supilo treated the Slovenes as merely adjuncts to Croatia. Furthermore, none of them would have agreed to give up the Adriatic lands Italy craved.

The Yugoslav Committee was in a similar position to that of the Polish government in exile during World War II. The only way the Poles could have reached an accommodation with Stalin would have been to recognize the 1941 borders. But the very reason the Poles went into exile in the first place was to protect 1939 Poland. For both the Poles and the Yugoslavs, the one thing they most needed to do was the one thing to which they would never consent.[34]

Politics may be the art of the possible, but in this case the only way the Yugoslav Committee could have succeeded would have been to practice the art of the impossible. The committee needed to accept the Treaty of London and break with the Serbs. Had the Yugoslavs accepted the Italian claims they would not have lost much more territory than they did anyway, but they would have opened up enormous positive possibilities. One of the constant and unsuccessful struggles of the committee, for example, was to create a Yugoslav Legion from Habsburg prisoners of war in Italy.[35] The experience of the Czech Committee in exile showed how important it was to have such a force in being. In the spring of 1918, when the manpower shortage was critical on the western front, the Czechs had been able to extract concessions from the Allies because they controlled Czech legions that could be assigned to the front. Sonnino did not want the Yugoslavs to have such legions because he feared they would be used on behalf of the South Slavs in the lands Italy had been promised in 1915. But if the committee had accepted the Treaty of London, this fear would have been allayed and perhaps Sonnino would have let the Yugoslavs form their legions. With these forces at their back, the committee might have been recognized in mid-1918 at the same time the Czechs were.

This is all the more likely because of a second result acceptance of the London Treaty would have produced. From the beginning, the fact that many Slavs lived in the territories the Italians claimed by the Treaty of London threatened the Italian aims. They needed some group that spoke for these Slavs to agree to Italian rule. The Yugoslav Committee was such a group. But acceptance of the Italian territorial demands by, the committee would gain legal significance only if it were a legal entity, not just an émigré group. It is almost certain, therefore, that if the committee had accepted the London Treaty the Italians would have favored recognition, because in that way any possible ethnic stain on the Italian claims would have been wiped clean.

Naturally, acceptance of the Treaty of London would have meant breaking with Serbia, as Supilo suggested. Difficult though this would have been, it too would have had positive effects. For example, Pašić's opposition to recognition would have been much less effective if the committee was not seen as subordinate to the Serbian government. As the war drew to a close and the *narodno vijeće* came into being, the Yugoslav Committee could have offered the new state its assets: military forces and formal recognition, a combination that would have been hard to resist. Two possibilities would have opened up. Either two South Slavic states would have been established at the end of the war, or Serbia would have had to meet the Yugoslav Committee and *narodno vijeće* on equal terms and work out a mutually satisfactory agreement. In either case, the chances that Serbia could dominate Croatia and Slovenia in a post-war state wouid have been greatly lessened, and the goal of the Yugoslav Committee would have come much closer to realization.

In fact, of course, none of this happened. Frano Supilo was willing to break with Serbia and even to make concessions to Italy, but most of his colleagues, including Ante Trumbić, were not. Trumbić believed that the exclusion of Serbia from a South Slavic movement would eviscerate the entire idea of Yugoslavism. Therefore, he was alway willing to make one more effort to work out an agreement with Pašić. The irony of this position was that precisely his belief that Serbia was necessary to a new Yugoslavia made it impossible for Trumbić to make the cold-blooded decision that could have made an equal partnership possible. This, coupled with his inability to negotiate realistically with Italy, prevented the committee from transcending its émigré status and reduced its historical role to that of a propaganda agent for Yugoslavism.

In this capacity, the Yugoslav Committee was extremely successful. But in its political goal, it was not. One's evaluation of this outcome depends a good deal on whether one is a pessimist or an optimist. The pessimists will say that Trumbić failed because he did not have the greatness to correctly evaluate the situation and lead his committee to the extremely difficult decisions that hindsight shows were necessary. The optimists will point out that Trumbić always kept before his eyes the ultimate goal of a unified Yugoslavia, successfully created a climate of opinion in Europe favorable to that idea, and had the charity and vision to refuse to consider a new Yugoslavia without Serbia. Both evaluations are correct, but in either case, the result did not turn out as Trumbić had hoped.

NOTES

1. Some of the research for this article was done at the Illinois Summer Research Laboratory for 1978. I would like to thank both the Russian Center at the University of Illinois and Rice University for making my stay at the Laboratory possible.

2. The extensive efforts on behalf of the Yugoslav movement by South Slavic emigrants in North and South America will not be discussed in this article. For their influence on American policy see Victor S. Mamatey, *The United States and East Central Europe, 1914–1918: A Study in Wilsonian Diplomacy and Propaganda* (Princeton: Princeton University Press, 1957) and George J. Prpić, "The South Slavs," in Joseph P. O'Grady, *The Immigrants' Influence on Wilson's Peace Policies* (Lexington: University of Kentucky Press, 1967). I am not aware of similatly extensive treatments of the strong Yugoslav movement in South America, although Paulova discusses it briefly (pp. 226–35).

3. The first major interpretation of the Yugoslav Committee was Milada Paulovà, *Jugoslavenski odbor [The Yugoslav Committee]* (Zagreb: Prosvjetna nakladna zadruga, 1925). It remains important, even though it is an *apologio* for Trumbić and the committee. A basic bibliography may be found in the superb study, which is now the standard interpretation of the period, Dragovan Šepić, *Italija saveznici i Jugoslavensko pitanje, 1914–1918 [Italy, the Allies, and the Yugoslav Question, 1914–1918* (Zagreb: Školska knjiga, 1970). The two standard studies in English are Michael B. Petrovich, *A History of Modern Serbia, 1804–1918* (New York: Harcourt. Brace, Jovanovich, 1976), Volume II, pp. 621–682 , and Ivo J. Lederer, *Yugoslavia at the Paris Peace Conference: A Study in Frontiermaking* (New Haven: Yale University Press, 1963), pp. 3–78. Two collections of documents are Ferdo Šišić *Dokumenti o postanku Krajlevine Srba, Hrvata i Slovenaca 1914–1919 [Documents on the Creation of the Kingdom of the Serbs, Croates, and Slovenes, 1914–1919]* (Zagreb, 1920), and Dragoslav Janković and Bodgan Krizman , eds., *Gradja o stvaranju juboslovenske države [Materials on the Creation of the Yugoslav State]* (Belgrade, 1964). Neither collection was available to me during the preparation of this article. See also Vaso Bogdanov, *et al.*, eds., *Jugoslovenski odbor u Londonu [The Yugoslav Committee in London]* (Zagreb: The Yugoslav Academy, 1966).

4. Milorad Ekmečić, *Ratni ciljevi Srbije 1914 [Serbian War Aims in 1914]* (Belgrade: Srpska kniževna zadruga, 1973), pp. 208–214. See also the solid study by Dragoslav Janković, *Srbija i jugoslovensko pitanje, 1914–1915 [Serbia and the Yugoslav Question, 1914–1915]* (Belgrade: Institut zu savremenu istoriju, 1973).

5. Šepić, *Italija, saveznici i jugoslavensko pitanje*, pp. 12–13 (map). Pašić's memorandum had been preceded by a note to the allied governments on September 4 in which he had said that the best way to assure the allied war aim, the containment of Germany, was to create a strong national state in the Balkans that would consist of all Serbs, Croats, and Slovenes (Ekmečić, pp. 88–89).

6. Šepić, *Italija, saveznici i jugoslavensko pitanje*, p. 32.

7. As late as October 1918, Pašić said that he had created the Yugoslav Committee and given it money "for propaganda and nothing more" (Šepić, *Italija, saveznici i jugoslavensko pitanje*, p. 358).

8. This is one of Ekmečić's main points. As he puts it, "In the war smoke of 1914, it was seen clearly in Serbia that her five minutes of history had come . . ." (p. 84). For a supportive biography of Pašić, see Alex Dragnich, *Serbia, Nikola Pašić, and Yugoslavia* (New Brunswick, NJ: Rutgers University Press, 1974).

9. The key statement of the declaration was that Serbia's war aim was "the liberation and unification of all our unliberated brothers: Serbs, Croats, and Slovenes." The Bulgarophile Noel Buxton, who was present, describes the event as follows: "The *skupshtina* met in a concert hall attached to a cafe. The deputies sat close together on rows of small wicker chairs facing the president. On his right along the wall sat the eight members of the new Cabinet which had just been formed, with a green baize table before them lit by two candles. . . . M. Pasich . . . then rose. . . . His long grey beard and somewhat threadbare frock coat made him a striking figure as he stood and read by the dim candle light his momentous declaration" (Noel and Charles Roden Buxton, *The War and the Balkans* [London: Allen and Unwin, 1915), pp. 41–42). The basic work on the Declaration is Dragoslav Jankovii, "Niška deklaracija" ["The Niv́ s Declaration"] *Istorija dvadestog veka* X (1969), pp. 7–111.

10. Ekmečić, *Ratni ciljevi* pp. 214–218.

11. The committee made this fear public at the very end of the war. when Trumbić had lost hope that Serbia would allow the committee to be recognized (Šepić, *Italija, saveznici i jugoslavensko pitanje*, p. 357).

12. Of the two main leaders of the Yugoslav Committee. Frano Supilo and Ante Trumbić. Supilo has occasioned the most interest among historians. Dragovan Šepić published his letters and memoranda from the war period in (1914–1917) (Belgrade: Serbian Academy of Arts and Sciences, 1967) and some further items in *Politički spisi [Political Writings]* (Zagreb: Znanje, 1970). The latter contains an extended biographical introduction on Supilo's life until 1914. See too Šepić, "Hrvatska u koncepcijama Frana Supila o ujedinjenju" ["Croatia in Fran Supilo's Conceptions of Unification"], *Forum*, 7 (1968), pp. 342–381, and Tereza Canza-Aras, "Frano Supilo u svjetlu najnovijih istraživanja ["Fran Supiio in the Light of the Latest Research"] *Historijski zbornik* XXV–XXVI (1972–3). pp. 387–406.

13. Šepić, "Hrvatska u koncepcijama Supila," pp. 355–356; Šepić, *Italija saveznici i jugoslavensko pitanjey*, pp. 26–34.

14. The provisions of the treaty did not become public until they were published by the Bolsheviks in 1917. But the main provisions were surmised almost immediately by the interested parties.

15. Šepić, *Italija, saveznici i jugoslavenski pitanje*, pp. 89–92.

16. Ibid., pp. 140–146; Šepić, "Hrvatska u koncepcijama Supila," pp. 357–65.

17. For an excellent review of the problems faced by Pašić see Vojislav J. Vučković, "Unutrašnje krize Srbije i prvi svetski rat" ['Serbia's Internal Crises and the First World War"], *Istorijski časopis,*, XIV–XV (1963–65), pp. 173–229.

18. Within a short while, however, Supilo realized that if the Habsburg South Slavs were to accomplish their goal of independence, accommodation with Italy was necessary. "I believe," he said, "that the Serbo-Croat-Slovene state, which has more need of Italian support than any other European power. must compensate for this collaboration with adequate concessions" (Leo Valiani, *The End of Austria-Hungary* (New York: Knopf, 1973), p. 418). Valiani believes that by 1917 Supilo would have conceded Italy dominance of the Adriatic, if not Dalmatia.

19. Supilo read his earlier memorandum of seven points to the committee, but the committee soundly rejected any idea of a separate Croatia as damaging to the ideal of Yugoslavism. For the texts of their statements. see *Nova Evropa [New Europe]* 13 (1926), pp. 85–86.

20. For Supilo's resignation statement, in which he accuses the Serbian government of supporting the committee with "pretty words" while thwarting it politically, see Paulová, *Jugoslavenski odbor*, pp.

211-14. Supilo's premature death a year later removed him from Yugoslav politics entirely.

21. The basic work is Dragoslav Jankković, *Jugoslovensko pitanje i krfska deklaracija 1917. godine [The Yugoslav Question and the Corfu Declaration, 1917* (Belgrade: Savremena administracija. 1967). For the text of the agreement see Petrovich, *History of Serbia*, pp. 644–45.

22. Vučković, "Ullutrašnje krize Srbije," pp. 203–23.

23. Šepi;c, *Italija, saveznici i jugoslavensko pitanje*, pp. 197–205.

24. Petrovich recognizes this: "Trumbić and others may have regarded it as the Magna Charta of Yugoslav unification. For Pašić it was a tactical move in response to a given political situation" (*History of Serbia*, p. 649).

25. For a succinct review of Sotlnino's career, see Salvatore Saladino, "In Search of Sidney Sonnino," *Reviews in European History*, 2 (1976), pp. 621–633.

26. Christopher Seton-Watson, *Italy from Liberalism to Fascism, 1870–1925* (London : Methuen and Company, 1967), p. 432.

27. English Yugoslavophiles such as R. W. Seton-Watson and Henry Wickham Steed are not discussed in this article, but they had a great impact on the success of the Yugoslav Committee in bringing its ideas before Europe. They founded a Serbian Society of Great Britain. established a journal to forward the cause of East European nationalism (*The New Europe*] and through official propaganda efforts in 1918 popularized the idea of destruction of Austria-Hungary (for the last, see Kenneth J. Calder, *Britain and the Origins of the New Europe, 1914–1918*, (Cambridge: Cambridge University Press. 1976). The fundamental narrative of this activity is Steed, *Through Thirty Years* (New York: Doubleday, Page and Company, 1925). Recently Hugh Seton-Watson has been investigating his father's role in Yugoslav affairs (e.g. "Robert William Seton-Watson i jugoslavaensko pitanje" ["Robert William Seton-Watson and the Yugoslav Question"] *Časopis za suvremenu povijest* II [1970]. pp. 75–96. In cooperation with the Seton-Watson family, the British Academy and the Institute of Croatian History of Zagreb University has published *R. W. Seton-Watson i Jugoslaveni: Korespondencija 1906–1941 [R. W. Seton-Watson and the Yugoslavs: Correspondence, 1906–1941* (Zagreb-London, 1976), 2 vols.

28. For the following see Valiani, *The End of Austria-Hungary*, pp. 199–256; Christopher Seton-Watson, *Italy from Liberalism to*

Fascism, pp. 492–97; Steed, *Through Thirty Years*, II, pp. 183–85; Šepić, *Italija, saveznici i jugoslavensko pitanje*, 289–96; and Paulová, *Jugoslavenski odbor* pp. 417–43.

29. Valiani, *The End of Austria-Hungary*, p. 240. Paulova's analysis (p. 442) is a good example of how even later supporters of the Yugoslav Committee overestimated its potential positive effect on Italian public opinion and policy.

30. Šepić, *Italija, saveznici i jugoslavensko pitanje*, 337–44.

31. Ibid., p. 358. Seton-Watson became so irritated with Pašić's unwillingness to recognize the Yugoslav Committee that he attacked him in a famous article, "Serbia's Choice," in *The New Europe*, 22 August 1918. "Any Serbian statesman who failed to perceive this truth [that the Austrian Slavs should be treated as an equal factor] would deserve to be regarded . . . as a traitor to the best interest of his race. In Serbia . . . our sympathy and support must be given. not to the old Oriental tendencies. now tottering to their fall, but to those new and democratic elements in whose hands the future of Jugoslavia lies." This was not an entirely fair criticism, since the Radical Party had long stood for constitutionalism and civilian government in Serbia, but when Stojan Protii responded that in his opinion "there is more reason to fear that we may encounter semi-Turkish [he is referring to Bosnia and Hercegovina] and semi-Austrian traditions nearer to you in the West," the justice of his reply was drowned out by cries of outrage. and Pašić's reputation was further weakened (*The New Europe*, 26 September 1918). The strong anti-Pašić feeling of the British Yugoslavophiles is obvious in Steed's description of his conversation with Pašić on October 8, 1918 (Steed, *Through Thirty Years*, II. 233–39).

32. For the foliowing see Bogdan Krizman, "Zenevska konferencija o ujedinjenju 1918. godine" ["The Geneva Conference of Unification, 1918"], *Istorijski glasnik*, 1958, no. 1–2, pp. 3–32. and Dragoslav Janković, "ženevska konferencija o stvaranju jugoslovenske zajednice 1918. godine" ["The Geneva Conference on the Creation of a Yugoslav Union, 1918"], *Istorija XX veka, Zbornik radova*, V (1963), pp. 225–63.

33. Petrovich, *A History of Modern Serbia*, pp. 663–82.

34. Compare the realistic and successful policy that Lenin forced on his unwilling comrades when he cajoled and bullied them into accepting severe losses at Brest-Litovsk, but in the process saved the Bolshevik Revolution.

35. Some Yugoslav legions were actually formed in Odessa. seeing action in the Dobrudja in 1916, but Sonnino consistently blocked the formation of such units in Italy (Paulová, *Jugoslavenski odbor, passim*). In English see Margot Lawrence, "The Serbian Divisions in Russia, 1916–1917," *Journal of Contemporary History*, 6 (1971), pp. 183–92.

HISTORIOGRAPHIC LITERATURE ON ITALIAN OCCUPIED DALMATIA, 1914–1943

Frank P. Verna

Although literature on the Italian participation in World War II is profuse and varied, that dealing specifically with Italian rule in Dalmatia is not as extensive. The primary sources of depicting Italian administration in Dalmatia are contained in those accessible documents conserved in the Italian state archives: the military archives, especially the *Ufficio Storico dello Stato Maggiore dell' Escerito Italialo* [Historical Office of the Chief of Staff of the Army]; *Archivio Storico de Ministero delli Affari Esteri Servizio Storico e Documnatazione* [Historical Office of the Minister of Foreign Affairs, Historical Service and Documentation].

Military matters pertaining to Dalmatia, conserved in the military archives, are principally the diaries of the former Second Army and its subordinate headquarters—the VI and XVIII Army Corps, which had operational jurisdiction in the Dalmatian region. Of particular interest are the reports of the civil affairs offices of the army corps. These reports contain comments on a variety of matters, including the political, social and economic aspects of the area. Access to these and similar reports is limited due to Italy's fifty-year rule regarding documents of a restricted nature. Most of the aforementioned material, however, is readily available from the United States National Archives collection of seized Italian military documents on microfilm – *Microcopy Publication T-821, "The Italian Military Records Collection."* Included in this collection is documentary material dealing with the jurisdictional conflict between the civil and military authorities in occupied Dalmatia. After the war, the historical office of the chief of staff of the Italian Army began publishing monographs dealing with the conflict, among them *Le Operazione Delle Unità Italiane in Jugoslavia (1941–1943).* This is a detailed study of the military operations in Yugoslavia from April 1941 to September 1943. The appendices of this publication contain reproductions of numerous military documents, including those of the former Second Army and its subordinate corps.

Preserved in the archives of the Ministry of Foreign Affairs is a large and heterogeneous collection, consisting principally of political and diplomatic papers, grouped by themes or serially within several sub-divisions. The documents of the political series, *Inventario delle Serie Affari Politici 1931–1945* [Inventory of the Political Affairs Series 1931–1945] are especially pertinent to the study of Dalmatia. This collection consists of a variety of materials, including situation reports, which relate specific incidents and economic matters; summaries of activities, which include partisan activities; staff papers; treaty agreements; proclamations issued by Mussolini; miscellaneous notes and memoranda; correspondence from the military government of Dalmatia to the *Presidenza de Consiglio dei Ministri* [Presidency of the Council of Ministers]; as well as copies of military directives and correspondence.

Information concerning the development of the political situation and guerrilla activities in Dalmatia is also contained in *Note relative all' occupazione Italiana in Jugoslavia* [Notes Relating to the Italian Occupation in Yugoslavia], issued by the Ministry of Foreign Affairs to counteract unfavorable propaganda regarding the alleged behavior of the Italian troops in the occupied areas of Yugoslavia.

The quantity, diversity, and intermingling of the documentary material conserved in the Italian state archives precludes placing them into a specific category. In general, this vast collection is grouped under the headings of the highest organs of the government responsible for their origin. Of direct interest to the study of Dalmatia are documents in three such groupings: *Presidenza del Consiglio Dei Ministri (1941–1943); Ministero dell'Interno – Direzione Generale della P.S., Divisione Affari Generale e Riservata* [Ministry of the Interior – General Headquarters of the Public Safety, Division of General and Confidential Matters]; and, to a lesser degree (because of the unavailability of certain documents), the *Secretaria Particolare dell'Duce* [Office of the Private Secretary to the Duce].

A substantial amount of documentary material useful to the study of Dalmatia is grouped under the heading *Presidenza del Consiglio Dei Ministri (1941–1943)*. This collection comprises a variety of materials initiated either by the Italian Government or the administration of Dalmatia, including the latter's periodic reports on communist activities and on various political, economic and military security aspects; miscellaneous correspondence on matters relating to the internal administration of the province, including public works initiated or completed; requests for funds for various purposes; the status of Jews in the area; personal letter from Governor Bastianini to Luigi Rossi, undersecretary to the council of ministers, and diverse memoranda addressed to *il Duce (Appunto Per il Duce)*, commenting on the local situation or requesting rectification of perceived deficiencies within certain military units stationed in the province; various decrees issued either by the Italian government, Mussolini himself, or the Fascist Party; military situation reports initiated by the former Second Army or its subordinate corps; miscellaneous material from the military establishment and civilian government agencies pertaining to the formation of the government of Dalmatia and its subsequent abolition.

An important reference in this collection is the official bilingual (Italian and Serbo-Croatian) publication of the Dalmatian government, *Giornale Ufficiale Del Governo Dalmazia (1941-1945)* [Official Journal of the Dalmatian Government (1941–1945)]. This journal includes, among other matters, a series of decrees and ordinances issued by Governor Bastianini that affected every aspect of the daily life of the province. Other important references, although not part of this Collection, are the Italian Government publications, *Gazzetta Ufficiale del Regno d'Italia* [Official Gazzette of the Kingdom of Italy] and *Raccolata Ufficiale delle leggi e dei Decreti del Regno d'Italia* [Official Collection of the Laws and Decrees of the Kingdom of Italy], which contains decrees and ordinances pertaining to Dalmatia.

The collection grouped in the *Ministero dell'Interno – Direzione Generale della P.S., Divisione Affari Generale e Riservata* consist mainly of material pertaining to anti-Italian and anti-fascist literature and activities, communist organizations, activities and propaganda; clandestine publications; various types of police reports; as well as political and economic reports received from the prefectures and other agencies.

There are other publications that are useful because they either have reproductions of Italian documents or contain some factual material pertinent to the study of Dalmatia. The official Yugoslav publication, *Zbornik Dokumenta i Potaka o Narodnosslobodilačkom Rata Jugoslovekih* [Collection of Documents and Information on the National Liberation War of the Yugoslav People], (Belgrade, 1949) includes, in addition to partisan material, some captured German and

Italian documents. It is a source frequently consulted by Yugoslav historians and specialists.

The volume by Raphael Lemkin, *Axis Rule in Occupied Europe*, (Washington, 1944) is useful for its collection, in English, of representative texts and decrees issued by the Axis powers and their puppets for the administration on their occupied territories in Europe. The publication is divided into three parts: Parts I and II present a synthesis of the techniques of occupation and an analysis of the administrative systems of the various occupied areas. Part III comprises the documentary material. An article, by Alberto Mori, "La Dalmazia," *Scienze Giuridice Politichie e Sociale*, VI, (Firenze, 1942) is a technical study which considers, among other things, the political boundaries, topographic features, economic structure, and natural resources, as well as the demographic and strategic aspects of Italian Dalmatia.

The United States Office of the Provost Marshal General, Army Service Forces Manual M 355-5, Civil Affairs Handbook, *Yugoslavia*, (Washington, 1944) is a reference manual of factual data concerning money and banking in Yugoslavia, including the territories annexed by Italy, prepared by the board of governors of the federal reserve system.

A very useful secondary work on Dalmatia is Dragovan Šepić, "La Politique Italienne d'Occupation en Dalmatie 1941–1943," *Les Systemes d'Occupation en Yougoslavie 1941–1945*, (Belgrade, 1963). This study is part of a collection of papers presented by Yugoslav historians at the Third International Congress on the history of European resistance, held in Czechoslovakia during early 1963. Based principally on documents from Yugoslav archives, the study critically examines the Italian occupation policies in Dalmatia. Another paper, also prepared for delivery at the Third International Conference, but part of a separate collection, is Pero Morača, "*I crimini commessi da occupanti e collabarazionisti in Jugoslavia durante la seconda guerra mondiale*," [The Crimes Committed by Occupiers and Collaborators in Yugoslavia during the Second World War], *L'occupaziolle nazista in Europa*, Enzo Collotti, ed. (Rome, 1964). This study examines the, policy of terror and persecution practiced by the Hungarian, German, and Italian authorities in their respective zones of occupation in Yugoslavia. It is based on documentation from Yugoslav archives and secondary works of other Yugoslav authors.

Another source of useful material for the study of Dalmatia are the memoirs and historical surveys concerning Italy's participation in World War II. This literature often amplifies or fills in gaps of the material found in official sources. The work of General Giacomo Zanussi, *Guerra e Catastrofe d'Italia, Giugno 1940 - Giugno 1943,* (Rome, 1945), discusses in great detail the military and political aspects of Italy's participation in the conflict. It is based on personal recollections and notes, as well as documentary sources. Of particular interest is the author's first-hand account of the Second Army's activities in Yugoslavia, and his personal observations concerning the civil and military jurisdictional conflict in the occupied areas. In Mario Roatta's *Otto Millioni di Baionette - l'Esercito Italiano in Guerra dal 1940 al 1944,* (Milan, 1946), the author examines the status and conditions of the Italian military forces before and during the war, the decisions made for the conduct of the campaigns (up to the signing of the armistice), as well as the situation after the war. Included in chapter VIII is an account of the protective measures extended by the units of the Italian army of occupation in Yugoslavia to the Serbs, Jews and Poles fleeing from the persecution of the Germans and the Croatian *Ustashi.* The work of Giorgio Bocca, *Storia d'Italia nella Guerra Fascista 1940-1945,* (Bari, 1969) is a well-documented history of Italy's war, written from an anti-fascist point of view, by an Italian journalist. Of special interest is chapter XXII, which deal with the activities of the Italian military forces in Yugoslavia. In these pages the author describes not only the conduct of the military operations and the reprisal measures used against the insurgents, but also recounts the atrocities committed by certain Italian military units, as well as the intensive Italianization measures instituted in the controlled areas. The author, however, also commends the Italian occupation for the vigorous measures adopted to protect the Jews.

A work by Giacomo Scotti, *Ventimilia Caduti - gli Italiani in Jugoslavia 1943 al 1945,* (Milan, 1970), is both a chronological survey of the events leading to the formation of military units in Yugoslavia by former members of the Italian army of occupation, and a detailed account of the sacrifice and contribution that these Italian units made by their collaboration with Tito's partisans in the liberation of Yugoslavia. The work is based on a variety of sources that include, in addition to Italian and Yugoslav documents, testimonies from ex-combatants and military publications. Pertinent to the study of Dalmatia are the author's observations concerning partisan activities against the Italian occupiers.

There are other secondary works of interest to the extent that a section or chapter provides some information that further illuminates an aspect of Italian Dalmatia. For example, Section IV of an article by Pietro Pastorelli, "L'Esaurimento dell' Iniziativa dell' Asse," *Alnuario di Politica Internazionale* (1939–1945), Vol. VI (Milan, 1967), is of interest because it contains an analysis of the contrasting views and aims held by Germany and Italy regarding the partition of Yugoslavia, as well as the resulting accommodations and steps taken by each state within its provisory zone of occupation. The article is based on German and Italian sources, as well as secondary publications. Kruno Menghello -Dincic's "L'Etat 'Oustachi' de Croatie (1941–1945)," *Revue d'Histoire de la Deuxième Guerre Mondiale*, XIX, #74 (April, 1969), based mainly on secondary works, is a study of the *Ustashi* regime. It examines the regime's structure and aims, its repressive measures used against Serbs, Jews, and others, as well as its relationship with the Catholic Church and its Axis allies. Edmond Paris' *Genocide in Satellite Croatia 1941–1945 – A Record of Racial and Religious Persecutions and Massacres* (trans. from the French by Lois Perkins), (Illinois, 1961), examines in detail the extreme ravages caused in the satellite state of Croatia by the *Ustascha* government and the Croatian Catholic hierarchy. It is based on testimonies, secondary works, as well as Yugoslav documentary sources. The studies of Menghello-Dinčić and Paris are useful for their background information on the Croatian racial policies that provoked the influx of Serbs and Jews into the Italian occupied zones and which, eventually, caused the Italian Government to react against the Croatian regime.

Another monograph by Leon Poliakov and Jacques Sabille, *Jews Under Italian Occupation*, (Paris, 1955), is useful for the information it provides regarding the attitude of the Italians toward the persecuted Jews in Europe, including Yugoslavia. Sabille, for his part, gives an account of the humane attitude and inventive methods used by the Italians to thwart German and *Ustashi* persecution of the Jews. The study, published by the Center of Contemporary Jewish Documentation, is well supported by French, German and Italian documentation. The publication, Luigi Missoni, *Duce ed Ombre sulle Dinarche – L'Italia nei Balcani*, (Bologna, 1942), is a pro-fascist work which, using historical, cultural and geographic arguments, develops the theme that the Dalmatian region is an integral part of the Italian Empire. Of practical interest is its inclusion of the address given by Giuseppe Bastianini, Governor of Dalmatia, on 12 April 1942 at Zara, in which he details the accomplishments achieved by his administration in Dalmatia.

The aforementioned literature, although not all-encompassing, does provide a basis for a meaningful understanding of the Italian occupation in Dalmatia. Undoubtedly, further light will be shed on the issue as additional documents conserved in the Italian archives become available for research.

THE PROMETHIAN MOVEMENT IN INTERWAR POLAND

Richard A. Woytak

In December, 1982, celebrating the sixtieth anniversary of the formation of the USSR held in the Kremlin Palace of Congresses, Yuri Andropov stated:

> For the first time in history, the multinational character of a country has turned from a source of weakness into a source of strength and prosperity.

Thus, according to Moscow, the Socialist nations have succeeded in forming and experiencing a new unified historical community. On the other hand, the press reports on the Soviet involvement in Afghanistan have thrown a different light on the non-Russian peoples who border that turmoiled land. On the whole, an image of a growing national self-awareness of the non-Greater Russian peoples from the Baltic to the Pacific has emerged from today's newspapers and academic journals.[1]

The struggle for national self-determination has been deeply rooted in Russian history; in the twentieth century it has become known as the Promethean movement. The movement was named after the Greek mythological figure, Prometheus, imprisoned and chained in the Caucasian mountains. Basically, it was a joint conspiratorial political action rooted within Soviet Russia and penetrating into the outside world. The movement had aimed to awaken the yearings for independence of the non-Russian peoples inhabiting Soviet Russia. It attempted to establish a common front made up of Byelo-Russians, Tartars, Cossacks, Georgians, Armenians, Azerbaijanis, Ukrainians, Caucasians, and many other peoples. The movement also aimed to organize the political-ethnic emigration centered in Paris, Turkey, Germany and Warsaw.[2]

The Promethean concept had been based on the assumption that the changes caused by the post-World War I national revolutions were still in progress; according to this view, the emergence of Soviet Russia was still an unfinished process. The followers of the movement hoped that the nationalist dynamism unleashed by the Great War would in time dissolve the new Soviet state. As a result, the non-Russians would have emerged in the West, Southeast and East. An independent Ukraine, Byelo-Russia and the Baltic peoples would have come into existence in the West, Turkish-Muhammedan states—in the Southeast, and an independent Siberian union in the East. On the whole, the dynamism of this movement in theory superceded a given ideology that happened to rule—be it Tsardom or Soviet Communisrn.[3]

Despite the fact that the inter-war roots of the Promethean ideology had stemmed directly from the period of the Russian Revolution and Civil War, the movement never experienced moderate or even lukewarm support from the Western countries. British or French intervention in Russia was in no respect Promethean in its goals to break up Russia; the multi-ethnic and political diversity of the peoples living within the former territories of the Tsarist Empire was ignored by Allied countries. Generally, they intended to rebuild a unified and indivisible pro-Entente Russia.[4]

The reborn Polish state was simply too weak to challenge openly these prevalent Western concepts of Russia. Poland's main goal was to retain her newly gained independence. Nevertheless, the ethnic national revolution stemming from World War I inherited the Promethean ideology and consequently Poland became one of the major centers of Promethean activities. One of the major creators of the modern Promethean school was none other than Josef Pi lsudski. As early as 1904, in his memorandum to the Japanese government he emphasized the importance of taking advantage of the many nationalities within the Russian Empire, with the Polish people in the forefront.[5]

The development of the Promethean movement in Poland can be characterized by an overview of four major phases: they encompass roughly the periods of 1918 to 1921, 1922 to 1926, 1926 to 1932, and 1932 to 1939.

During the first phase, extending from 1918 to 1922, Poland became actively involved in support of the Promethean movement. After regaining her independence, Poland signed a formal pact with Simon Petlura and the Ukrainian nationalist front. In addition, Warsaw recognized the national governments of Georgia, Azerbaijan, and Caucasus. The Polish government looked with approval upon the request of the Crimean Tartar government to the League of Nations in

1920 for a Polish protectorate and mandate over the Crimean Peninsula. During the same period, Poland permitted Cossack and Tartar official delegations to function in Warsaw.[6] Additionally, the Polish government invited numerous foreign military cadre to join the Polish army as special contract officers and soldiers and helped them to get organized. As early as 1922 the first officers from the Caucasus were permitted to join the Polish army.[7]

In the same time frame, Warsaw provided financial and technical assistance to the Promethean front. The Poles subsidized over a hundred irregular periodicals and more than twenty regularly published journals dealing with Promethean topics.[8] Contacts with the divergent peoples living within Soviet Russia were intensified by broadcasting propaganda material and use of courier passage mainly via Turkey and the Baltic states.[9] Additionally, Poland also granted help and diplomatic assistance to émigré Promethean representatives and refugee centers. A Ukrainian Institute was founded in Warsaw and major Promethean centers were established not only in Warsaw, but also in Paris, Helsinki, and Charbin China.[10]

During the second phase, 1922–1926, the Promethean movement in Poland suffered a setback. At that time, Piłsudski was cutting off his direct governmental ties and the internal political endeavors were shifted into other areas of interests; generally, thc Promethean nationalist concepts were played down. In contrast, the Moscow government fostered a broad cultural, language and educational enrichment among the ethnic peoples. This new Soviet policy was successful; it undermined the nationalist opposition. Yet, at the same time, the Soviets used the harshest methods to destroy national independence movements.

The events of 1926 initiated a third phase of the Promethean movement: that year Piłsudski staged and led a successful coup d'état against the Polish parliamentary system and his political opponents. The newly established Piłsudski regime supported the Promethean ideology. During this period, the Promethean front was expanding its activities. With Piłsudski's help, the Eastern Institute with Near East and Far East studies was set up in Warsaw. This institute became a major study center for Promethean scholars. It had affiliate centers in Cracow, Wilno, and Charbin. Subsequently, Promethean publications were expanded to monthlies, among them two Paris publications, *France Orient* and *Prométhée*. Additionally, the Polish government funded scholarships to promising Promethean students in

Warsaw, Poznań, Wilno, Paris, Berlin, and Cairo. Also an enlarged Ukrainian Institute was funded in Warsaw; it published in Paris and Bucharest. Similar undertakings—but on a lesser scale—were taking place in the Caucasus, Georgia, Tartary, and Azerbaijan; the inhabitants of these republics were contacted by Promethean agents via Turkish and Iranian bases. On the whole, by the late 1920s Polish influence played a dominant role in the Promethean front.[11]

Anti-Promethean reaction was swift and violent. The Paris assassination of Simon Petlura in May 1926 as well as several trials of Ukrainian nationalists in Kiev in 1928 constituted major blows to the Promethean front. Furthermore, the 1930 assassination of the Georgian leader, Noege Ramiszwili, in Paris, had considerably weakened the movement.

Fights between new and old Promethean factions as well as an increased competition between Berlin and Warsaw over the control of the movement had contributed to its downfall. In the early thirties, a number of Ukrainian factions had been formed on German territory. One of the factions, formed in 1929, was headed by Colonel Eugene Konowalec.[12] In time, the Polish-German competitive struggle for domination over the Promethean front turned into violence. On July 29, 1931, the Konowalec group in Poland assassinated the Ukrainophile Tadeusz Hołowko, chief of the Eastern Department of the Ministry of Foreign Affairs. Hołowko's death created a vacuum in the Promethean movement; it eliminated one of the key Polish "spiritual leaders" of the Promethean concept and an important contact between thc Foreign Ministry and Poiish intelligence.[13]

The Warsaw government reacted in kind to the terrorist actions by instituting military and police operations known as "pacification"; its violence in Eastern Galicia shocked even some of the most stalwart followers of Piłsudski and weakened the Promethean cause in Polish governmental circles. It is noteworthy that the Polish Promethean activists neither supported nor approved these actions.[14]

The final phase of the Promethean movement, beginning with the conclusion of the Polish-Soviet non-aggression pact in July 1932 and ending with the fourth partition of Poland in September of 1939, can be characterized as the most difficult. The Warsaw-Moscow agreements halted much of the open Promethean activities. The Polish Foreign Ministry and other government bureaus were forbidden to support the Promethean movement or attend its functions. The Promethean activists were further weakened by the Stalin famines and purges of 1933–1938 which caused great misery and dislocation among the divergent nationalities within Soviet Russia. During the late 1930s, the Promethean activities were beginning to lose their international flavor. Although the Promethean front was almost totally funded by Polish intelligence, its direction was being more and more controlled by Berlin.[15]

Polish support for the Promethean movement was scaled down by terrorism. On June 15, 1934, on a Warsaw street, Ukrainian nationalists assassinated a major Polish Promethean supporter, Bronisław Pieracki who at the time was the Minister of Interior. The suspected assassin received German assistance and subsequently fled to Swinemunde. In response to this terrorist act, the Polish government issued a strong demarche to Germany. Since the assassination occurred during an official trip of Propaganda Minister Goebbels to Poland, it could have caused serious consequences in Polish-German relations. To avoid a disaster, Berlin communicated promptly to Warsaw that the suspect would be extradicted immediately by a Polish plane.[16]

The death of Piłsudski in 1935 left a vacuum of support which was never filled. The the Promethean movement. The new Marshal Rydz-Smigly and his last chief of intelligence, Colonel Józef Smoliński, never fully supported the Promethean ideology. Also the Polish political parties from the left to the right did not have any genuine understanding or even sympathy for this movement. Basically the same can be stated of Polish interwar public opinion,[17]

It is noteworthy that the Promethean harvest was reaped by none other than Hitler in his invasion of Soviet Russia in June 1941 when the peoples of that country—not understanding the real intentions of the Nazi Germans—greeted the aggressors as liberators. Finally, the crucial event putting an end to the Promethean movement was brought about at the end of World War II at the Yalta Conference: the Crimea agreements resulted in the mandatory Allied repatriation of thousands of people to the Union of Soviet Socialist Republics.

NOTES

(An earlier version of this paper was delivered in May of 1983 on the occasion of the Forty-First Annual Meeting of the Polish Institute of Arts snd Science of America at the City University of New York, Hunter College, New York.)

1. The most recent comprehensive work on the Soviet Socialist Republics has been written by Helen Carrere d'Encausse, *Decline of*

an Empire (New York, 1979).

2. Edmund Cheraszkiewicz, "Przebudowa wshodu Europy" ("Rebuilding Eastern Europe") *Niepodległość* (London, 1955). pp. 125–167. Major Charaszkiewicz of Polish military intelligence department *Oddzial II* [Second Department] was a key figure and an expert on the Promethean movement in Polish intelligence circles.

3. Sergiusz Mikulicz, *Prometeizm w polityce II Rzeczypospolitej* ("Prometheism in the Politics of the Polish Republic") (Warsaw, 1971). pp. 11–12. Also see George F. Kennan, *Russia Leaves the War*, Vol. 1 (Princeton, 1956), pp. 160–190.

4. Piotr S. Wendycz, *Soviet-Polish Relations 1917–1921* (Harvard, 1969), pp. 100–101.

5. Piłsudski's ideas toward Russia reflected his early Socialist outlook, in which he considered the destruction of Tsarism by all methods including separatism. See Waclaw Jedrzejewicz, *Sprawa wieczoru: Józef Piłsudski a wojna rosyjsko-japonska 1904–1905* ("The Evening Affair: Józef Piłsudski and the Russo-Japanese War 1904–1905") (Paris, 1974). pp. 45–46.

6. Edmund Charaszkiewicz, *Zagadnienia Prometejskie* ("Promethean Question"), (hereafter cited Charaszkiewicz, *Zagadnienia*).

7. Thirty officers from the Caucasus were accepted by the Polish Staff College. For a complete list of the foreign officers from 1922 to 1938 see *W 50-lecie powstania Wyższej Szkoly Wojennej w Warszawie* ("On the Occasion of the 50th Anniversary of the Staff College in Warsaw") (London, 1969), pp. 239–243 (hereafter cited as *WSW*).

8. Charaszkiewicz, *Zagadnienia*

9. L. Sadowski, *Oddziat II Sztagu Głównego: Rezultaty pracy pokojowej i udziałw przygotowaniu do wojny*)"Section II of the Polish General Staff: The Results of Peace Work and Participation in the Preparation for War"), unpublished typescript, 1940 (Warsaw, Wojskowy Instytut Historyzny) (hereafter cited as *Sadowski Report*).

10. The Armenian people were least affected by the Promethean philosophy because of the Turkish massacres and their traditional pro-Russian attitude. See Charaszkiewicz, *Zagadnienia*, p. 6.

11. Charaszkiewicz, *Zagadnienia*, pp. 11–14. In 1931 the first Petlura Ukrainians were contracted into the Polish Army, *WSW*, p. 241.

12. Ibid., pp. 21 and 22.

13. *Sadowski Report*, p. 92.

14. It is noteworthy that the Polish Prometheans did not support or approve these actions, *Sadowski Report*, p. 95.

15. Between 1927 and 1939 the Promethean movement had cost the Polish goverment approximately 15 million zlotys. *Sadowski Report*, p. 97.

16. Józef Lipski, *Diplomat in Berlin* (New York, 1968), pp. 135–142. Richard Torzecki, *Kwestia ukraińska w polityce III Rzeszy 1933–1945* ("The Ukrainian Question in the Policy of the Third Reich") (Warsaw, 1972), pp. 138–139.

17. Taped interview with General Józef Smoleński, London, England (January 16, 1976). In the author's files.

PART V

OTHER FIELDS

FRANK A. GOLDER, COLLECTING DOCUMENTS FOR THE RUSSIAN SECTION OF THE HOOVER WAR LIBRARY,* 1920–1923: A BIBLIOPHILE'S DREAM AND DRAMA

Alain Dubie

After the signing of the Treaty of Versailles in 1919, American scholars had their hands full. Enormous changes had occurred in Europe as result of World War I—the departure of kings, the breakup of empires, and the rise of radical and conservative protests in response to catastrophic social and economic conditions. One monumental series of changes involved the downfall of tsardom in Russia in 1917, the establishment of the Provisional Government (PG), and its disintegretion six months later when the Bolsheviks came to power in November. American scholars who wished to dig into U.S. archives in an effort to unravel what had happened to bring about such an upheaval as the Russian Revolution and to describe the radical changes that had taken place in Soviet Russia could not do so. No archival center in the U. S. had any major documentary holdings about recent Russian history.[1]

In 1920, the Hoover War Library sought to reduce this important documentary gap. Founded in 1919 by D. Ephraim D. Adams, a professor of history at Stanford University, and the Herbert Hoover Library was originally established on the Stanford campus as an archival center focusing on the documentation of the Great War from diplomatic, military, political, econfortune in the mining industry, had directed the Belgian Relief Administration (ARA), which supplied food and medicine to victims of war, provided the bulk of the Library's financial support. Adams, while directing the overseas operations of

---

*Now called the Hoover Institution on War, Revolution, and Peace.

the library, was the curator of the East European section; Ralph H. Lutz[2] a professor of German history at Stanford University, was curator of the Central European section. In 1920, a year after the library's inauguration, he hired Frank Golder, a professor of American and Russian history in his early thirties who had been teaching at Washington State College in Pullman, to develop and to oversee the Eastern European section. This paper will discuss Golder's three-year document collecting trip to Europe, from 1920 to 1923, describing in general the kinds of documents he collected and the tactics he used, what problems he faced, and what experiences he had as a collector who eventually culled millions of documents involving Russian/Soviet history.[3]

But first, who was Frank Golder? He was born in 1877 in the Ukraine, close to Odessa, where his Jewish parents had settled after leaving their German homeland. Although Frank's parents lived in poverty, it was the fear of pogroms which compelled them to immigrate to America when their son was eight-years-old. His father tried farming in New Jersey but could not make a go of it; the family then moved on to city life in Philadelphia, where hard times continued to press them, especially after the addition of two sons and four daughters. Frank, though, managed to excel in school and went on to earn a bachelor's degree from Bucknell University.

After graduation he accepted a position teaching native children in remote Unge, Alaska, and he lived there for three years. Even though he experienced success as a teacher and earned the respect of the population for his many kind acts, the isolating harsh winters and the violence among the native Alaskans and the Caucasian traders evaporated his intent of staying longer. Golder resigned his teaching position in 1901 and returned to the less hazardous world of scholarly life in New England. He attended Harvard University, earning an M.A. in 1903 and a Ph.D. in 1909 under the direction of Archibald Cary Coolidge, who inspired Golder to study Russian history, to research European archives for his dissertation, and to learn French in Paris and German in Berlin, languages which supplemented his knowledge of Russian. It was Coolidge's students of Eastern European history who provided new directions in Russian studies as teachers, scholars, and bibliophiles.[4]

Golder then taught briefly at Boston College and the University of Chicago. In 1911, he joined the history faculty at Washington

State College in Pullman, where he stayed for nine years. During this period, he undertook two research trips to Russia, having in mind to establish a scholarly reputation for himself. In 1914, he researched the archives of St. Petersburg and Moscow on topics dealing with Russo-American relations; from this information he published several original articles in 1915 end 1916; while in St. Petersburg he also did research on Russian expansion in the Pacific and Alaska, his dissertation topic, which was published in 1914 was the first monograph on Russian history written by an American. Besides acquainting himself with Russian archival centers, Golder gained valuable impressions of Russian politics, society, and culture. But one event in particular stood out in Golder's mind after this trip: Russia's entrance into World War I. Golder had witnessed Tsar Nicholas II deliver his emotional war declaration from a balcony over a square jammed, as the historian had noted in his diary, with a mildly enthusiastic crowd.[5]

In March 1917, Golder returned to Russia for further research. After his arrival, he observed what effects the year had had on the capital: long bread lines, a severe coal shortage, and complaints from every class about the lack of leadership in a murderous war that was draining Russia of its men and resources. Yet, paradoxically, Golder noted that the capital had a strange normlalcy: it was lively with fashionably attired Russians and with an array of bright-lighted theaters and restaurants. Within a few days of his arrival, however, Golder felt this illusory atmosphere recede into the beckground as popular protest flared up from the deep crisis affecting Russia and escalated into a revolution, the March Revolution, which led to the downfall of tsarist rule and to the establishment of the so-called dual government the Provisional Government (PG) and its counterpart the Petrograd Soviet. While Golder favored the transition of this internal dual government into constitutionally democratic institutions, he feared that extreme radicalism might gain the upper hand if the war further eroded confidence in leadership. By November 1917, in a matter of seven months, Golder's fear became reality when Lenin's Communist Bolshevik Party overthrew the existing order. Golder, who had departed Russia in late August to undertake teaching responsibilities at Pullman, did not get to observe what became known as the November Russian Revolution; notwithstanding his absence, the momentous transforniation of Russia influenced the rest of his life.[6]

In December 1917, Golder was chosen as a member of the Inquiry Commission, an organization set in motion by President Wilson to prepare the U. S. government's case for the peace settlement of World War I. He worked with the Inquiry's Eastern European Division at Cambridge, Massachusetts, where he contributed reports on former tsarist provinces Lithuania, the Ukraine, and Siberia. But his experience with the Inquiry proved to be a frustrating one. He was accustomed to working at his own pace, in pursuit of objectivity, and with relevent primary sources; instead, he confronted bureaucratic deadlines, Wilsonian ideology, and the scarcity of relevant source materials. The final blow was the news that he would not be included as a delegate to the Paris Peace Conference. Nevertheless, his experience was not without benefit. He gained wider knowledge of the social, economic, and political problems facing the post-war world. Above all, he was aware of the dearth of source materials on c on temporary Russian history, a problem which had plagued him throughout his tenure with the Inquiry.

Little did Golder know at the time that one day he would personally correct this document vacuum. In the summer of 1920 Adams brought Golder to Stanford, integrated him into the history department and in the Hoover Library, and prepared him for a document collecting trip to Soviet Russia for the acquisition of materials on the late tsarist period, Russia in World War I, the March and November Revolutions, and the Russian Civil War. There was, however, a considerable hitch in the new assignment. The Soviet government had closed its borders to traveling Americans because of the U. S. nonrecognition policy directed at the Soviet Government since its seizure of power in 1917 and because the U. S. had supported the white counterrevolutionary armies with soldiers, money, and military equipment during the Russian Civil War. Golder therefore decided to collect what documents he could on Russia elsewhere in Europe, while intermittently negotiating with Soviet authorities for permission to enter Russia.[8]

Golder departed from Stanford on 20 August 1920. After his train arrived in New York City, he booked passage on the steamship *Imperator*. He then contacted Ludwig Martens, who had been sent by the Soviet Government to the U. S. to act as an unofficial diplomat and to establish commercial ties with Americen businessmen. Whereas the State Department viewed Martens as a subversive and was harassing him, Golder had no qualms about asking Martens for assistance in entering Russia. Golder, although no admirer of the

Soviet government's centralized ecnomic system and lack of political democracy, put practical objectives above politics in this case. When the two men met, Martens treated the historian cordially and said that he would send a message to a Soviet representative in London concerning his request. Even if this meeting was inconclusive, Golder had some expectations of future success.[9]

When Golder arrived in London, he looked up the Russian émigré Paul Miliukov, whom he had met in Russia in 1917. Miliukov had been foreign minister of the Provisional Government and, after the Bolsheviks came to power, had fled into exile. Over lunch Miliukov told Golder that before he had left Russia he had transferred various archival materials to Rostov and Kiev but that they had vanished during the civil war. He added, though, that another collection, which consisted of personal papers and rare books in eighteen boxes, had survived and were hidden in a village in Finland. He offered to let the Hoover buy the collection if Golder wished to take the trouble of securing it. Golder agreed to do so.[10]

The following day, Golder called on Leonid Krassin, head of a Soviet trade delegation in London. A note from Martens in New York may have helped bring about this meeting. Golder gave Kressin an introductory letter from the director of the ARA office in London, Walter Brown; the letter asked that Golder be given permission to collect documents in Soviet Russia and to write a report on food conditions there for Hoover's evaluation; Hoover, who was not averse to using food as a political weapon (to inspire anti-communist sentiment among a population by way of the beneficance of capitalism), was apparently considering at this time aiding Russia where the destruction of crops during the Russian Civil War and drought had brought about a severe food shortage. Golder, who viewed the ARA in nonpolitical terms, thought that he could use the prospect of ARA aid a way of getting into Russia. But Kressin repeated to Golder that he already knew the Soviet government prohibited Americans from traveling into Russia because of U. S. hostility. Golder then portrayed his collecting mission as purely nonpolitical and his food investigative mission as purely humanitarian. In response, Kressin promised to communicate Golder's overture to the Soviet government and to inform the ARA London office of the result. Golder wrote, "[Perhaps] Kressin's efforts will not be in vain."[11]

That evening, Golder had dinner with a Count Benningson and his wife. The Count worked at the consulate of the former Russian

Provisional Government in London, which continued to keep its doors open in the capacity of an information center for émigrés. The count told Golder that he and his wife had suffered many privations in Russia. After the Bolshevik Revolution, but, unlike other émigrés, Golder noted in his diary, "They have little bitterness toward the new order, and give their enemies credit for their good points."[12] Golder also learned that life abroad for the émigrés had not been easy; they had no consistent income and depended heavily on the generosity of Russians who visited the consulate. The count's wife, who spoke several languages, asked Golder if he could help her find translating work. While sympathetic, Golder related that translating work was scarce, the applicants many; he could do nothing. Even though Golder hopes did not bring new hopes to the Benningsons' lives, the count did understand the importance of Golder's documentary quest and gave him a package of Bolshevik and White Russian propaganda which he had collected in northern Russia in 1918. Golder accepted, knowing that the gift was not of great value but it was a beginning.

A few days later, Golder departed London for Paris. There he visited the embassy of the Provisional Government. Like London, the Soviet government had no embassy in Paris, because of a nonrecognition policy. At the Russian embassy Golder approached several staff members about offering any records that had a bearing on recent Russian/Soviet history. The staff members proved to be helpful, no doubt because of their grievances against the Bolsheviks who had ousted them from positions of power and influence. They gave Golder a number of packages which had documents regarding World War I, the Provisional Government, and the Bolsheviks. Gradually, Golder's Russian collection was growing.[13]

From Paris, Golder made stopovers at Coblenz and Berlin, and then traveled on to Riga, the capital of Latvia. As yet, he had no idea of what had happened to Krassin's promise of contacting the Soviet government. Being so close to Russia, Golder itched to go there. He therefore decided to contact Adolf Yoffe, head of e Soviet delegetion in Riga for the settlement of the recent war between Soviet Russia and Poland. But at Yoffe's office a secretary barred him from seeing the diplomat. On top of this, he received a telegram at the American Red Cross which stated that Hoover considered Russia unsafe for him to enter because the Bolsheviks had recently imprisoned several Americans, accusing them of spying.[14] Such a risk, though, failed to impress Golder, because a great sense of urgency gripped him;

at Riga several Europeans who had traveled to Russia told him of the desperate situation prevailing there: famine in the countryside, bread riots in the cities, and severe fuel shortages. He wished to help starving Russians and to collect valuable materials before chaos consumed Russia.[15]

Unfortunately, for the moment, Golder could do nothing. In another telegram Hoover suggested that Golder collect documents on the Baltic states regarding Bolshevik influence from within and from without. When Golder tried to follow this advice in Latvia, he discovered that the government had outlawed the sale of any book, newspaper, or pamphlet which concerned Bolshevism, But he wanted materials so eagerly that he decided to circumvent the law, arranging a rendezvous with a bookseller who, one night, slipped him a file of newspapers, *Die Rote Fahne (The Red Flag)*, which the Bolsheviks had published during their occupation of Riga in 1916. To avoid arrest, Golder stored the illegal newspaper in the safest place he could think of: the headquarters of the American Commission for the Baltic States.

While at the headquarters, Golder asked commissioner Evan Young if he could add any materials, gathered by his organization, which covered Bolshevik activities in the Baltic. Young said that he could and contributed everything through his organization. Golder, having successfully outwitted the Latvian authorities and secured documents from Young, was pleased.[16]

Cheered by success, Golder now considered tracking down Miliukov's collection. To begin this adventure, he traveled to Helsingfors (Helsinki), Finland. There he met with Rudolf Holsti, the foreign minister, to assist him in his quest. Holsti was certainly the right choice, for Holsti owed Hoover a favor; it was Hoover, who, as food adnmnistrator of the Supreme Economic Council in Paris in 1919, had ordered food shipments to Finland to aid the destitute as well of preventing the rise of Bolshevism; Hoover had also been instrumental in bringing about the independence of Finland during during the Paris Peace Conference.[17] Moreover, Miliukov had contacted Holti, informing him of the collection and its location. To Golder's delight, Holsti provided him with an army officer to escort him to Terijoki where the documents were located and fired a message to the town's commandant explaining Golder's mission.

In the evening, Golder and the officer took the train to Terijoki. After they arrived, Golder learned from the local commandant that

the caretaker of Miliukov's collection had threatened to sell it because
of the accumulating storage fees. The next day, Golder, the officer,
and the commandant drove to a secluded tree in a forest. The commandant then led Golder to a barn where the collection was stored.
Shortly the caretaker, a German farmer appeared and greeted Golder.
As soon as Golder indicated his interest in Miliukov's collection, the
caretaker stubbornly demanded payment of all storage fees. Golder,
although eager to pay the storage fees and thereby acquire the collection, first wanted to inspect the collection for weather damage; but
growing darkness prevented him from doing so. In spite of the risk
of weather damage, Golder paid the storage fees and then persuaded
the caretaker to strengthen the boxes and to haul them to the railway
station. Everything was settled; yet Golder could not help wondering
if his hastiness might lead to disaster.

A few days later, Golder located the collection at a Helsingfors
railway station. He counted the number of boxes, which came to
thirty-four. This number surprised him because Miliukov had mentioned only eighteen. He opened one box and saw for himself that
there was no weather damage; he was dismayed by the contents, which
led him to believe that Miliukov had been unaware that the collection
involved a greater variety of materials than rare books and personal
papers.[18] As he later found out, in addition to rare books and personal
papers, there were government documents, manuscripts, periodicals,
pamphlets, leaflets, and broadsides, some 4,000 titles in all, excluding
the leaflets and broadsides.[19] Golder wrote optimistically to Adams,
"Miliukov's collection is a beginning and in [time] I may say with
certainty that Stanford will have the best Russian collection west of
the Atlantic."[20]

After his trip to Finland, Golder traveled to Constantinople,
which he reached in February 1921. From there he planned to travel
on to Georgia, a country which bordered the Black Sea, to collect
documents. Georgia, a former tsarist province, had declared its independence when the Bolsheviks had seized power, establishing a Menshevik government, which first came into conflict with Soviet political
exclusiveness and later with its expansionist practices. Recently, border disputes had brought the two countries close to war. Via ship and
train, Golder traveled through this uncertain part of the world, omi-
nously experiencing two exhausting weeks of snowbound countryside,
rickety train cars, and unscheduled stops.

When Golder finally arrived at Tiflis, Georgia's capital, he secured a room at the headquarters of the Near East Relief. The next day, a staff member arranged a meeting between Golder and the President of Georgia, Noah Zhordania, an arrangement which elevated the collector's spirits. After the tiring train ride, Golder called on him, stating his case, "in a way that would appeal to him,"[21] playing up the importance of Georgia's history, even though a small country, and the necessity of preserving its recorded past for historical study. Zhordania's response stunned Golder; Zhordania issued a memorandum to every government department, every public institution, and every learned society to be as flexible and as responsive as possible to Golder's want lists. To find out if the President's memorandum would produce results, he visited a number of ministers of state and they showered the bibliophile with friendliness, filling his want list without exception. He wrote to Adams that they considered themselves flattered that "a great man like Hoover, a great institution like Stanford, and a great country like the United States should be interested in Georgia and its ministers.[22]

Golder then wished to add a series of a Georgian newspaper to his collection. Approaching one editor, Golder solicited copies of his newspaper which covered Tsar Nicholas II's rule over Georgia, World War I, the two Russian revolutions, and the Russian Civil War. Without offering any explanation, the editor flatly refused to cooperate. Knowing how the art of flattery could work wonders in Georgia, Golder proceeded to praise the quality of the editor's newspaper and then the editor himself for that quality. The editor did not disappoint Golder; he dropped all opposition and gave the American a Russian edition of the newspaper, editions in two other languages, pamphlets, maps, and, lastly, a photograph of himself. Golder wrote Adams:

> At times I am really ashamed of myself, not because I do anything underhanded, for I treat the Georgians as I do Frenchmen and Germans, but because they concede so easily and let themselves open to childish flattery that it makes me feel somewhat guilty.[23]

After two days, Golder had concluded his Georgian collection. While happy over the outcome, he knew that this particular collection, scattered and large, would require at least two months of on-the-spot supervision to collect, organize, and prepare it for shipment. He therefore hired two Georgian scholars to take care of the many necessary details.

With a sense of accomplishment, Golder began the trip back to Constantinople. He took a train to Batum, where he boarded the USS *Barker*. From there he sailed to Sakham for a brief stopover; there he heard a rumor—the Red enemy was invading Georgia. He had expected the Bolsheviks to invade Georgia because of political-territorial disputes, but not so soon, and he returned to Istanbul to find out what was actually happening. At Batum, he learned that the invasion had, in fact, taken place. He wrote, "alarming reports reached us of the Bolo (Bolshevik) invasion, of the flight of the diplomatic missions, and of the removal of the Georgian (Menshevik) government."[24] His easily-won collection of documents would not go through. The following day, Golder boarded the USS *Tracy*, a ship bound for Constantinople.

When Golder arrived at Constantinople, he was suffering from a sense of failure and depression. Soon, though, he treated the whole affair philosophically, writing:

> Had I remained two days in [Tiflis, the Bolsheviks] would have been attacking me. Luckily, I escaped just in time. This explains why I am here instead of feeding the small animals which infest the Bolshcvik Prisons. Though the Reds did not make a home run in only case, they got a hit and spoiled all my efforts of a month and have secured some documents to which I had better right than they. *C'est le guerre.* The first round between us ended in a draw and I look forward to more decisive fights in the future.[25]

During the next four months, Golder continued his travels in Europe, collecting documents, mostly materials unrelated to Russian history. Yet the difficulty of getting into Russia was often on his mind. In June, he managed to set in motion a scheme that he hoped would let him do just that. He persuaded Holtsi to act as an intermediary between him and the Soviet government in negotiating an agreement that would permit him to investigate the famine in Russia for the purpose of writing a report that would be delivered to Hoover. The Soviets gave him permission because the famine was taking e heavy toll on the population. But when Golder transmitted the news of the successful negotiations to the ARA London office, ARA officials there ordered him not to enter Russia. It was a disheartening rebuff.[26]

Then, in early August, he made a stopover in Vienna; there his whirl of collecting activity came to a momentary halt; illness had beset him. In his letters to the Hoover Library, he did not specify what was wrong with him, except to say that he would be having an operation on his "breathing apparatus."

After his release from the hospital, the convalescing Golder figured out why the ARA had refused him permission to go into Russia. In a local newspaper, he read that ARA and Soviet officials were in Riga discussing plans that involved food relief shipments to Russia and the use of ARA members to distribute the food. The ARA had not wanted Golder interferring with its plans.

Still determined to get into Russia, Golder sent several telegrams to Walter Brown, head of the ARA Office in London, asking to be included in the initial ARA expeditions into Russia in the event of a signed agreement. Brown did not respond to any of the telegrams, though. In anger, Golder wrote Lutz at the Hoover Library, "I wish that damn ARA director would act. It is getting on my nerves and in addition it is wasting valuable time for me."[27] On 20 August, Golder learned that the ARA and the Soviet government had signed the so-called Riga Agreement which permitted ARA personnel and relief shipments into Russia. Believing he had sufficiently recovered from his operation and anxious to take matters into his own hands, Golder traveled by train to Riga. After he arrived there, he convinced ARA officials not only to allow him to accompany a group of ARA members to Moscow, but also to grant him status as a member of that organization. Notwithstanding this success, he complained to Adams that the ARA viewed him as a nuisance, a man of words in his professional capacity rather than a man of action who had had ARA field experience.[28]

A few days after Golder reached Moscow, his status in the ARA changed expeditiously. The ARA needed someone who spoke Russian, had a knowledge of Russian society, and had wide travel experience in Russia. None of the ARA members fit the bill. ARA leaders elevated Golder to the rank of special representative, a position which placed him among the highest ARA members in the Russian unit. Thus, Golder now had what he had so eagerly desired, a dual function in Russia: collecting documents and investigating famine conditions. At first his ARA role took precedence because of the famine's gravity; Golder traveled along the Volga River to Samara, where he encountered hordes of wandering Russians who were clothed in rags and suffering from disease end starvation. His ARA reports of this tragic plight contributed to saving thousands of lives.[29]

When Golder returned to Moscow, he began the long-anticipated endeavor of collecting documents inside Russia. On 6 October, he met the Commissar of Education, Mikhail Pokrovsky. Like Golder, Pokrovsky was a historian and could easily grasp the importance of Golder's archival mission. And, too, the fact that Golder represented the ARA and that the Soviets wished to broaden trade relations with Western powers was not lost on Prokovsky; perhaps the release of documents could influence political ends? The professor/commissar informed Golder that he had control of *all* government publications. Golder could have what he wanted. Of this generosity, he wrote Lutz:

> Everything of importance since 1917 was published by the government, and [Pokrovsky] gave orders that two copies of every book and pamphlet should be set aside for us.[30]

In this single meeting, Golder had added substantially to the Hoover's documentary depth and range of diplomatic, administrative, and military sources involving Russia from 1917 to 1921. As he wrote to Lutz, "Our prospects in the line of collecting in Russia are very bright."[31]

Optimstic of further success, Golder wanted to collect books that covered the period of late tsardom to contemporary Soviet history. Such a goal, though, placed Golder in marginal conflict with Adams. Previously, during his collecting sojourn in Europe, Golder had wired Adams requesting funds to buy books for Stanford's main library, hoping to take advantage of the deflationary postwar European economy, which offered the buyer an inexpensive book market. The president of Stanford University, Lynlen Wilbur, had approved a sum of $2,000 for Golder's proposal, while Adams, Although he sent the money to Golder, had reservations; he viewed the main library, where the Hoover's holding were located, as a threat to the Hoover War Collection's independence. Even the head of the main library, George Clark, took a dim view of a Hoover representative buying books for the main library, since he resented the Hoover's independence, growing holdings, and influence in his realm. But Golder, far from local and administrative politics, envisioned a university library with extensive secondery sources dovetailing the Hoover's primary sources; linked together, the two institutions might bring Stanford University world-wide recognition as a unique research center.[32] Golder had acted on that premise; in the Baltic States and elsewhere in Europe, he hed purchased estate and even institutional library collections of books for a fraction of their original value. Now, in Russia, Golder planned to use part of the controversial $2,000 to buy precious books. Circumstances there certainly favored his intent. Lenin's New Economic Policy, a measure set in motion in 1921 to alleviate some of the pressures of the economic crisis, permitted small businesses to flourish; this concession to capitalism encouraged many Moscovites to sell their books to bookdealers as a way of acquiring extra money for food and fuel. Golder wrote to Lutz:

> I have been watching the book market, and it makes my intellectual mouth water. Rare editions, beautiful bindings, heirlooms of great value are thrown on the market. I have decided to cast prudence aside, and spend some of the two thousand on purchases here. Tell . . . Adams . . . and all the others they might as well begin abusing me and get done with it, for they cannot stop me. In a century from now, when I am dead of a broken heart caused by their reproaches, the scholars of 2000 will thank me.[33]

In a few weeks, Golder purchased thousands of books. He boasted to Adams: " I am glad that I got here, for we are making a clean-up which those who follow after us cannot duplicate."[34]

Even though Golder was collecting materials with apparent ease, he experienced his share of apprehensions. The Soviet secret police, the *Cheka*, shadowed him everywhere in Moscow. He wrote Adams: "My great crime is that I understand the language and talk with people, something that most ARA men cannot do." [35] Before long, he learned that the *Cheka* had accused him of criticizing the Soviet government (true) and of having fought with Admiral Alexander Kolchak's White army in Siberia during the Civil War (false) Golder refused to let his awareness of the *Cheka*, even with its reputation of imprisoning and shooting dissidents, inhibit his collecting momentum. All the same, he could not ignore the *Cheka* either. "I walk around as if a sword hung over me,"[36] he wrote Adams.

By December, Golder had a bountiful Russian collection and began working toward shipping it safely out of Russia. In this endeavor, he consulted his loyal supporter, Pokrovsky. The Soviet historian assured Golder that he had authority to issue a train-shipment permit for such an unusual cargo. But when Golder contacted Soviet transportation officials about this permit, they told him that the Commissar of Education had exceeded his power. They would not issue

Golder the necessary permit, and he surmised that the *Cheka* was pulling strings behind the scenes. While distressed by this snag, he tried to obtain assistance from the ARA and Soviet political leaders; they would not aid him either. Golder had nowhere else to turn; it just was not an auspicious time for helpful assistance: the ARA hierarchy was preoccupied by the distribution of food ne relief and Soviet political leaders by the Ninth All-Russian Congress of Soviets. A few days before Christmas, Golder indicated his general frustration in a letter to Adams: "The Bolos are having their big powwow,and it is difficult to get them to pay attention to anything practical."[37]

His shipment plans stalled, Golder traveled to Petrograd after Christmas in search of more documents. There he found a city, like Moscow, impoverished by war and famine. Although a gloomy atmosphere pervaded the former Tsarist capital, he kept in sight the reason behind his visit. During his month-long stay, Golder covered as much archival ground as he could. First, he went to the Revolutionary Museum and its staff gave him a set of revolutionary newspapers from 1917 to 1918, which complemented his Moscow files from 1919 to 1922. The museum staff also gave him a large collection of pamphlets and posters. He then visited the Soviet printing press and its staff opened their stacks to him. From there, he proceeded to the Academy of Sciences and on to other learned societies where he secured a variety of publications. Next, he saw friends at archival centers, who, he wrote, "loaded me down with sets off publications until I was ashamed to take them, but I took."[38] Lastly, he invaded the book market, finding books in Petrograd even cheaper than in Moscow. His selection of books filled some fifty boxes. At the end of this trip, Golder wrote Adams, "We are getting now what cannot again be had."[39]

Golder returned to Moscow in 30 January 1922. Then, after a seven week trip to Georgia and Azerbaijan, he focused again on the elusive shipment permit. This time new factors favored his goal. The Commissar of Transportation, Feliks Dzerzhinski, who also headed the *Cheka*, had joined the ARA in a coordinated effort to deliver food and supplies to famine stricken areas all over Russia; taking advantege of this cooperation, Golder appealed to the ARA hierarchy to provide some leverage on the Soviets regarding a shipment permit. Golder wrote Lutz of what happened next:

> Colonel Haskel (director of the ARA in Russia) and his men
> have taken the needed interest, and the Soviet officials have
> come through. During the last few days, I have purposely

kept in the background and let the ARA do it all. Last night, [Alexander Eiduk, the Soviet plenipotentiary assigned to the ARA unit] impressed upon my mind that a very special favor had been granted in letting us take out the [materials]. I thanked him that we appreciated it and let it go at that, for I could have added a word or two.[40]

The Soviet authorities proceeded efficiently in guaranteeing the shipments packing and safe delivery outside Russia. Russian workers double-sealed fifty-five crates of government publications, archival materials, newspapers, periodicals, diaries, pamphlets, memoirs, posters, and books.[41] and loaded onto train cars this documentery cargo that would prove invaluable to historians in bringing Russia's past to life on the printed page. Then, a special convoy accompanied the train to the northern Soviet border, continuing on to Riga, where the ARA office would transship the documents to the U. S. Golder wrote Lutz. "It is a good collection and you had better tell librarian Clark to get ready to have an exhibition of Russian bindings, for, all things being equal, I took beautiful bindings.[42] Joyful? Yes; and relieved.

Lutz acknowledged:

My feeling is that you have covered the ground thoroughly. I do not believe that any scholar in the U.S. would have accomplished two-thirds of the results which you heve achieved since you left Stanford. As for the Bolsheviks, you will be the greatest authority in America on them when you return.[43]

Lutz' appraisal and estimation of Golder was fitting, indeed.

In 1923, Golder left Russia, returning to Stanford University to teach and to act as one of the directors of the Hoover Library. At Stanford he sought to promote Russian studies in the U. S. through teaching Russian history, inviting European and American scholars to do research at the Hoover, and establishing a Russian-American Institute for the study of the Russian Revolution. It was with special pride that he saw students and scholars using the Russian Collection for research projects in the small room the Hoover had in the main library. While all this was taking place, Golder precipitated by way of correspondence a steady flow of documents to Stanford from all over Europe and of course Russia. And trips to Russia in 1924 and 1927 deepened the Russian Collection still further. The flow of documents came as a result of what had made Golder a successful collector in the first place: determination, affability, persuasiveness, and awareness.

Not least of all, he had his share of luck, too. For the Soviet political situation had favored him—chaotic, liberal, vengeful, and proud.

Luck, one might also add, has a certain consistency with preparedness. For example, Golder's Harvard mentor, Archibald Cary Coolidge, who worked briefly in Moscow for the ARA when Golder was there, had in mind to collect materials for the Widener Library, but passed up the chance of buying in the inexpensive book market (prices did rise as NEP succeeded), deciding instead to buy duplicates of the Hoover's Russian Collection; he reasoned that this approach would be less wasteful, less troublesome. Golder thought differently; as he wrote Adams:

> Our policy is wiser. . . . From the great abundance of materials that we have we can sift and select what we need, and with the remainder we can trade for what we do not have.[44]

While Coolidge missed a unique opportunity in Russia, he acknowledged the Hoover Library's significance. He told Golder: "Stanford is going to be the place for the study of history since 1914."[45] To be sure, the totality of Golder's Russian Collection established the Hoover as the most exemplary repository of sources on Russian/Soviet history in the world, outside of Russia itself.

Sadly, in 1929, this pioneer historian died of lung cancer at the age of fifty-one.

NOTES

1. See, the author's, "Frank A. Golder, the Inquiry, and Soviet Russie," in *War, Revolution, and Peace: Essays in Honor of Charles B. Burdick* Joachim Reemak, ed. (New York: University Press of America, 1987), pp. 102–03. Cited hereafter as Wachhold, "Golder and the Inquiry."

2. For a biography of Lutz, see, Charles B. Burdick, *Ralph H. Lutz and the Hoover Institution* (Stanford: Hoover Institution, 1974).

3. Wachhold, "Golder and the Inquiry," pp. 89–98, 107.

4. Ibid. Robert F. Byrnes, *Awakening American Education to the World: The Role of Archibald Cary Coolidge. 1866–1928* (Indiana: Indiana University Press, 1982) p. 49. Cited hereafter as Byrnes, Coolidge.

5. Golder, "1917 Diary," Golder Papers, Hoover Institution, Stanford, CA, Box 19. Cited hereafter as GP.

6. Ibid.

7. Wachhold, "Golder and the Inquiry," pp. 102–107.

8. Golder to Adams, 17 August 1920, p. 1, GP, Box 32. Golder to Adams, 19 August 1920, p 1; ibid., Golder to Adams, 30 August 1920, p.1, ibid., Ephraim Adams, "Digest of the Work of F. A. Golder in Connection eith the American Relief Administration and Hoover War Collection, no date, ibid. Cited hereafter as Adams, "Digest" Adams to Golder, 12 November 1920, p. 2, ibid. Frederick Schuman, *American Policy toward Russia since 1917* (New York: International Publishers, 1928). Cited hereafter as Schuman, *American Policy Toward Russia.*

9. Adams, "Digest,"p. 1. Schuman, *American Policy toward Russia*, pp. 185–95.

10. Golder to Adams, 21 September 1920, p. 1, GP, Box 32. Arthur P. Mendel, ed., *Paul Miliukov: Politics Memoirs, 1905–1917* (Ann Arbor University of Michigan Press, 1967) pp. xiv, 198.

11. Adams, "Digest," p. 2.

12. Golder, "Diary," 21 September 1920, GP, Box 19. Golder to Adams, 25 September 1920, p. 1, GP, Box 32. Adams, "Digest," p. 2.

13. Ephriam Adams, *The Hoover War Collection: A Report and Analysis* (Stanford: Stanford University Press, 1921), pp. 10–15. cited hereafter as Adams, *Report.*

14. Walter Brown to Golder, 11 October 1920, Telegram, BAEF papers, Correspondence Series, Hoover Presidential Library, West Branch, Iowa. Cited hereafter as HPL. Golder, "Diary," 13 October 1920, GP, Box 19.

15. Golder to H. Eliot, 17 October 1920, p. 1, GP, Box 12. Golder to Walter Brown, 18 August 1920, p. 1, BAEF papers, Correspondence Series, HPL. Golder to Walter Brown, 31 December 1920, p. 1, ibid.

16. Golder to Adams, 17 October 1920, p. 11, GP, Box 33. Golder to Adams, 19 October 1920, p. 14; ibid., Adams, *Report*, p. 73. Adams, "Digest," p. 7.

17. Golder, "Diary," 1 November 1920, GP, Box 19. Herbert Hoover, *The Order of Woodrow Wilson* (New York: McGraw-Hill, 1956), pp. 126–34. Herbert Hoover, *An American Epic* , Vol. 3: *The Battle on the Front Line and the Famine in Forty-Nine Nations* (Chicago: Henry Regnery, 1961) pp. 27–29. Cited hereafter as, Hoover, *An American Epic.*

18. Golder, "Miliukov Collection," 6 November 1920, pp. 1–2, GP, Box 32.

19. After Golder had recovered Miliukov's collection, the Russian scholar later demanded several thousand dollars as a purchasing price from the Hoover. The Hoover could not afford to pay such a large price for one private collection; Golder haggled with Miliukov but to no avail. According to Wojciech Zelewski, "Golder [by 1926] gave up altogether his hopes that the Miliukov collection would remain at Stanford. He prepared a list of its contents to facilitate its sale to another library. When the list was ready in July 1922, he wrote to Miliukov: "I am impressed with the value of it, but am sorry to say that we at Stanford have no money to purchase it. Much as we regret it, we all have to let it go." Soon after, Miliukov did sell his collection to the library of the University of California, Berkeley, where it remains today. See, Wiojciech Zalewski, unpublished monograph on, "Slavic collections at Stanford libraries and the Hoover Institution," p. 74. Gary Paul, "The Development of the Hoover Institution on War, Revolution, and Peace Library, 1919–1944," (Ph.D. dissertation, University of California, Berkeley, 1974) pp. 158–59.

20. Adams, "Digest," p. 7.

21. Golder to Adams, 20 February 1921, p. 1, GP, Box 33.

22. Ibid.

23. Ibid.

24. Golder to Adams, 30 January 1921, p. 38, GP, Box 32.

25. Golder to Adams, 20 February 1921, p. 2, GP, Box 33.

26. Golder to Adams, 30 Apil 1921, p. 1, GP, Box 32. Golder to Walter Brown, 18 August 1921, p. 1, BAEF papers, Correspondence Series, Golder, HPL. Logan to Walter Brown, 26 July 1921, Cablegram, ibid. Walter Brown to Edgar Rickard, 29 July 1921, ibid.

27. Golder to Lutz, 18 August 1921, p. 1, GP, Box 32.

28. Golder to Adams, 27 August 1921, p. 1, ibid. Walter Brown to Miller, 26 August 1921, Telegram, BAEF papers, Correspondence Papers, Golder, HPL.

29. See, Golder's memoir, *On the Trail of the Russian Famine* (Stanford University Press, 1927).

30. Golder to Lutz, 3 October 1921, p. 115, GP, Box 33.

31. Ibid. Golder to Adams, 16 November 1921, p. 1, BAEF Papers, Hoover Institutions Collectors, Golder, HPL.

32. Golder to Adams, 19 October 1921, p.14, GP, Box 33. Adams, "Digest," p. 6. Adams to Golder, 4 December 1920, p. 2,

ibid. Golder to Adams, 21 December 1920, pp. 1–2, General Correspondence, Internal Records of the Hoover Institution, Box 6. Cited hereafter as HIR. Lutz to Adams, 20 July 1922,p. 1, Administrative Subject File, ibid, Box 156.

33. Golder to Adams, 6 October 1921, p. 116, GP, Box 33.

34. Golder to Adams, 30 December 1921, p. 143, ibid.

35. Golder to Adams, 2 December 1921, p. 132, ibid.

36. Golder to Adams, 22 December 1921, p. 136, ibid.

37. Ibid.

38. Golder to Adams, 30 January 1922, p. 212, ibid. Golder humbly added, "I am telling you all this not to praise my work, for I have made mistakes, but to explain what we have, for it will please you." Golder to Adams, 4 January 1922, p. 3, ibid.

39. Golder to Adams, 30 January 1922, p. 210, ibid.

40. Golder to Lutz, 2 April 1922, p. 240, ibid.

41. Under Golder's direction , the Russian Collection at the Hoover Library consisted, by 1925, of 1,000,000 letters and documents, 20,340 manuscripts, 127,500 pamphlets, 29,500 printed volumes, 172,000 newspapers and periodicals,15,150 posters, photographs, and watercolors. See, "Summary of materials in the Hoover War Library," 4 August 1925, Russian Collection, HIR, Box 156. Ralph H. Lutz, "The Hoover War Library Grows Yearly in Importance as a Great Field for Historical Research," *Stanford Illustrated Review* (June 1923) 465.

42. Golder to Lutz, 1 April 1922, p. 231, GP, Box 33.

43. Lutz to Golder, 15 April 1922, p. 2, ibid

44. Golder to Adams, 3 April 1922, p. 240, GP, Box 33. William Bentinck-Smith, *Buiiding a Great Library: The Coolidge Years at Harvard* (Cambridge: Harvard University Press, 1976), pp. 126–28.

45. Golder to Adams, 22 December 1921, p. 138, GP, Box 32.

SOMETHING NEW AND SOMETHING OLD
ESTABLISHMENT OF THE *REICHSHEER*

S. J. Lewis

> Our deeds still travel with us from afar,
> And what we have been makes us what we are.
>
> George Eliot, Middlemarch

World War I ended with the defeat of the German Army and popular uprisings against the government in the larger cities across Germany. In the tumultuous days of November 1918, Kaiser Wilhelm II abdicated and in Berlin Philipp Scheidemann, the leader of the Social Democratic Party, proclaimed a republic. In the rear areas of the army, among the replacement units, supply and signal troops, many soldiers followed the example of their former opponents in the Russian Army, forming Soldiers Councils, demanding abolition of military rank and discipline, and immediate demobilization. The unthinkable had occurred and it appeared to many that Germany would soon follow the path of Lenin and Trotsky in Russia. Germany, however, was not Russia.

The Social Democrats dutifully set about establishing a new government in Berlin, encountering virtually no conservative opposition. Indeed, the old order appeared bankrupt in the winter of 1918/19; no doubt the result of the sacrifices of the long and costly war, the Imperial government's misleading propaganda, the Kaiser's arrogation of authority to the General Staff, and the bewildering rapidity of the conclusion of hostilities. The Social Democrats themselves officially remained a party of social and economic revolution. In reality, however, the Party had come to accept the existence of Germany's social institutions—not that it was fond of them, but rather that it did not know how to replace these institutions. The Social Democrats were a party of reform, not of revolution. Their new Chancellor was Friedrich Ebert, a decent, hardworking, and practical man nearing the age of fifty. He and his colleagues knew of the course of events in Russia and they were determined to prevent such an occurrence in Germany. Opposition to the Social Democrats came from the left wing socialists, or Spartacists, under the leadership of Karl Liebknecht and Rosa Luxemburg, who desired a revolution based upon the bolshevik model. The Spartacists controlled many of the larger cities, having driven the police underground, and leaving the ruling Social Democrats without means of self-defense.

Under such circumstances the role of the military establishment would prove to be of major importance. Germany's junior service, the Imperial Navy, had already voted with its feet, joining the Spartacist camp following its mutiny in Kiel in early November. Sailors of the Peoples Marine Division constituted one of the chief radical military formations. The German Army remained under the command of its Chief of Staff, Field Marshal Paul von Hindenburg, with his headquarters in Spa. The actual center of power within the General Staff, however, resided in the office of von Hindeburg's deputy, the First Quartermaster. This post had been held by General Erich Lundendorff until October 26, 1918, when von Hindenburg relieved him of office as a result of Ludendorff's emotional exhaustion. Von Hindenburg received the names of five generals qualified for the position from the Central Branch of the General Staff. The Field Marshal selected General Wilhelm Groener, an intelligent and able staff officer from Württemberg, whose democratic sympathies made him more suited for the times than a number of his Prussian colleagues.[1]

On the evening of November 9, 1918, Chancellor Ebert reached an agreement with the Army High Command. In a telephone conversation with General Groener, Ebert promised to assist the army in its withdrawal to Germany and to help combat the spread of bolshevism. In return Groener agreed to attempt to bring the field army back to Germany in proper order and discipline.[2]

A number of historians (John W. Wheeler-Bennett[3] for one) maintain that from his supposedly sinister act the fate of the Weimar Republic was sealed. Yet on that November day the decision contained a certain logic and was in the interest of both the Social Democratic Party and the Army High Command. Neither party wished to see a real revolution on the bolshevik model and both desired the maintenance of order. The officer corps had owed its allegiance to its king and emperor; now that the monarchy was gone, to whom did it own its allegiance? The Army High command decided that its allegiance belonged to the government in Berlin, and that meant Ebert's Social Democrats. The gentlemen of the General Staff had had personal dealings with the Social Democratic leadership during the war and in the course of parliamentary hearings and other business. They knew that the Social Democrats were not devils. Social Democrats were not the sort of people a Prussian officer would choose to associate with; nevertheless, they were people with whom one could do business. In addition, neither side wished to see the German Army return undisciplined and carrying red flags.[4]

The final act of the Prussian General Staff was the organization, planning, and execution of the withdrawal of the German Army from foreign territory. The army's combat units were relatively unaffected by left-wing unrest, but the *Etappe*, or rear area troops, had already formed Soldiers Councils and posed a threat to the retreating forces. Nevertheless, the Army High Command succeeded in restoring discipline on the march back to Germany. Upon being confronted by delegates of the Soldiers Councils, staff officers would present a copy of a letter from Chancellor Ebert requesting compliance with traditional military order in the interest of the fledgling democracy. Often delegates received copies of allied threats regarding any possible German noncompliance with withdrawal procedures and timetables. The end result was that the delegates themselves often requested the troops to maintain order and discipline. Thus, when the German Army crossed over the Rhine bridges at Köln, Mainz, and Koblenz, it was indeed *in Ordung* with colors flying. This final success, however, created two new problems. It was well and good that the army marched back in such fine fashion; but memory of such orderliness would later reinforce the notion that the army had not been beaten on the field of battle but rather betrayed by traitors in the rear areas. The second problem was that although the army returned in good order, it was an instrument of questionable value. The war had been long and costly and many soldiers took the first opportunity to return to their homes and civilian life, even if that meant desertion. In short, the Ebert government still found itself surrounded by enemies and without effective military support.[5]

The relationship between Ebert and the Army High Command was not an easy one, for each party found it difficult to live up to its agreement. On December 1, the congress of Frontline Soldiers meeting at Ems denounced the army's efforts to restore discipline and demanded immediate demobilization. Several days later the first returned army units reached Berlin, a force of nine divisions under the command of General Arnold Lequis which included elements of the Prussian Guards. Many of the troops were born and raised in the area and took the first opportunity to desert, within days reducing Lequis' force to a palry 800 men. And on December 12, Ebert's cabinet under pressure from the left promulgated a decree for the creation of an 11,000 man National Guard which would stand outside the jurisdiction of the army. The situation deteriorated even further when on December 23, 1918, the Peoples Naval Divison, which had lingered about Berlin for some time, revolted against the Ebert regime and surrounded the Chancellory. On Christmas eve General Lequis' small force attempted to surprise the insurgent force and actually penetrated as far as the latter's headquarters in the formal Imperial Stables. There they were overwhelmed by the radicals after a two-hour fight. No additional army units could reach Berlin quickly, and it had become apparent that the returning army units were of dubious value.[6]

In this crisis, the Ebert government gained a reprieve only through the inactivity of its opponents, who immediately began to argue among themselves. Already in December a number of officers had begun to form volunteer military organizations to combat the spread of what they considered to be "anarchy." Originally suggested by von Hindeburg, these formations drew an odd assortment of adherents: former officers, students, professional men, adventurers, but mostly soldiers. Realizing the unreliability of the army, the High Command chose to support these volunteer units, the *Freikorps*, and named General Walther von Lüttwitz commander of the *Freikorps* in the Berlin area. Chancellor Ebert also took the opportunity to bring Gustav Noske from Kiel to Berlin to assume the functions of Minister of Defense. Noske was a former woodcutter and editor of a Social Democratic newspaper who had successfully quelled the sailors' disturbance at Kiel. He was a hard-nosed realist, a former noncommissioned officer, and a man of intelligence who gained the respect of his military counterparts. So as the radical left squabbled, the Social Democrats marshalled their forces and prepared for the next onslaught.[7]

When the Spartacists, or Communists as they now called themselves, rose against the Ebert government in January, Noske and the *Freikorps* were prepared. In the following six months in battles across the breadth of Germany, the *Freikorps* triumphed over the

Spartacists. It was a victory for the old army, whose officers, noncommissioned officers, and men filled the ranks of the *Freikorps*. There still remains the question, however, of why the Social Democrats did not attempt to create and utilize their own, democratically based, military formations. Ebert and Noske ignored this possibility and chose rather to use the *Freikorps*, which were certainly more efficient than any other military formations in Germany, but which would do little to encourage the development of a more democratic military system. In all probability Ebert chose the *Freikorps* in an attempt to adhere to his agreement with General Groener of November 9th, and in his desire to obtain the most effective military units.[8]

The end result was predictable. Following the January 1919 elections the National Assembly authorized the future German Army, or *Reichsheer*, to be formed from the existing *Freikorps*. How then would the *Reichsheer* differ from the old army? Was not the *Reichsheer* simply the old army with a new name? The same men, the same traditions, doctrines, and organization? The answer is not an easy one, for the army did undergo a number of significant reforms. The Constitution of the Weimar Republic required its soldiers to swear an oath of allegiance to the republic. It also stipulated that the military would be responsible to civilian authorities, the President of the Republic and the Minister of Defense. Soldiers would henceforth (except during wartime) be subject to civil rather than military law, and "Courts of Honor" were finally eliminated. There would no longer be Prussian, Saxon, Bavarian, and Württembergian Armies, but rather one German Army under the direction of a Ministry of Defense in Berlin. In addition, on January 19, 1919, the army abolished officer epaulettes, the long hated symbol of military authority.[9]

In spite of these reforms the *Reichsheer* remained a miniature Imperial Army. It wore the same gray uniforms, lived in the same barracks, and carried the same equipment as the former Imperial Army. More importantly, the army abolished Soldiers' Councils, returning undiminished authority to the officer corps; and entrance into the officer corps itself would be determined by its regimental commanders.[10] The *Reichsheer* would be led by officers of the former Imperial Army. At the request of the Army High Command in February 1919, one of the army's ablest staff officers, General Hans von Seeckt, designed a reorganization plan for the new army. He foresaw the *Reichsheer* consisting of only 200,000 men serving for a period of two years and backed up by a militia based upon a three-month training period.[11]

General von Seeckt has been widely credited as the creator of the *Reichsheer*. But the Weimar Republic's army was also a creation of David Lloyd George, Marshall Ferdinand Foch, and Georges Clemenceau, who in early 1919 dictated the size, organization, and armament of the future German Army at the Paris Peace Conference. The victorious Allies agreed that their main task was to insure that the German Army be incapable of threatening European security again. How this was to be accomplished, however, proved to be no easy question to solve. Marshal Foch wished the German Army to be a militia composed of volunteers serving for a period of from six months to one year. The English maintained that Germany should possess an army like their own, small and professional. Foch strongly objected to the English position, emphasizing that such a force would soon become a "citadel of Prussiandom." Ultimately, they settled upon a compromise. The *Reichsheer* would consist of a professional army, but one of only 100,000 men, of whom 4,000 would be officers (half the force Foch suggested). This force would be organized in seven infantry and three cavalry divisions, with no more than two corps headquarters staffs. Soldiers would enlist for a period of twelve years, while officers would serve for twenty-five. The General Staff, War Academy, and cadet schools were to be abolished. Conscription was prohibited. The army was not allowed to manufacture or purchase tanks, aircraft, heavy artillery, and other modern weapons. And to insure that Germany conformed to these stipulations, the Allies created a commission to observe the German military.[12]

The Treaty of Versailles succeeded in reducing Germany to the status of second-rate military power. Besides reducing the army to a mere 100,000 men Germany also lost 14 percent of its territory, almost all of its navy, and its overseas colonies. An allied occupation force established bridgeheads over the Rhine River and the Rhineland itself became demilitarized. The dissolution of the Austro-Hungarian Empire created a number of independent nation-states in Central and Eastern Europe. Two of these, Poland and Czechoslovakia, occupied salients on Germany's southern and eastern borders and soon became client states of France. Poland posed a particular concern, for the newly created Polish corridor, giving Poland access to the seaport of Danzig, isolated the German province of East Prussia. In the event of war, Germany would have to expect to lose quickly its industrial centers, nearly all of which were situated in threatened border areas.[13]

In March 1920, the Minister of Defense and Chief of the Army

Command resigned following the abortive Kapp *Putsch*. Otto Gessler became the Minister of Defense, but the man who would mold and shape the new German Army was General Hans von Seeckt, the new Chief of Army Command (*Chef der Heeresleitung*). Von Seeckt was born in Schleswig in 1866, although his family came from Pomerania. He did not attend a cadet school (attending a cadet school was *de rigueur* for a career in the Prussian Army), but instead attended a secondary school in Strasbourg. He entered his father's regiment (Emperor Alexander 1st Prussian Guard Grenadier Regiment) in 1886 and received his general staff training at the age of thirty-three. Von Seeckt was a thinking man's soldier. The English Ambassador to Berlin, Lord D'Abernon, went so far as to remark that von Seeckt's enemies believed him to be too intelligent to be a general. D'Abernon also observed that von Seeckt's emaciated and austere appearance camouflaged an "honorable and punctilious gentleman."[14] He was also egotistical, ambitious, and a very difficult superior officer. Von Seeckt possessed an unusual and enigmatic personality, marked by a profound reticence which obscured his true thoughts and feelings behind a sphinx-like face and a wall of silence. He rapidly gained the reputation as one of the finest minds in the German Army during Wor!d War I, directing German arms to victory at Soissons, Gorlice, and Riga.[15]

Von Seeckt learned of the Kaiser's abdication while returning to Germany from Turkey, where he had served as a military advisor. The news reduced him to tears. He never fully reconciled himself to the Weimar Republic, treating it as a temporary misfortune. Nevertheless, he devoted his full energy and considerable talent to the creation of a reliable military force and a more secure Germany. The general isolated the *Reichsheer* from all outside influences, including the influence of his civilian employers. Not only did the army not allow officers to participate in politics, but officers were prohibited from membership in social organizations. Any hope of creating a more democratically based army ended with the arrival of Hans von Seeckt as Chief of the Army Command, for he created a miniature Imperial Army while attempting to evade the restrictions of the Versailles Treaty. Von Seeekt retained as many General Staff officers as possible and used the *Truppenamt* (Troop Office) to assume the duties of the outlawed General Staff. With the abolition of the War Academy, the military district (*Wehrkreise*) headquarters assumed the duties of selecting and training talented young officers for the

General Staff.[16] Von Seeckt followed the advice of General Bernhard von Lossberg to maintain the traditions of the Prussian, Bavarian, Saxon, and Württembergian Armies. Each *Reichsheer* unit became the heir to the traditions, honors, and history of an Imperial Army unit. The 9th Infantry Regiment from the Berlin area, for example, assumed the heritage of the Prussian Guards.[17] Contrary to these appearances, however, the German Army leadership did not complacently seek to create a small Imperial Army or to live in the past, but rather began a period of intense and critical self-examination. We have seen how von Seeckt in February 1919, proposed forming a 200,000 man army based upon a two-year enlistment. This proposal reflected von Seeckt's distrust for a mass army and a preference for a small professional force. There were generals who maintained the accepted tenets of World War I, that victory could only be secured by overwhelming firepower and "the nation in arms." Von Seeckt's predecessor as *Chef der Heeresleitung*, General Walther Reinhardt, operating upon these presuppositions, concluded that the age of strategic mobility had passed.[18]

Lessons of the Great War

Von Seeckt and the remains of the General Staff faced the task of evaluating the army's defeat in World War I, while at the same time creating a doctrine suitable for a small professional army. World War I had forced the German Army to undertake numerous changes in doctrine, tactics, clothing, weaponry, and discipline. The General Staff now had to evaluate those changes and select which to maintain and which to discard. Von Seeckt rejected the concept of positional warfare, describing trench warfare as "the opposite of real war."[19] He desired a return to the concept of maneuver leading to the battle of annihilation, harkening back to the ideas of Frederick the Great, the Elder Moltke, and von Schlieffen.[20]

Since the age of Napoleon the basic tactical military formation of European armies had been the corps, which consisted of from two to five divisions, in addition to cavalry, artillery, engineer, and (later) signal troops. The German Army of 1914 possessed twenty-five corps of regular army troops and thirteen corps of trained reservists. The corps possessed the traditional "square" organization, with two infantry divisions, each consisting of two infantry brigades, and each brigade possessing two infantry regiments.[21] This form of organization proved successful in the army's rapid advance through Belgium and northern France, in spite of the revelation of increased firepower and the resultant high casualties. German organization and tactics suffered later in 1915, however, when Generai Erich von Falkenhayn, the new Chief of the General Staff, ordered the western forces into trenches. German corps and divisional commanders on the West Front soon adopted the practice of placing two of their major formations in the front line and the remaining two formations in reserve. Massive artillery bombardments preceded attacks, the bombardments occasionally lasting for days. The defender, fully alerted to the threat by the artillery preparation, countered by massing his own reserves of men and artillery. The final result was organized slaughter without the possibility of victory. The artillery bombardment created massive casualties among the men in the trenches, but even the heaviest shelling could not eliminate all opposition. As long as the defender possessed his own artillery and reserves in the rear areas and several machine guns at the front remained in operation, the attacker could not gain a decisive victory. Trenches exchanged hands, the front would occasionally shift several hundred yards, casualties mounted.[22]

Military historians acknowledge little or no change in allied or central power military doctrine until 1917, following the replacement of von Falkenhayn by von Hindenburg and Ludendorff. The accepted thesis states that Ludendorff in 1917 instituted the use of defense in depth. This was facilitated earlier in 1915 when von Falkenhayn began a reorganization of the army by placing a greater emphasis upon the infantry division rather than the corps, and by adopting a "triangular" organization for the infantry division. In addition, the army bolstered the firepower of its battalions with the addition of a machine gun company and trench mortars.[23] The triangular organization reduced the number of infantry regiments from four to three, eliminating brigades, thereby reducing the number of men in the division. This proved to be advantageous, because, ironically, the more men in a unit, the denser the formation, and therefore the more casualties received from artillery barrages and machine gunfire. Ludendorff carried the idea to its logical conclusion, reducing the number of men in the trenches and echeloning them in a checkerboard formation behind the front line. Again, the traditional account explains that the German defensive successes of 1917 in the West convinced the Aliies of the wisdom of the defense in depth, resulting in their utilization of the doctrine in 1918. Then genius entered the picture in the form of General Oskar von Hutier.[24]

According to the accepted thesis, General von Hutier invented a new tactical innovation at the Battle of Riga in 1917 on the Eastern Front. Ludendorff then brought von Hutier and his new tactics west for the great Spring offensive, which came so close to knocking the Allies out of the war. The key ingredients to the new tactics were surprise, a massive but short artillery barrage, and infantry infiltration through and around enemy strong points. In June 1918, one Paris magazine proclaimed Oskar von Hutier, "Germany's new strategic genius."[25] In 1920 a distinguished French military thinker modified the explanation of "Hutier Tactics" claiming that von Hutier was aided by his brilliant artillery commander, Colonel Georg Bruchmiller.[26] The result was the tacit recognition in France, England, and the United States by established military historians that von Hutier revolutionized warfare through his tactical innovations. And in 1940 in his book *Blitzkrieg*, S. L. A. Marshall hailed von Hutier as the father of the Blitzkrieg.[27]

Oskar von Hutier was a very talented general whose victories led Kaiser Wilhelm to award him the coveted *Pour le Mérite*. Nevertheless, he did not create a new tactical system. How he came to be selected as the Great War's tactical genius remains open to conjecture. German military literature and documents reveal von Hutier to be a capable general, a cousin of Ludendorff, but no tactical innovator.[28] In all probability the new German tactics resulted from a gradual evolution. What we do know for certain was that by late 1916 both the Allies and Central Powers had suffered severe losses and consequently had difficulty in maintaining the authorized strength of their divisions. In an attempt to minimize losses Ludendorff in 1917 began to experiment with varied defensive alignments. His memoirs make no indication of his use of defense in depth and give the impression that the German Army had not yet attained a suitable method of defense.[29] Nevertheless, army regulations of March 1917 specifically stated the necessity of defending a position in depth.[30] As early as April 1916, the German 2nd Army directed its forces to deploy machine guns in depth behind the front line, so the idea was not entirely new.[31]

The German method of attack in 1918 also had its origins in previous experience. Ironically, it was at the battle of Verdun in 1916 that the first significant steps were taken to escape the infantry malaise of trench warfare. Under the command of Crown Prince Wilhelm special assault groups withdrew for refitting behind the front, where they undertook detailed rehearsals of their attacks. The success of this measure led the General Staff to authorize publication of Captain Cordt von Brandis' *Der Sturmangriff* in 1917.[32] The Crown Prince's forces retained these methods and improved upon them during the defensive fighting in 1917. Following the French failure on the Aisne, the German XI Corps faced the task of launching several limited counterattacks to improve its situation. In a series of minor operations in May and June it largely succeeded in creating what has come to be known as "Hutier Tactics." The attacks were methodically prepared and rehearsed beforehand; then special assault troops (*Stossruppen*) drove secretly at night to assembly areas, from where they walked to the front line. The artillery preparation was heavy, but of short duration, with gas shells fired against enemy artillery positions. Timing was critical, and the *Stosstruppen* aimed and often succeeded in entering the enemy positions as the last artillery shell detonated. When executed correctly, the attack surprised the enemy, rendered enemy artillery inoperative until the poison gas blew away, and the *Stosstuppen* assaulted the enemy infantry before the latter could leave their dugouts. The assault force, carrying its own machine guns, then deployed in depth to repel the inevitable enemy counterattack.[33]

Ludendorff issued the army new regulations for offensive action in early January 1918. He included the innovations of the XI Corps without significant changes, mentioning the unit by name in the regulations. Ludendorff added several other measures, the most important of which was the idea that infantry must continue to advance into the enemy's rear, leaving the task of reducing bypassed enemy strong points to the second or third attack wave. German infantry regiments would hereafter possess their own cannon company, whose task it was to accompany the infantry and destroy nests of enemy resistance with direct fire. Engineers, usually equipped with flame throwers and explosives, would also support the attacking infantry along with additional signal troops, liaison officers, runners, and orderlies. Through these measures Ludendorff hoped not only to win a decisive victory over the French and English, but to abandon trench warfare and return to a war of movement.[34]

The German offensives in France of 1918 exhausted Germany's remaining war potential and, coupled with the collapse of the Austro-Hungarian Army, ensured a rapid end to hostilities. Ludendorff's last offensives had ended as a dismal strategic defeat, but ironically they succeeded in recreating a war of movement. The French and English, like Ludendorff, had also reexamined their military experiences. When the German Marne offensive spent itself, massed French tanks counterattacked the German flank without an artillery barrage. The German Army reeled backwards. By August the understrength and worn-out German divisions along the Western Front faced a numerically superior enemy utilizing surprise and supported by tanks and air superiority.[35]

Writing shortly after the conclusion of hostilities, Basil H. Liddell-Hart, the noted English military critic, observed that although the tactics of 1918, used first by Ludendorff and later by the Allies, were a major improvement in tactical doctrine, they were still insufficient to penetrate a modern defense in depth. He concluded that what was lacking in the 1918 tactics were the weapons to exploit the rupture of the enemy's line. His friend and colleague, General J. F. C. Fuller soon convinced him that the required weapon already existed, the lowly tank, that with its continued development it would dominate the world's future battlefields.[36]

Through the 1920s and 1930s Fuller and Liddell-Hart fought a running battle over the role of the tank with England's military establishment. Fuller, the more radical of the two, soon alienated many of his colleagues with his notion that the tank would and should replace the horse in the army. A similar but far less acrimonious debate occurred within the French Army. How could such a debate transpire within the German Army, which was prohibited from possessing tanks? Why would a police force need to discuss the role of tanks and aircraft?[37]

NOTES

1. F. L. Carsten, *The Reichswehr and Politics 1918 to 1933* (Oxford: Clarendon Press, 1966), pp. 3–10; and Waldemar Erfurth, *Die Geschichte des deutschen Generalstabes 1918–1945* (Göttingen: Musterschmidt Verlag, 1957), pp. 13–15.

2. Erich Otto Volksmann, *Revolution über Deutschland* (Oldenburg: Stalling, 1930), p. 68.

3. John W. Wheeler-Bennett, *The Nemesis of Power: The German Army in Politics, 1918–1945* (London: Macmillan & Co., 1953), p. 21.

4. See Gordon A. Craig, *The Politics of the Prussian Army 1640–1945* (New York: Oxford University Press, 1968), pp. 342–360; and

Golo Mann, *The History of Germany since 1789* (New York: Praeger, 1968), trans. by Marian Jackson, pp. 330–341.

5. Erfurth, *Geschichte des deutschen Generalstabes*, pp. 17–21.

6. Erfurth, *op. cit.*, pp. 21–25; and Craig, *op. cit.*, 347–354. It is no longer possible to determine the numerical strength of von Lequis' force of nine divisions or to trace the rapidity of its troops leaving the service.

7. Carsten, *op. cit.*, pp. 12–24.

8. Ibid., pp. 22-25.

9. Craig, *op. cit.*, pp. 360–364.

10. Carsten, *op. cit.*, pp. 23–34.

11. Friedrich von Rabenau, *Seeckt aus Seinem Leben 1918–1936* (Leipzig: Hase & Koehler, 1940), p. 147.

12. Erfurth, *op. cit.*, pp. 38–39; *Traiteé de Paix entre les Puissances alliées et Associées et l'Allemagne et Protocole Signés à Versailles, le juin 1919*, Articles 160, 164, 170, 171, 174–178, 180, 181, 183, and 191–198, pp. 77–96; David Lloyd George, *Memoirs of the Peace Conference*, Vol. I (New York: Howard Fertig, 1972), pp. 389–402; and Walter Goerlitz, *History of the German General Staff,*. translated by Brian Battershaw (New York: Frederick A. Praeger, 1953), pp. 214–216.

13. Burkhard Müller-Hillebrand, *Das Heer 1933–1945, Entwicklung des organisatorischen Aufbaues*, Vol. 1 (Darmstadt: E. S. Mittler & Sohn, 1954), pp. 15–17.

14. Lord D'Abernon, *An Ambassador of Peace: Lord D'Abernon's Diary*, Vol. II (London: Hodder and Stoughton, 1929), p. 271.

15. Hans von Seeckt, *Aus meinem, Leben 1866–1917* (Leipzig: Hase & Koehler, 1938); von Rabenau, *op.cit.*, pp. 114–203; and Carsten, *op. cit.*, pp. 103–140.

16. Carsten, *op. cit.*, pp. 103–124; and Goerlitz, *op. cit.*, pp. 222–228.

17. National Archives, Papers of Hans von Seeckt, Microcopy M-132, *Abschrift* from General von Lossberg to von Seeckt of September 30, 1919, *Stück*, 130.

18. Walter Reinhardt, *Wehrkraft und Wehrwille* (Berlin: E. S. Mittler & Sohn, 1932), pp. 170–175.

19. Hans von Seeckt, *Thoughts of a Soldier*, trans. by Gilbert Waterhouse (London: Ernest Benn Ltd., 1930), p. 84.

20. Ibid., p. 62.

21. Each regiment possessed three battalions and one machine gun company. Divisional units included one *Jäger* battalion (with infantry, machine gun, and bicycle companies), a cavalry regiment containing two to four squadrons, and an artillery brigade of two artillery regiments (each regiment consisting of six batteries of cannons and/or field howitzers). German Reichsarchiv, *Der Weltkrieg 1914 bis 1918, Kriegswirtschaft*, Vol. 1 (Berlin: E. S. Mittler & Sohn, 1930), pp. 9–22, 211–213, and table 18.

22. "Die Entwicklung der deutschen Infanterie im Weltkrieg 1914–1917," compiled by the Seventh Branch of the Army General Staff, *Militärwissenschaftliche Rundschau, dritte Jahrgang* (Berlin: E. S. Mittler & Sohn, 1938), pp. 367–419.

23. German Reicharchiv, *Der Weltkreig*, Vol. VII, *Die Operationen des Jahres 1915*, p. 303; see also Goerlitz, *op. cit.*, p. 169.

24. Hubert Essame, *The Battle for Europe 1918* (New York: Charles Scribner's Sons, 1972), pp. 17–51. In particular, see Timothy T. Lupfer, *The Dynamics of Doctrine: The Changes in German Tactical Doctrine during the First World War*, Leavenworth Papers No. 4 (Fort Leavenworth, Kansas: U. S. Army Command and General Staff College, 1918).

25. "Comment attaquent les allemands: la manoevre de von Hutier (March 21–April 5, 1918)," *L'Illustration*, Paris, June 1, 1918, pp. 534–537.

26. Laszlo M. Alfoldi, "The Hutier Legend," *Perameters Journal of the U. S. Army War College*, Vol. V, no. 2, 1976, pp. 69–74. Few data have survived regarding Colonel Bruchmuüller, other than the facts that he was born on December 11, 1863, and died on February 26, 1948. A brilliant gunner, he received the oak leaves to the *Pour le Mérite* from the Kaiser. Evidence suggests he was a Prussian.

27. S. L. A. Marshall, *Blitzkrieg: Its History, Strategy, and Challenge to America* (New York: W. Morrow & Co., 1940), pp. 85–87.

28. Alvoldi, "The Hutier Legent," pp. 69–74.

29. Erich von Ludendorff, *Ludendorff's Own Story, August 1915–November 1918*, Vol. II (New York: Harper & Bros., Publs., 1919), pp. 163–174.

30. National Archives, Record Group 120, American Expeditionary Force, AEF General Headquarters G-2, A-2, Translations, Entry 86, Box No. 5236, Manual of Position Warfare for All Arms Part 8, of March 1, 1917, p. 607; and Lupfer, *op. cit.*

31. National Archives, same series Box 5367, Armee-Oberkom-

mando 2, 1a, No. 189 geh. v. 18.4.16, signed by von Below (presumably Fritz von Below).

32. Cordt von Brandis, *Der Sturmangriff Kriegserfahrungen eines Frontoffziers* (Berlin: Chef des Generalstabaes, 15 September 1917).

33. National Archives, Record Group 120, American expeditionary Force, AEF General Headquarters G-2, A-2, translations, Entry 86, Box No. 5230, No. 219. Accounts of minor offensive operations carried out by the Vailly Group (XI Corps) during May and June 1917, introduction by Ludendorff.

34. National Archives, same series, Box 5236, Manual of Position Warfare for all Arms, Part 14, The Attack in Position Wafare, 1 January 1918; and *Der Weltkrief*, Vol. XIV, *Die Kriegführung an der Westfront in Jahre 1918*, pp. 40–50.

35. Essame, *op. cit.*

36. Basil H. Liddel-Hart, *The Liddel Hart Memoirs 1895–1938*, Vol. I (New York: G. P. Putnam's Sons, 1965), pp. 43–44.

37. Ibid., pp. 65–156; and John F. C. Fuller, *Tanks in the General War, 1914–1918* (New York: E. P. Dutton and Company, 1920).

About the Author

S. J. Lewis was born in Stockton, California, on October 15, 1948. He received his A.B. and M.A. degrees in history from San Jose State University. He studied modern European history at the University of California, Santa Barbara, where he received his Ph.D. in 1983. A career civil servant, Dr. Lewis has served as an archivist at the National Archives and as an historian at McClellan Air Force Base and at the U. S. Army John F. Kennedy Special Warfare Center at Fort Bragg, North Carolina. He is currently affiliated with the Combat Studies Institute of the U. S. Army Command and General Staff College. Dr. Lewis is the author of *Forgotten Legions: German Army Infantry Policy, 1918–1941* (New York: Praeger, 1985) and *Jedburgh Operations in Support of the 12th Army Group, August 1944* (Leavenworth, KS: 1991), USACGSC.

PARTISAN WARFARE 1845
ULRICH OCHSENBEIN AND THE RAID ON LUCERNE

Joachim Remak

The year 1848 arrived ahead of schedule in two of the nations of Europe. One was Poland, and what happened there in 1846 and after is fairly well known. The other was Switzerland, and events here have received next to no attention in the English-speaking world. Yet what took place in Switzerland between 1845 and 1847 offered much of a preview of what was to come on the rest of the continent.

As the President of the Diet, Switzerland's highest political authority, put it in the summer of 1847, a battle was going on in his country "between progress and stability," a battle between the advocates of "a new intellectual order" promoting freedom in all areas of life, and "the mummy-like social institutions that are part of long-gone views, concepts, and realities."[1]

After paying tribute to "Helvetia's sister, the Republic of Cracow, whose independence has been trampled underfoot . . . and destroyed counter to all international law,"[2] he predicted that the end of the story still remained to be told, and that the confrontation between opposing forces was as active as ever. And in that confrontation, he said, "the picture which Europe presents on a large scale finds its counterpart on a smaller one in our fatherland."[3]

The Background: 1815 And The Triumph of States' Rights

The background against which he spoke was this: Switzerland, in the first half of the nineteenth century was far from being the peaceable, sensible polity that would later make it the envy of many other states. Its problems, rather, were many. The most crucial perhaps was the weakness of its central government. Its basic constitution—the so-called Federal Treaty concluded between the cantons in 1815 after Napoleon's earlier intervention in Swiss affairs was safely past—provided for only the loosest association between the cantons. It made Switzerland, in the all to accurate words of a contemporary scholar, scarcely more than an alliance, and a weak one at that, "of largely independent rural republics and city states."[4]

All received an equal voice in the Federal Diet, whether it was Uri with its population of 12,000 or Bern with its 300,000. And quite accurately, the Diet's members carried the title of envoy, not of deputy or representative, for envoys they were, representing their sovereign cantons, with their vote determined by the instructions received from their respective cantonal capitals.

Yet the Diet, for all its limitations, provided one of the very few joint institutions created in 1815. Thus, there was no common monetary system; coinage, Baedeker advised its readers, was "in very poor shape; it would be in vain to go into detail about the different currencies of the different cantons."[5] Nor was there a common trading area; instead, each canton was at liberty to impose its own internal duties and other restrictions on the movement of goods and services, a right of which most of them made liberal use. There was in fact not even a common postal system, so that, in the eighteen-thirties, it cost more to mail a letter from Geneva to Appenzell than from Geneva to Constantinople.

What best summed it all up perhaps was that the negotiators of the Federal Treaty of 1815 had not been able to agree on a permanent capital for the country. Instead, they compromised by deciding that the federal capital was to shift every two years between the three cantons of Bern, Lucerne, and Zürich. Each of them was to rotate in hosting the Diet for that two-year term, during which time it would act as *Vorort,* or presiding city. Switzerland thus was the only country in Europe which even avoided the word capital.

Subsequent years saw many an effort to correct the obvious short-comings of the 1815 arrangement. None were successful; opposition to change was too ingrained. As was the case elsewhere on the continent too, the modernizers were facing some very determined defenders of the status quo, believers in the ancient verities who were unwilling to barter away traditional rights and customs for the promised blessings of a supposedly more effective new order of things.

What exacerbated the conflict was that it involved a struggle between country and city, and between uncompromisingly Catholic cantons and Protestant or at least less conservatively Catholic ones. It was an argument that might have gone on for years without coming close to any resolution had it not been for an issue that triggered it in the early eighteen-forties. That issue was the recall of the members of the Society of Jesus to Lucerne.

"Look, They Are Riding Upon Snakes": The Jesuits Re-Enter Lucerne

The Jesuits had been banned from Lucerne as they had been from most of the regions of Europe during the preceding century. But there were those who now thought of them as "the radical cure for modernism," and after some years of acrimonious debate they succeeded, in 1844, in having a group of Jesuits invited to Lucerne to run a substantial part of the canton's educational system.

The reaction was furious and immediate. Rightly or wrongly, few groups were as thoroughly disliked in nineteenth century Europe as were the members of the Society of Jesus, and Switzerland was no exception. It certainly was a problem of which the Jesuits themselves were well aware. The Swiss Provincial had counseled against a return to Lucerne "under present circumstances," and the General of the Order in Rome told associates that he wished that the issue which was being discussed *sans nous*.

How right he was was shown by the polemics that followed. The Jesuits, wrote the normally temperate Jacob Burckhardt during the debate over the recall, "appeared to be a plague on those nations and individuals that fall under their power."[8] And that was the language of restraint compared to the articles, poems, and broadsides that followed.

> Damned corrupters of men's minds
> Falsehood's satanic teachers
> Reason's sinister enemy
> From the gild of hocus-pocus[9]

began one such anonymous poem. Another, which was fully signed, was written by Switzerland's most prominent nineteenth century author, Gottfried Keller. Just two stanzas may suffice to convey the tone of his "Jesuit Parade," a long poetic diatribe that became popular enough to invite countless imitations. They went:

> Look they are riding upon snakes
> Followed by those on dragons and pigs
> Oh what jolly fellows they are
> Though the child's sore afraid in his mother's womb
> The Jesuits are coming!
>
> Phoo how it crawls and slithers and creeps

> And ugh for that infernal smell
> Gone now is our peaceful rest
> Come, Margaret, close the window please
> The Jesuits are coming![10]

Before long, violent action followed violent language, especially after an effort launched in the Diet to compel the expulsion of the Jesuits had failed. Some of the more determined opponents of the Order decided, early in 1845, that force would have to be applied. Or as the slogan shouted at one of the many public protest meetings put it

> Nix diète
> bayonettes![11]

They hence agreed to launch a great partisan raid on Lucerne and bring down both its Conservative government and the Jesuits with it.

December 1844: The First Partisan Raid

Actually, it was not the first such raid. In December 1844, a group of Lucerne Radicals had attempted an anti-government coup in which they had had the help of armed *Freischärler*, or partisans, from surrounding cantons, especially from Bern and Aargau. But both the incursion into Lucerne and the coup itself suffered from poor preparation. As a result, the enterprise quickly collapsed and many of its participants, rather than being acclaimed as liberators, found themselves in jail or exile.

But this second raid would be different—well equipped, well organized, and well led. If nothing else, the qualities of the man chosen to take charge of the raid would see to that. He was Johann Ulrich Ochsenbein, and he possessed some remarkable qualities indeed.

"The Romantic Chivalry of His Character": Johann Ulrich Ochsenbein

Ulrich Ochsenbein was thirty-three years old at the time, and something of a rising politician. He had worked his way up from poverty to a flourishing law practice in Nidau, a small town not far from Bern. (During the first few years, he spent much of the proceeds from that practice to pay off the one thing he had inherited from his father—his debts.) He had run for office with equal success, becoming President of Nidau's General Assembly at the age of twenty-seven, and going on from there to wider cantonal and national office, first as a member of Bern's governing body, the Great Council, and then as Bern's envoy to the Federal Diet.

His talents showed up equally well in his military career. He had joined a student regiment while still in law school in Bern, where his performance earned him a second lieutenant's commission at twenty-three. Further promotions followed, but the most signal recognition of his talents came in 1842, when he was invited to join the General Staff School in Thun. He was graduated a year later, and in 1844 received his appointment as Captain in the General Staff.

He clearly was helped in this threefold success—in law, in politics, in the military—by his obvious intelligence and drive. Nor did it hurt that he possessed both pleasing looks—he had been called "the handsomest man of his time"[12]—and an easy manner. And what people noted was that behind that easy manner lay a genuine generosity of spirit. One of his most striking traits, noted a contemporary, was "the romantic chivalry of his character,"[13] and one of his sharpest political adversaries paused to laud his "open and noble nature."[14]

The historian Anton von Tillier, who knew him well, perhaps summed it up best. Tillier's usual style runs to something between sober and dry, but in writing about Ochsenbein he for once permitted himself what for him was almost lyrical prose. Ochsenbein's easy manners, he wrote,

> enabled him to cut a fine figure in the higher reaches of society, and it was this same adroitness which—together with a noble and winning character—brought him the applause of the crowd and in particular the favorable interest of the fair sex.[15]

He obviously relished both. But the ambition that drove him was anything but limited to his own person or career. There also was the commitment to serve others; "the romantic chivalry of his character" was no illusion. Found among the papers he left behind was an undated note headed "Ambition," and reading:

> It is my ambition to have contributed more than anyone else toward unifying and strengthening our fatherland, and to make it appear as one to the outside world. That is what I want to achieve, or die.[16]

In 1845, that ambition seemed best served by putting together a force that would invade Lucerne.

A Masterpiece of Strategy": Ochsenbein's Plan of Operations Against Lucerne

He was not the only one to think so. A committee had been formed composed of militant liberals and anti-Jesuits to finance and organize such an incursion.

When the committee invited him to lead it, he readily accepted, even though he felt that he was facing a far from easy task. What particularly concerned him was the contribution to be expected from the Lucerne refugees—the people who had been forced to flee after the December coup, and who now were among the most active of proponents of another *Freischärler* raid. They might be talking a good war, he thought, but he feared that their verbal eagerness for action was not necessarily matched by an equal readiness to fight. Still, he set about preparing for a victorious campaign as well as he could, determined to avoid the amateurishness of the earlier coup.

He did so first by a conscious effort to rally public opinion. Thus, as the new year began, he wrote an open letter to his "dear fellow-citizens" which read in part:

> If ever there was a need for the true friends of our fatherland to avert the danger threatening it from the Society of Jesus it is now. . . .

> The grave question before us is this: Shall we bend like cowards to this yoke, do we want to be robbed by devious means of the work of Luther and Zwingli, and thus submit to the oppressive, sinister rule of papacy and aristocracy?

> No . . .! For as our fathers before us took an oath not to rest until the Austrian overlords had been driven from our beautiful land . . . so we have sworn not to rest, but to risk everything until our beloved Switzerland has been freed from the Jesuits.[17]

Ochsenbein followed this with a plan of attack against Lucerne which indeed had none of the haphazardness of the original *Freischärler* raid. Provided with false identity papers, he first secretly reconnoitered Lucerne and its surrounding countryside. This allowed him to make an appraisal of the opponent's strength, and to draw up what he considered a realistic estimate of the manpower and supplies his own force would need. The next step was to design the actual strategic plan use of force, aided by speed and deception.

He would, as expected, march his men the roughly twelve miles South from Aargau to Lucerne; but would avoid the easy route leading by way of Sursee that Lucerne's defenders might expect him to take. Instead, he would bear slightly East by way of the village of Ettiswil and the river Emme (located in the Emme Valley, or *Emmental*, which has given its name to one of Switzerland's most famous exports). From there, he would move on to Lucerne with the greatest possible dispatch and force the city's surrender.

On paper, it was an excellent plan, which did his general staff training proud. It was, wrote his usually quite critical biographer, "generally recognized as a masterpiece," displaying as it did

> the most basic principles of strategy: the concentration and application of all available force, the use of time, speed and the quick pursuit of the defeated enemy, and finally measures to secure a retreat.[18]

March 31, 1845: The Attack Opens

And initially, the plan worked. On the evening of March 31, 1845, a 450–men strong advance guard of his partisan army, which numbered about 3,500 in all, began its march on the canton of Lucerne. The first village through which it passed, Dagmersellen, surrendered without resistance. In the second, that of Altishoren, the mayor did order the citizens' guard to open fire. But no one was hit; the only consequence was that the mayor and his council found themselves under arrest.

But then both the advance guard and the men who followed it began to sense trouble ahead. The most obvious, perhaps, was that the troops, in their march south, found most or the villages deserted. The few men who remained proved resistant to efforts to recruit them. The tone was set by the response of an old farmer in Castelan who when asked whether he would not like to come along and help liberate Lucerne said: "You go ahead, we'll catch up with you later."[19] (Warfare, regular and irregular, has changed mightily over the years, but it was perhaps the classic response of the reluctant bystander who prefers peace to a cause.)

There were other portents as well. The invasion, it was turning out, was proceeding so smoothly in large part because it had purposely gone unresisted—the commander of Lucerne's forces, General Ludwig von Sonnenberg, had withdrawn many of his troops to the city for its expected defense. Where there *was* resistance, as there was on the bridge across the Emme, it halted the advance. When concentrated enemy fire made the raiders realize how well that bridge was defended, some of the braver among them dove into the river, to make their crossing that way. But a shower or bullets forced them to turn back before they had reached the opposite side. Nor were they helped by the reluctance or the rest of the men to join them in so risky an enterprise.

March 31: "Not As A Conqueror": The Attack Falters

The upshot was that the bridge remained in the defenders' hands. What was more, the encounter demoralized the attackers. For most of them, it had been the first time they had heard shots fired in anger, and experienced the fear and confusion that is likely to follow such an unfriendly act. As a result, many of them were in a mood to forget about their mission and head back to Aargau. "It was not without effort," noted a contemporary chronicler, that their commanding officer, a Major Billo from Bern, "managed to stop those who had begun their rearward movement."[20]

Still, the main part of Ochsenbein's force, by battling their way across another part of the river, managed to reach the outskirts of Lucerne by nightfall of March 31.

The question now arose of what to do next. Some of his officers urged Ochsenbein to press his advantage, and to proceed to an immediate artillery bombardment of Lucerne. Ochsenbein hesitated. One reason he gave was his reluctance to operate in the dark of night with his tired and hungry troops. But an even weightier one, he later explained in his report on the expedition, was that he had

> not advanced on Lucerne as a conqueror, who does not care whether one city or one village more or less is burned to the ground or shot to pieces.

Rather, he had come "to plant the flag of law and humaneness instead of that of despotic force." But one could hardly do that in a burning city. "Howitzer grenades, as everyone knows, contain flammable material . . . and at this time of night, I could not limit their effect." Hence the consequence of a bombardment might well be a great conflagration ruinous to Lucerne, and that, he thought, would have been "a travesty of our purpose."[21]

This was true. It also was Purest Ochsenbein; the concept of "we had to destroy the village in order to save it" was foreign to his way of thinking. Still, it was not the whole truth. For what was to be the next step after he had bombarded his way into the city? During the day's advance, he had become acutely aware of some grave deficiencies in his partisan forces. He did not have the manpower he needed; as he had feared, many of the Lucerne refugees had second thoughts about the enterprise and stayed behind in Aargau. Nor were they the only men missing. As he noted laconically in his report on the raid

> of the six hundred men from Zürich who had promised to occupy the Gislikon bridge, and who had been ordered to advance on Lucerne, I received no news, and could have received none, since they had stayed at home.[22]

And among those who had decided to join him after all, not a few turned out to be spies and agents of Lucerne. Besides, some of his troops now were drunk as well as tired; there had been too many inns along the way. And even without the aid of alcohol, the day's march had displayed a conspicuous lack of discipline. What had contributed to the disaster at the Emme bridge, recalled one of its veterans, was that it seemed as though "everyone preferred discussion to action. Everyone wanted to give orders; no one wanted to follow them."[23]

Nor should that have been surprising perhaps. The expedition, after all, was made up not of regular army troops but of volunteers. No courtsmartial awaited them if they should follow their own drummer, not even if the sound they heard was that of a call to go home.

But no matter what the reasons for Ochsenbein decision, it cost him the advantage of one of his strategy's essential components, that of speed. He had lost momentum, and the campaign with it.

We know now that if he had proceeded with the bombardment, Lucerne might well have surrendered. For on the night of March 31, several Conservative members of Lucerne's government were ready to resign in order to open the way for negotiations with the city's attackers. But Ochsenbein was unaware of that. He had no intelligence to that effect. If any of his Lucerne sympathizers in town had heard about it, they had failed to pass along the information.

April 1, 1845: Lucerne Strikes Back

The next morning, April 1, everything was different. The Council members had a change of heart. They were reassured by the forces Sonnenberg had assembled in the city. They were even more cheered when those troops—augmented by men from the neighboring Catholic cantons of Zug and Uri began their counterattack.

It was a well organized attack; Lucerne had had the advantage of advance warnings about the coming raid. Faced by Sonnenberg's disciplined and strongly armed force, Ochsenbein and his partisans began their retreat. It was a panicky one, and soon turned into a rout. Some of the partisans fleeing Lucerne's forces kept ahead of their pursuers and made it safely back to Aargau and Bern, either in small groups or individually. Others were not so lucky. Occasionally, they would try to counterattack their pursuers. They were outfought every time; the casualties they took changed nothing. And more often, they were set upon by Lucerne's troops.

April 1, 1845: Massacre at Malters

The worst such incident took place at Malters, a small town on the road to Bern. Here government forces surprised a large group of partisans, surrounded them, and opened fire from all sides. Several of the partisans shouted that they were ready to surrender, but whether because of the confusion or the rage of the moment their attackers ignored their pleas. As more partisans and refugees stumbled onto the scene "they were shot without resistance," to quote the contemporary historian Anton von Tillier.

> In wild haste, men and horses, cannons, carts with explosives and supplies fell in heaps, and the frightful nocturnal fight ended with the complete defeat of the partisans.[24]

> They had lost twenty-five dead, Lucerne's forces one. Their wounded numbered thirty, Lucerne's four. The government forces also captured "370 prisoners, eight cannon, a great many other weapons and thirty horses."[25]

But where was Ochsenbein in all this? Only a day before, he had been jubilant. On the march to Lucerne he had turned to a fellow officer riding next to him, Eduard Rothpletz of Aargau, and said,

> Dear Colonel, we've won. You must support me in my command, I am tired and I've shouted myself hoarse; this is the first time I've been in command.[26]

Now he was in flight like everyone else.

He was not giving up without a fight, however. At Littau, close to Lucerne, he joined a partisan attack on government troops, fighting with "a courage that bordered on the foolhardy," as an enemy officer who watched him in action testified.[27] The attack was bloodily repelled; it was as hopeless as the rest would be. Still Ochsenbein did not give up. He led what remained of his column to look for the detachment of Colonel Billo—the commander at the Emme bridge—so that they might join forces. But before he could do so, enemy fire dispersed his group.

April 1–4, 1845: Flight

His force now had dwindled to three, as along with two companions he tried to make his way back to Bern. Since the enemy obviously was on the lookout for him, the group abandoned their horses and proceeded on foot. For two days, they wandered about. Except for some herbs and melted snow, they were without food and drink. They also, since they kept going through the night and were avoiding places where they thought they might be recognized, soon found themselves without clear directions. At one point, they realized in their daze that they had spent hours walking in circles.

They finally reached an isolated farmhouse. His companions walked ahead and asked for shelter. It was a mistake. The residents were furious at the partisans, and took the two men prisoner.

Only Ochsenbein escaped. He had hidden under some straw in a nearby barn, and even managed to catch a few hours' sleep. The next morning, on April 3, he still did not know precisely where he was, but he sensed—rightly so—that he was approaching the Bernese border. Ahead, he could see a few farm houses. He walked up to one of them at random. He had no way of knowing whether he would be any luckier than his two companions had been if he came out in the open. But he also knew that he needed help, and he decided to ask for it.

He did not identify himself, but the elderly farmer who greeted him, Niklaus Zimmerli, had little difficulty recognizing him by his unkempt appearance, and by the saber he was still carrying. "I am not with you," said the farmer, "but I won't betray you. At my neighbor's, you would have been lost. Your people shot his only son."[28]

Zimmerli then made him some soup. It was "spiced with horse grease," and tasted like a feast to Ochsenbein. The following day his host led him across the border. Ochsenbein was safely back at his home in Nidau. Safely, and deeply depressed. He was, he wrote that April 4, physically and morally crushed."[29]

The Aftermath

Yet he was alive, and he was home. By contrast, more than a fourth of his men had remained behind; 104 of them were dead, perhaps twice that number were wounded, and 785 had been taken prisoner. Their treatment was often brutal. Since they were considered to be rebels and law-breakers, they seldom received the protection that regular soldiers might have. A few reportedly were shot out of hand; others were cursed and beaten.

One of the prisoners later confided to a friend what had happened to him after his capture; and many essentially similar stories would be told by others. Four soldiers, he recalled, had taken him to Lucerne

> amidst curses, insults, and invective. "You filthy animal, you traitor, you perjurer; you wanted to steal our religion from us. It'll be a pleasure to put a bullet through your head. . . ."

While they were conversing with me in the another hit me with his gun; one member of my escort then proposed shackling me. But I was too desperate and tired of life by then to let that happen. I tore open my coat and shirt so that my chest lay bare and said, "You have a right to shoot me but not to torment me. Do your duty!" The result was that the sergeant in charge would not let them tie me up. But the result, too, was that my mistreatment got to be twice as rough. The soldier following me from time to time kicked me with his feet and pushed me from behind with his bayonet, accompanying this with the foulest of curses. As a result, I had to jump forward, whereupon the soldier in front of me hit me in the chest with the barrel of his gun. The two walking on either side of me meanwhile pulled me by my hair and ears until I was bleeding; my ears still have not healed.[30]

Anton Wapf, a young militiaman who was among Lucerne's defenders, meanwhile was witnessing some even more pitiless behavior. He recalled how along with some of the other members of his company he was detailed to guard the school house in the village of Neuenkirch.

> It was almost entirely filled with partisans. Sharpshooters of the militia and the reserve led away groups of sixty to

eighty prisoners in pairs. Their hands were tied with ropes, and all were again tied to great carriage ropes. . . ."[31]

Colonel Rothpletz, his beard half torn out, was lying in the firehouse in fetters. North of the main road, at the barn of a locksmith named Widmer, lay nine corpses. Their wounds made it obvious that the barrels of the guns had been placed directly on their bodies at the point of entry, leaving burn marks even on their clothing.[32]

No "Courtesy in Return": The Fate of the Prisoners

Nor did the prisoners who managed to reach Lucerne necessarily find safety, even though the commander or the canton's forces, General von Sonnenberg, on April 2 issued an order of the day reminding his men that "Christian charity demanded the humane treatment even of an enemy," and that it was a soldier's duty "to protect prisoners from any harm."[33]

Yet trouble still awaited many of them, even after the initial anger had spent itself. "Invasions of peaceful regions do not call for courtesy in return,"[33] was the adage that guided Lucerne. Those partisans who were citizens of the canton were tried and sentenced to jail terms, although the majority of them soon were free again under a partial amnesty. Their leader, the popular Dr. Steiger, who had fought alongside Ochsenbein, received the death sentence, however. As for those who did not hold citizenship in Lucerne, they ultimately were released, although only against payment of a ransom, which was put up either by themselves and their families, or by contributions from political sympathizers. But in the meantime, they still were regarded not as captive soldiers but as marauders, and often treated accordingly.

Medical care remained something of a lottery; most of the wounded were adequately treated, but others apparently were allowed to die of neglect. Food and shelter for the bulk of the prisoners were often primitive. Many of them were taken to Lucerne's Jesuit Church, which was made to serve as a temporary holding area. "The first few days were the worst," one of the men recalled.

> Almost nothing to eat, almost no straw, instead cold stone plates. We had to lie beneath the pews, almost like pickled herrings. If anyone raised his head a bit, or talked loudly, the riflemen posted in the gallery . . . would shout the most obscene threats and curses.

Even when we were finally heading for home, we were treated quite barbarously, despite the Fr. 35,000 ransom. No food between eight in the morning when we got some rough oatmeal and late at night. . . . Before every inn we passed a rider was posted who had been dispatched ahead to deny us entry. In Sursee . . . some of the people tried to invite us to a meal, but Colonel Goldlin angrily intervened and declared that if we did not continue on our march that very instant, it was back to Lucerne and to jail![35]

In sum, the second partisan raid had been no more successful than the first. It had merely been more painful.

Aftermath: Civil War

Yet it was not the end of the matter. In the aftermath of the raid, the Catholic-Conservative cantons, fearful of more such attacks, formed a separate alliance, the *Sonderbund*, for their joint protection. This in turn angered the Liberal cantons, who declared that alliance to be in violation of the constitution. In the end, a large-scale civil war had to settle the issue in 1847—in a way that brought victory to thc partisans' cause after all. It was fought in the spirit that Ochsenbein had displayed before Lucerne—with a minimum of destructiveness— and under Ochsenbein's Presidency's; the words opening this chapter are his.

NOTES

1. Enclosure to *Auszug aus dem Abschied der ordentlichen Tagsatzung des Jahres 1847*, I, Litt. B. (hereafter cited as *AT*), p. 1. Federal Archive Bern.

2. Encl. to *AT*, pp. 1–2.

3. Encl. to *AT*, p. 4.

4. Lionel Grossman, "Success Story," *The New York Review of Books* (October 26, 1989), p. 56.

5. *Die Schweiz, Handbuch für Reisende, nach eigener Anschauung und den besten Hüfsquellen bearbeitet* (Koblenz, 1848), p. XII.

6. Quoted in Ferdinand Strobel, *Die Jesuiten in der Schweiz im XIX. Jahrhundert* (Olten, 1954), p. 71.

7. Strobel, p. 100.

8. *Basler Zeitung*, June 30, 1844; cited in Emil Dürr, *Jakob Burckhardt als politischer Publizist* (Zürich, 1937), p. 50.

9. Quoted in Strobel, p. 684.

10. Translated, alas without the rhyme, from "Jesuitenzug" in Gottfried Keller, *Sämtliche Werke*, Jonas Fränkel, ed,, Vol. I (Bern, 1931), 336–337.

11. *Neue Zürcher Zeitung*, 1845, No. 2; quoted in Hans Spreng's doctoral dissertation *Ulrich Ochsenbein, I, Teil, 1811–1848* (Bern, 1918), p. 33.

12. Gallus Jakob Baumgartner, *Die Schweiz in ihren Kämpfen und Umgestaltungen von 1830–1850* (Zürich, 1853–1866), III, 167.

13. Cited in Erwin Bucher, *Die Geschichte des Sonderbundskrieges* (Zürich, 1966), p. 499.

14. Anton Philipp von Segesser, *Sammlung kleiner Schriften*, III (Bern, 1879), p. XV.

15. Anton von Tillier, *Geschichte der Eidgenossenschaft während der Zeit des sogenannten Fortschritts von dem Jahre 1830 bis zur Einführung der Bundesverfassung im Herbste 1848* (Bern, 1854–1855), II, 359.

16. "Nachlass Ulrich Ochsenbein," Staatsarchiv des Kantons Bern. I am particularly indebted to Dr. Peter Martig of the Archive for locating this quotation.

17. *Seeländer Zeitung*, 1845, No. 3; quoted in Spreng, p. 34.

18. Spreng, p. 45.

19. Tillier, II, 251.

20. Tillier, II, 255.

21. Ulrich Ochsenbein, *Zweiter Bericht Ober den Kampf der luzernischen Flüchtlinge und ihrer Freunde am 31.März und 1 April 1845* (Bern, 1845), p. 73.

22. Ochsenbein, *Zweiter Bericht*, p. 93.

23. Bernhard Zeerleder von Steinegg, *Der Freischarenzug gegen Luzern im Jahre 1845 ,Notizen eines Zeitgenossen* (Bern, 1893), p. 53.

24. Tillier, II, 257.

25. Ibid.

26. Zeerleder, *Freischarenzug*, p. 59.

27. Franz von Elgger, *Des Kantons Luzern und sener Bundesgenossen Kampf gegen den Radikalismus von 8. Dezember 1844 bis 24. November 1847 und mein Antheil an demselben* (Schaffhausen, 1850), p. 58.

28. Zeerleder, p. 116.

29. Spreng, p. 83.

30. Leemann, *Der Freischarenzug und das Schicksal der Gefangenen im März und April 1845* (Bern, 1845), p. 118.

31. The officer who had ridden next to Ochsenbein on the advance to Lucerne, and whom Ochsenbein had asked for help since his voice was getting hoarse.

32. Anton Wapf, *Ernste und heitere Bilder aus dem Soldatenleben zur Zeit der Freischarenzüge und des Sonderbundes* (Lucerne, 1878), p. 34.

33. Tillier, II, 261; and see the grateful reference to the order in Leemann, p. 30. And it should in fairness be mentioned that by no means all witnesses agreed that the prisoners were being treated badly, at least once they reached the city. Jacob Burckhardt, who was present, wrote that despite the magnitude of the task facing Lucerne, "the wounded of both sides are being fed equally well, and humanitarians of all parties try to do what they can to ease the prisoners' unfortunate situation." (Dürr, pp. 113–114.)

34. Zeerleder, p. 123.

35. Leemann, p. 135.

CONTRIBUTORS

JELISAVETA ALLEN holds degrees from the University of Belgrade and the Catholic University of America in Washington D.C. For over thirty years she has been affiliated with Dumbarton Oaks where she is the bibliographer in charge of the Dumbarton Oaks Bibliography and numerous other publications. Mrs. Allen is a childhood friend of Professor Djordjević.

NIKOLAY G. ALTANKOV received his Ph.D in history at the with the Special Research Corporation in Santa Barbara. His numerous published works include *The Bulgarian-Americans* (1981), "The Bulgarian Press in the U. S." in *The Immigrant Labor Press, 1840–1970* (1983), and "The Bulgarian Churches in the U. S." in *Bulgaria Past and Present* (1980).

NINA BAKISIAN is currently a fellow of the Institute for Global Conflict and Cooperation, University of California–Santa Barbara. Her research interests focus on self-determination of minorities within the Habsburg Empire. Her article on "Oscar Jaszi in Exile: Danubian Europe Reconsidered" has been accepted for publication in *Culture and Society in 20th Century Hungary*, forthcoming from Westview Press.

CORNELIA BODEA is a senior member of the Nikolai Iorga Institute in Bucharest and is a recently elected member of the Rumanian Academy of Sciences. Dr. Bodea and Hugh Seton-Watson are co-editors of a two-volume work, *Correspondence of Robert R. W. Seton-Watson and the Rumanians, 1906–20.*

LYNN CURTRIGHT received his Ph.D. in history from the University of California–Santa Barbara in 1980. His major publications are *Muddle, Indecision and Setback: British Policy and the Balkan States, August 1914 to the Inception of the Dardanelles Campaign*

(Thessaloniki, 1986), and "Great Britain, the Balkans, and Turkey in the Autumn of 1939," *The International History Review*, X, 3 (August 1988). Dr. Curtright is a member of the history faculty at Tallahassee Commuunity College.

MILORAD M. DRACHKOVITCH is a Senior Fellow at the Hoover Institution of War, Revolution and Peace at Stanford University. He is a historian of political movements in Europe and has published extensively in the United States and abroad.

ALEX N. DRAGNICH received his M.A. and Ph.D. degrees from the University of California at Berkeley. He is professor emeritus of political science, Vanderbilt University. His research interests have focused on comparative politics, especially the major European political system. While he has written on those systems, the majority of his books deal with Serbian and Yugoslav political history. Dr. Dragnich now lives in retirement near Washington, D.C.

STEPHEN FISCHER-GALATI is Distinguished Professor of History, Emeritus, at the University of Colorado and the editor of *East European Quarterly* and *East European Monographs*. Author of numerous books and articles on Eastern European history, he has just completed a new edition of *Twentieth Century Rumania* (Columbia University Press, 1991) and is nearing completion of a book on religion and modernization in the Balkans.

BERND J. FISCHER completed the Ph.D in History at the University of California–Santa Barbara in 1982. In addition to his monograph, *King Zog and the Struggle for Stability in Albania* (1984), he has published numerous articles on Albanian history and has contributed to collective works in that field. Dr. Fischer is currently an Assistant Professor of History at the University of Hartford in Connecticut.

KIMBERLY FRANCEV completed her Ph.D. at the University of California–Santa Barabara in 1988. Her dissertation topic was "France and the Montengrin Government-in-Exile, 1916–1921." She is currently pursuing a law degree.

ELPIDA HADJlDAK earned her B.A. and M.A. degrees in Ancient History and Maritime Archeology from the University of Manchester, England, and her Ph.D in History and Maritime Archaeology from the University of California, Santa Barbara. She is director of ongoing research at the excavation site of a classical Hellenistic era port in the ancient town of Phalasarna in Western Crete. In 1991 she was appointed as the Director of the Department of Maritime Antiquities in the Greek Ministry of Culture.

BARISA KREKIĆ was educated at the University of Belgrade, the Serbian Academy of Sciences (Ph.D.) and at the Sorbonne. Since 1970 he has been a Professor of History at UCLA where he teaches the modern and medieval history of Southeastern Europe, history of Medieval Russia, History of Medieval and Renaissance Dalmatian and Italian cities, and Byzantine History. Dr. Krekić has conducted research and published on late medieval and Renaissance urban history, focusing on the social and cultural history of Dubrovnik.

S. J. LEWIS received his B.A. and M.A. degrees in history from San Jose State University and his Ph.D. from the University of California–Santa Barbara in 1983. A career civil servant, Dr. Lewis has been on the faculty of the U. S. Army command and General Staff College at Fort Leavenworth, Kansas since 1985. He is the author of *Forgotten Legions: German Army Infantry Police 1918–1941* (New York: Praeger, 1985), and *Jedburgh Team Operations in Support of the 12th Army Group, August 1944* (Fort Leavenworth: U. S. Army Command and General Staff College, 1991).

RENI NADEAU earned his bachelor's degree in American History at Stanford University in 1942 and his Ph.D. in European history at the University of California–Santa Barbara in 1987. From 1942–45 he served as an intelligence officer and gunnery officer with the U. S. Air Force in the Mediterranean and European theaters. He has published seven books and contributed to anthologies on Western American History. His work is *Stalin, Churchill and Roosevelt Divide Europe* (Praeger, 1990).

LINDA L. NELSON is presently completing her dissertation on "Nationalism and Gender Identity: The Bulgarian National Revival, Women's Consciousness, Women's Activism." Her other research and publication areas include Yugoslav history, gender studies, and film studies. She is currently on the faculty of the Center for Liberal Studies at Clarkson University, Potsdam, New York.

LJUBICA D. POPOVICH received her diploma from the University of Belgrade and her Ph.D. from Bryn Mawr College. Her research and publications concern Byzantine and Serbian Art. Dr. Popovich is currently an Associate Professor in the Department of Fine Arts at Vanderbilt University.

MILAN PROTIĆ obtained a B.A. in the Faculty of Law at Belgrade, Yugoslavia, and completed a Ph.D. in History at the University of California–Santa Barbara in 1987. He is the recipient of distinguished fellowships and has published in the United States, Yugoslavia, and Europe. He is currently a Research Fellow of the Institute for Balkan Studies of the Serbian Academy of Sciences and Arts in Belgrade.

JOACHIM REMAK, a member of the History Department of the University of California–Santa Barbara since 1965, has been interested in both the Western and Southeastern European fields. His most recent book is *Another Germany: A Reconsideration of the Imperial Era* (Boulder, 1988) which he edited with Jack Dukes.

RADOVAN SAMARDZIĆ is one of the most distinguished Yugoslav historians. He studied history in Belgrade where he became a Professor of the University, member of the Serbian Academy of Sciences, Directory of the Institute for Balkan Studies, and Secretary of the Serbian Academy's Historical Department. He is the author of numerous books and papers dealing with Serbian, Yugoslav, and Balkan hisiory from the eighteenth to twentieth centuries which have been published throughout Europe and in the United States.

RICHARD B. SPENCE received his Ph.D. from the University of California–Santa Barbara in 1981, completing a dissertation on "The Yugoslavs in the Austro-Hungarian Army during World War I." He is currently an Associate Professor of History at the University of Idaho–Moscow. Dr. Spence is the author of *Boris Savinkov: Renegade on the Left* published by *East European Monographs* in 1991.

GALE STOKES is a Professor of History at Rice University. His most recent publications include *Politics as Development* (Duke, 1990) and *From Stalinism to Pluralism* (Oxford 1991).

NIKOLAI TODOROV holds degrees in history from the Universities of Sofia and Moscow and is a specialist in economic and urban history of the Balkans. He has published many works on these topics including *The Balkan City, 1400–1900* (University of Washington Press, 1983) with previous editions in Bulgarian, French, Russian, and Greek, and numerous works on nineteenth century inter-Balkan relations, focusing on Bulgarian-Greek relations. From 1979–1983 he served as the Bulgarian ambassador to Greece. A founder and longtime director of the Institute of Balkan Studies at the Bulgarian Academy of Sciences until 1989, he is currently President of the Bulgarian National Assembly.

MARIA TODOROVA holds a degree in history from the University of Sofia where she has been a professor of Balkan history. Her publications include *England, Russia and the Tanzimat* (Sofia, 1980 and Moscow, 1983); *Britishers Travelers' Accounts of the Balkans, 16th–19th Centuries* (Sofia, 1987); and *Balkan Family History and the European Pattern: Demographic Developments in Ottoman Bulgaria* (forthcoming from American University Press). She has recently joined the History Department Faculty at the University of Florida–Gainesville.

FRANK P. VERNA attended the University of Cincinnati and, at the outbreak of World War II, joined the armed forces as a commissioned infantry officer in the southwest Pacific theater of operations. In the postwar period he served as an Army Intelligence Officer (Counterintelligence). Upon his retirement as a Lieutenant Colonel he resumed his academic studies earning his M.A. (1973) and Ph.D. (1985) degrees in history from the University of California–Santa Barbara. His latest publication is an article entitled "Notes on Italian Rule in Dalmatia under Bastianini, 1941–1943" in *The International History Review*.

NICK VUCINICH has a B.A. from Stanford University and an M.A. from the University of California–Santa Barbara. He is currently the California State Senate's Senior Consultant on international trade. He came to government service with experience in private consulting, college teaching and research. As a consultant for the Center for Planning and Research, a Palo Alto consulting firm, he worked on trade, economic development and transportation issues.

He has also researched and written extensively on Yugoslav ethnic communities in California.

WAYNE S. VUCINICH received his doctorate from the University of California at Berkeley in 1941. He then served in the U. S. Navy, Office of Strategic Services and Department of State as an intelligence officer specializing in Eastern Europe and the Soviet Union. He has taught at Stanford University since 1946, becoming a professor emeritus in 1978. He was the Director of Stanford's Center for Russian and East European Studies from 1972–1985. Among his numerous publications are *Serbia between East and West. 1903-19. A Study in Social Survival: Katun*, and *The Ottoman Empire*. He was honored upon his retirement with a *Festschrift* entitled *Nation and Ideology*.

ALLEN WACHHOLD earned his Ph.D. under Dr. Djordjević in 1984. He lives in Santa Barbara where he works in the University of California library. He has published his dissertation—a biography of historian Frank A. Golder—and a number of related articles. He is currently conducting a study of Ambassador David R. Francis and the American Embassy in Petrograd in 1917.

RICHARD WOYTAK completed a M.A. at the Monterey Institute of Foreign Studies and earned his doctorate at the University of California–Santa Barbara in 1977. His dissertation, "On the Border of War and Peace: the Role of Intelligence and the Frontier in Polish Foreign Policy, 1938–1939" has been published.

DOCTORAL DISSERTATIONS DEALING WITH MODERN BALKAN HISTORY PRESENTED IN THE HISTORY DEPARTMENT OF THE UNIVERSITY OF CALIFORNIA–SANTA BARBARA

During his teaching at UCSB Professor Djordjević was the major comprehensive examiner of forty-three students in Modern European history. He participated as a member of eleven Ph.D. Committees and chaired nineteen Ph.D. Committees in Balkan history.

Frances Radovich, Aftermath of the Regicide: British Policy and Serbian Conspiracy Question, 1903–1906 (1975)**

James Barringer, Alexander Petrovich Izvolsky, 1906–1908: A Revaluation. (1975)

Nikolai Altankov, The Bulgarian Americans, (1977)*

Richard Woytak, On the Border of War and Peace: The Role of Intelligence and the Frontier in Polish Foreign Policy, 1938–1939, (1977)*

Lynn Curtright, Muddle, Indecision and Setback: British Policy and the Balkan States, August 1914 to the Inception of the Dardanelles Campaign (1980)*

Horst Lorscheider, The German Economic Penetration in the Balkans, 1871–1914 (1980)**

Richard B. Spence, The Yugoslavs in the Austro-Hungarian Army during World War I, (1981)**

Bernd Fischer, King Zog and the Struggle for Stability in Albania, (1982)*

Kathy Bangerter, Three Prominent Philhellenists in the Greek Struggle for Independence, (1982)

Leonard Friedman, The Anglo-Axis Rivalry in Greece on the Eve of World War II, (1984)

Alain Dubie, Frank Golder, (1984)*

Frank Verna, Yugoslavia under Italian Rule 1941–43: Civil and Military Aspects of the Italian Occupation (1985)**

Eric Knudsen, Great Britain, Constantinople and the Turkish Peace Treaty 1919–1922, (1985)*

Thaeib Elbhloul, Italian Colonialism, the Young Turks and the Lybian Resistance 1908–1918, (1986)

Remi Nadeau, The Big Three and the Partition of Europe 1941–45, (1987)

Milan Protić, The Ideology of the Serbian Radical Movement 1881–1903: Sources Characteristics, Developments, (1987)*

Kimberley Francev, France and the Montenegrin Government in Exile 1916–1921, (1988)**

Linda Nelson, Nationalism and Gender Identity: The Bulgarian National Revival, Women's Consciousness, Women's Activism (Anticipated completion 1992)

Nina Bakisian, The Danubian Federation Projects: Motion for Unity in an Age of Nationalism and Dissent (Anticipated completion 1992)

DISSERTATIONS IN ANCIENT HISTORY

Elpida Hadjidaki, The Classical and Hellenistic Harbor at Phalasarna: A Pirate's Port (1988)

Robert Frakes, Audience and Meaning in the *Res Gestae* of Ammianus Marcellinus (1991)

M.A.. THESES DEALING WITH MODERN BALKAN HISTORY PRESENTED IN THE HISTORY DEPARTMENT OF THE UNIVERSITY OF CALIFORNIA SANTA BARBARA

Steve Harding, The OSS and American Covert Operations in Yugoslavia, (1979)

Chester Biedul, The April War in Yugoslavia (1941), (1979)

Eric Knudsen, The Failure of European Diplomacy and the Greek-Turkish War 1919–1923, (1979)

Kim daKuhna, Comparative Study of Serbian, Bulgarian, Greek and Montenegrin Constitutions in the 19th Century, (1980)

Thaeib Elbhloul, The Italian Colonial Expansion: A Study of the Italian-Turkish War over Lybia 1911–12, (1980)

Nicholas Vucinich, From the Adriatic to the Pacific Coast: The Yugoslavs of California, (1983)

Milan Protić, The Characteristics and Ideology of the People's Radical Party in Serbia 1881–1903, (1983)

Linda Nelson, The Yugoslav Government in Exile and the United States, 1941–44, (1983)

Patricia Brown, European Immigrations in Rural Illinois 1860–1910, (1990)

*Published
**Partially published

TABULA GRATULATORIA

Ronelle Akexander
Jelisaveta Stanojevich Allen
Nikolai Altankov
American Association for the Advancement of Slavic Studies
Dorothy Atkinson
Atlantic Research and Publishing
Nina Bakisian
George Barany
Jim Barringer
Ivan T. Berend
Dan Berindei
Jon Billigmeier
Henrik and Marianna Birnbaum
Cornelia Bodea
Sava Bosnitch
Mr. and Mrs. Pavle Botica
Robert F. Byrnes
Virgil Candea
Georges Castellan
Anna N. Cienciala
Sima N. Cirković
Richard Clogg
RichardJ.Crampton
Lynn Curtright
Istvan Deak
Burris Debenning
Alexander and Glace DeConde
Dimitrios J. Delivanis
Mr. and Mrs. Paul Demeure
Petar Dimitrijević
Nan Fletcher Djordjević
Nikola and Spomenka Djordjević
Vera and Sasha Djordjević
Mihailo Dordević

Basil Dmytryshyn
Domna Dontas
Milorad N. Drachkovitch
Alex N. Dragnich
Alain Dubie
Elsie Ivancich Dunin
M. Kamil Dziewanowski
Thomas Eekman
Milorad Ekmecić
Thomas A. Emmert
Faculty of Philosophy and History, Department of History,
    Belgrade University
Bozhidar Ferjancić
Alexandr Filippenko
Vladimir Filippenko
Bernd Fischer
Stephen Fischer-Galati
Ann Sloan Fletcher
Robert Frakes
Kimberly Francev
Tibor Frank
Lenny Friedmian
Amlanda Clark Frost
Frank Frost
Milutin Garasanin
Imanuel Geiss
Aleksander Gieysztor
Radmlila Jovanović Gorup
H. C. Grothuysen
Elpida Hadjidaki
Bojana Hill
History Department, University of California, Santa Barbara
Mr. and Mrs. Robert Hixson, Jr.
International Research and Exchanges Board
Institute for Balkan Studies, Serbian Academy of Sciences and
    Arts
Institute for Balkan Studies, Thessaloniki
Institute for Byzantine Studies, Serbian Academy of Sciences
    and Arts
Barbara Jelavich

Charles Jelavich
Geza Jeszensky
Miodrag Jovicić
Jovanka Kalić
Cynthia S. Kaplan
Bela Kiraly
Mr. and Mrs. Adrian Kisovec
Evangelos Kofos
Andrzej Korbonski
Ruzica and Aleksandar Kostić
Frances and Mstislav Kostruba
Barisa Krekić
Ladis D. Kristof
John Lampe
Dejan Lazarević
Ken Leonard
Sam Lewis
Al and Barbara Lindemann
Karlheinz Mack
David MacKenzie
Victor S. Mamatey
Daniela Marković
Jelena and Rade Marković
Vladimir Marković
Miroslav Marcovich
Gordon McDaniel
J. Sears McGee
Dejan Medaković
Vasa D. Mihailovich
Ankica and Misha Milosavljević
Remi and Margaret Nadeau
Nicholas N. Nagy-Talavera
Maria Negreponti-Delivanis
Linda Nelson
Sybil and Jovan Nikolić
North American Society for Serbian Studies
Stephanos Papadopoulos
Aleksandar Pavković
Roger V. Paxton
James S. Peters (Zivka Petrovich)

Margaret L. Peters
Zorica and Sveta Petrović
Richard G. Plaschka
Ljubica D. Popovich
Ruzica Popovitch-Krekić
Milan Protić
Marin V.Pundeff
Sabrina Petra Ramet
R. John Rath
Joachim and Roberta Remak
Diana M. Russell
Jeffrey B. Russell
Radovan Samardzić
Nina Sloan Sarguis
Milan and Jelena Savić
Gordon Schaeffer
Allan and Marina Scholl
Serbian Academy of Sciences
Boyd and Carol Shafer
Jo Anne and Rod P. Sharpe
Philip Shasko
Biljana Sljivić-Sinisić
Rick and Ingrid Spence
Dragoslav Stankovich
Olga Stankovich
Theofanis G. Stavrou
Gale Stokes
Peter F. Sugar
Arnold Suppan
C. Svolopoulos
Nikola Tasić
Slavenko Terzić
Nikoloi Todorov
Maria Todorova
George Todorovich
Harold Tollefson
George Vid Tomashevich
Donald W. Treadgold
E. Turczynski
Barbara S. Uehling

Apostolos Vakalopoulos
Constantinos Vavouskos
Milos Velimirović
Frank Verna
V. N. Vinogradov
Slobodanka Vladiv-Glover
Miheilo Vojvodić
Speros Vryonis   Alexander Vucinich
Nicholas and Lisa Vucinich
Wayne S. Vucinich
Ana and Zvoniniir Vucković
Desa Tomashevich Wakeman
Richard Woytak
William E. Wright
Gordana Zivanović
Srbislav Zivanović
Dragoljub Zivojinović